Democratization and Research Methods

Democratization and Research Methods is a coherent survey and critique of both democratization research and the methodology of comparative politics. The two themes enhance each other: the democratization literature illustrates the advantages and disadvantages of various methodological approaches, and the critique of methods makes sense of the vast and bewildering democratization field. Michael Coppedge argues that each of the three main approaches in comparative politics – case studies and comparative histories, formal modeling, and large-sample statistical analysis – accomplishes one fundamental research goal relatively well, "thickness," integration, and generalization, respectively, but the other two poorly. Chapters cover conceptualization and measurement, case studies and comparative histories, formal models and theories, political culture and survey research, and quantitative testing. The final chapter summarizes the state of knowledge about democratization and lays out an agenda for multimethod research.

Michael Coppedge is professor of political science at the University of Notre Dame. He is one of the principal investigators for the Varieties of Democracy Project at the Kellogg Institute, a collaboration producing many new indicators of democracy. He chaired the American Political Science Association's Task Force on Indicators of Democracy and Governance. His first book, *Strong Parties and Lame Ducks: Presidential Partyarchy and Factionalism in Venezuela* (1994), analyzes institutional problems underlying the crisis of Venezuelan democracy. He has published articles on comparative and Latin American politics in *Journal of Politics, Perspectives on Politics, Comparative Politics, Comparative Political Studies, Journal of Democracy, Party Politics, Studies in Comparative International Development*, and other journals and books. He is a past recipient of grants from Fulbright-Hayes, the Tinker Foundation, the World Society Foundation, and the Research Council of Norway, and he has taught at Johns Hopkins School of Advanced International Studies, Princeton, Yale, and Georgetown. Coppedge received his PhD from Yale University in 1988.

Strategies for Social Inquiry

Editors

Colin Elman, *Maxwell School of Syracuse University*
John Gerring, *Boston University*
James Mahoney, *Northwestern University*

Editorial Board

Bear Braumoeller, David Collier, Francesco Guala, Peter Hedström, Theodore
Hopf, Uskali Maki, Rose McDermott, Charles Ragin, Theda Skocpol, Peter Spiegler,
David Waldner, Lisa Wedeen, Christopher Winship

This new book series presents texts on a wide range of issues bearing upon the
practice of social inquiry. Strategies are construed broadly to embrace the full
spectrum of approaches to analysis, as well as relevant issues in philosophy of social
science.

Published Titles

John Gerring, *Social Science Methodology: A Unified Framework*, 2nd edition

Democratization and Research Methods

Michael Coppedge

University of Notre Dame

CAMBRIDGE
UNIVERSITY PRESS

CAMBRIDGE UNIVERSITY PRESS
Cambridge, New York, Melbourne, Madrid, Cape Town,
Singapore, São Paulo, Delhi, Mexico City

Cambridge University Press
32 Avenue of the Americas, New York, NY 10013-2473, USA

www.cambridge.org
Information on this title: www.cambridge.org/9780521537278

First published 2012

Printed in the United States of America

A catalog record for this publication is available from the British Library.

Library of Congress Cataloging in Publication data

Coppedge, Michael, 1957–
Democratization and research methods / Michael Coppedge.
    p.   cm. – (Strategies for social inquiry)
Includes bibliographical references and index.
ISBN 978-0-521-83032-4 (hardback) – ISBN 978-0-521-53727-8 (paperback)
1. Democratization – Research – Methodology.   2. Comparative government – Research –
Methodology.   I. Title.
JC423.C7173   2012
321.8–dc23   2012003497

ISBN 978-0-521-83032-4 Hardback
ISBN 978-0-521-53727-8 Paperback

Contents

List of tables

List of figures

Acknowledgments

This book has been in gestation more than ten years – how much more, I cannot bear to calculate. In a sense, it began when I was a graduate student thirty years ago. I remember wanting to believe that the research I was reading was giving me real insights into comparative politics, but at the same time I had a nagging feeling that it rested on a shaky foundation that people were trying hard to ignore. I remember wondering, "How do we know what we think we know?" In subsequent years I undertook a long, slow journey through methodology and the philosophy of science to satisfy my own curiosity and eventually found the answers I sought. This is the book I wish I had had. I hope it will be useful to beginning graduate students who are now where I was then.

During the decade-plus that I have been writing this book, I have accumulated too many debts to enumerate exhaustively. Among them are general intellectual debts to great scholars whose insights on methodology or regimes I have appropriated and remixed: Kenneth Bollen, Henry Brady, David Collier, Robert Dahl, Larry Diamond, Barbara Geddes, Alexander George, John Gerring, Gary Goertz, Donald Green, Peter Hall, David Held, Carl Hempel, Jonathan Katz, Robert Keohane, Gary King, Thomas Kuhn, Imre Lakatos, Evan Lieberman, Juan Linz, James Mahoney, Gerardo Munck, Guillermo O'Donnell, Karl Popper, Adam Przeworski, Charles Ragin, Giovanni Sartori, Phillippe Schmitter, Ian Shapiro, Theda Skocpol, Alfred Stepan, and Sidney Verba.

I owe more specific debts to the many people who commented on draft chapters, corresponded with me, or followed up on presentations of the work in progress, most generously Neal Beck, Andrew Bennett, Michael Bernhard, Daniel Brinks, Matthew Cleary, Ruth Collier, Kathleen Collins, Alan Dowty, Robert Fishman, Rob Franzese, Mark Gasiorowski, John Gerring, Carlos Gervasoni, Andrew Gould, Thomas Gresik, Frances Hagopian, Jonathan Hartlyn, Evelyne Huber, Wendy Hunter, Herbert Kitschelt, Evan Lieberman, Scott Mainwaring, Xavier Márquez, Monika Nalepa, Gabriela Nava-Campos,

David Nickerson, the late Guillermo O'Donnell, Valeria Palanza, Richard Rose, Ben Ross-Schneider, Sanjay Ruparelia, Jason Seawright, Richard Snyder, John Stephens, J. Samuel Valenzuela, Kurt Weyland, and an anonymous referee. I extend general thanks as well to the dozens of graduate students who took the two graduate seminars on which this book is based, "Comparing Democracies" and "Comparative Research on Democratization." I am also grateful to FLACSO-Quito, the Institute for Development Studies in Sussex, and the Duke-UNC Working Group on Political and Economic Regimes for the opportunity to lecture on selected draft chapters.

This book benefited greatly from research assistance provided by Angel Alvarez, Victoria Anglin, Annabella España Nájera, Cora Fernández-Anderson, Ezequiel González Ocantos, Lucas González, Courtney Isaak, Claudia Maldonado, and Erik Wang. It also benefited indirectly from research assistance by Sandra Botero, Chad Kiewiet de Jonge, and Cecilia Pe Lero, whose work on other projects freed me up to finish the book. I owe institutional debts to the Helen Kellogg Institute for International Studies, the Department of Political Science, and the College of Arts and Letters at the University of Notre Dame for leaves, course reductions, and other kinds of material and moral support.

During the years of work on this book, I made many people wait for many things much longer than they would have liked. They include colleagues, department chairs, deans, journal editors, advisees, my collaborators in the Varieties of Democracy project, the members of the APSA Task Force on Indicators of Democracy and Government, Lewis Bateman of Cambridge University Press, and, most frequently and importantly, my wife and family. They handled my delays with patience and understanding more often than I deserved. I can only hope that in the long run the book will have been worth the wait.

Some portions of this book were previously published elsewhere and are reprinted with permission, for which I am grateful. Portions of Chapters 2, 3, and 7 were first published as Michael Coppedge, "Thickening Thin Concepts and Theories: Combining Large N and Small in Comparative Politics," *Comparative Politics* (July 1999): 465–476. Portions of Chapter 2 were first published by SAGE/SOCIETY as Michael Coppedge, "Democracy and Dimensions: Comments on Munck and Verkuilen," *Comparative Political Studies* 35: 1 (February 2002): 35–39. Figure 2.2 and Tables 2.1 and 2.2 were previously published in Michael Coppedge, "Thickening Thin Concepts: Issues in Large-N Data Generation," in *Regimes and Democracy in Latin America: Theories and Methods*, 105–122, ed. Gerardo L. Munck (New York: Oxford

University Press, 2007). Portions of Chapter 3 were previously published in Michael Coppedge, "Theory Building and Hypothesis Testing: Large-N Versus Small-N Research on Democratization," in *Regimes and Democracy in Latin America: Theories and Methods*, 163–177, ed. Gerardo L. Munck (New York: Oxford University Press, 2007).

1 Research methods and democratization

Why are some countries democracies while others are not? Why do some democracies survive while others fail? These are core questions in political science, sociology, history, and economics. Scholars have been trying to answer them ever since Aristotle. After 2,500 years of research, what do we know? How do we know it? This book answers the latter two questions.

Rationale

After so much has been written on these matters, I am obliged to explain why we need this particular book on democracy. The answer is simple: to distill this vast literature down to a comprehensible critical survey! Democratization has been studied for so long and in so many different ways that the literature is overwhelming and bewildering. It encompasses ideas borrowed from the study of early modern Europe, strategic bargaining games, Asian cultures, measurement theory, public opinion about economic trends, legacies of colonialism, geographic networks, theories of class struggle, demographic trends, war and peace, and many other phenomena. There are dozens of hypotheses about the causes of democracy (Chapter 4 summarizes fifty-five of them). The first step toward digesting this mountain of scholarship is taking a comprehensive inventory of all the possible explanations.

This book is not just about democratization, however; it is equally devoted to evaluating research methods in comparative politics. This is another area in which it might seem that there is already a superabundance of reading material (Brady and Collier 2004; Geddes 2003; George and Bennett 2005; Gerring 2001; Goertz 2006; Green and Shapiro 1994; King et al. 1994; Landman 2008; Lave and March 1993; Lichbach and Zuckerman 2009; Peters 1998; Przeworski and Teune 1970; Ragin 1987, 2000; Shively 1998). The past fifteen years have been especially embroiled in debates about political science methodology. There is a growing feeling, however, that in the latter part of this decade, the polarization is abating in favor of a hopeful methodological pluralism. I believe that the time is right to articulate a unified vision of research methods that recognizes the strengths and weaknesses of each approach with respect to the shared fundamental aims of all social science research.[1] This book proposes such a vision and uses its standards to evaluate three basic approaches in comparative politics: case studies and comparative history, formal models and theories, and quantitative testing.

The principal virtue of this book, however, is not its grouping of research methods into a single framework. There are many alternatives that offer their own classification schemes and others that go much deeper into each method. Neither is its virtue the breadth or depth of its survey of democratization research; there are worthy alternatives for this purpose as well (Diamond 1999; Geddes 2007; Haerpfer et al. 2009; Teorell 2009; Whitehead 2002). Rather, the uniqueness of this book is that it combines a survey of democratization research with a critique of research methods.

These two tasks can be better accomplished together than separately, for two reasons. First, it is often difficult to appreciate the implications of research methods until they are applied to a substantive theme. Examples of actual research demonstrate how choices about research methods can decisively affect substantive conclusions. Democratization is the ideal application for this purpose. Because it has been studied for decades, if not centuries, and studied with almost every method employed in comparative politics, it can supply examples that illustrate and illuminate every conceivable approach in comparative politics. It also has the advantage of being interesting to most people who do research in comparative politics.

Second, a survey of this bewildering literature demands explicit attention to methodology. Precisely because such diverse methods have been used, the literature is a hodgepodge of disparate findings that are difficult to integrate into a comprehensive summary of what we know. Students of democratization have employed class analysis, structural functionalism, case studies, conceptual analysis, game theory, survey research, advanced statistical analysis, and the occasional lab or field experiment. How can we extract any meaningful conclusions from such disparate types of knowledge?

---

[1] I use the term *approach* loosely and sometimes interchangeably with *method* or even *school of thought*. When a distinction matters, however, I think of an approach as a path to a goal or a means to an end. In this context, methods are the means and the ends are the goals of a research project or program, whether they are as narrow as explaining a particular coup or as broad as integrating models into a theory or testing the general truth of hypotheses.

The key that makes a comprehensive assessment possible is attention to the strengths and weaknesses of different methodological approaches relative to absolute standards for good research. If the assessments in this book sometimes sound harsh, it is because the book uses standards of evaluation that are very high – close to perfection. To evaluate research in other contexts, scholars use *relative* (movable) standards, which are appropriate for those contexts. To judge which articles deserve to be published, we judge them relative to other publications; to judge whether colleagues deserve tenure or promotion, we judge them relative to other scholars at an equivalent stage of their careers; to judge whether to be impressed by a research project, we judge what it accomplished relative to the difficulty of carrying it out. But if we need to judge how much we have explained about democratization, we must judge our explanations by absolute standards for what a true, complete, and certain explanation would be. Relative standards can tell us whether we are making progress, but only an absolute standard can tell us how far from perfection we are and what we must improve to get there.

Although democratization research has made great progress, it still falls far short of perfection. Too often incautious students and scholars develop exaggerated confidence in the conclusions of published research, and authors, understandably enough, tend to downplay the limitations of their own findings. This leaves the impression that our knowledge is more complete and certain than it really is. A careful, comprehensive methodological critique of this literature encourages a more mature and modest appreciation of what we know about democratization and how well we know it. Explicit acknowledgment of what a method is supposed to accomplish creates a standard for evaluating how well it works. Having a unified, comprehensive set of standards makes it possible also to evaluate methods against one another, thus revealing the kinds of insights each one reveals and the kinds it conceals. This book uses these standards in the final chapter to lay out an agenda for future research on democratization. Thus, readers of this book can expect to come away with balanced judgment about what each method can teach us, a comprehensive synthesis of what is known about democratization, and a sober appreciation of the limitations of that knowledge.

Although democratization research is probably the best application for this critique of research methods, it has a few limitations. First, it does not lend itself to experiments. It would be neither feasible nor ethical to split countries or populations into treatment and control groups to examine the impact of economic development, religious traditions, or other supposed causes of democracy (although various split or merged states may provide opportunities for "natural experiments" – such as Germany, Czechoslovakia, Yemen, Vietnam, and Korea).[2] Therefore, almost all the research discussed in this book is based on observational data, and my arguments about the challenges to inference are correspondingly more cautionary than they would be about experimental data.

Second, because democracy is a feature of national states, most of the research reviewed here pertains to the national level of analysis. Research on subnational phenomena – movements, parties, classes, regions, individuals – would encounter some different issues. Chapters 4, 5, 6, and especially Chapter 8 do touch on some of these issues, but I have not attempted to address them systematically.

Third, formal theorizing about democratization is relatively recent. As I note in Chapter 6, it is too early to draw conclusions about the long-term potential of this approach for understanding democratization.

Fourth, most research on democratization, including the quantitative research, performs frequentist hypothesis testing, which tells us how likely it is that a hypothesis is true, given the evidence. There is growing support in the social sciences for the Bayesian approach, which seeks conclusions about how evidence changes our prior beliefs about hypotheses.

Finally, as noted in Chapter 4, there is too little research on democratization using Boolean or fuzzy-set Boolean methods to judge how well it works in practice. In all of these respects, however, the limitations of democratization research are also found in research on other topics, from political economy to institutions to ethnic conflict to state building. Democratization research is more the rule than the exception.

Overview

I ground all of my judgments in an exacting philosophy of the social sciences. I start from a commonsense belief that politics is extremely complex. It is complex in that many forces are in play, constantly interacting, and varying by time and place; and often unique events have powerful consequences, further undermining our ability to build useful theories. All social sciences must grapple with this complexity, but the subfield that must grapple with it most

---

[2] Susan Hyde's field experiment on the impact of election observation is one example of experimental research that helps understand an aspect of democratization (Hyde 2007).

fully is comparative politics, which takes the entire world and all of human history as its domain. No parsimonious theory can possibly encompass all of the relevant phenomena or explain any piece of it completely. For this reason, any student of comparative politics must learn to be comfortable with theories that are probabilistic, partial, conditional, and provisional. Our theories are necessarily probabilistic because there are always exceptions, due to unknown causes that we cannot model systematically. Our theories are partial because no political outcome worth explaining has just one cause: many causes help explain it, and none determines it alone. Our theories are conditional because causal relationships often vary according to time, place, and other conditions. Finally, comparative theories are provisional, because we have no choice but to build on probable, partial, conditional knowledge that will change when a better theory comes along.

My stance could be called sadder-but-wiser positivism. I believe in the scientific method for understanding society and politics, but I also understand the challenges it faces. I am not a naive positivist who believes that everything is reducible to a set of eternal equations whose truth can be objectively demonstrated and replicated. Our reality is complex and ever changing, and it appears very different to different observers. As social scientists, we will never understand any phenomenon fully, and we will always have our own subjective biases. I can understand why some in my profession would conclude that scientific methods are inappropriate for understanding politics and society and that the search for theory is futile. Nevertheless, I am convinced that rather than giving up, we must do the best we can; that rather than giving in to our biases, we must struggle against them. We cannot explain everything we observe, but we can hope to explain big pieces of it; we cannot perceive the world objectively, but we can test our perceptions against others' and against evidence, and adjust them. In the process, we will create social and political science that responds to antipositivist critiques of naive positivism by developing more nuanced concepts and theories. In my view, the most useful corrective for poor science is better science.

In comparative politics, the fundamental division of labor is between what I call thick and thin approaches. Thick approaches entertain many intricately intertwined causes, they seek to explain multifaceted outcomes, and they rely on elaborate theoretical assumptions. Anthropological, interpretive, thick description is the extreme case of such an approach; in comparative politics, it approximated by case studies, area studies, comparative history, and some approaches to understanding political culture. At the other extreme, thin approaches consist of simple, theoretically neutral propositions considered in isolation from the surrounding complex reality. Good examples are econometric analyses of the impact of per capita gross domestic product or presidential constitutions on the age of democratic regimes. Thick approaches lend themselves to rich understanding of specific events; thin approaches lend themselves to hypothesis testing and generalization. In principle, we can strive to combine the best of both approaches by thickening thin concepts and theories (Coppedge 1999). In practice, however, this is difficult, so there is a trade-off. I illustrate this trade-off in Chapter 2 by demonstrating the advantages and disadvantages of thick definitions of democracy and thin quantitative indicators of democracy. I argue that existing quantitative indicators are adequate for some purposes but that we cannot measure democracy much better until we thicken the concept that we are operationalizing to take multiple dimensions of democracy into account (Coppedge 2002). Recognizing the distinct dimensions of democracy would also help us measure each one more accurately.

The three subsequent chapters focus on theory building. I argue in Chapter 3 that, ideally, theory is thick, general, and integrated. Thick theory is rich, descriptively accurate, and sensitive to local and historical variation in concepts and causal relationships. General theory applies to as many times and places as possible; it approaches universality. A truly universal theory of politics does not exist and, if it did, it would not be a set of simple propositions. Rather, a general theory would be a set of interlocking middle-range theories knit together by more general propositions that identify the circumstances in which each middle-range theory is relevant. Integrated propositions are clear, logical, formal, and systematic, which aids the accumulation of theoretical knowledge and creates a fecund mechanism for generating hypotheses. We have no theory that possesses all three qualities; these are merely characteristics of an ideal theory that would explain practically everything in politics well. Although this is an unattainable goal, it points us toward better theory. I then argue that there are three major sources of theory in comparative politics: case studies, large-sample comparisons, and formal theories. However, each source supplies a kind of theory that meets one of these three criteria well but the other two only poorly. Case studies suggest theory that is thick but not general or integrated. Large-sample comparisons, although we tend to regard them as tests rather than sources of theory, do supply a kind of theory: empirically confirmed generalizations that are thin and undertheorized. Formal theory is clear, logical, and systematic but neither thick nor truly general.

The following three chapters illustrate these arguments. Chapter 4 compiles a master checklist of proposed causes of democratization. It defines *democratization* generously to include any process in which countries become democracies or not, become more democratic or less so, survive as democracies, or break down. There are many conventional wisdoms (the plural is deliberate) about the factors that prepare countries for democracy, spur transitions, and help democracies survive. Explanations have suggested dozens of causes related to mass political culture, leadership, the economy, society, the state, various political institutions, and the international system. If we, foxlike, took all of these suggested factors into account, we could make surprisingly reliable predictions about which countries are democracies and which are not, but we would not be able to predict the intermediate or mixed cases well, and we would not be able to say which factors mattered, how much they mattered, why they mattered, or in which combinations. These limitations of checklists justify political scientists' emphasis on developing theory and testing hypotheses. Chapter 4 also describes and evaluates the Linz (1978) breakdowns framework; the O'Donnell and Schmitter (1986) transitions framework; and the Linz and Stepan (1996) consolidation framework, which take steps toward integrated theory. This chapter concludes with a brief critique of Boolean analysis, which can be used to test checklist-type arguments (Ragin 1987).

Chapter 5 begins by contrasting histories and case studies. It praises case studies as the thickest method for generating and intensively testing competing explanations of specific events but notes that the voluminous knowledge they produce is difficult to integrate into general theory and tends to overemphasize dynamic, idiosyncratic factors and underemphasize static, structural factors. Most of the chapter critiques comparative histories, which are intended to represent a compromise between case studies and large-sample comparisons. The result, I argue, is an approach that is probably the best way to generate more general explanations that are likely to survive testing but also one of the worst ways to test them. Examples include books by Moore (1966); Skocpol (1979); Rueschemeyer, Stephens, and Stephens (1992); Ruth and David Collier (1991); Luebbert (1991); Downing (1992); and Ertman (1997).

Chapter 6 surveys formal models and theories of political liberalization, transition, and survival. It distinguishes positional models, in which regimes are ends in themselves, from economic models, in which regimes are a means to economic ends. This approach has the potential to generate a large, logically connected body of well-integrated theory. It has, however, integrated these models far less than one would expect, although the economic models are much more integrated than the positional ones. Nevertheless, these models have placed new puzzles on the research agenda. Why would authoritarian rulers ever ease repression if this might snowball into a loss of power to the democratic opposition? Why would the opposition ever take the risk of challenging a dictator? How can the rich assure the poor that democracy will be preserved, and how can the poor assure the rich that a democratic government would not confiscate their assets? The downside of this approach is that it works with extremely thin concepts, and its predictions are largely untested, and perhaps untestable. The chapter discusses models developed by Przeworski (1986, 1991), Marks (1992), Colomer (2000), Boix (2003), Acemoglu and Robinson (2001, 2006), and others.

Theories should meet the requirements laid out in Chapter 3, but they must also survive rigorous testing. Chapter 7 proposes comprehensive criteria for rigorous testing and uses them to explain why rigorous testing of theories of democratization is so challenging. The core principle is that we can "prove" causal relationships only indirectly, by disconfirming any alternative hypothesis that other scholars consider plausible. Unfortunately, democratization is presumably so complex that the number of alternative hypotheses is huge. The chapter develops a fundamental distinction between extensive testing, which evaluates whether we can generalize propositions about average causal effects, and intensive testing, which evaluates which of several alternative stories best explains a specific outcome in a single case. Ideally, our theories should survive both extensive and intensive testing.

Chapters 8 and 9 survey the results of testing, mostly extensive. (Because case-study conclusions cannot be summarized without taking them out of context, this book largely ignores the findings of their intensive tests.) Chapter 8 evaluates research on political culture and democratization. It first explains why the method of studying culture that is derived from psychology – survey research – is more useful for developing general theory than methods derived from anthropology. Survey research findings are riddled with paradoxes. Support for democracy as the best form of government remains high even though citizens in the West have lost trust in democratic institutions; in fact, critical citizens tend to support democracy more than their complacent peers (Norris 1999a). Average levels of support for democracy have almost no association with how democratic a country is or how long democracy has survived in a country. And there are striking cross-national differences in certain syndromes, such as institutional trust and belief in self-expression, that do not exist at the level of individual attitudes (Davis and Davenport 1999; Inglehart and Welzel 2005; Muller and Seligson 1994). A major difficulty in this area is the lack of a theory that could link individual-level attitudes to both behavior and system-level outcomes such as democracy.

Chapter 9 surveys quantitative testing of democratization hypotheses, which has accelerated and deepened in technical sophistication in the past two decades as democracy data have become more abundant. Because I value confirmed generalizations more than untested theories, I tend to be more positive about the large-sample statistical approach. However, it is no exception to my central claim that each approach has one strength and two weaknesses, as each tends to be general but thin and poorly integrated. Quantitative research has unearthed dozens of general empirical regularities, but because the concepts and theories tend to be thin, the findings tend to be consistent with many possible theoretical interpretations. The most robust discoveries, such as geographic diffusion and the logarithmic association between per capita gross domestic product and levels of democracy, have been followed by lengthy debates about what the causal mechanisms (if any) might be. Quantitative researchers tend to crunch first and ask questions later. It has become clear that there are striking and stable cross-national differences in levels of democracy that constitute much of the variance to be explained; identifying their causes will probably have to be a task for case studies and comparative histories. Over the decades, this approach has proliferated new dependent variables that force us to be more precise in our definitions of democratization. It has also given us a detailed and varied empirical basis for judging which explanations are intuitively plausible and which are not.

The concluding chapter, Chapter 10, pulls all the preceding analyses together in an agenda for future research on democratization and for future methodological development. Each approach could, of course, continue to do what it does best and strive to do it better. Case studies and comparative histories can become ever more nuanced, formal models could integrate themselves into a more coherent body of theory, survey research could cover more countries and more questions more frequently, and quantitative testing could bring ever more sophisticated data and estimation techniques to bear on democratization hypotheses. The most fruitful advances, however, will come from efforts to transcend the typical limitations of each approach. Those who immerse themselves in cases could do more to contribute to, and be guided by, broader theoretical debates. Those who develop formal models could try to make them more realistic and testable. And those who do statistical testing could rely on theory to resist the curve-fitting temptation and collaborate with area specialists to develop thicker indicators of key concepts such as democracy. All of these tasks are difficult, but I believe that our understanding of democracy will deepen only to the degree that we accomplish them.

2 Defining and measuring democracy

Scholars who set out to study a political phenomenon talk past one another if they define the phenomenon differently. Suppose two scholars want to understand "democracy," but one understands "democracy" to refer to the liberal political democracies of advanced capitalist economies, whereas the other considers only the "people's democracies" of communist regimes to be truly democratic. They will end up studying completely different countries and will probably come to opposite conclusions. If they try to reconcile their findings, they will discover that they are not really studying the same phenomenon at all. In practice, the difference in definitions is rarely so stark, but clear and consistent conceptualization is essential for preventing misunderstandings.

Unfortunately, one of the most difficult challenges in studying democratization has been reaching agreement on what "democracy" is. In fact, W. B. Gallie once argued that democracy is one of the best examples of an "essentially contested" concept: a concept that is the focus of endless disputes that, "although not resolvable by argument of any kind, are nevertheless sustained by perfectly respectable arguments and evidence" (Gallie 1956). Democracy is a contested concept because nearly everyone values the label, but there are different reasonable and legitimate, yet incompatible, criteria for judging whether the label is deserved.

As though conceptualization were not enough of a challenge, empirical research requires us to carry out a second and a third step – operationalization and measurement. To operationalize a concept, we define a procedure for mapping a label or values of a variable onto observations in the real world. To measure a concept, we actually perform that operational procedure. The result is an indicator. Indicators are not necessarily numerical variables (although some are). Even a simple classification of a country as a democracy is an indicator, even when the operation that produced that classification is not explicitly defined.

Democracy has been defined in hundreds of ways.[1] However, almost all definitions fit into one of six overlapping models: socioeconomic, people's, participatory, representative, liberal, and deliberative democracy.[2] Socio-economic democracy emphasizes the equalization of wealth, income, and status, both as a prerequisite for political equality and as an end in itself. Many of its advocates define it in ways that are compatible with liberal representative or, especially, participatory democracy; but the people's democracy subtype claimed by communist regimes denies significant political authority derived from Western institutions such as popular elections. Participatory democracy emphasizes the value of citizen involvement that goes beyond mere voting in general elections. This model holds that both society and citizens themselves benefit from participation in referenda, primaries, local hearings, and civil society organizations (Pateman 1970). Some versions of participatory democracy stress socioeconomic equality as well. Extreme versions of participatory democracy – applicable only in small societies – may reject the delegation of authority to representatives, insisting instead that the people must rule directly; but most versions seek only to complement and enhance representative democracy. Deliberative democracy also seeks to enhance representation and, especially, participation, by promoting well-informed and rational discussion of what is in the public interest (Held 2006). Its advocates deplore the poor quality of political debate and competition that takes place when citizens passively choose among superficial slogans; instead, they propose, the state should select representative samples of the public, educate them about the issues, enable them to listen and take part in policy debates, and then publicize their recommendations to the general public. Deliberative democracy is still experimental, participatory democracy is practiced only to a limited extent except in a few places, and socioeconomic equality is considered relevant for democracy in some cultures but not others. But all democratic national states today have a form of representative democracy, which contains a range running from popular sovereignty to liberal democracy. The principle of popular sovereignty holds that the majority rules: whatever the people want becomes the law. In Figure 2.1, popular sovereignty would be the part of representative democracy that excludes liberal democracy, although in extreme form it can also include versions of deliberative, participatory, and socio-economic democracy that do not require representation. Liberal democracy limits the power of the majority by guaranteeing some fundamental rights of

---

[1] See Collier and Levitsky (1997); Katz (1997); and my summary of Held (1996) in Table 2.2.
[2] This conceptual scheme is adapted from that in Coppedge and Gerring (2011).

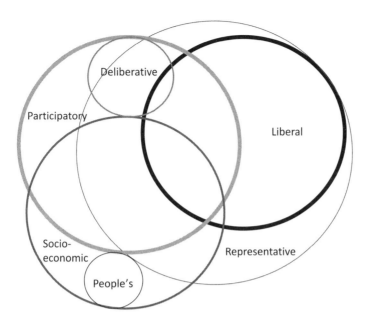

Figure 2.1   Models of Democracy. *Note*: This figure represents only which of these models have some similarities and which have distinctive elements. The sizes, shades, and thicknesses of the circles are not intended to represent the importance, complexity, or legitimacy of any of these versions of democracy.

individuals (and sometimes groups) and by creating constitutional checks on executive, legislative, and judicial powers.

This set of types and subtypes is neither exhaustive nor universally accepted; one could make additional distinctions in the set of liberal representative democracies to distinguish consolidated democracies from transitional ones, parliamentary from presidential democracies, unitary from federal democracies, high-quality from low-quality democracies, and so on. However, this basic typology is useful for describing how political scientists have faced the challenge of measuring democracy.

Although scholars would be better off if democracy were not an essentially contested concept, research on democratization is still possible. Research can proceed if, at a minimum, we are always very clear about what we mean by "democracy" so that we do not become entangled in semantic confusion. Beyond that, it is desirable to develop a consensus on a manageable number of types of democracy so that at least some research projects address the same questions. But what is ultimately most important is to have concepts and indicators that are useful: ones that establish an easy and natural correspondence between the symbols in our minds and the observable features of the real political world that play important roles in causal processes. Scholars make choices whenever they define or measure a concept, and their choices have consequences for their research findings. This chapter surveys the range of possible choices regarding conceptualization, levels of measurement, procedures to ensure reliability, and the aggregation of dimensions, and it uses democracy indicators to illustrate the consequences of those choices.

Operationalizing concepts

In a perfect world, comparativists would use concepts that reflect the uniqueness of each country and yet are simple enough to be relevant and measurable in every country. In practice, the difficulty of gathering political information usually prevents us from achieving both goals, so we tend to settle for concepts that are either thick or thin. Thick concepts have many facets; that is, they refer to many aspects of what we observe. Thin concepts have few facets: they focus attention on only one or a few characteristics. Conceptual thickness is relative and can be understood as a matter of degree. Even a relatively thin version of democracy, one of the thickest concepts in political science, can refer to half a dozen characteristics. A thick version can refer to dozens. For example, David Held's 1996 *Models of Democracy* defines twelve different models of democracy, all of which, he argues, possess some claim to the democratic label. Between them, the twelve models refer to seventy-two different characteristics, which are listed in Table 2.1.

Definitions of regimes are typically thick. A good example is Juan Linz's definition of an authoritarian regime:

[Political systems without] free competition between leaders to validate at regular intervals by nonviolent means their claim to rule...with limited, not responsible, political pluralism; without elaborate and guiding ideology, but with distinctive mentalities; without extensive nor intensive political mobilization, except at some points in their development; and in which a leader or occasionally a small group exercises power within formally ill-defined limits but actually quite predictable ones.[3]

---

[3] Linz (1975) quoting the definition from his own "An Authoritarian Regime: The Case of Spain" from 1964. This element is implied by Linz's explicit statements that authoritarian regimes are by definition nondemocratic. The language comes from his own definition of a democratic political system (Linz 1975).

Table 2.1. Elements of Held's models of democracy

Institutions
    Regular elections
    Elections for many offices
    Secret ballot
    Strong executive
    Party politics
    One person, one vote
    Multiple or different voting rights
    Representation
    Constitutional limits to state power
    Separation of powers/checks and balances
    Rule of law
    Internal party democracy
    Mixed government
    Direct participation in decision making
    Some appointments by lot
    Strict term limits
    Payment for participation
    Public campaign finance
    Innovative feedback mechanisms
    Universal adult suffrage
    Proportional representation
    Independent, professional bureaucracy
    Professional bureaucracy
    Limited bureaucracy
    Guarantees of civil liberties
    Guarantees of political rights
    Workplace democracy
    Minimization of unaccountable power centers
    Representation of corporate interests/representation of the powerful
    Restriction of some interest groups
    Jury service
International System
    Global state
    International competition
    Pluralist, free-market international order
    Unequal international order
Social Structure
    Small community
    Patriarchal family or society
    Intense societal conflict
    Autonomous civil society

(continued)

Table 2.1 (*continued*)

Free-market society
Maintenance of religious worship
Interest-group pluralism
Economic System
   Private property
   Market economy
   Industrial society
   Nonindustrial society
   Economic inequality
   Priority of economic interests
   Exclusion of some from effective participation by economic inequalities
   Redistribution of resources
   Experiments with collective property
Culture and Participation
   Public debates
   Participation in local government
   Competition for power
   Openness to institutional reform
   Transparency
   No distinction between citizens and officials
   Individualism
   Poorly informed or emotional voters
   Culture of toleration
   Consensus on legitimate scope of politics
   Procedural consensus
   Moderate level of participation
   Liberal leadership
Miscellaneous
   Strong leadership
   Popular sovereignty
   Unbiased state
   State with interests of its own
   Large nation-state
   Right to child care
   Demilitarization

Note: Table 2.1 was previously published as Table 4.1 in Michael Coppedge, "Thickening Thin Concepts: Issues in Large-*N* Data Generation" in *Regimes and Democracy in Latin America: Theories and Methods*, 106, ed. Gerardo L. Munck (New York: Oxford University Press, 2007).
Source: Author's compilation of elements discussed in Held (1996).

Compare this with one set of criteria for a threshold on a democracy-nondemocracy continuum that corresponds closely to authoritarianism. I have chosen the Polyarchy Scale for this purpose because its criteria are explicitly stated. (These coding criteria are reproduced in Table 2.2.) The first two components of each definition are nearly interchangeable, even though the Polyarchy Scale is more explicit here about what limited pluralism means in practice. (Obviously, Linz's legendary 237-page essay is far more elaborate than the brief definition quoted in Table 2.2.) The Polyarchy Scale, however, omits three additional components that are included in Linz's definition – the nature of the leaders' belief systems, the absence of active political mobilization by the regime, and some degree of institutionalization. The Polyarchy Scale is therefore thinner.

A trade-off between validity and extension

Operational definitions of concepts are valid to the extent that they refer to all the aspects of the concept that we have in mind when we use it and no aspects that we do not have in mind. This implies that thicker concepts are not necessarily more valid. Adding a criterion to a definition makes it more valid only if the new criterion is a relevant one. For example, in the 1960s, a series of scholars made the mistake of considering countries more democratic if they maintained democracy over a long period of time (Arat 1988; Cutright 1963; Cutright and Wiley 1969; Lipset 1959). This practice only confounded democracy with stability, thus resulting in a loss of conceptual validity (Bollen 1980).

There is a trade-off between the thickness of an indicator and its applicability to a variety of countries. Comparative research on democratization employs some thick concepts of democracy that are deeply and richly descriptive of some countries but not others, and some thin concepts of democracy that describe many countries equally well but less revealingly. As Sartori explained, there is a trade-off between a concept's intension (the number of defining attributes it has) and its extension (the range of countries to which it can be applied) (1970).[4] We often say that thin concepts travel farther. Thick concepts do not travel as far because they carry more baggage, but they are better equipped for the places to which they do travel.

---

[4] As Collier and Levitsky (1997) note, the trade-off between intension and extension that Sartori identified applies only to classical definitions (Sartori 1970), in which defining attributes are all required ($Y = X_1$ AND X_2 AND $\ldots X_n$). It does not apply to what Goertz calls "family resemblance" definitions, which describe alternative attributes ($Y = X_1$ OR X_2 OR $\ldots X_n$) (Goertz 2006). For the latter type of definition, increasing (alternative) intension increases extension.

Table 2.2. Definitions of authoritarian regime and a low degree of polyarchy contrasted

Authoritarian regime	Polyarchy Scale score 5
"[Political systems without] free competition between leaders to validate at regular intervals by nonviolent means their claim to rule."	"[There are] no meaningful elections: elections without choice of candidates or parties, or no elections at all."
"Political systems with limited, not responsible, political pluralism."	"Some political parties are banned and trade unions or interest groups are harassed or banned, but membership in some alternatives to official organizations is permitted. Dissent is discouraged, whether by informal pressure or by systematic censorship, but control is incomplete. The extent of control may range from selective punishment of dissidents on a limited number of issues to a situation in which only determined critics manage to make themselves heard. There is some freedom of private discussion. Alternative sources of information are widely available but government versions are presented in preferential fashion. This may be the result of partiality in and greater availability of government-controlled media; selective closure, punishment, harassment, or censorship of dissident reporters, publishers, or broadcasters; or mild self-censorship resulting from any of these."
"Without elaborate and guiding ideology, but with distinctive mentalities."	
"Without extensive nor intensive political mobilization, except at some points in their development."	
"And in which a leader or occasionally a small group exercises power within formally ill-defined limits but actually quite predictable ones."	
Source: Juan J. Linz, "Nondemocratic Regimes," in *Handbook of Political Science*, vol. 3: *Macropolitical Theory*, 264, ed. Fred I. Greenstein and Nelson W. Polsby (Reading, MA: Addison-Wesley, 1975).	*Source*: Michael Coppedge and Wolfgang Reinicke, "Measuring Polyarchy," *Studies in Comparative International Development* 25:1 (Spring 1990): 53–54.

Note: Table 2.2 was originally published in Michael Coppedge, "Thickening Thin Concepts: Issues in Large-*N* Data Generation" in *Regimes and Democracy in Latin America: Theories and Method*, 105–122, ed. Gerardo L. Munck (New York: Oxford University Press, 2007).

Figure 2.2 illustrates this trade-off in extension using Linz's definitions of the basic democratic, authoritarian, and totalitarian regimes. Linz contrasted each regime with reference to five characteristics: the selection of leaders through elections, the degree of pluralism, the nature of participation, the ideological mind-set of the leaders, and the degree to which the political system was institutionalized. The figure simplifies his scheme a bit by allowing each characteristic to have only two or three possible variations. This conceptual scheme tells us a great deal about the regimes that match these characteristics. But, at the same time, as the figure illustrates, the multiple requirements for each regime type limit the applicability of his definitions to just 3 of the 108 theoretically possible combinations.[5] To be more realistic about the severity of the problem, the cells in Figure 2.2 that are unlikely to contain any countries are shaded dark gray; the largest number of countries would fall in the white and light-gray cells. This shading also helps illustrate the strength and weakness of thin concepts. A slightly thinner conceptual scheme that distinguished among democracy, authoritarianism, and totalitarianism based simply on elections, pluralism, and participation would probably cover all of the cases in the white or light-gray cells. However, to do so, it would tell us nothing about the omitted characteristics – institutionalization and the leaders' ideological mind-set.

The ability of concepts to travel applies to travel in time as well as space. The ancient Athenians understood their own democracy in terms that are alien to us today. Athenians restricted democratic rights to a small minority of the adult males; they voted directly on laws rather than for representatives; they considered democracy impossible in states with more than a few thousand citizens; and they considered public-spirited harmony, not a competition among interests, essential to the nature of democracy (Katz 1997). By these criteria, there are no democracies in the twenty-first century. Today's emphasis on liberal representative democracy is the result of an eighteenth-century adaptation of the concept to large states and the struggle against absolutist monarchy. In the nineteenth century, writers (Tocqueville and Marx, for example) considered social and economic equality a defining characteristic of democracy. Most U.S. political scientists turned their backs on this tradition in the twentieth century when a purely political, procedural version

---

[5] Linz wrote hundreds of pages describing political systems that differed from these basic three. Some, such as authoritarian situations, could fit in Figure 2.2 without any revisions to the characteristics around which it is structured. Others, such as sultanistic regimes and posttotalitarian regimes, had defining characteristics that were not part of Figure 2.2 and therefore suggest that Linz's underlying classificatory scheme was still more complex.

Ideology of Leaders	Participation	Institutionalized?	Full Pluralism		Limited Pluralism		Monistic Control	
			Elections	Not	Elections	Not	Elections	Not
Indeterminate ideology	Welcome but not forced	Yes	Democratic					
		No						
	Discouraged	Yes						
		No						
	Forced	Yes						
		No						
Distinctive mentality	Welcome but not forced	Yes						
		No						
	Discouraged	Yes				Authoritarian		
		No						
	Forced	Yes						
		No						
Elaborate and guiding ideology	Welcome but not forced	Yes						
		No						
	Discouraged	Yes						
		No						
	Forced	Yes						Totalitarian
		No						

Figure 2.2 Intension and Extension in Linz's Definitions of Regime Types. *Note:* Previously published in Michael Coppedge, "Thickening Thin Concepts: Issues in Large-*N* Data Generation," in *Regimes and Democracy in Latin America: Theories and Methods*, 105–122, ed. Gerardo L. Munck (New York: Oxford University Press, 2007).

of democracy more effectively distinguished the West from its fascist and communist rivals (Purcell 1973). Over the centuries, therefore, the concept of democracy has lost component after component, leaving us with today's very thin, minimal standard that many diverse countries can satisfy.

Thin concepts of democracy are well represented by Robert Dahl's concept of polyarchy. Polyarchy has eight components, or "institutional requirements"[6]: (1) almost all adult citizens have the right to vote; (2) almost all adult citizens are eligible for public office; (3) political leaders have the right to compete for votes; (4) elections are free and fair; (5) all citizens are free to form and join political parties and other organizations; (6) all citizens are free to express themselves on all political issues; (7) diverse sources of information about politics exist and are protected by law; and (8) government policies depend on votes and other expressions of preference (Dahl 1971). This version of democracy is not accepted by all comparativists, but it is a well-known point of reference, and many scholars who do not wish to write their own definitions have cited polyarchy as what they mean by democracy. With eight components, polyarchy is not the thinnest concept in the discipline, but it is thin enough to omit mention of many qualities that are commonly associated with democracy, such as majority rule, judicial independence, separation of powers, local autonomy, jury trials, and numerous personal rights, not to mention socioeconomic equality, direct democracy, small population, and public-spirited harmony.

One consequence of using a minimal concept of democracy is that many countries qualify as democracies even though some subjectively seem more democratic than others. For example, in 2009, Freedom House assigned its highest ratings to countries as diverse as Switzerland, Uruguay, Greek Cyprus, Cape Verde, Finland, Poland, and Andorra.[7] Such results have stimulated a reaction against minimal concepts of democracy. Some scholars therefore remind us of components of democracy that have been dropped or taken for granted in the past fifty years and quite understandably call for them to be restored or made explicit. Thus, Schmitter and Karl include institutionalization and a viable civil society ("cooperation and deliberation via autonomous group activity") among their criteria for "what democracy is"

---

[6] In his later work, *Democracy and Its Critics*, Dahl amended "government policies depend on votes and other expressions of preference" to "control over governmental decisions about policy is constitutionally vested in elected officials" (Dahl 1989, 221). This small change in wording made more explicit Dahl's acceptance of representative democracy.

[7] Freedom House claims to consider a very long list of characteristics in its ratings, but its procedures are not transparent, and its ratings are similar to other indicators that take few characteristics into account. Complete Freedom House ratings are available at http://www.freedomhouse.org.

(1991, 79). Similarly, others stress the centrality of the rule of law and an independent judiciary (Diamond et al. 1995; Hartlyn and Valenzuela 1994; O'Donnell 1994). Valenzuela and others also argue that democracy requires elected officials to enjoy autonomy from unelected veto groups, whether they are economic conglomerates, international powers, or the military; and impartial respect for basic citizenship rights (O'Donnell 1993; Valenzuela 1992). Guillermo O'Donnell, building on the work of Amartya Sen, has come full circle by arguing that satisfaction of some basic economic and social needs is necessary for any meaningful democracy to exist (O'Donnell 2002).

The choice of thick or thin concepts also affects the potential theoretical significance of research. Thick concepts are often meaningful only when embedded in a well-defined theory; many of them contain elaborate theoretical assumptions as elements of their definitions. They are shorthand for theories or parts of theories. Thin concepts are more theoretically adaptable: they lend themselves more easily for use in diverse theories. Philosophers of science like to remind us that all concepts are theoretical, as all constructs require making assumptions about pieces of reality that we imagine to be especially relevant for certain descriptive or explanatory purposes (Lakatos 1970). But some concepts are more theoretically involved than others.

A good way to appreciate the difference is to think of theory in the social sciences as selective storytelling. As social scientists, we craft stylized accounts of events. The elements we emphasize are the elements of theater and fiction: who the relevant actors are, what the time and the place is (the setting), which instruments (props) can be used by the actors, the nature of their preferences or goals (motives), how they strategize to achieve their goals (plot), and a process (action) leading to a particular outcome (denouement). The thinnest concepts refer only to individual elements of a story; thick concepts tend to link together several elements. Thick concepts can be stories in themselves, sometimes complete with morals. "Dependency" was one (Cardoso and Faletto 1971). Guillermo O'Donnell has formulated a series of others – bureaucratic-authoritarianism (1973), delegative democracy (1994), and horizontal accountability (1998); Collier and Collier's (1991) mode of incorporation is yet another. Some thick concepts would qualify as conflicting imperatives, Andrew Gould's (1999) term for complex concepts possessing a tension that can be used to generate hypotheses. All of these could be considered either very thick concepts or shorthand for theories.[8]

---

[8] Because thick concepts contain more ambitious theory, they should be subjected to testing, just as theories are. Calling a theory a concept does not render it immune to testing. Thin concepts, in

Unfortunately, different preferences for thin or thick concepts lead scholars to talk past one another: when qualitative and quantitative analysts say "democracy," they literally mean different things. Strictly speaking, research on the causes of thin democracy speaks only to other research on thin democratization; research on the causes of thick democracy has relevance for a longer and richer theoretical tradition. As we shall see herein, the practical consequences of defining democracy differently are not serious when the elements of different dimensions are all strongly correlated with a common underlying dimension. But sometimes changing the criteria for democracy makes a huge difference. For example, Paxton (2000) has shown that using women's suffrage as an essential criterion for democracy changes the age of some democratic regimes by more than a century.

It is important to bear in mind that the trade-offs between thick and thin concepts are consequences of the difficulty and expense of gathering political information. If political scientists had more resources, we could probably develop concepts of democraticness that would be richly descriptive of all countries (and all historical periods) to an equal degree. For the present, however, we have to choose between thick and thin concepts, and these choices have repercussions for theoretical understanding and measurement. Choices about measurement, in turn, affect the kinds of causal analysis that can be carried out. These are profoundly pivotal choices that have caused the qualitative and quantitative approaches in political science to diverge. Scholars who prefer thick concepts tend to engage in qualitative research, whereas those who are comfortable with thin concepts tend to promote quantitative research, and these approaches have evolved on partially separate tracks. Although these approaches have never completely lost touch with each other, it is increasingly difficult to perceive how each is relevant for the other. One of the purposes of this book is to clarify their mutual relevance.

Measurement

The choice that comparativists make between thick and thin concepts affects the number of dimensions that underlie their measurements. Thick concepts tend to be multidimensional, whereas thin concepts tend to be unidimensional. When a concept is unidimensional, its components vary together.

contrast, are less theoretically ambitious; they assume less (and say less), and therefore leave more to induction. The thinner the concept, the less testing is required to achieve a similar level of readiness for theory building.

Intuitively, this means that if component A is present to a high degree, then component B is present to a high degree as well, and vice versa. In bivariate tables and scatterplots, unidimensional components show a strong diagonal relationship, but multidimensional components show a more uniform dispersion of cases in all four quadrants. Intuitively, it is easy to imagine low-high or high-low combinations of multidimensional components that would not be rare exceptions. In a 2 × 2 table, cases are spread out among at least three of the four cells; in a scatterplot, they form no diagonal pattern. There is no way to represent such patterns faithfully without employing at least two dimensions; attempting to do so would be oversimplification or reductionism. But the higher the degree of association, the more reasonable it is to reduce the two components to one simpler concept or a single dimension.

Even minimal concepts of democracy are usually multidimensional. Dahl, for example, argued explicitly that polyarchy had two dimensions: contestation ("the extent of permissible opposition, public contestation, or political competition") and inclusiveness ("the proportion of the population entitled to participate on a more or less equal plane in controlling and contesting the conduct of government") (Dahl 1971). They are separate dimensions because countries that have high contestation are not necessarily highly inclusive and vice versa. Rather, mixed combinations can be observed: closed hegemonies, competitive oligarchies, inclusive hegemonies, and polyarchies. Subsequent empirical research has confirmed Dahl's intuition. Figure 2.3 is a scatterplot of countries in 2000 on indicators of Dahl's dimensions, contestation and inclusiveness (using indicators described in Coppedge et al. 2008). The plot shows that some countries, the polyarchies, such as Norway, Cyprus, Sweden, Italy, and Canada, are high on both contestation and inclusiveness; and some are low on both dimensions, the closed hegemonies, such as Afghanistan, Saudi Arabia, Libya, and Burma. However, some other countries are low on contestation but high on inclusiveness. Countries such as Cuba, Syria, Vietnam, Iraq, and China include citizens in elections but do not permit competition.[9] These off-diagonal cases are evidence of a second dimension. Just as the points in the plot cannot be joined by a straight line, the information in these two indicators cannot be reduced to a single meaningful number for each country. Contestation and inclusiveness therefore lie on two different dimensions.

---

[9] Obviously, there are intermediate cases as well. It is interesting that in 2000 there were no countries with high contestation and low inclusiveness – what Dahl called competitive oligarchies (Dahl 1971). This combination was common before the extension of the suffrage in the early twentieth century, but it is extinct today.

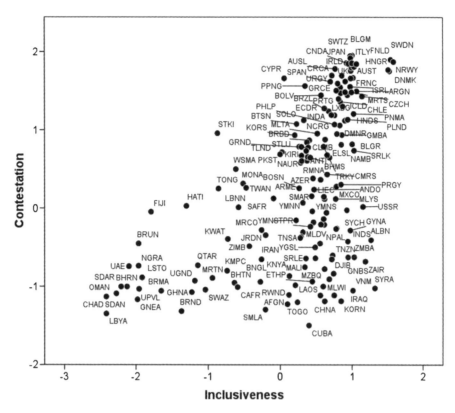

Figure 2.3   Distribution of Countries on Two Dimensions of Democracy, 2000. Both indicators were estimated by exploratory Principal Components Analysis of fourteen democracy indicators. The units of measurement are standard deviations. The estimation procedure and justifications for interpreting these as indicators of Dahl's two dimensions of polyarchy are in Coppedge, Alvarez, and Maldonado (2008).

A thicker version of democracy would have more than two dimensions. I suspect that a thicker concept of democracy would possess five dimensions. The first two would be thick versions of Dahl's dimensions of polyarchy – contestation and inclusiveness. There is probably more to contestation than becoming informed and making a simple choice among parties or candidates every few years. Contestation could also depend on the number and quality of choices presented on a ballot, democratic selection of candidates, certain kinds of public campaign financing, guaranteed media access for all parties, and opportunities for opposition parties to gain a foothold at lower levels of government.

Similarly, inclusiveness – the proportion of the adult citizens who have effective opportunities to participate equally in the available opportunities for decision making – need not be confined to voting for representatives and running for office. In reality, there are or could be many other opportunities for citizens to participate equally in decision making: in judicial proceedings, at public hearings, in primaries, and in referenda and plebiscites. It could also include a judicial system that provides equal protection under the law. To complicate matters, inclusiveness itself may consist of two dimensions – the proportion of people possessing a right and the degree to which they possess it – which together would define a distribution of rights akin to a distribution of wealth.

To these three dimensions – contestation, breadth of inclusion, and fullness of inclusion – I would add two more: the division of powers and the scope of democratic authority. The division of powers corresponds to the unitary-federal dimension of Lijphart's concept of consensual democracy. Lijphart has established that federalism, regional autonomy, bicameralism, and local self-government cohere as one dimension and that this dimension is distinct from his executives-parties dimension (Lijphart 1999). Whether one considers a division of powers more democratic or merely differently democratic than unitary government is a matter of opinion, but the separateness of this dimension is beyond dispute.

A fifth dimension – the scope of democratic authority – reflects the agenda of issues that the democratic government may decide without consulting unelected actors. This dimension reflects any constraints on governmental authority imposed by the military, business groups, religious authorities, foreign powers, or international organizations regarding issues of importance to them. A broad scope of democratic authority also requires that civil servants be willing and able to implement the policies made by elected officials because it does not matter how a government was chosen if it has no power to carry out its decisions. The fewer the issues that are in practice off-limits to final decision making by relatively inclusive bodies, the broader the scope of democratic authority. These five dimensions taken together would define democracy as a regime in which a large proportion of the citizens have an equal and effective chance to participate in making final decisions on a full range of issues at an appropriate level of government.[10]

Ultimately, however, the number of dimensions in a concept is an empirical question. Sometimes components that seem to be conceptually distinct are

---

[10]   For an even thicker definition of the quality of democracy that includes the satisfaction of basic human needs and respectful treatment of citizens by fellow citizens and the state, see O'Donnell (2002) and the Citizen's Audit of the Quality of Democracy in Costa Rica (Proyecto Estado de la Nación 2001).

Table 2.3. Two unidimensional components of polyarchy

		Freedom of expression		
		Free expression	Dissent discouraged	Dissent forbidden
Media pluralism	Media are diverse and protected by law	40	3	0
	Media have a progovernment bias	11	24	0
	Diversity allowed only when harmless	0	45	1
	Complete official domination	0	6	29

Note: Numbers in cells are the number of countries that had both the row and the column characteristic in 1985.

Source: Data used in Michael Coppedge and Wolfgang Reinicke, "Measuring Polyarchy," *Studies in Comparative International Development* 25:1 (Spring 1990): 51–72, and available online at http://www.nd.edu/~mcoppedg/crd.

empirically associated closely enough that one can treat them as unidimensional. This is the case with the many items that are often used to measure contestation, which include regular competitive and fair elections, party competition, freedom to form and join parties and other political organizations, freedom to express diverse political positions private and publicly, and freedom for newspapers and broadcast media to express diverse points of view, especially those critical of the government. Table 2.3 provides an example of such a close association using an indicator of pluralism in the media and an indicator of freedom of expression. Most countries are arrayed along the diagonal running from the upper left to the lower right. This means that regimes that permit free expression also have laws to protect diverse media; those that forbid dissent also tend to have official media that present only the state's versions of the news; and so on. Because of this close association, both indicators can be treated as measuring the same underlying dimension, contestation. The Polyarchy Scale is a good general example of unidimensionality (Coppedge and Reinicke 1990). All four of its components – indicators of fair elections, freedom of organization, freedom of expression, and pluralism in the media – are closely associated. For instance, it happens that almost all countries that have many alternatives to official information also have leaders chosen in fair elections and a high degree of freedom of organization and expression, whereas countries in which citizens are afraid to criticize the government even privately also tend not to have meaningful elections, do not permit opposition parties or other organizations, and maintain tight official control over the media. Because of these empirical associations, it makes sense

Table 2.4. Principal components analysis of democracy indicators for 1990

Indicator and source	Contestation	Inclusiveness
Civil liberties (Freedom House 2002)	**0.98**	0.13
Political rights (Freedom House 2002)	**0.97**	0.07
Competitiveness of participation (Marshall and Jaggers 2002)	**0.93**	0.02
Competition (Vanhanen 2000)	**0.92**	0.01
Type of regime (Cheibub and Gandhi 2004)	**0.88**	0.02
Executive constraints (Marshall and Jaggers 2002)	**0.86**	0.04
Competitiveness of executive recruitment (Marshall and Jaggers 2002)	**0.80**	0.12
Freedom of assembly and association (Cingranelli and Richards 2004)	**0.80**	0.05
Workers' rights (Cingranelli and Richards 2004)	**0.77**	0.05
Freedom of speech (Cingranelli and Richards 2004)	**0.67**	0.05
Political participation (Cingranelli and Richards 2004)	**0.62**	0.31
Adult suffrage (%) (Bollen 1998)	0.12	**0.94**
Women's political rights (Cingranelli and Richards 2004)	0.06	**0.69**
Openness of executive recruitment (Marshall and Jaggers 2002)	0.20	**0.59**
Participation (Vanhanen 2000)	0.51	**0.37**
Eigenvalue	9.30	1.21
Percentage of variance explained	62.0	8.0

Note: Exploratory principal components analysis with direct oblimin (oblique) rotation. The two components have a correlation of 0.549. All variables come from two merged compilations (Bollen 1998; Teorell et al. 2006). Only the absolute values of the component weights are reported.

to treat the four components as reflections of a single underlying dimension, which can be called contestation.

Most of the commonly used indicators of democracy are primarily indicators of contestation. Table 2.4 reports an exploratory principal components analysis of fifteen indicators. This analysis tells us how closely each indicator is aligned with two dimensions of democracy, which have been identified as contestation and inclusiveness (Coppedge, Alvarez, and Maldonado 2008): the closer the weight in the table is to 1, the closer the alignment is. Most of the indicators, including both Freedom House indices (Political Rights and Civil Liberties); three of the four components of Polity; and Cheibub and Gandhi's update of the Alvarez and colleagues' (2004) democracy-dictatorship dichotomy, measure contestation more than inclusiveness. Half as many indicators measure inclusiveness more than contestation, although less well, except for the percentage of adults who can vote; and these indicators have not been used nearly as often. This emphasis on the contestation dimension is the reason that many democracy indicators are highly correlated: almost always at .800 or better. Researchers who need indicators of contestation therefore have many from which to choose.

But how accurately do they measure contestation? In measurement theory, accuracy has two aspects – validity and reliability. Validity – the extent to which an indicator measures what one claims it measures – has already been discussed, and it seems clear that these indicators are valid as long as we treat them as indicators of contestation rather than of democracy in all of its aspects. Reliability is the degree to which a measurement procedure produces the same measurements every time, regardless of who is performing it. Reliability depends on many qualities of the measurement procedure: the reliability of the source information, the clarity of coding criteria, the skill and care of the coders, the degree of agreement among coders, and so on. But reliability is also a function of the unidimensionality of the components of an indicator because, in practice, unidimensionality is a matter of degree. The looser the associations among any of the components of an indicator, the less reliable the indicator is.

Most existing democracy indicators are very reliable for identifying large differences in democracy but less reliable for measuring intermediate values and small differences (Pemstein et al. 2010). All of the indicators we have can easily distinguish between Sweden and China or even between Costa Rica and Pakistan, but none can very reliably distinguish the degrees of democracy in Greece and India in the 1990s or the small change in Mexico from 1994 to 1997. These indicators are very useful for research on democratization that uses large samples of nearly global extension, but less useful for comparing the quality of democracy in fairly homogeneous world regions or tracking short-term changes in single countries.

The limitations of existing democracy indicators are partly the result of the multidimensionality of democracy. Multidimensionality forces scholars to choose between two measurement strategies. One option is to create distinct indicators for distinct dimensions. For example, principal components or factor analyses like the one reported in Table 2.4 enable researchers to create an indicator of each dimension by combining all of the indicators that went into the analysis, giving more weight to those closely aligned with the dimension and less weight to those only loosely correlated with it. Indicators produced in this way are more valid and more reliable because they measure the commonalities among many indicators and exclude the random or idiosyncratic variation in each indicator that is not found in other indicators (Pemstein et al. 2010). With two collaborators, I have produced such indicators of contestation and inclusiveness for nearly all countries covering all of the years from 1950 to 2000 (Coppedge, Alvarez, and Maldonado 2008). I use these indicators occasionally in this book, especially in Chapter 9.

The other strategy is to combine all of the dimensions into a single indicator. Combining dimensions is much harder to do well, so those who measure democracy have usually taken the easier path of reducing democracy to the most unidimensional set of indicators: contestation. Nevertheless, here and there scholars have created variables to measure other dimensions of democratization. Kenneth Bollen and others have created a sophisticated suffrage time-series (Bollen 1996); Munck and Verkuilen (2002) have created an appealing indicator of the relative strength of elected and unelected powers in Latin America; Arend Lijphart has constructed a valid indicator of the division of powers in thirty-six countries (Lijphart 1999); and the World Bank and Transparency International have built data sets containing many indicators of corruption, bureaucratic efficiency, and other items that would be relevant for measuring the chance that the state will implement democratic decisions faithfully (Kaufmann et al. 2007; Transparency International 2008). All of these indicators are relevant for measuring democracy, broadly defined, but they are not integrated into a single comprehensive indicator of democracy. This strategy has the advantage of avoiding any assumptions about how these dimensions might combine to determine a country's degree of democracy. The disadvantage is that this strategy stops short of producing a single summary indicator of democracy. Paradoxically, therefore, one way to measure democracy better is to stop measuring democracy and simply measure its component dimensions instead.

This disaggregated strategy has the additional advantage of making it possible to explore empirically the interrelationships among dimensions, which would open up a fascinating new avenue for research. Do elected officials enjoy greater autonomy vis-à-vis the military when they are backed by a broad electoral base of support? Does federalism really allow citizens to be better represented on certain issues? Does possession of the suffrage translate into effective possession of other civil and political rights? All of these are questions that should be addressed by empirical research. Such questions must be answered before any unified indicator of democracy can be developed, and it would be desirable for the answers to come from empirical research rather than mere assumptions.

The development of separate indicators is, in fact, a prerequisite for the second option: appropriate aggregation of dimensions into a single indicator of democracy. Doing this requires a stronger theory about how dimensions of democracy combine, from which one might derive a mathematical formula. Goertz has written the best guide to aggregation rules: correspondences between certain logical relationships and certain mathematical operations (Goertz 2006, chap. 2). Most indices and scales combine indicators by adding or averaging them. Goertz, however, shows that these operations are rarely consistent with the concepts, which are typically defined in terms of necessary and sufficient conditions. Such definitions correspond more naturally to the mathematical minimum function or the logical "AND" function, when the country is only as democratic as its least democratic feature; or to the mathematical maximum function or the logical "OR" function, when the country is as democratic as its most democratic feature. These two functions define the most divergent ways of combining indicators. Averaging produces intermediate scores because it allows substitutability: high scores on some indicators can compensate for low scores on others. Multiplication allows for some substitution as well but is closer to the minimum. There are many other possible aggregation rules (Goertz 2006).

I suspect that a workable rule is likely to be more complex than addition and subtraction. If so, component indicators will have to be interval, if not ratio, data; otherwise, it would not be legitimate to subject them to multiplication or division, not to mention logging or exponentials (Stevens 1946).[11] Most measurement of democracy now is ordinal, so if we wish to develop a single indicator of democracy in several dimensions, we will have to find ways of measuring dimensions at the interval level or higher. One way to do this is to reformulate the attributes of democracy in terms of probabilities. This would entail measuring, for example, the probability that a citizen will be allowed to vote, that votes will be counted fairly, that a writer can criticize the government without being punished, and so on. These probabilities could be either estimated reasonably or calculated from actual practices. The rules for aggregating probabilities are then straightforward.

A few scholars have taken steps in this direction. Axel Hadenius made a start by combining indicators of contestation and participation in an innovative and promising fashion (Hadenius 1992). Hadenius's index of democracy is an average of an indicator of open, correct, and effective elections and an indicator of various freedoms. What makes this index interesting is that before the elections component is averaged, it is multiplied by the proportion of the population that is eligible to vote and the proportion of national legislative seats that is filled by election. This mathematical operation implemented

---

[11] Differences on interval indicators become ratio data, so for some applications, interval-level measurement is a legitimate starting point for higher-level mathematical operations.

Hadenius's theoretical assumption that freedoms contribute to democracy independently of elections and that elections matter for democracy only to the extent that they select real decision makers and that all citizens are eligible to vote. This is the kind of theory that is necessary for aggregating dimensions. However, it is not the only possible theory for doing so. Kenneth Bollen made different assumptions when combining contestation indicators with suffrage in his "Liberal Democracy" series (Bollen 1993). Bollen's formula, although complex, had the effect of giving much lower scores to countries that allow competition but restrict the suffrage to about a quarter of the population or less.[12]

I believe that it would be useful to think in terms of a floor and a ceiling for democracy. Fundamental civil liberties constitute a floor for democracy in the sense that the freedom of individual citizens to speak, write, read, associate, and so on is valuable even if they are not allowed to compete in elections or choose representatives to make policy. A regime cannot be less democratic than the individual freedoms it allows. By a similar logic, the state's willingness and capacity to execute policies faithfully constitutes a ceiling. No matter how representative and democratic a government is, if its policies are ignored and undermined by the bureaucracy, the police, and the courts, then the whole representative process comes to nothing. Therefore, a regime cannot be more democratic than its actual execution of any policies that are adopted democratically. Between the floor and the ceiling, what matters for democracy are all of the institutions and processes designed to translate the will of the people into public policy – party competition, elections, electoral systems, legislative procedures, and executive-legislative relations.[13]

Unfortunately, there is as yet no scholarly consensus on a thicker definition that convincingly incorporates components such as the rule of law,

---

[12] Bollen's index first calculates an indicator that we can call political and legislative rights, composed of an average of a Freedom House–based political rights variable and the product of legislative effectiveness and legislative selection, two variables from the Arthur Banks data set. All are weighted so that this average ranges from 0 to 100. If this indicator of political and legislative rights is less than the percentage of adults enjoying suffrage, then liberal democracy is the average of political and legislative rights, and Banks's party legitimacy is variable. However, if political and legislative rights are greater than suffrage, then liberal democracy is simply the average of suffrage and party legitimacy. If suffrage is high, therefore, liberal democracy is a weighted average of several contestation variables; and if suffrage is very low, suffrage drags down the liberal democracy series more powerfully (Bollen 1998).

[13] This theory would imply a formula something like $[kF + (1 - k)P]S$, where F is an indicator of individual freedom, P is an indicator of competition to make public policy, S is the probability that the state will faithfully execute policies, and k is the maximum possible height of the floor; that is, the highest degree of democracy a regime can provide if it does not allow elections. All variables are scaled to a 0–1 interval, although k should be small, around 0.25.

the autonomy of elected officials, decentralization, and national sovereignty. Progress toward consensus would be aided by empirical analysis of the number and nature of any dimensions that structure these concepts or components. Empirical analysis is crucial because the number and nature of dimensions in a thick concept is determined more by the real world than by our imaginations. In theory, every facet of a concept could lie on a separate dimension from every other facet. In theory, for example, there could be cases in every cell of Figure 2.2: even poorly institutionalized regimes with highly ideological leaders who welcome participation and permit fair elections but practice monistic control. It is only in practice that such combinations become odd and rare and that other combinations become more common. We do not always know the reason for this. They may cause each other, or they may have a common historical cause. In any case, the dimensions that structure a thick concept are best thought of as handy bundles of a larger number of potential dimensions. Such bundles probably hold together only for selected periods and places. The more diverse the sample and the longer the expanse of time it covers, the more likely it is to resist reduction to a small number of dimensions.

Consequences for analysis

The choices that scholars make about how to define and measure their concepts have consequences for the kinds of analysis that are possible and desirable. This section examines consequences for the selection of cases and models, for descriptive and causal inferences, and for levels of measurement.

Data-driven research

In comparative politics, data are scarce because the costs of collecting data are high, especially quantitative data that cover a large number of countries over a long span of time using consistent measurement criteria. The practical consequence of scarce data is that comparativists who would like to do large-sample (i.e., large-N), quantitative studies inevitably run up against severe constraints. They find that the variables they want to use are simply not available for many of the cases they would like to study, or that some of the variables they would like to use do not exist for any of the cases in their study, or both. If this does not lead them to give up on the project altogether, they may choose to do research on just the cases for which all of their variables are available, or they may choose to drop some of their variables to keep a larger sample. The result is research that is data-driven: the choice of indicators influences the selection of cases and the set of hypotheses to be tested.

Research on democratization has always been heavily data-driven. For example, almost every quantitative study of democratization excludes some cases because they are communist countries, countries with small populations, countries in civil war, or countries too far back in time for good data to exist. Another example of data-driven research is the prevalence of purely cross-sectional analyses before time-series indicators of democracy became generally available in the late 1980s. Before then, researchers settled for data that measured democracy in a large number of countries for one year – snapshots of democratization frozen at one moment in time. There was no good methodological reason to do this; in fact, we shall see in Chapters 5, 7, and 9 that there are good reasons to prefer comparisons over time. In fact, scholars would have preferred time-series data all along. When international-relations scholars developed the Polity time-series and Freedom House country ratings covered a sufficiently long span of years, time-series analysis quickly became de rigueur for quantitative research on democratization. Another characteristic of data scarcity has been the widespread use of indicators of debatable validity and reliability. Examples abound: studies have used per capita energy consumption or per capita gross domestic product as proxies for economic development; they have measured income inequality with mixed individual- and household-based data; and they have employed regional dummy variables as proxies for culture or world-system position. To their credit, democratization researchers have always eagerly used better variables and more cases as soon as they have become available; but, in the meantime, the scarcity of data has always constrained their choices.

Consequences of measurement error

How do measurement problems affect research findings? One would expect conclusions based on somewhat unreliable indicators to inspire less confidence, but the consequences of measurement problems are not so simple. The nature of the consequences depends on whether one is trying to describe or explain; whether the measurement error is systematic or random; and, if the error is systematic, what the pattern of error is.

Description and explanation are fundamentally different tasks. Description focuses on characteristics or variables one at a time, serially, whereas explanation focuses on the relationships among two or more variables.

When we are describing, that is, reporting measurements on one variable at a time, there are two kinds of errors we can commit: *systematic* or *random*. Random errors have no pattern to them; the kind or degree of error made in one measurement has nothing to do with errors made in other measurements on the same variable. If we rate some countries too high and others too low and there is no particular reason for our mistakes, then we have created random measurement error. When errors are systematic, there are reasons for our mistakes, even if we are unaware of them. We may be too tough and therefore classify some democracies as dictatorships, or we may be ethnocentric and rate presidential democracies higher than otherwise-similar parliamentary democracies. Systematic measurement error leads to biased descriptions, which are "off" in a systematic way. Random measurement error leads to inefficient or fuzzy descriptions, which may be unbiased on average but are less certain. Figure 2.4 illustrates this difference by contrasting the positions of little white diamonds, representing a set of measurements on one variable, with the big black diamond, which shows the true value that we are attempting to measure and therefore describe. In part a, the biased measurements are to the right of the true value, showing how systematic error can lead to an overrating. When there is random error (part b), the measurements are dispersed more broadly around the true value, even though the average measurement is very close to the true value. Of course, measurement error can be biased and inefficient at the same time. All comparative indicators are probably biased and inefficient to some degree; the question is whether they are too biased or inefficient to be useful.

Democracy indicators certainly contain some measurement error, but is it random or systematic? A number of scholars have raised questions about the specific ratings of specific countries. Scott Mainwaring has questioned Przeworski and colleagues' decision to code some authoritarian regimes as democracies if they eventually surrendered power after an electoral loss, such as the military regime in Brazil from 1979 to 1984 (Mainwaring et al. 2001). This is an example of systematic error leading to bias. In fact, Przeworski and colleagues explicitly acknowledge and defend the systematic measurement error in their indicator on the grounds that it is known and correctable (2000, 28). Freedom House indicators have also been criticized for some questionable ratings. For example, Scott Mainwaring has argued that Freedom House was too harsh on leftist Latin American governments in the 1980s and seems to have used stricter criteria in the 1990s than before, with the result that its ratings fail to reflect improvement in Mexico, Colombia, the Dominican Republic, El Salvador, and Guatemala in

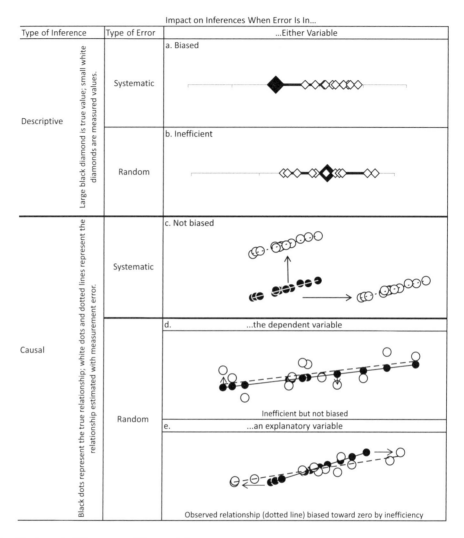

Figure 2.4   The Impact of Measurement Error on Inferences

those years (Mainwaring et al. 2001). Jonathan Hartlyn (2002) identifies the same discrepancies by correlating Freedom House and Polity scores for these countries. Such discrepancies reinforce the conclusion that such indicators are less reliable for small, intraregional differences and changes than they are for large, cross-regional comparisons. If these errors are random, then this is all the caution that is necessary.

However, the only way to know whether there is systematic measurement error is to analyze many measurements systematically. Two of the most sophisticated such analyses did find systematic error in several common indicators in the 1970s and 1980s (Bollen and Paxton 1998; Gleditsch and Ward 1997).[14] The democracy indicators found in the Cross-National Time-Series Data Archive (Banks 1979), which continued the Banks and Textor Cross-Polity Survey (Banks and Textor 1963), tended to be more favorable to Eastern Europe or communist countries and harsher on countries with recent coups, whereas Freedom House tended to overrate Catholic monarchies and under-rate communist regimes. However, the degree of systematic error was, with one exception, 22 percent or less. Five of the eight indicators were at least 70 percent valid, and two – Freedom House's Index of Political Rights and Banks's freedom of group opposition – were more than 87 percent valid.[15] This is fairly reassuring. Furthermore, the high loadings on the first principal component reported in Table 2.4 suggest that even if none of these indicators is very reliable for small-N studies, quite a few of them are sufficiently reliable for large-N comparisons.[16]

The consequences of measurement error for causal inferences are surprising, in principle. There are three basic patterns of error: (1) the addition of a constant to either variable, (2) random error in the dependent variable, and (3) random error in the explanatory variable. Figure 2.4 illustrates these three situations using black dots for the points measured without error, white dots for points measured with error, a solid line for the true regression line, and a dashed line for the regression line affected by measurement error.

1. As King, Keohane, and Verba have pointed out, causal inferences about the magnitudes of effects are not affected if the dependent or independent

---

[14] The Bollen and Paxton article replicates and extends somewhat on Bollen (1993). These articles report confirmatory factor analyses to estimate the source bias and random measurement error in eight indicators that were presumed to measure political liberties and democratic rule; see also Hadenius and Teorell (2005).

[15] Bollen calculated validity as 100 percent minus the sum of the systematic and random measurement error percentages (1993). The worst of the eight indicators were Banks's chief executive elected, with 76 percent random error, and Banks's competitiveness of the nomination process, with 38.5 percent systematic error (1979). At the most valid extreme, Sussman's indicator freedom of print media (1988) had only 9 percent random error and Freedom House's political rights (2003) had 6.4 percent systematic error and no random error. It is important to keep in mind that these estimates have meaning only with respect to the indicators on which they are based.

[16] Munck and Verkuilen (2002) have argued that high correlations should not be very reassuring for two reasons. First, one can obtain high correlations when two indicators agree at the extremes but are completely unrelated in the middle. This point reinforces my conclusion that these indicators are useful for large-sample comparisons but not to measure small differences or changes. Second, correlations (or Bollen's confirmatory factor analysis, for that matter) cannot detect any systematic bias that is shared by all of the indicators. I believe that there is such a systematic bias but that it is the tendency to focus on contestation rather than other aspects of democracy; hence, my caveats about interpreting these indicators.

variable is systematically too high or too low (King et al. 1994). Part c of Figure 2.4 illustrates this result: when a constant bias is added (or subtracted) from either variable, a new line must be drawn to fit the points, but its slope (its angle of inclination, representing the change in Y for each unit change in X) is the same.[17]

2. When there is only random error in the dependent variable, the impact (measured by its slope) of the independent variable is unchanged, but we become less confident that the impact is really there. Part d of Figure 2.4 illustrates this result: the same slope fits both the true (black) and measured (white) dots, but it does not fit them equally well. If we find a significant relationship despite suspected random error in the dependent variable, it is actually more impressive than detecting a relationship when there is no such error. By the same reasoning, if we fail to find a relationship, we need not abandon hope because the relationship may be hidden by the measurement error.

3. When there is only random error in the independent variable, the slope estimate is biased as well as inefficient. But, in all cases, the slope (the dotted line, which fits the white dots) is biased toward zero, as shown in part e of Figure 2.4. Once again, if we find a significant effect despite suspected random error in the independent variable, then it is all the more impressive; if we find no relationship, then it may be that random error is hiding it.

This analysis suggests that what seems like a big problem for descriptive inference is less of a problem for causal inference. To the extent that there is systematic error, it has no effect on our estimates of the marginal effect of any cause on democracy. To the extent that there is random error, it should increase confidence in the many findings that have achieved statistical significance despite the error, although it does cloud the interpretation of other findings that are only marginally or occasionally significant. It might

---

[17] If either variable is multiplied by a constant, the new estimate of the slope will be changed. To be precise, the estimated slope will be the true slope times the constant if the error is in the dependent variable, or the true slope divided by the constant if the error is in the independent variable. In practice, the only instances in which a variable is multiplied or divided by a constant occur when one changes the units of measurement, for example from miles to kilometers or from 1970 dollars to 1990 yen. In any case, the substantive interpretation of the slope would be unchanged, so these are trivial possibilities. Similarly, point predictions would be substantively unaffected provided that the bias is systematic; that is, it affects all observations, and it is present for both the estimation of the model and the generation of predictions. Of course, point predictions are misleading when measurement error biases some observations but not others.

seem, therefore, that if criticisms of measurement error in democracy indicators were intended to undermine confidence in analyses of the causes of democracy, then they have backfired: the worse the measurement, the more we should believe any significant findings, and the more we should give the benefit of the doubt to findings that are marginally insignificant.

This is true in principle. In practice, however, it is very unlikely that systematic measurement error is limited to adding or subtracting constants or that what we treat as random error is purely random. It is more likely that we overrate democracy in some clusters of countries and underrate it in others, and that there is a pattern to our over- and underratings, as Bollen found with respect to various regions. If so, this is neither purely random nor purely systematic measurement error but rather error that is correlated with some unspecified explanatory factor. It is always tempting to dismiss as random variation whatever aspects of democracy that are not well accounted for by our explanations, but it is far more likely that we have not yet discovered the keys to those aspects that would reveal their systematic components. Rather than discuss these issues under the heading of measurement error, however, I save them for later examination of model specification and omitted variable bias in Chapter 9.

Levels of measurement

In addition to their consequences for case and model selection and inferences, choices about concepts influence the level of measurement that can be attempted. Thick concepts are most easily measured with nominal or ordinal data, whereas thin concepts lend themselves more naturally to interval or ratio data.

Ratio indicators are numerical measures with a meaningful zero point and intervals of equal size. Because the intervals are of uniform size, an increase from 2 to 3 is equivalent to an increase from 100 to 101. That is, a one-unit increase is the same no matter what the initial value is. Because ratio indicators have a meaningful zero, ratios are also meaningful: a score of 4 is twice as large as a score of 2. Few democracy indicators are truly at the ratio level of measurement, but one good example is Bollen's suffrage indicator (Bollen 1998). This variable measures the percentage of the adult population that is entitled to vote. An increase from 25 to 50 percent of the adult population is an increase of 25 percentage points, as is an increase from 50 to 75 percent. It also makes sense to say that a country with a score of 90 percent has suffrage that is three times as extensive as that of a country with a score of 30 percent. Another example is Vanhanen's Index of Democratization, which is the product of turnout and the proportion of the legislative vote not won by the largest party (Vanhanen 1990).[18] A zero on this index would mean that either no one voted in the election or that the largest party received all the votes. Many independent variables are ratio data, especially socioeconomic variables such as per capita gross domestic product, economic growth rates, inflation rates, and literacy rates.[19]

Interval indicators, like ratio indicators, have equal intervals but, unlike ratio indicators, lack an absolute zero point. Outside of the political world, the best example is the Fahrenheit temperature scale. An increase of ten degrees is an increase of ten degrees no matter what the starting temperature is; but it is not correct to say that ninety degrees is three times as hot as thirty degrees. One interval-level democracy indicator is Bollen's Liberal Democracy Series. This variable takes on many possible values between 0 and 100, so its intervals can be assumed to be approximately equal.[20] However, a value of 0 on this indicator does not qualify it as ratio data unless it corresponds to situations of zero liberal democracy, that is, the complete absence of liberal democracy. Highly repressive regimes such as that of the Soviet Union under Stalin, Nazi Germany, China during the Cultural Revolution, Cambodia under the Khmer Rouge, and North Korea could be considered antitheses of liberal democracy, but it is hard to imagine no freedom of any kind, the complete exclusion of all citizens from any role in policy making, and the complete lack of any information whatsoever about politics.

Ordinal indicators are rankings: they reflect relative positions on some dimension, but the distances between ranks are assumed to be unknown. The third-best score could be a close third or a distant third; the top score could be the best by far or nearly a tie with the second-best score. Most democracy indicators are technically at the ordinal level of measurement.[21] A good example is Mainwaring, Brinks, and Pérez Liñán's classification of Latin American regimes as democratic, semidemocratic, or authoritarian: three ranges on an underlying dimension from democratic to authoritarian

---

[18] The validity of this index is dubious, but it is clearly ratio data.

[19] I have suggested here that democracy could be reconceptualized in terms of probabilities. If so, one could imagine a zero probability of free citizens influencing policy decisions. We lack such an indicator at present, but if one were created, it would qualify as ratio data.

[20] This variable has more than twenty values, and Bollen made extraordinary efforts to make the sizes of differences in scores correspond to the sizes of differences in democraticness.

[21] Gurr's and Hadenius's indicators are built from both interval- and ordinal-level components, but when the components are combined, the lower level of measurement prevails in the aggregated indicator.

(Mainwaring et al. 2001). Others include Wesson's Democracy Classification (five ranks), the Freedom House Indexes of Political Rights and Civil Liberties (seven ranks each), Gurr's Polity Indexes of Democracy and Autocracy (ten ranks each), and the Coppedge-Reinicke Polyarchy Scale (eleven ranks) (Bollen 1998). When an ordinal indicator has a small number of ranks, its ordinal nature should be respected. However, the more ranks it has, the more closely it approximates interval data (Labovitz 1970).[22] For this reason, scholars have often combined the two Freedom House indicators into an index ranging from 2 (least freedom) to 14 (most freedom) and the two Polity variables into an index ranging from -10 (full autocracy) to 10 (full democracy). Hadenius's index has so many levels between 0 and 10 (e.g., 7.2, 9.4) that he considered it accurate to within 0.6 points (Hadenius 1992, 76).

Classifications, labels, or typologies that do not imply any ranking on an underlying dimension are nominal indicators. For example, Hannan and Carroll categorized regimes as multiparty, one-party, military, or traditional no-party regimes (Hannan and Carroll 1981). Similarly, Linz and Stepan defined a typology of democratic, authoritarian, totalitarian, posttotalitarian, and sultanistic regimes (Linz and Stepan 1996). In both examples, the first regime in each list is democratic, but there is no implicit ordering of the other regimes on a democracy-nondemocracy dimension. Nominal indicators contain the least amount of quantitative information, but they often compensate by representing a great deal of qualitative information. Nominal indicators can even be used to measure multidimensional phenomena, simply by establishing thresholds on each dimension and labels or types that correspond to being above or below the threshold on certain dimensions. Figure 2.2 shows all the nominal classifications that might be generated with Linz's four criteria. Linz himself labeled three of these types that lie on a democracy-totalitarianism continuum, but if the other possible types were labeled, there would be no underlying ordering.

Dichotomies are the simplest nominal indicators, in which all cases are either above the threshold on all of the criteria or assigned to a residual category. Any list of democracies qualifies as a dichotomous nominal indicator. The best recent example is the classification of democracies and dictatorships by Alvarez, Cheibub, Limongi, and Przeworski (1996). If a regime had an elected executive and legislature, more than one party, and the opposition had a real chance to win the next election, then they coded it a

---

[22] Scholars disagree about the number of ranks required for an ordinal indicator to approximate interval data. Some are comfortable with as few as five; others prefer at least twenty.

democracy; otherwise, they assigned it to a residual (i.e., leftover) category of dictatorships. Note that although dichotomies can handle thick criteria, this particular indicator is based on rather thin criteria.

No level of measurement is inherently superior to another. Nevertheless, there have been heated debates about whether democracy should be measured by dichotomous or continuous indicators. On one side, Sartori (1987) and Przeworski (2000) argue that democracy is inherently dichotomous: a country is either democratic or it is not; there are no degrees of democracy. Therefore, measuring democracy as a matter of degree implies conceptual confusion and increases measurement error. On the other side, Dahl (1971), Bollen (1990), and others argue that there are degrees of democracy and a continuum of democraticness, ranging from very democratic to highly undemocratic regimes. For them, higher levels of measurement improve the accuracy and reliability of democracy indicators. I agree more with Collier and Adcock (1999), who argue that almost any concept can be considered as either categorical or continuous. Contrary to the best-known example of a supposedly inherent dichotomy, it is not strictly true that a woman cannot be half pregnant, for it depends on how one defines pregnant. She can be 4.5 months pregnant; she can have delivered one of two twins; she can, for a brief moment during labor, have the baby half in and half out; she can be heading for a miscarriage or a stillbirth; and so on. If pregnancy can be defined as a matter of degree, so can anything else. Of course, the distribution of the data also matters: the more bimodal the distribution is, the less information is lost by treating the concept as a dichotomy. But the real issue is not whether a concept is a priori categorical or continuous but rather which level of measurement is most useful for the analysis one wishes to do, using the concepts that are most appropriate for the theory.

Precision

The usefulness of an indicator depends on how valid and reliable it is, which we have already discussed; but it also depends on how precise the indicator is. Precision is a criterion separate from considerations of validity, reliability, and level of measurement.[23] Precision is the fineness of the distinctions made by an indicator: the amount of detail. Measurements can be precise

[23] One meaning of *precision* is "level of measurement." This is what Shively calls precision in measurement. Because this definition can be confusing, what I mean by precision is what Shively calls precision in *measures* (Shively 1998).

or imprecise whether they are quantitative or qualitative. A statement that a country is 91.8 percent democratic would be extremely precise in quantitative terms (if such a statement could be made reliably). But it would also be very qualitatively precise to describe that country's democratic institutions in sufficient detail to establish that the d'Hondt system of proportional representation is used in a single national district for legislative elections, opposition parties receive equal broadcast time during campaigns, citizens legislate directly in referendums several times a year, city council meetings are open to the public, and so on.

There is, in practice, a trade-off between quantitative and qualitative precision. Quantitative precision usually entails a loss of qualitative information, and qualitative precision usually entails a loss of quantitative information. If both continuous and categorical indicators measured exactly the same concept, then we would prefer the continuous one on the grounds that it is more informative, more flexible, and better suited for sophisticated testing. For example, if the concept of interest were breadth of the suffrage, then we might choose between two indicators: a qualitative indicator that divided countries into two categories such as universal adult suffrage and suffrage with restrictions, and a quantitative index of the percentage of the adult population that is eligible to vote. Of the two, we should prefer the quantitative indicator because it measures the concept with finer gradations, which give us more quantitative information. If one wanted a categorical measure, it could always be derived from the continuous one by identifying one or more thresholds that correspond to the categories desired, such as at least 95 percent of adults are eligible to vote. A dichotomized indicator would sort cases and interact with other variables the same way a dichotomy would – again, assuming that they measured exactly the same concept. The continuous indicator contains more information about degrees of the suffrage, which we could choose to ignore, but the reverse is not true: one cannot derive a continuous measure from a categorical one without adding new information about gradations.

However, this argument has a flip side: if a qualitative and a quantitative indicator measured a concept with equally fine gradations, we would prefer the qualitative indicator on the grounds that it provided more information about the qualities that are being represented. Let us suppose that we have, on the one hand, a threefold typology dividing regimes into democratic, authoritarian, and totalitarian regimes; and, on the other hand, a three-point scale of, say, degrees of accountability. In this example, we could derive a quantitative indicator from the qualitative typology, but we could not derive the typology from the accountability indicator without adding qualitative information about regime qualities beyond accountability.

Quantitative precision affects how appropriate an indicator is for the kind of analysis one intends to carry out.[24] There is a hierarchy among the levels of measurement based on the kinds of mathematical operations that can be meaningfully performed with them. Nominal measurements can be used only for identity relations; ordinal measurements can establish identity and inequalities; interval measurements are useful for identities and inequalities and can be counted or added and subtracted; and ratio measurements are useful for identities and inequalities and can be counted, added and subtracted, multiplied and divided, and subjected to higher-order transformations such as logarithms and exponentials. These possibilities for mathematical manipulation constrain the ways that indicators can be used in quantitative analysis. Table 2.5 lists various types of descriptive and explanatory quantitative analysis that are appropriate for each level of measurement.

These analytic constraints have important implications for democratization research. On the one hand, dichotomies – because they are categorical and because they can take into account multiple criteria – correspond most naturally to the concept of regimes, which can persist without relevant alteration for years. Dichotomies therefore lend themselves to analyses of rare and dramatic changes such as democratic transitions and breakdowns and to the related concept of regime life expectancy, as in the important work by Przeworski and colleagues (2000). On the other hand, analysis of subtle, short-term, or partial changes in democracy such as political liberalization, democratic deepening, institutional crisis, and quality of democracy requires a higher level of measurement.

Thickening thin concepts

It is tempting to conclude that different types of measurement are appropriate for different kinds of research and that there is no best kind of measurement.

---

[24] There is some debate about this. Some argue that numbers are numbers regardless of the measurement procedures that produced them, so any numbers can be used in any quantitative analysis. Others argue that the measurement theory that guided the generation of the numbers dictates the kinds of analysis that are appropriate. I lean toward the intermediate position that indicators can be used as though they were at a higher level of measurement when the measurement theory allows a reasonable interpretation of the results. This is not always possible, so scholars must be cautious. As Winkler and Hays observed, "the road from objects to numbers may be easy, but the return trip from numbers to properties of objects is not" (Winkler and Hays 1975, 282).

Table 2.5. Appropriate uses of indicators at different levels of measurement

	Dichotomous	Nominal	Ordinal	Interval	Ratio
Description					
Percentage change					X
Standard deviation and variance				X	X
Factor analysis			X[a]	X	X
Mean			X[a]	X	X
Median			X	X	X
Mode	X	X	X	X	X
As an independent variable					
Complex transformations					X
Multiplicative interactions					X
Differenced variable				X	X
Random variable				X	X
Dummy-variable interaction	X	X	X		
Dummy variable	X	X	X		
As a dependent variable					
Regression				X	X
Product-moment correlation				X	X
Rank-order correlation			X		
Ordered logit or probit			X		
Multinomial logit		X			
Logit or probit	X	X			
Cross-tabulation	X	X	X		
Discriminant and log-linear analysis	X				
Event-history and Boolean analysis	X				

[a] Technically, one should not calculate means or perform factor analysis with ordinal data. Nevertheless, we have become accustomed to the unnatural concept of an average rank. Also, a factor analysis will yield meaningful results only to the degree that any ordinal variables in the analysis approximate interval data. In practice, they often do.

Again, the problem with that view is that it impedes the accumulation of knowledge. Qualitative and quantitative researchers have no choice but to talk past each other as long as their evidence measures qualitatively different concepts. Therefore, there is a great need to overcome this division. It can be done by developing quantitative indicators of thick concepts.

The idea may be offensive to those who are comfortable with fine qualitative distinctions and distrust numbers. Their attitude is reminiscent of skeptics who argued years ago that one could not reduce, for example, Beethoven to a string of numbers. Now it can be done, and is done, in digital recordings. With enough technology, laboriously developed over a century at great expense, we can sample multiple frequencies thousands of times per second, convert it into digital code, and then reproduce the sound so well that it is virtually indistinguishable from a live performance of Beethoven's music.

In social science, we already do something like this with dichotomies. Any dichotomous concept can be perfectly operationalized as a dummy variable, which takes on values of 0 or 1. We can pile as many components as we like onto a dummy variable and still represent them with these two values without suffering any loss of information. The components do not even have to be unidimensional because one cut point can be picked on each component and the dummy defined to equal 1 only when every component equals 1. This is the exact mathematical equivalent of a multifaceted, categorical distinction. Quantitative indicators do not strip away qualitative meaning; rather, they establish a correspondence between meaningful qualitative information and numbers.

In principle, we should also be able to create polytomous, ordinal, interval, or (in some cases) ratio-data indicators of thick concepts. The challenge is threefold. The first challenge is to ensure that every element that contributes to the definition of a thick concept is measured by a quantitative variable. The second challenge is to reconceptualize each of these elements as a matter of degree, not as just an either-or difference. The third challenge in bringing about the best of the qualitative and quantitative approaches is to preserve the structure of the qualitative concept. This requires grouping components into dimensions correctly and combining them into a single index for each dimension.[25]

I suspect that we are not likely to achieve much improvement in reliable and valid measurement until we begin working with a thicker, multidimensional concept of democracy. If democracy is multidimensional, then democracy indicators must be multidimensional as well; otherwise, measurements are compromised by measurement error or validity problems. The worst tactic for coping with multidimensionality is to assume blindly that all of the components are unidimensional and barrel on, adding or averaging these apples and oranges. The fruit of such efforts may turn out to be reasonable at the extremes but is likely to be a meaningless mess in the middle.

A more acceptable tactic is to tolerate a low level of measurement: interval rather than ratio data, ordinal rather than interval, a three-point scale rather

---

[25] It is sometimes possible to combine multidimensional components into a single indicator. Doing so, however, requires a theory that tells one how to combine them properly. In geometry, for example, "volume" is a single indicator of a multidimensional quality, but it cannot be calculated unless one knows the appropriate formula for the shape of the object in question.

than a ten-point scale, or a dichotomy rather than a scale. This tactic is available because unidimensionality is a matter of degree. Sometimes dimensions are distinct but parallel, or bundled. The tighter the bundle, the less measurement error is created when they are combined simply into an allegedly unidimensional indicator. If one is content to produce an indicator of democracy at a low level of measurement – say, a three-point scale of democracies, semidemocracies, and nondemocracies – one can aggregate components that lie on different and fairly weakly correlated dimensions.

As noted previously, dichotomies are the limiting case of this tactic. But dichotomizing is radical surgery. It amputates every dimension below the cutoff and tosses all that information into a residual bin labeled "nondemocracy." If this information is truly not worth knowing, such radical surgery can be justified – for example, if it is the only way to salvage a viable indicator. But if there is serious doubt about where to cut, caution is advised.

Obviously, we lack the rich data that would be needed to measure any thick concept of democracy in a large sample.[26] Comparative politics is still data poor, and the problem is not limited to democratization research. Correcting the situation will take an enormous investment in rigorous, systematic data collection on a large scale. Resources to make it possible may not be available now, but to obtain the resources it is first necessary to decide that such data are meaningful; desirable; and, in principle, feasible to create. In the meantime, it is useful to keep in mind even today that small- and large-N analysis, thick and thin, are parts of a whole, and that as data collection improves, we can expect them to converge rather than diverge into entirely separate camps.

Conclusion

Democracy can be measured, and has been measured, in many different ways. However, the indicators in our possession today capture only a thin version of democracy. Despite the fact that democracy is demonstrably a multidimensional phenomenon, and probably more multidimensional the more richly it is defined, most existing indicators focus on just one of its dimensions – contestation. The bright side is that contestation has been measured adequately for very large-sample comparisons. The existing indicators may not

---

[26] At this writing, however, I am part of a large collaborative effort, Varieties of Democracy, to generate exactly this sort of rich data: hundreds of attributes of multiple conceptions of democracy for all countries from 1900 to 2011 (see https://v-dem.net).

be sufficiently reliable to be useful for intraregional comparisons, but to the extent that there is measurement error, it does not seem to pose much of a problem for research on causes of democracy in large and diverse samples. In fact, the knowledge that there is some measurement error should actually increase our confidence in findings that turn out to be statistically significant despite such error. Nevertheless, we need thicker indicators, over a longer span of time, with greater attention to reliability and additional dimensions of democracy.

3 Criteria for evaluating causal theories

Much of our knowledge about politics is factual or descriptive. It requires useful concepts and valid, reliable measurement, as discussed in Chapter 2. Often, it goes beyond describing static, unchanging situations and constructs narrative accounts of specific events. These accounts can be richly detailed, amounting to histories of events and processes that enable us to feel that we understand what happened and why. Much of our understanding of the birth and death of democracies consists of this kind of knowledge. If one wants to understand how democracy evolved in Great Britain, there are hundreds of books that recount the process in exhaustive detail. Most other countries are not quite as well studied, but there are still dozens of books on democratization in Brazil and Japan and even a healthy number of books or articles on relatively neglected cases such as Paraguay, Botswana, Sri Lanka, and Mongolia. The knowledge contained in these works is essential and extremely valuable; it is a scholarly achievement that deserves greater appreciation.

This literature is so massive that it would be foolish to attempt to summarize it in this book. Instead, I focus here on attempts to develop a theoretical understanding of democratization, which is a quite different kind of knowledge. I do not argue with readers who prefer an idiographic, every-case-is-unique understanding to any attempt to develop a nomothetic, or theoretical, understanding. However, those who seek a theoretical understanding must develop and test theory.

Theory plays an indispensable role in any science. A theory is a mental model designed to make sense of reality: to describe and explain or predict what we observe. Theories do this by proposing logical analogies for empirical relationships. Theories give us reasons to say that what did happen, had to happen. When we can see parallels between observed sequences and logical consequences, we feel that we understand. Of course, we may be mistaken: some theories are not very useful for explaining or predicting reality. Science is a process of continually testing theories against evidence, and revising them, to make them ever more useful.

Theories have three elements. First, they have theoretical terms, which are intellectual constructs that need not refer to anything that is directly observable – the observational terms. Geometry has points and lines; physics has gravity and electromagnetic fields; comparative politics has legitimacy, stability, and other somewhat abstract constructs, including democracy. Second, theories have correspondence rules, which connect theoretical terms to observational terms. For some theoretical terms, the correspondence rules are obvious: the empirical referents of trade union and prime minister are rarely disputed. But the correspondence rules for some other theoretical terms require more thought. As we have seen, identifying democracies is no simple matter. Third, theories have a heuristic, that is, a procedure that enables one to derive necessary connections among the theoretical terms. Usually logic and mathematics are the heuristics, which are preferred because they remain faithful to the assumptions.[1] But many political theories employ less formal and mechanical heuristics, such as consensual, conventional understandings of how the world works. Such theories risk reaching conclusions that are not actually strictly entailed by the assumptions. This is a problem that is remedied only by subsequent challenges and corrections.

Theories help us make causal inferences. Although I am a philosophical realist in most respects (I believe that the political world is really out there as an object we can study), I treat causality as a property that we attribute to observed relationships rather than as a force or entity with an independent existence. We can infer that A causes B when we observe (1) constant conjunction (B is present if and only if A is present, or B changes when A changes), (2) temporal priority (A appears or changes before B appears or changes), and (3) contiguity (A and B are close together in space and time); and when we have a theory that provides reasons for expecting A to cause B (Holowchak 2007). Causal inference therefore requires both observation and theory.

The foregoing describes a deterministic theory that is appropriate in the natural sciences. This is also a mode of thinking practiced by those who search for necessary causes, sufficient causes, or complex combinations thereof.[2] In

[1] This quality is more commonly called truth preserving, which is a misnomer, because logic and mathematics can preserve either truth or fiction, depending on the nature of the assumptions. This characteristic would be better called fidelity to assumptions.

[2] Mahoney, for example, categorizes case-oriented causes as (1) necessary and sufficient, (2) necessary but not sufficient, (3) sufficient but not necessary, (4) insufficient but necessary parts of a condition that is unnecessary but sufficient (INUS causes), or (5) sufficient but unnecessary parts of a factor that is insufficient but necessary (SUIN causes) (Mahoney 2008). He also recognizes population-oriented causes that are not deterministic. Although the logic of necessary and sufficient conditions has been viewed as deterministic, the recent application of fuzzy-set logic to comparative politics provides a probabilistic alternative (Ragin 2000).

political science, it is not practical to search for such deterministic relationships because there are few, if any, statements about politics that are universally true (Hempel 1965, 173–177). Whether political life is inherently probabilistic because of free will or quantum mechanics, or only apparently probabilistic because of our inability to trace causal processes down to the molecular level, we must treat it as probabilistic and regard our explanations as incomplete. Useful theories about politics, therefore, are intended to be understood as only partially true, other things being equal (ceteris paribus), and expected to be inconsistent with some of the evidence. Theories of necessary or sufficient conditions are not, in my view, useful ways of thinking about complex political reality.

There does not seem to be a well-accepted, clear-cut distinction between theories and models, so I take a cue from Hempel and say that a model "has the character of a theory with a more or less limited scope of application" (Hempel 1965, 446). Models are more specific and bounded than theories. Theories do not necessarily have any direct application; models do. Models explain a class of observations. Also, models use only a subset of the propositions in a theory. However, the more specialized and applied a theory is, the more the boundary between theories and models blurs. These concepts should be understood relative to each other rather than in absolute terms. We could speak of a theory of democratization and a model of transitions to democracy within it; but we could also speak of a theory of transitions to democracy and a model of transitions from electoral authoritarian regimes within it.

Theoretical understanding is knowledge of the general (probabilistic) laws that give rise to the specific events we observe. If we had perfect theoretical understanding, we could claim that the causes singled out in our explanations would have the same effects in cases that we have not yet observed and would have the same effects even in hypothetical situations that we can never observe. We do not have this quality of understanding yet, and we may never have it about politics. But the goal of political science, just like physics or biology or meteorology, is constantly to improve our theoretical understanding and to learn useful things along the way.

Practitioners of different approaches to comparative politics have jealously disputed one another's claims to theoretical understanding. Area studies specialists have accused quantitative comparativists of either comparing the incomparable or quantifying the obvious. Statistical analysts have condescendingly thanked country experts for digging up the anecdotal evidence that only multicountry comparisons can transmute into theory. Both complain about the lack of realism in rational-choice theory, yet formal theorists have tried to brand propositions in both large-sample and case-study approaches as atheoretical because they are not integrated into a larger, systematic body of propositions. All of these charges reflect a narrow view of theory. In reality, all three approaches make indispensable contributions to good theorizing.

In this chapter, I define three fundamental criteria for good theories, and I use these criteria to evaluate three approaches in comparative politics – formal theory, case studies and small-sample comparisons, and large-sample statistical analysis. My purpose in doing so is to advocate a broader view of theory, in which each approach has one unique strength and two weaknesses. Their strengths and weaknesses stem from the goals of the researchers who use them. Those who do case studies and small-sample comparisons are trailblazers who are primarily interested in developing innovative explanations; this leads them to favor thickness over generality or integration. Rational-choice theorists are more interested in adding to a large body of integrated theory; they must keep their theories simple to keep from straying too far from what others have said and, because they are less interested in testing, they feel little pressure to specify how generally their theories apply. Quantitative researchers, by contrast, are principally interested in testing; theoretical innovation is a low priority for them, and the imperative of controlling for competing explanations compels them to consider disparate propositions that are not integrated into a single coherent theory. From this broad perspective, our three main approaches can be considered complementary. I illustrate the trade-offs with examples from research on democratization, which has been studied so long and in so many different ways that it affords examples of the strengths and weaknesses of every method.

Three fundamental criteria for good theory

An overview of criteria for good theorizing provides a good foundation for a comparison of the advantages and disadvantages of different approaches. In a literature too voluminous to summarize here, scholars have defined more than a dozen criteria for good theory.[3] However, I contend that three criteria are especially central: generality, integration, and thickness.[4] They are central

---

[3] John Gerring (2001), in one of the most comprehensive discussions of what good theory is, mentions generality (breadth), integration (analytical utility or logical economy), and thickness (depth), but he also lists specification, accuracy, precision, parsimony, innovation, intelligibility, and relevance.

[4] Gerring's (2001) specification and accuracy are more pertinent to testing, discussed later in this chapter. I discuss precision as a characteristic of conceptualization and measurement elsewhere.

in the sense that each of the three major approaches in comparative politics achieves one at the expense of the others. Case studies and small-sample comparisons produce thick propositions, large-sample statistical research produces general propositions, and formal theory integrates propositions. This division of labor has developed because these three criteria are locked in a three-way trade-off: it is very difficult, in practice, to do a good job of satisfying more than one criterion at a time.

Generality

A general theory is one that is intended to apply to all relevant cases, both all those that have been observed and all that could be observed.[5] (A general theory must also be correct for all cases; see Chapter 7 on testing.) Some scholars claim not to seek general knowledge and consider the goal of generalization a matter of taste. Sir Isaiah Berlin once suggested that people are either foxes, who know many small things, or hedgehogs, who know one big thing (Berlin 1953). A better analogy for comparative political theories would contrast whales and octopuses. Both are renowned for their intelligence, but they use their intelligence in different ways. Whales come to know great swaths of the earth in their tours of the globe; they lack limbs that would allow them to experience objects firsthand; and their eyesight is too poor to perceive fine detail. They acquire a surface knowledge of general things. Octopuses, in contrast, dwell in one place and use their fine eyesight and eight flexible arms to gain an intimate knowledge of local, specific things. (To buttress the analogy, there is the additional, although not apropos, parallel that octopuses are well equipped to blend into their surroundings, whereas whales are as conspicuous as creatures can be; however, I ask readers not to overinterpret the octopus's tendency to spread clouds of ink when threatened.) I do not wish to suggest that scholars who emulate the octopus should emulate the whale instead, or vice versa. Rather, my point is that each kind of knowledge is limited in its own way, and the most complete kind of knowledge would result from pooling both kinds.

Innovation and intelligibility are lesser methodological virtues, and I do not consider parsimony a virtue at all.

[5] Distinguishing between relevant and irrelevant cases is a crucial consideration. The rule of thumb is that a theory should not be arbitrarily bounded. In comparative politics, a theory is arbitrarily bounded when its application is restricted to certain objects for reasons that are not integral to the theory. A theory that applies only to Asian countries for no potentially theorizable reason is arbitrarily bounded, but one that explains how certain unique features of Asian countries condition the causal relationships is properly bounded.

For decades, the proponents of middle-range theory have fostered the view that generalization is at best optional and at worst impossible and pernicious. This is false.

Generality is an indispensable characteristic of theory. In the deductive-nomological view of the role of theory in explanation – which is, despite the philosophical critiques of Hempel (Gerring 2001), the dominant view in political science (Clarke and Primo 2007) – an explanation is an interpretation of an event or a tendency as a specific instance of universal laws. If the laws are not universal, then there is no solid foundation for the explanation; the explanation itself then requires explanation, and that explanation requires explanation, and so on. The phenomenon is not fully explained until it is understood as a necessary consequence of laws recognized as universally true.

Because true universals are unattainable in social science today, practicality forces us to confine our theories to bounded times and places. We always work with bounded laws even though our ultimate goal is universal law. But the universal law toward which we are advancing is not a simple, one-size-fits-all law; rather, it is a complex, multitiered set of laws. At the lowest tier, one law applies in certain contexts and other laws apply in others. But at a higher tier, there is a prior law that determines which law applies in each context. The more heterogeneous reality is, the more it may be necessary to postulate additional tiers of laws determining laws determining laws until eventually this complex hierarchy of laws accounts for all of the variation we observe.

A perhaps too-literal example: speed limits vary within a town. Suppose we find that in Squaresville, speed limits correspond perfectly to public safety considerations: how wide the street is, how straight and flat, the distance between intersections, proximity to schools and playing children, and so forth. In neighboring Bearburg, however, we find that public safety is not the only consideration: the speed limit on the main drag is artificially low so that cops can operate a profitable speed trap. To account for speed limits in these two locations, therefore, we need at least a law about public safety explanation and a law about speed traps, but we also need a metalaw explaining why some towns have speed traps and others do not. In this case, perhaps a shrinking tax base led the town government to pressure its police to raise revenues by collecting fines. If a different town, Greasepalmyra, had a speed trap for a different reason, such as police soliciting bribes, then a meta-metalaw would be needed to explain the different motivations for speed traps. If we succeeded in explaining the variation in speed limits within each town and across all towns, all over the world, then the resulting layers of laws nested within laws could be considered a single, complex, universal law. This is the kind of universal law that I consider the goal of comparative politics.

Until we develop such composite, complex laws, we must settle for bounded theories. In the meantime, we must take care not to bound our theories arbitrarily, that is, for no good theoretical reason. But as long as we can presume that there is potentially a good theoretical reason for limiting a theory to, say, postwar Europe, even if the reason is vague or implicit, then we can treat the theory as provisionally valid, pending completion (and empirical confirmation). All actual theories in comparative politics are therefore incomplete and provisional. The admission that they are works in progress is not damning because this is all that one can claim about any scientific theory. Even physicists are still searching for a theory of everything that could overturn the insights of Einstein and quantum mechanics. Generalizations in comparative politics are less elegant than those in physics, but we still have an obligation to generalize, for generalization is a defining characteristic of theory. This does not mean that all of us must generalize, only that some of us must. Generalization is a collective obligation.

The notion of a truly general theory of democratization in units as diverse as countries is difficult to imagine. Even those who dare to generalize about a region typically take care to disclaim any application beyond that region. After all, it is very likely that the nature and causes of democratization were fundamentally different in nineteenth-century Western Europe than they were in Latin America in the 1980s. In Europe, democratization required extending the suffrage to all adults in elections that were already competitive; in Latin America, it required restoring electoral competition to countries that had usually already practiced universal adult suffrage. These were fundamentally different processes involving different sets of actors, interests, and goals. A general theory can fit both processes only if it includes a reason for knowing where to apply which part of the theory. A general theory might state, for example, that the European variant of the theory applies only to the first countries to develop mass liberal democracy, whereas a different version of the theory applies to the latecomers, because prodemocracy elites among the latecomers benefited from the example of the first democracies. Without such a reason, a theory would be arbitrarily bounded. It would state, in effect, that the theory applies everywhere except where it doesn't, or that it applies only in Western Europe because we say so. The justification for bounding a theory does not have to be fully developed because general theory is a work in progress; but scholars have an obligation at least to recognize this issue and to suggest possible reasons for circumscribing the relevance of their theories to certain times and places.

Integration

Generalization to the entirety of observed reality is not enough. To explain, we must also generalize to what is unobserved and hypothetical (Moon 1975, 243). As Donald Moon wrote:

> The nomological pattern of explanation, as its name implies, requires the presence of general laws in any explanatory account. . . . But not just any kind of general statement can perform this explanatory function. Not only must laws be unrestricted universals (i.e., they must be in universal form and must apply to an unrestricted class of objects), but they must also support "counter-to-fact" and subjunctive conditional statements. . . . But to make such an assertion requires a great deal more information than that conveyed by a particular law, and so in order to understand the explanatory force of laws, we [must] examine them in relation to scientific theories. (Moon 1975, 153–154)

In other words, instead of saying that a law is generally true because we have observed it to be generally true, theory says that a law is generally true because it is necessarily entailed by other laws that are generally true. (Those other laws are in turn subject to the same standards of confirmation.) Thus, a generalization must be integrated into a systematic set of other laws – a theory – to be truly general.

Two qualities and two consequences of this integration deserve to be highlighted. The two qualities are logical consistency and internal completeness. The statements of a theory are logically consistent when they do not contradict one another. Consistency can refer either to the internal consistency (the statements of this theory do not contradict one another) or to external consistency (the statements of this theory do not contradict statements in other theories).[6] A theory is internally complete when it defines a prediction for every logically entailed premise: a *then* for every *if*. Theories that raise a lot of ifs but predict few thens are incomplete. For example, O'Donnell and Schmitter's framework from *Transitions from Authoritarian Rule* (discussed in greater detail in Chapter 4) posits that successful transitions to democracy begin with (1) a division between the authoritarian hard-liners and

---

[6] Internal integration of statements in the same theory could also be called vertical, and external integration with statements from other theories at the same level of generality could be called horizontal.

soft-liners, and (2) an opening (*abertura*) that permits (3) the resurrection of civil society, which (4) tilts negotiations toward an alliance between soft-liners and the opposition (O'Donnell and Schmitter 1986). This provides a good account for cases that meet all four criteria. But this sequence of events is, according to the authors, highly uncertain. What if the division between hard-liners and soft-liners does not lead to an opening? What if civil society does not take advantage of the political opening? What if the soft-liners fail to ally with the opposition? The framework's predictions for these scenarios are undefined. In this sense, it is incomplete (which is one reason for calling it a framework rather than a theory).

In a sense, regime typologies could be considered extremely incomplete theories. They highlight selective characteristics of regimes, such as elections, competition, and freedom, but they do not specify what difference it makes whether or not a regime possesses these characteristics. A more complete theory would tell us that if a regime is democratic, then something specific will result, such as extensive social security coverage or peaceful relations with other democracies.

If a theory is internally and externally consistent and internally complete, then two highly desirable consequences follow. First, consistency makes it possible for a theoretical understanding to cumulate. When the propositions of one theory are logically consistent with one another and with the propositions of another theory, the two theories are integrated with each other, merging into a larger, more complex, and more comprehensive theory that attempts to explain more of the world. As John Gerring notes, "The proposition that sits by itself in a corner is likely to be dismissed as 'ad hoc,' or 'idiosyncratic.' It does not fit with our present understanding of the world. It refuses to cumulate" (2001, 107). The more ways in which a proposition meshes with other propositions, the richer our understanding becomes.

Second, consistent and complete theories are more fertile: they generate a larger number of observable implications. This results in part from the completeness of the theory, but it is also a by-product of the number of propositions that are integrated together. The greater the number of propositions that are linked together, the more hypotheses they can generate. One can derive more theorems from fifty axioms than from three. As a result, complete, well-integrated theories have many observable implications and are therefore potentially more testable.[7]

---

[7] All this presumes that the empirical referents of the propositions are clear. If it is unclear how the concepts in the theory correspond to observable phenomena, the theory is untestable for other reasons.

The basis for the systematic structure of a theory is often logic, but it can be other branches of mathematics as well, such as calculus, game theory, or probability theory. I believe that it can also be, and typically and unavoidably is, common sense: our own informal understandings of how the world works. No elaborate proof is needed to show that money talks, that united organizations are stronger than divided ones, or that you can fool some of the people some of the time. These understandings of how the world works are less reliable than mathematical or logical tools but, consciously or not, we rely on them all of the time. For example, if a general calls for the overthrow of an elected president, we may not know exactly what will happen, but the range of possible consequences is actually quite small. The general may be forced to retire or sent overseas, other officers may rally around him, the U.S. ambassador will weigh in on one side or another, and so on; but we know the consequences will not include the discovery of a platinum mine, a major earthquake, the outbreak of world peace and harmony, or talking butterflies. Our common sense guides the translation of theoretical symbols into meaningful referents (interpretive theory) and informs and constrains the range of possible causal connections (causal theory). In fact, few hypotheses in comparative politics have been derived purely from the formal assumptions of a theory. In almost all cases, at some point, researchers have had to draw on their commonsense knowledge of the political world to translate the logical implications of a theory into observable implications.

Thickness

Finally, theory should be thick. A thick theory is a thorough one, a theory that provides a complete explanation for the phenomenon in question. It is useful to think of theoretical thickness as having two dimensions: depth and breadth. A theory is deep if it traces the chain of causation far back from the eventual effect. Depth is desirable to avoid overly proximate explanations, which tend to be superficial or trivial. For example, Higley and Burton argued that "a disunified national elite . . . produces a series of unstable regimes that tend to oscillate between authoritarian and democratic forms," whereas "a consensually unified national elite . . . produces a stable regime that may evolve into a modern democracy" (Higley and Burton 1989, 17). Although their argument fit their cases well, the authors never explained why a country's elite is divided or consensually unified. The cause is suspiciously close to the effect, so the explanation is unsatisfying. It avoids the more interesting, and more difficult, question of what causes elite unity or disunity. A deeper explanation that took us farther back along the causal chain would be more useful and satisfying.

The breadth or complexity of a theory concerns the number of parameters it includes and the degree of interconnection among them. Every theoretical model in social science has five parameters. First, every model pertains to a certain level of analysis – individual, group, national, global, or some intermediate gradation. Second, it has one or more dependent variables. Third, it has one or more explanatory variables. Fourth, it applies to a certain relevant universe of cases. And fifth, it applies to events or processes that take place during a certain period of time. We can refer to the definitions of each of these five parameters as possessing zero-order complexity because no relationships among parameters are involved. In the study of democratization, however, even at the zero order there is great leeway for defining what democracy is, how to measure it and any explanatory factors, which sample of countries is relevant for testing any given set of explanations, and the period of time to which such explanations apply. And this is just at the national level of analysis; with smaller or larger units of analysis, one would use completely different variables, cases, and time frames.

First-order complexity involves any causal relationship between any of these parameters and itself. These relationships include the following:

1. Causation bridging levels of analysis, or aggregation and disaggregation
2. Causal relationships among dependent variables, or endogeneity
3. Interactions among independent variables
4. Impacts of one time period on another, called lagged effects or temporal autocorrelation
5. The impact of one case on another, called diffusion or spatial autocorrelation

Such relationships may sound overly technical and irrelevant but, in reality, examples of all of them can be found in the democratization literature. O'Donnell and Schmitter (1986) proposed aggregation in the theory of democratization at the national level as the outcome of strategic maneuvering among elites at the group or individual level. Also, their argument that political liberalization is a prerequisite for transition asserted an endogenous relationship between the two outcomes. Anyone who has studied modernization as a cause of democracy assumes that the components of modernization, such as education, wealth, urbanization, and secularization, interact to produce democracy. Many quantitative studies assume that democratization is a process of incremental change from a country's previous level of freedom

(Burkhart and Lewis-Beck 1994; Przeworski et al. 1996). These are lagged effects. Finally, a number of recent studies have examined the democratic-diffusion hypothesis that conditions in other countries influence democratization (Brinks and Coppedge 2006; Li and Thompson 1975; O'Loughlin et al. 1998; Przeworski et al. 1996; Starr 1991). First-order complexity is common.

Second-order complexity involves causal relationships between two different parameters. All hypotheses about an independent variable causing democracy (or democracy causing something else) are of this order, but so are various complications that could be introduced into a model. If the meaning of democracy varies over time or if the best way to operationalize an independent variable depends on the world region, then one is dealing with this degree of complexity. Third-order complexity comes into play when there are plausible hypotheses relating three parameters. Most common among these are hypotheses that the relationship between the dependent variables and an independent variable is partly a function of time or place. A good example is the hypothesis that the impact of economic development on democratization depends on a country's world-system position (Bollen 1983; Burkhart and Lewis-Beck 1994; Hadenius 1992; O'Donnell 1973). With fourth-order complexity, a causal relationship could be a function of both time and place (or level of analysis). This may sound far-fetched, but in small-sample comparisons such relationships are fairly commonly asserted – for example, the notion that increasing wealth has not favored democracy in the Arab oil-producing states since World War II (Karl 1997), or the claim that the United States has become more sincerely interested in promoting democracy in the Caribbean Basin since the end of the Cold War (Huntington 1991). Increasing complexity does not render a theory more esoteric; on the contrary, it is only by increasing complexity that a theory begins to approximate common sense.

Orders of complexity can increase only so far. Eventually, one arrives at the extremely inelegant saturated model that explains each outcome perfectly by providing different and unique explanations for each case. Laypersons who have not been socialized into social science know that the saturated model is the truth: every country is unique, history never repeats itself exactly, and every event is the product of a long and densely tangled chain of causation stretching back to the beginning of time. We political scientists know on some level that a true and complete explanation for the things that fascinate us would be impossibly complex. But we willfully ignore this disturbing fact and persist in our research. We are a community of eccentrics who share the delusion that politics is simpler than it appears. Although I would be as delighted as any other political scientist to discover simple, elegant, and powerful explanations, I think the common sense of the layperson is correct: we must presume that politics is extremely complex, and the burden of proof rests on those who claim that it is not. Understanding the political world, in my view, requires theory that is deeply and broadly thick.

Guided by our own experience in the world, we should presume that most of these complex possibilities could be true and that only a thick theory can explain politics well. Unfortunately, this is a controversial position. Most influential works on the methodology of comparative politics emphasize the fact that all models necessarily simplify reality, and these texts usually exalt parsimony as a methodological virtue. However, parsimony is often misunderstood. It is not a rule that we should always prefer the simpler of two theories; properly understood, it is a rule that if two theories explain a phenomenon equally well, then we should prefer the simpler one.[8] In my experience in comparative politics, simplifications almost always sacrifice some accuracy. I see no reason to prefer a simple but less accurate theory over a complex but more accurate one. Of course, theoretical thickness does not guarantee a grasp of the truth; any creative person could dream up ten complex theories that are wrong for every one that is right. But very few of the right theories are likely to be simple. We should not let a misguided preference for parsimony blind us to the truth. We have to consider complex theories; the trick is to find the right ones. This is the role of testing, which is discussed in Chapter 7.

My understanding of causation diverges from some conventional efforts to sort out, categorically, which factors are causal and which are not, or to distinguish between necessary and sufficient causes, binary and scalar causes, deterministic and probabilistic causes, individual and joint causes, causes-in-fact and causes-in-general, causes-of-effects and effects-of-causes. (For an excellent overview of the literature on causation, see Gerring 2001.) Such distinctions are the product of rather scholastic efforts to focus attention on limited, simplified causal stories. Such simplified accounts are useful and essential to personal-injury lawyers and they may interest philosophers, but I think it is unproductive to draw arbitrary lines separating causes from non-causes when we could agree that countless factors are linked in an immense web of probabilistic causation. Some factors are more proximate, some more

---

[8] William of Occam's instruction, "Pluralitas non est ponenda sine necessitas" ("Plurality should not be posited without necessity"), does imply that a more complex explanation would be preferred when it is necessary to account for the facts at hand.

distant; some are powerful, others weak; some matter individually, others jointly – but they all matter. This is the most comprehensive and accurate, and therefore realistic, way to understand causation – albeit not the most practical way! Limited time, resources, and patience force us to focus on smaller regions of the web, but we should never forget that, in principle, such narrowing always simplifies the truth.

Multiple paths to theory

All approaches in comparative politics are deficient in satisfying some requirements for theory. In fact, each of the three major approaches excels in a different respect and is deficient on the other two. This is why they are competing approaches. Formal theory integrates propositions into a larger web of theory but neglects generalization and is thin; large-sample statistical analysis establishes general empirical fit but in thin and unsystematic ad hoc ways; and case studies and small-sample comparisons generate thick knowledge that may not be generally true and tends to be only loosely integrated into a larger theory. These are appropriate emphases, given the different and complementary goals of these approaches: incrementally accumulating an integrated body of theory, testing implications of theory, and developing novel theory, respectively. Nevertheless, all three approaches contribute to theory in their own way. The following sections elaborate on this evaluation of each approach according to these three criteria, with illustrations from research on democratization.

Theory in small-sample studies

Case studies and small-sample comparisons sometimes have been dismissed as "merely" descriptive, anecdotal, historical, or journalistic, and therefore atheoretical. But the harshest critic of such studies would have to concede that they at least generate "facts." Facts may seem atheoretical, but they are not. In reality, we cannot even observe facts until we have a conceptual framework to help us make sense of what we perceive (Lakatos 1978). Such a framework is an interpretive theory that helps us identify what to observe, defines the relevant and meaningful characteristics of actors and institutions, and fills in the connections between action and reaction so that we can plausibly reconstruct events and processes. We are unconscious of much of this theory; we develop it and refine it by trial and error from birth onward. If the test of a good theory is that it enables us to predict consequences, common sense is a magnificent theory. With it, we successfully walk, talk, drive, work, parent, and invest, negotiating our way around a thousand daily challenges throughout whole lifetimes. With the benefit of this commonsense understanding of how the world works, we feel that we can understand political events that we did not experience in person, as long as someone supplies us with the crucial details.

The more descriptive case studies and small-sample comparisons consist of propositions that are integrated into this intuitive interpretive theory. The bulk of democratization research consists of case studies and small-sample (usually within-region) comparisons. Every transition to democracy in the past two decades has been thoroughly analyzed in several books and numerous articles. Some of the most influential books in the field have been compendia of case studies (Linz and Stepan 1978; O'Donnell et al. 1986; Diamond et al. 1988; Domínguez and Lowenthal 1996). Scholars seeking a thorough knowledge of a particular transition, breakdown, or regime survival are practically cursed with a superabundance of information. Often such studies prefer specific concepts to general ones: Duma to parliament, Clinton to president, Quebec to province; however, such precision reflects not a simple interpretive theory but rather a more elaborate one that captures some of the idiosyncrasies of each case.

What is striking at this level is that we collectively know so much and disagree so little. Research of this type has created what is probably the most thorough understanding of specific democratic transitions, breakdowns, and survival, and has done so for practically every country one could mention. These works, whether they are academic research in a historical or anthropological tradition, current history, or journalistic analyses, do an excellent job of recounting events, identifying key actors and their motives, assessing the strength of organizations, and tracing connections among causal forces. The authority of this work is such that we rarely argue about who the key players were, what the basic chronology was, or who won and who lost. Ironically, the lack of controversy about these inferences diminishes the prestige of the scholars who make them. But the high degree of consensus around their work makes their accomplishment more impressive, not less so. All theories should be as convincing as these.

But these studies are just one pole of a continuum in small-sample research. At the opposite pole, some small-sample studies interpret every specific actor, institution, trend, and situation as a specific instance of a general type. They take literally Przeworski and Teune's call to "replace proper names of social systems" with "the relevant variables" (Przeworski and Teune 1970, 8). The kind of theory generated by this type of research tends to have two character-istics. First, most of it is qualitative and categorical. The causal relationships it identifies link types to types and kinds to kinds rather than matching quan-tities or degrees. Relationships are hypothesized to be true or false, necessary or sufficient, rather than partially true, stronger or weaker, likely or iffy.

Second, the theoretical propositions that emerge from these studies, if examined with care, turn out to possess a high order of complexity. The more faithfully a theory represents our complex world, the more complex it must be. (How faithfully, of course, is a question to be resolved by testing.) In the Latin American democratization literature, the conventional wisdom presumes that each wave of democratization is different, that each country has derived different lessons from its distinct political and economic history, that corporate actors vary greatly in power and tactics from country to coun-try, and that both individual politicians and international actors can have a decisive impact on the outcome. This is the stuff of thick theory, and com-parative politics as a whole benefits when a regional specialization generates such rich possibilities.

For these two reasons, case and area studies have made many of the best-known and most original contributions to comparative political the-ory. Dependency theory germinated in a study of Argentina's terms of trade (Sikkink 1988; Prebisch 1949). The concept of consociational democracy was inspired by Lijphart's Dutch origins (Lijphart 1977). The debate about the impact of parliamentary and presidential constitutions began as an effort to understand the fall of the Weimar Republic, and its renewal was inspired by the success of the Spanish transition (Hermens 1972; Linz and Valenzuela 1994).

The hypotheses generated by this literature have reflected high-order, com-plex theorizing.[9] Daniel Lerner's seminal work on modernization was cen-tered on a case study of Turkey that identified parallel trends in the complex processes of urbanization, secularization, and education (Lerner 1958). Juan Linz's theorizing about the breakdown of democratic regimes described a detailed sequence of events – crisis, growing belief in the ineffectiveness of the democratic regime, overpromising by semiloyal leaders, polarization of public opinion, irresponsible behavior by democratic elites, culminating in either breakdown or reequilibration. He saw each step as necessary but not sufficient for the next and described various options available to elites at each

---

[9] The seminal article by Dankwart Rustow (1970) anticipated many of the complex relationships discussed herein.

stage, as well as structural and historical conditions that made certain options more or less likely. This was a theory that assumed endogeneity, aggregation across levels of analysis, and conditional interactions among causal factors (Linz 1978). O'Donnell and Schmitter bridged levels of analysis when they theorized about democratization at the national level as the outcome of strategic maneuvering among elites at the group or individual level; they contemplated endogeneity or path dependence when they asserted that political liberalization was a prerequisite for regime transition (O'Donnell and Schmitter 1986). Huntington's thesis that there are waves of democratization required a transnational causal process in addition to multiple domestic causes (Huntington 1991). Collier and Collier's *Shaping the Political Arena* identified four similar processes or periods – reform, incorporation, aftermath, and heritage – in eight cases but allowed them to start and end at different times in each country. It was particularly exacting in describing the nature of oligarchic states, organized labor, and political parties and in specifying how they interacted with one another, and with many other aspects of their political contexts in the twentieth century, to affect the course of democratization (Collier and Collier 1991). Case studies of democratization, such as those collected in the Diamond, Linz, and Lipset projects and dozens of country monographs, weave together social, economic, cultural, institutional, and often transnational causes into coherent, case-specific narratives (Diamond et al. 1988). This literature has been the source of most of what we think we understand about democratization.

Nevertheless, the small-sample approach has two weaknesses. First, although its propositions are integrated with theory, they are integrated more loosely. By "loosely," I mean that such propositions are not derived from other propositions according to any strict logic. Rather, they are borrowed from other theories and taken out of their original theoretical context or generated by observation, induction, and intuition. Loose integration has two consequences. One is that the facts can be used to support an embarrassing variety of theories. This happens because the question "What is this a case of?" has many possible answers. The leap from specific to general can go in many different directions. What, for example, was Venezuela in 1989 a case of? Every theoretical framework suggests a different direction. To a progressive political economist, it was an oil-dependent economy (Karl 1997); to an institutionalist, it was a presidential partyarchy (Coppedge 1994); to a liberal political economist, it was a case of delayed structural adjustment (Naím 1993); to a student of labor, it was a corporatist system (McCoy 1989); to a cultural theorist, a nation with unrealistic trust in a magical state (Coronil and Skurski 1991). In reality, all these labels may have been accurate. The point is that moving from the specific to the general forces us to describe our cases more selectively, and we make our selections so as to integrate the case into a larger body of theory.

The second consequence of loose theoretical integration is that it is less clear which tests would confirm or disconfirm the theory. Without rigorous logic or mathematical tools to generate hypotheses, there is no straightforward way to derive necessary implications: what must be true if the theory is true. In contrast to formal theory, the theories of small-sample analysis are less clear about their assumptions; they rely more on the tacit assumptions of common sense, which leads to conditional and vaguely probabilistic predictions that are hard to falsify.

The second weakness of small-sample theories is that they are, by definition, not general. These propositions (when they are explicitly integrated into a theory) merely assert generality; whether or not such assertions are empirically valid is a matter for large-sample testing to decide. Until the testing takes place, these are only general hypotheses, not generally confirmed theory. Replacing proper names with variables is indeed our goal, but generalizing is far more difficult than affixing general labels to particulars. It is one thing to call the United States a presidential democracy, but it is quite another to assert that what one observes in the United States is true of presidential democracies in general. The former is a description of one case; the latter is an inference about a population (all presidential democracies) from one case (the United States), which is not justified.

To summarize, case studies and small-sample comparisons yield a type of theory that is qualitatively thick and empirically well grounded and, therefore, plausible in bounded times and places, but also provisional, pending extension to more general samples, and often ambiguous in its theoretical implications and, therefore, difficult to test decisively, especially beyond its original boundaries. It is, to caricature a bit, soft theory built on a hard foundation.

Brian Downing's *The Military Revolution and Political Change* (1992) is a small-sample comparison that illustrates this trade-off well. As we have come to expect of comparative historical analysis, it is admirably thick and well grounded. Downing delves deeply into the resurrection of Roman law in medieval constitutionalism, the rights of towns in the Holy Roman Empire, the terms of feudal levies, the advantages of Swiss pikemen over mounted knights, the powers of the estates of Brandenburg and Pomerania, seventeenth-century French tax farming, the consensus voting rule in the

Polish Seym, the financing of English wars, and the logistics of Swedish armies. The specificity of his arguments, however, forces him to eschew generalizations beyond Europe:

To say that European social, political, and economic history is markedly different from that of the rest of the world is to say nothing new.... Three principal conditions in medieval Europe provided a predisposition to democracy: a rough balance between crown and nobility, decentralized military systems, and peasant property rights and reciprocal ties to the landlord. Though one or more of these may have obtained in other parts of the world, the combination of all three, as well as the strength of each, was unique to Western Europe. (Downing 1992, 18–19)

It is also difficult to imagine the testable hypotheses that might spring from his theory. A condensed version of his theory is that (1) late-medieval institutions unique to Europe predisposed the region to eventual democratization; but (2) absolutist rulers destroyed these institutions to keep up with an arms race in the seventeenth century; although (3) absolutism was avoided in states that were protected by mountains (Switzerland) or water (England), or that could finance the military buildup through trade (Holland). Testing would be difficult in part because the theory is confined to Europe, where there are few cases left unexamined. Testing would also be difficult because the concepts on which the theory rests are so specific that considerable interpretation would be required to apply them to additional cases. Was the country's late-medieval constitutionalism of the right variety? Was the country under greater military threat than England? Did it earn enough from trade to expand its standing army without raising taxes? One gets the feeling that any apparent exception could be explained away by going more deeply into some obscure and unique sixteenth-century land-tenure arrangement. Theories based on case studies and small-sample comparisons invite constant reformulation and ad hoc defenses. Nevertheless, they have theoretical content. In fact, they are superior to other theories with respect to thickness, particularly in offering guidance about why different explanations are relevant in different contexts.

Theory in large-sample comparisons

Many scholars tend to view large-sample, statistical research as an exercise in testing only rather than as a source of theoretical innovation. But even though the original motivation for applying statistics to comparative politics may have been to test hypotheses generated by other methods, this kind of research actually does contribute to theory in distinct and novel ways. The mathematical tools used in hypothesis testing encourage, and sometimes require, conversion of theories from a qualitative logic to a quantitative logic. Theories become less about kinds and types and true-false or necessary-sufficient relations and more about the magnitudes of impacts, partial impacts, probabilities, and curvilinear relationships. These relationships are difficult to handle in a qualitative idiom. The reverse is not true, fortunately. Statistical analysis can also handle the kinds of relationships found in qualitative theories, such as conditional relations, necessary or sufficient conditions, and the direction of causation.

Examples of distinctly quantitative theory abound in democratization research. The qualitative hypothesis that wealthy countries tend to be democracies has been converted into a rococo variety of quantitative hypotheses:

1. The wealthier the country is, the more democratic it is.
2. The wealthier the country is, the more democratic it is, but to a logarithmically diminishing degree.
3. The wealthier the country is, the more democratic it is, but with logarithmically diminishing increases and a dip at an intermediate level of wealth (the N-curve hypothesis).
4. The wealthier the country is, the more democratic it is, except when economic growth temporarily worsens inequality, which undermines democracy.
5. The wealthier the country is, the more democratic it is, although the impact of wealth is mediated by state size, which has an inverted-U relationship with democracy.
6. Increasing wealth does not make countries become more democratic but improves the life expectancy of any regime.

Another line of research has begun to explore the notion of democratic diffusion. Although Rustow and Huntington wrote about various possible types of transnational influences on democratization, quantitative scholars have found that democratic diffusion can refer to a tremendous variety of causal paths (Brinks and Coppedge 1999; O'Loughlin et al. 1998; Starr 1991). In the course of testing for them, they have had to refine the theory to distinguish among neighbor effects, regional effects, and superpower effects; impacts on the probability of change, change versus stasis, the direction of change, and the magnitude of change; and change influenced by ideas, trade, investment, population movement, military pressure, and national reputations, many of which were not contemplated in smaller-sample or qualitative research.

The principal advantage of the kind of theory that emerges from large-sample work is that it is relatively general, both in its aspirations and in its empirical grounding. The degree to which it is general varies depending on the coverage of the universe by the sample, of course, but it is by definition more general than small-sample research. Formal theory makes universalistic assumptions, which are even more general, but large-sample research has the advantage of making at least some assumptions that are guaranteed to have empirical support. (The assumptions of statistical analysis are rarely fully supported, such as the assumption of normally distributed random errors. I discuss the consequences of this problem in Chapter 9.) For example, the most consistent finding in the large-sample statistical literature is that democracy is associated with high levels of economic development. The association is a rough one, not strong enough to predict small differences in democracy or differences between any two cases with a high degree of certainty, but it remains a very general statement.

The two weaknesses of large-sample comparisons are thinness and loose theoretical integration. A thin proposition is a simple statement that assumes very little about the world and identifies an association between just two narrowly conceived phenomena, such as democracy and development. Both could be, and originally were, thick concepts that would require thick theory. But large-sample research typically has reduced the concept of democracy to a few easily measured institutions – fair and competitive elections, some basic freedoms – that reflect just one dimension of democracy: Dahl's notion of contestation. Similarly, economic development has been reduced in this research to per capita gross national product, per capita gross domestic product, or energy consumption. Thin concepts make for thin theory. Although the bivariate relationship between thin development and thin democracy has undergone elaborate permutations in statistical testing, many other hypotheses about the causes of democracy have been neglected. None of the large-sample literature really addresses theories that are cast at a subnational level of analysis, such as the very influential O'Donnell-Schmitter-Whitehead project. Large-sample research concerns the national, and occasionally international, levels of analysis, and it will continue to do so until subnational data are collected systematically – an enterprise that has barely begun. In addition, there are quite a few hypotheses about causes of democratization that have not yet been addressed in large-sample research. Among them are U.S. support for democracy or authoritarian governments (Blasier 1985; Lowenthal 1991), relations between the party in power and elite interests (Rueschemeyer et al. 1992), the mode of incorporation of the working class (Collier and Collier

1991), interactions with different historical periods, U.S. military training (Loveman 1994; Stepan 1971), and elite strategies in response to crisis (Linz 1978; O'Donnell and Schmitter 1986). In this sense, the large-sample literature lags behind the theories developed in other approaches.

The second weakness is loose integration with a body of systematic theory. Mathematics is an inherently systematic tool but by itself it has no political content, and the political content that has been inserted into the mathematical framework lacks system. Large-sample theory consists of a handful of isolated, disembodied propositions. Each one by itself can generate many necessary implications by simply plugging different numbers into simulated predictions. But there is no theory in the gaps between the propositions that would enable us to combine them to make predictions. For example, we know that rich countries tend to be democratic and that countries tend to become more like their neighbors. But there is no overarching theory that would enable us to predict how democratic a country should be if it is poor and surrounded by democracies or rich and surrounded by authoritarian regimes. Lacking such a theory, quantitative researchers tend simply to accept whatever estimates they obtain as reflections of the true weights of different causal factors; these estimates are then absorbed into the conventional wisdom about what matters. It is a fundamentally inductive process of discovery. The problem with induction, as David Hume observed centuries ago, is that even if a hypothesis is confirmed in 10,000 cases, there is no guarantee that it will be true in the 10,001st case unless one has a very good theory that predicts that it must.[10]

Most of the large-sample research on democratization has concerned two debates: one about whether the relationship between development and democracy is linear, logarithmic, or some sort of N-curve (Jackman 1973; Lipset et al. 1993; O'Donnell 1973; Przeworski and Limongi 1997) and one examining interactions among per capita gross domestic product, economic inequality, and democracy (Bollen and Jackman 1985; Burkhart 1997; Muller 1988). The lack of integration in this area is so great that after nearly forty years of repeated confirmation, a group of scholars was able to make a credible case that the association is spurious (Przeworski and Limongi

---

[10] Or, as John Stuart Mill put it, "That all swans are white, cannot have been a good induction, since the conclusion has turned out erroneous. The experience, however, on which the conclusion rested was genuine. From the earliest records, the testimony of all the inhabitants of the known world was unanimous on the point. The uniform experience, therefore, of the inhabitants of the known world, agreeing in a common result, without one known instance of deviation from that result, is not always sufficient to establish a general conclusion" (Mill 1843, 378–9).

1997).[11] Similar criticisms could be leveled against the emerging evidence for democratic diffusion (the spread of democracy from country to country): we are pretty sure it is happening, but we do not know what the causal mechanisms are (Brinks and Coppedge 2006; Elkins and Simmons 2005; Starr 1991; Whitehead 1986).

This quality of knowing things but not knowing why is what inspires the accusation that large-sample research leads to empirical generalizations but not to theory. Again, I consider such criticism to be based on excessively narrow criteria for theory, one that privileges integration over general empirical confirmation and thickness. The propositions that spring from large-sample analysis may be thin and disjointed, but they are still theories, albeit of a distinct kind, with the advantage of empirically grounded generality.

Formal theory

Formal (rational-choice) theories achieve levels of integration that elude small- and large-sample research. Three standards for good theorizing often touted by formal theorists are universal scope; clear, simple, and explicit assumptions; and the potential to generate testable hypotheses derived from theory. Formal theorists aspire to universal scope by refraining from limiting the applicability of their theories to certain times and places: what is true for one committee is assumed to be true for all committees as long as the assumptions of the model are met. Formal theorists also make their assumptions simple and explicit, which makes it easier for other scholars to follow the logic of the theory and derive the consequences of modifying some assumptions. Because of its deductive method, formal theory also lends itself to the generation of many hypotheses, especially about eventual, stable patterns of collective behavior. Because a whole community of scholars follows this logic and works within it, new research builds explicitly on what has gone before. Theory cumulates.

However, the theory that cumulates is far from thick. Formal theories of democratic transitions, for example, narrow their focus to the final stage of

---

[11] To be fair, the economic development hypothesis was originally embedded in the rather elaborate theory of modernization, which held that democratization was a trend parallel to development, urbanization, education, secularization, and industrialization. These trends were held to be causally linked in complex ways, although the nature of the actors driving the processes was not well specified. Lipset's (1959) seminal article developed various additional arguments about the relationship. However, over the years, as the demands of testing thinned concepts, noneconomic aspects of modernization encountered inconsistent confirmation and the inevitability of modernization came into question, the theory was reduced to a simple, underspecified hypothesis.

the process in which a small set of elites is bargaining about whether or not to found a democratic regime (Casper and Taylor 1996; Cohen 1994; Colomer 1991; Crescenzi 1999; Przeworski 1991; Weingast 1997). This is an extremely thin view of democratization. A thick theory would assume less and attempt to explain more. A thick theory would not limit the identities of the actors or the options before them to a fixed menu of choices. Game-theoretic explanations do not tell us how to know which actors are the elites and how they got their seats at the bargaining table. They do not explain where the bargainers' preferences came from or how they might change. They do not account for the number of rounds of bargaining to begin with or why democracy is one of the options on the table. A thicker theory would offer explanations (whether cultural, institutional, international, social, or economic) for at least some of these elements; formal theories simply assume them. Formal theory, as currently practiced, has difficulty developing thick explanations because it is anchored at the individual level. It aspires to make predictions about larger groups, but only within very restrictive assumptions about the rules of the game and the preferences of the players. It is the mirror image of small-sample theory: a hard theory built on a soft base. It is difficult to extrapolate from these small settings to macrophenomena like regime change. Indeed, Barbara Geddes has called on scholars to stop trying to theorize about "big structures, large processes, and huge comparisons," such as democratization, for the time being (Geddes 1997, 19–20).

Formal theories have universalistic aspirations; in this sense, they are even more general than large-sample theories, which are confined to the cases actually observed. However, generality is not, or should not be, merely an assertion or assumption of generality. It should be accompanied by empirical confirmation. A theory is only as good as the evidence that supports it. A theoretical model cannot be said to explain something just because it generated one possible explanation for an outcome. We don't actually know whether it might explain anything until we test it with fresh evidence. And even that is a low standard for explanation; it would be better to test it against a competing explanation.

Formal theories encounter two obstacles to empirical generality. First, if taken literally, the assumptions of these models render them inapplicable to the real world. All these theories are of the form "if W and X and Y are true, then Z must also be true." But if W is something like "this is a game with two and only two players," X is something like "players have complete information about each other's preferences," and Y is something like "this is a one-shot game," then the assumptions of the model cannot be met by actual cases. The assumptions may fit some cases approximately, or capture the most important features of most cases, but the theory makes no predictions about approximate fits. All bets are off. So if a case conforms to the prediction, it may be for the wrong reasons; if it doesn't fit, it may be that the theory is wrong, or it may be that it wasn't a fair test in the first place. Maybe there was a third significant player. Maybe one of the players was missing a key bit of information. Maybe this wasn't the first time these players had strategized about this game. These doubts undermine the relevance of any testing. Such premises cannot be said to hold in real-world situations and therefore any test of predictions derived from them could be ruled unfair (Green and Shapiro 1994). One could object that in practice, formal theorists constantly adjust their assumptions and predictions to what they observe in the world to make it as realistic and relevant as possible. But this backdoor induction is so unsystematic that it is prone to all the errors and biases found in the least rigorous testing methods.

Second, unlike small- and large-sample methods, formal theory is not a method of testing; it is only a method of generating theory (Blossfeld 1996). Their predictions can be tested; but if they are, they are tested using some version of small- or large-sample research, so the latter provide the only assurances of empirical support. Even if formal theories are generously credited with any empirical support their predictions may find, it must be confessed that testing is the weak suit of formal theorists. As Green and Shapiro argue, "a large proportion of the theoretical conjectures of rational choice theorists have not been tested empirically. Those tests that have been undertaken have either failed on their own terms or garnered support for other propositions that, on reflection, can only be characterized as banal: they do little more than state existing knowledge in rational choice terminology" (Green and Shapiro 1994, 6).

Nevertheless, the systematic, interlocking, cumulative nature of formal theory is an essential quality of theory, just as thickness and generality are. Even if its assumptions are false, or its predictions are false, or it has no empirical referents at all, it is necessary for developing other theories. But if a theory does not ultimately lead to propositions that survive rigorous testing, developing it does not constitute progress, just as making good time on the highway is not progress if one is driving in the wrong direction. There should be some effort to theorize in directions that are likely to lead to explanations that are consistent with evidence. I think that it would be a good idea to start

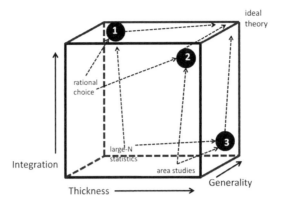

Figure 3.1   Paths to Thick, General, and Integrated Theory

with premises that are true, or mostly true. At any rate, the only way to know this is to test everything: predictions and assumptions. This is the scientific equivalent of stopping to ask for directions.

Toward theoretical perfection

Each approach has a different primary goal that lends it one strength and two weaknesses, which complement the strengths and weaknesses of the other two approaches. Formal theory is integrated but thin and lacking in general empirical support; large-sample analysis is relatively general but thin and theoretically disjointed; and case studies and small-sample research are admirably thick but drastically bounded and loosely integrated with a systematic set of theoretical propositions. Practical problems have kept these approaches separate in the past, but there is no necessary reason for them to remain separate. All three goals (innovating theory, articulating theory, and testing theory) are essential to any science. Although we can never achieve a perfect theory, we can move in that direction, toward a theory that would be thick, integrated, and general.

Figure 3.1 depicts where we are now and what we would have to do to improve our theories. The figure shows a cube whose three dimensions are the three fundamental criteria for good theory – integration, thickness, and generality. Each dimension ranges from little achievement of the criterion to full achievement of the criterion. I have placed the three major approaches in comparative politics at an approximate position on these three dimensions.

Rational-choice theory occupies a space of high integration, little generality, and thinness. Area studies are associated with thickness but weak integration and little generality. Finally, large-sample statistical analysis occupies a region of high generality but little integration and considerable thinness. At the opposite corner rests our goal: theory that is very thick, fully integrated, and general.

The figure traces two paths from each approach to the unattainable ideal. Formal theory could move toward empirical generalization through testing (bubble 1), which is increasingly common. Alternatively, formal theorists could thicken their concepts and make their models more complex so that they apply more naturally to real-world situations (bubble 2). This is one of the aims of the analytic-narratives approach. Scholars who do case studies and small-sample comparisons could meet them halfway by formalizing the complex models they generate inductively, integrating them with a larger and more systematic body of theory (bubble 2). But other area studies scholars will probably prefer to move toward generalization by testing their complex hypotheses in increasingly large samples (bubble 3). Quantitative comparativists, who have been testing hypotheses in large samples for a long time, could continue to increase the complexity of the hypotheses they examine (bubble 3). Or, to come full circle, quantitative scholars could develop formal models to explain the empirical regularities they have documented so consistently, integrating their research with the growing body of formal theory (bubble 1). These paths would lead to new kinds of theory that are integrated and general, thick and integrated, or general and thick (bubbles 1, 2, and 3, respectively), any of which would be superior to the theories we have now. Even this much progress may be too much to hope for in the next generation of scholarship, but it would still leave us with the challenge of achieving all three criteria for good theory in one approach. This map of the difficult course ahead may be discouraging. Nevertheless, it makes it understandable why different approaches exist now and defines some basic criteria for judging future progress in generating good theories.

4 Checklists, frameworks, and Boolean analysis

On some level, we political scientists think we understand some things about the causes of democratization; we share a conventional wisdom. However, the conventional wisdom is fragmented and not well integrated: it consists of dozens of propositions about the conditions that favor democracy. Although there is a core of propositions that most scholars consider credible, this conventional wisdom is poorly integrated. Some propositions can be grouped into competing schools of thought but, as we consume, interpret, test, and cite the literature, we tend to consider each proposition in isolation, as though it could stand or fall on its own without affecting our belief in other propositions. What passes for the conventional wisdom is not, therefore, an integrated theory of interwoven propositions; the plural, conventional wisdoms would be more accurate. Our collective beliefs about democratization resemble checklists: lists of independent, unconnected items. Checklists are useful for reminding us about all of the varied factors that may be important. Unfortunately, just as a grocery list is not a short story, a checklist is not a coherent and integrated explanation.

There is no official screening committee that certifies that a proposition is generally true and rigorously supported before it joins one of the conventional wisdoms. Rather, our conventional wisdoms are just that: matters of convention. Whatever ideas many scholars have found convincing at one time or another come to be part of what we believe. Because different scholars are convinced by different things, conventional wisdoms are a hodgepodge of ideas originating from diverse sources. To be sure, some propositions have survived repeated testing in large samples using the most rigorous techniques in our toolkits. But many of them are the conclusions of less rigorous studies that were so convincing, in their way, that we have incautiously assumed the conclusions to be generally true. Many comparativists are impressed by intimate knowledge of the politics of a particular country or a region, so the conclusions of case studies and intraregional comparisons sometimes yield insights of a particularly solid kind, and we sometimes elevate these insights to the status of universal truth. Some ideas have been treated as received wisdom since the infancy of comparative politics, when the field was limited to comparisons of Britain, France, and Germany. Other propositions originate in logically persuasive arguments, which are universally true, once you grant their premises; but the questionable truth of the premises is fine print that compilers of the conventional wisdom sometimes overlook. Quite a few propositions survive simply because they resonate well with common sense – our informal theory, as discussed in Chapter 3 – or with ideological convictions (e.g., "Free markets and free societies go together"). In a few cases, we frail and fallible humans have been convinced by our own wishful thinking: it must be true because we need it to be true. What is striking is that, despite the diverse origins and uneven rigor of these ideas, scholars who periodically take inventory of what we believe about democratization tend to list many overlapping propositions. I do not pretend that all of these authors arrived at their conclusions independently; clearly, they were all drawing on many of the same sources. But this is my point: scholars tend to accept, and repeat, propositions that they have not independently confirmed and that may not have been rigorously confirmed in the first place. This is a good starting point, but we must strive to do better.

This chapter begins with a summary of the major schools of thought, followed by a critique of this checklist-style knowledge. Checklists are indispensable memory-jogging aids, and they can even make reliable predictions at the extremes, but they are much less useful for the intermediate cases, and they fall short of the standards for integrated theory. This section contains a demonstration of what a checklist can and cannot do. The chapter then summarizes and critiques several efforts to integrate disparate propositions into a more coherent theory: Linz and Stepan's *The Breakdown of Democratic Regimes* (1978); O'Donnell, Schmitter, and Whitehead's *Transitions from Authoritarian Rule* (1986); and Linz and Stepan's *Problems of Democratic Transition and Consolidation* (1996). Although all are steps in the direction of integration, they are ultimately theoretical frameworks – stylized inductions – that continue to share some characteristics with checklists. The chapter concludes with a critique of Boolean analysis, which is useful for testing checklists and other large sets of qualitative hypotheses but also highlights the limitations of inductive approaches.

Conventional wisdoms

Because democratization is one of the central puzzles of comparative politics, there is a periodic need for leading scholars to take inventory of findings.

My summary of conventional wisdoms is based on eight well-known inventories of this type by Dankwart Rustow (1970); Robert Dahl (1971); Larry Diamond (1995); Seymour Martin Lipset (1994); Larry Diamond, Juan Linz, and Seymour Martin Lipset (1995); Samuel Huntington (1991); and Doh Chull Shin (1994). This should be an authoritative survey of conventional wisdoms because the list includes several of the most cited social scientists in the world and three past presidents of the American Political Science Association. These authors did not intend their essays to be merely checklists; often they linked some propositions together, speculated about which ones were more important than others, and in some cases discussed propositions they found unconvincing. Nevertheless, it is reasonable to use these works as my sources for the content of checklists because they are consumed as checklists: other scholars pick up propositions from them selectively in their literature reviews, tests, and citations. These works are not themselves the checklists; the checklists exist in the minds and practices of the scholars who consume such inventories.

One of the constants of the conventional wisdom is that it is important to distinguish among stages of democratization. At the very least, we must distinguish between the conditions that favor transitions to democratic regimes and conditions that make it possible for democracy to survive. Ever since Rustow's 1970 article, the conventional wisdom has warned that the forces that help democracies survive may be quite different from the forces that enabled them to become democracies in the first place. We should also treat the preparation for democracy as a separate stage, as a great deal of research focuses on conditions that laid the necessary groundwork for democracy (especially in early modern Europe) but that, in themselves, were not sufficient for a transition to mass political democracy. Other ways of defining the research question identify other possible stages of democratization, although there is less agreement on their importance. O'Donnell and Schmitter claimed that liberalization of an authoritarian regime was a necessary stage before transition. Breakdown can also be a stage if democratization includes reversals; according to Linz, a crisis of a democratic regime is a stage before breakdown, and reequilibration is an alternative to breakdown. Many scholars have written about the consolidation of democratic regimes in ways that suggest that consolidation is something more ambitious than mere survival. Notions of consolidation often stipulate that beyond surviving, regimes undergo legitimation and may achieve democratic deepening or improve the quality of democracy, and that these achievements favor regime survival. Each of these stages – preparation, liberalization, transition, crisis, reequilibration or breakdown, legitimation, consolidation, deepening, improving quality, and survival – may have its own set of causes, distinct from the causes of other stages. To simplify my discussion, however, I reduce all of these to just three basic stages – preparation, transition, and survival. Different authors discuss different stages and use different terminology, but almost everyone recognizes the divisions among the transition, pretransition, and posttransition stages.

I survey the conventional explanations for these stages of democratization under four convenient headings: culture and leadership, economy and society, the state and institutions, and international influences. Table 4.1 lists the major hypotheses involving mass political culture or elite leadership. It also identifies the sources that mention each hypothesis, or one in a very similar vein, and the stage of democratization that is affected, according to each source. I have listed only hypotheses that were mentioned by more than one source, but I suspect that most of these sources would list all of these ideas if they were all equally comprehensive. A few additional stray hypotheses are mentioned in the source notes. Similar tables accompany the discussion of other kinds of hypotheses. Altogether, these tables list fifty-five different supposed causes of democracy.

Culture and leadership

One of the oldest hypotheses is that democratic regimes spring from and are sustained by a democratic political culture. Table 4.1 lists these hypotheses. This notion goes back at least to Alexis de Tocqueville's *Democracy in America*, the French nobleman's 1835 description of what was then a novel regime. Although Tocqueville discussed the geography and laws of the United States as conditions that favored democracy, in the end he gave the greatest weight to the mores of its citizens: "the sum of the moral and intellectual dispositions of men in society," particularly Christian religion and the widespread understanding of the basic procedures of self-government, reinforced by constant practice (Tocqueville 1969, chap. 9).

Tocqueville saw the democratic culture of the United States in historical perspective, as the vanguard of inexorable human progress toward equality: "the gradual progress of equality is something fated. The main features of this progress are the following: it is universal and permanent, it is daily passing beyond human control, and every event and every man helps it along" (Tocqueville 1969, 12). The rise of fascism in the early twentieth century destroyed the belief in unstoppable progress, but this thinking survives more modestly in propositions that there is a democratic *Zeitgeist* or spirit of

Table 4.1. Leadership and cultural causes of democracy

Cause	Stages affected, according to each source							
Mass political culture source	A	B	C	D	E	F	G	H
Mass support for democracy in general and rejection of nondemocracy	S			T3	T	S	S	S
Toleration and pluralist values		X	X				TS	S
Social capital, public trust, civility, cooperation				T3			S	S
Mass support for this specific regime and rejection of prior regime				T3				S
Pragmatism and flexibility							TS	S
Protestantism			X	T1				
Christianity; at least, not Islam or Confucianism				T3	X			
Elite leadership								
Elite belief in the superiority of democracy	S	X	X	T1	T		S	S
Divisions among the preceding nondemocratic leaders	PT			T3	P		T	
Moderate leadership that is willing to compromise		X	X				TS	S
Nonviolent leadership that works within the system			X				TS	S
Efficacious leadership	S		X				S	
Continual adjustment, reform, and renewal	S						S	S
Pacts	T					T	TS	
Contingency and strategy						T	X	T
Cooperative and competitive political relationships			X					S

Note: The letters in the right-hand columns denote the stage of democratization that each cause is thought to affect. P = preparation, T = transition, S = survival, X = any or all stages. Huntington (column D) specifies different causal processes for each wave of democracy. The numbers in this column refer to waves of democracy: T1 = first wave, T2 = second wave, and T3 = third wave.

Sources: A: Rustow 1970, 337–363. Rustow also believed that democracy arises as a convenient solution to a prolonged conflict between two camps but argued that the nature of the conflict varies by country. B: Dahl 1971, 203. C: Huntington 1991, 37–38. In this passage, Huntington summarizes the conventional wisdom without endorsing it. He also mentions an "instrumental rather than consummatory culture" and both consensus and absence of consensus on political and social values. D: Huntington 1991, 106–107. In this passage, Huntington summarizes his own understanding of the causes of each of the three waves of democratization. E: Lipset 1994. Lipset also mentions individualism and the separation of church and state. F: Shin 1994, 135–170. G: Diamond et al. 1995. The authors also mention strong leadership, in particular the depoliticization of cleavages by leaders. H: Diamond 1999. Diamond also mentions a participatory culture.

the times that ebbs and flows, shaping every national culture's openness to democracy. Some scholars have turned to this idea to account for waves of democracy and its reversal. Most scholars believe that the defeat of the Axis powers in World War II discredited fascism and vindicated democracy; during the Cold War, democracy sometimes took a back seat to anticommunist authoritarianism; and an international bias for democracy fostered and sustained the third wave longer than expected, even in unlikely places (Fukuyama 1992; Huntington 1991).

The behavioral revolution in the social sciences in the 1960s made this view look simplistic. To study "culture," scholars conducted national surveys, which established that culture does not ebb and flow uniformly in all countries. Furthermore, to measure culture in these surveys, researchers had to define it more precisely. They reduced democratic culture to a set of attitudes, beliefs, behaviors, and norms, such as tolerance, open-mindedness, pragmatism, participation, efficacy, civility, trust, cooperation, and support for democracy and democratic institutions. Where these cultural traits prevail among the mass population, democracy is more likely to be founded and less likely to fall victim to bitter or violent clashes.

Much of the theorizing about culture has been inspired by the fact that modern democracy first arose in the states of the northwest of Europe and in some of the (principally British) colonies that they founded. The most obvious difference between Northwestern Europe and Southern or Eastern Europe is religion, so religion has always been an important strand of thinking about democratization. Protestantism, it is alleged, encourages individualism and resistance to state control, whereas Roman Catholicism requires submission to a hierarchical authority. Protestantism also, according to Max Weber, gave rise to capitalism (Weber 1958), which then favored democratization by empowering a bourgeoisie to the point that it was able to check state authority. More recently, Lipset and Huntington have argued that both Protestant and Catholic forms of Christianity, and perhaps Hinduism as well, favor democracy, whereas Orthodox Christianity, Islam, and Confucianism work against it, at least for the present (Huntington 1993; Lipset 1959). This shift in thinking clearly corresponds to the spread of democracy to the Catholic countries of Southern Europe and Latin America and the continuing resistance to democracy in the Middle East and China. Whether it is a causal relationship remains an open question.

An unintended consequence of the behavioral revolution was a weakening of the claim that a mass civic culture was necessary for democracy because survey research documented an appalling lack of democratic values in the United States and other stable democracies. In actual democracies, voters' "belief in liberal democratic values does not extend beyond limited recognition of platitudes; given a concrete situation, ordinary people see nothing wrong with abrogating freedom of speech, press, or religion for those with whom they disagree" (Katz 1997, 52). Methodological objections to cultural hypotheses (to be discussed in Chapter 8) reinforced the decline of this school of thought. By 1970, Rustow and Dahl were emphasizing that elite values and beliefs were far more important than mass culture and, for the following fifteen years, mass culture received little attention (Diamond 1993b). The lower panel of Table 4.1 lists hypotheses about elite leadership. Elites could bring democracy into being and hold it together as long as they were tolerant, moderate, ready to compromise, pacific, successful at finding solutions to pressing problems and, above all, convinced that democracy is a better form of government than any other (Diamond 1993b; Lijphart 1977; Linz 1978). This emphasis on elites gathered additional strength during the third wave, as O'Donnell and Schmitter portrayed transitions from authoritarian rule as complex yet voluntaristic processes in which elite strategizing could have a decisive impact. At the extreme, some scholars also argued that there were democracies without democrats: democratic regimes founded as peaceful solutions to conflicts between leaders who had, at best, only an instrumental commitment to democracy (DiPalma 1990; Przeworski 1987; Waterbury 1999).[1] In time, they argued, these leaders might come to value democracy as an end in itself, but democratic values did not create democracy; it was the other way around.

In the meantime, however, other scholars revived speculation about the importance of a democratic mass political culture for regime survival. They granted that democracies could come into being without a mass democratic culture, but they argued that if mass culture did not become democratic, the quality of democracy would be compromised and the regime would be in danger of breaking down. Robert Putnam, for example, reported that democratic government is more efficient and responsive where citizens participate in secondary associations that link them to broader networks of trust (Putnam et al. 1993). Linz and Stepan included in their definition of consolidation the requirement that "attitudinally, a democratic regime is consolidated when a strong majority of public opinion holds the belief that democratic procedures and institutions are the most appropriate way to govern collective life in a society such as theirs and when the support for antisystem alternatives is quite small or more or less isolated from the pro-democratic forces" (Linz and Stepan 1996, 6). Similarly, Larry Diamond wrote, "The essence of democratic consolidation is a behavioral and attitudinal embrace of democratic principles and methods by both elites and mass," and warned that many of the new democracies fall short of this standard, leading to "illiberal," "pseudo-,"

---

[1] Waterbury notes that Rustow's 1970 article stated this position first.

or "hollow" democracies (Diamond 1999, 20).[2] Some current thinking synthesizes both recent strands of theory into a hypothesis that elite leadership matters more for transitions and mass culture matters more for consolidation, deepening, and survival.

Economy and society

Aside from Rustow, who explicitly rejected most structural determinants of democracy, comparativists agree that the economic characteristics of countries affect their chances of becoming or remaining democratic. Table 4.2 lists several of these economic hypotheses. Three of them have been particularly prominent in the literature: that democracy is associated with (1) economic equality, (2) a high standard of living, and (3) capitalism (Table 4.2). Initially, these were mentioned as preparation for democracy but since the 1980s, scholars have emphasized their association with transitions or survival instead because democracy is increasingly found in some very poor or inegalitarian economies, such as India and Brazil. The association between democracy and wealth (measured by per capita energy consumption, gross domestic product, or gross national product) has received the most attention, and because practically all large-sample statistical studies have confirmed it, it is almost an article of faith in democratization research (Diamond 1992; Rueschemeyer 1991).

Within this conventional wisdom, however, there are two areas of profound disagreement. First, scholars disagree over whether wealth promotes both transitions and survival, or survival only. Before the 1990s, almost everyone agreed that a high standard of living helped democracies survive and made transitions more likely in nondemocracies. But Adam Przeworski and Fernando Limongi's (1997) article, "Modernization: Theories and Facts," challenged this long-standing conventional wisdom with its claim that the observed association between wealth and democracy is entirely due to the tendency of wealthy countries to remain democratic once they experience transitions, which are caused by many factors other than economic development (Przeworski et al. 2000). Others have since come to the defense of the older view, so this debate continues (Boix and Stokes 2003; Brinks and Coppedge 1999).

The second area of disagreement concerns the reasons for the association between wealth and democracy. The disagreement arises because the

---

[2] Diamond (1999) develops this argument in more detail in pp. 161–217.

Table 4.2. Economic and social causes of democracy

Cause								
	Stages affected, according to each source							
The economy source	A	B	C	D	E	F	G	H
Socioeconomic equality and poverty reduction	no	X	X	T1	P	S	S	S
High standard of living	no	X	X	T1	TS	T		TS
Market economy; limited state ownership and control		X	X		P	S	TS	TS
Recent good economic performance; no economic crisis			X	T3		S	S	S
Economic crisis				T3	T	T		
Rapid growth				T3	TS	T		
Low or decreasing relative deprivation		X				S		
Society								
Strong civil society vis-à-vis the state; checks on state power			X	T1	S	TS	TS	S
Either no deep ethnic divisions or crosscutting ones	S	X	X		S		S	
Literacy and education	no		X	T1&3		T	TS	
Large middle class, especially small business, professionals, and students			X	T1&3		T	TS	
No permanent minority excluded completely or indefinitely					S		S	S
Urbanization				T1		T	TS	
If commercial and/or industrial, then decentralized economy				T1		T		
Dispersed inequalities; crosscutting cleavages		X			S			
Nonclientelistic elite-mass relationships		X						S

Note: The letters in the right-hand columns denote the stage of democratization that each cause is thought to affect. P = preparation, T = transition, S = survival, X = any or all stages. Huntington (column D) specifies different causal processes for each wave of democracy. The numbers in this column refer to waves of democracy: T1 = first wave, T2 = second wave, and T3 = third wave.

Sources: A: Rustow (1970, 337–363). B: Dahl 1971, 203. Dahl also argued that polyarchy was more likely in agrarian societies if farmers were independent smallholders. C: Huntington 1991, 37–38. In this passage, Huntington summarizes the conventional wisdom without endorsing it. His list also included a feudal aristocratic past (from Barrington Moore). D: Huntington 1991, 106–107. In this passage, Huntington summarizes his own understanding of the causes of each of the three waves of democratization. Unlike other authors, he also claims that third-wave transitions are more likely in an intermediate zone of development. E: Lipset 1994. F: Shin 1994, 135–170. G: Diamond, Linz, and Lipset (1995). H: Diamond 1999. Diamond also argues that democracy is more common in small states and that this tendency accounts for the disproportionate success of former British colonies.

association is an empirical generalization, not a complete theory with actors, motives, context, and mechanisms, and is therefore compatible with many different stories. Some of these stories stay close to economics. One theory is that wealthy countries have fewer economic crises, which would increase feelings of relative deprivation, deprive governments of legitimacy, and make a regime breakdown more likely (Gasiorowski 1995; Haggard and Kaufman 1995). Freedom from economic crises is therefore the reason that wealthy countries tend to be more democratic. The opposite side of this coin is that transitions are more likely when authoritarian regimes experience the same kind of delegitimating economic crisis.[3] Some other stories connect the economy to cultural explanations already discussed. Lipset, for example, proposed that wealth, economic security, and education encouraged a belief in secular reformist gradualism, fostered cross-pressures that would diminish radicalism, and diversified opinions in society and increased interest in politics, all of which favored democratic survival (Lipset 1959).

The most prominent theories connecting economy and democracy, however, have claimed that economic development – first the commercialization of agriculture, later industrialization and rising standards of living – transforms social structure, creating new social actors and interests who promote and protect democracy. These actors – the bourgeoisie (owners and managers of capital), petty bourgeoisie (shopkeepers and craftspeople), free agricultural laborers, the middle class, and eventually the industrial working class – formed class alliances to reduce the power of the monarch and the bureaucracy, increase the power of parliament, and eventually extend the suffrage to all adult males. There have been many variations on this theme. Johnson argued that the middle sectors were the bearers of democracy in Latin America (Johnson 1958). Moore, saying "no bourgeoisie, no democracy," argued that in Western Europe the bourgeoisie played a pivotal role by allying with the landed aristocracy to check the crown, but only where the aristocracy participated in the commercialization of agriculture instead of repressing its agricultural workforce (Moore 1966, 418). Rueschemeyer, Stephens, and Stephens disagreed, arguing that the working class was the most consistent promoter of democracy and that the middle class often resisted democratic progress (although less so in Latin America) (Rueschemeyer, Stephens, and Stephens 1992, 1–29). Ruth Collier identified a variety of different roles that

---

[3] Some formal theorists have developed arguments that economic elites force regime changes in order to maximize their tax-adjusted rate of profit. For example, see Acemoglu and Robinson (2001). However, this way of thinking has not yet entered the conventional wisdom.

organized labor has played in democratization in Europe and the Americas (Collier 1999). Nevertheless, all of these authors share the belief that social classes created by capitalist development are among the presumptive agents of democratization, whether they advance democracy or obstruct it.

The rise of communist states in the twentieth century reinforced the belief in capitalism itself as a precondition for democracy because this modern alternative to capitalism is also nondemocratic. The idea is further reinforced by classic liberal ideology, which holds that free markets and free societies are inseparable components of freedom. However, even most advocates of the capitalist development hypothesis recognize an important qualifier: if economic growth inevitably or initially increases inequality (the Kuznets hypothesis), then democracy is less likely to arise, less likely to be stable, or more likely to be of poor quality. There are three reasons for this qualification. First, unequal development should create only a small middle class and an impoverished working class, both of which would be too weak to achieve their desire for political rights. Second, even if democratic institutions were adopted in an unequal society, inequalities would generate zero-sum conflict, distrust, demagoguery, and extremism, thus making a regime breakdown more likely. Finally, in a socially unequal democracy, many citizens would remain subject to oppressive clientelistic social relationships that would prevent them from exercising their full rights as citizens (Muller 1988).

As Table 4.2 notes, the conventional wisdom about democratization also includes several hypotheses about societal characteristics that are not necessarily related to the economy. These hypotheses spring from the belief that most noneconomic social cleavages are less tractable than class divisions. Economic conflicts can often be settled by redistributing resources; noneconomic conflicts, in contrast, usually involve ascriptive differences that are categorical, acquired at birth or otherwise not freely chosen, immutable, and therefore nonnegotiable (Horowitz 1985). These ethnic, religious, linguistic, and racial conflicts are thought to be especially likely to end in violence, a prospect that can both discourage attempts to inaugurate democracy (especially in states that have not resolved the nationality question) and precipitate regime breakdowns. However, the conventional wisdom is not quite so bleak. Aside from the obvious hypothesis that democracy is easier to achieve and sustain in homogeneous societies, it holds out two hopes for democracy despite these cleavages. First, social (and economic) cleavages are less threatening to democracy if they are crosscutting rather than overlapping. When cleavages overlap, they reinforce one another and increase the chance of deep, unresolvable conflict; when they cut across one another, each cleavage by itself is less salient, less deeply felt, and therefore less likely to become a major source of political tension (Lipset 1960). Second, the literature supports the hope that political institutions such as federalism and grand coalitions can dampen or manage social cleavages well enough to enable democracy to survive (Lijphart 1977). This takes us into the next section, but the basic principle is that the survival of democratic regimes requires that no significant minority be relegated to permanent opposition status. Institutions must allocate every group a share of power, at least some of the time.

The state and political institutions

Table 4.3 summarizes the major democratization hypotheses that concern the state and political institutions. Few of these hypotheses concern transitions to democracy; some concern preparation, but most promise to explain the survival of democratic regimes once they are established. Theories about state characteristics posit that there are certain basic functions that any viable state must perform regardless of the type of regime. If the state lacks the capacity to perform these functions adequately, the regime cannot survive. The most fundamental characteristic is simply being a state, that is, in Weber's definition, "a human community that (successfully) claims the monopoly of the legitimate use of physical force within a given territory" (Weber 1958, 78). This hypothesis would seem to be true by definition because regimes can exist only within states but, in practice, stateness can be partial or a matter of degree. In relative terms, then, democracy is less likely to survive where there are secessionist forces that challenge the boundaries of the state or where insurgents or large numbers of less violent citizens refuse to recognize the regime's claim to a monopoly of the legitimate use of force. Similarly, democracy is thought to be at risk where the state is unable to maintain public order or the civilian government does not command the obedience of the armed forces.

By a similar but less extreme logic, democratic regimes are more likely to survive where poor state capacity does not hobble governmental performance. More specifically, some desirable state capacities are the faithful execution of the laws by the bureaucracy, predictable policy making and implementation, the uniform and impartial application of the law to all citizens, and the absence of widespread corruption. Any regime, democratic or not, can be found in a state lacking these qualities; and, as in any other regime, citizens tend to blame the regime for the failings of the state.

Specific democratic institutions logically cannot be preparation for democracy or causes of democratic transitions because institutions are precisely the

Table 4.3. State and institutional causes of democracy

Cause	Stages affected, according to each source							
State characteristics source	A	B	C	D	E	F	G	H
Effective control over national territory; national sovereignty	P		X				PS	S
Ability to maintain public order		X				S	PS	S
Absence of widespread corruption					X		S	S
Rule of law				X	S			S
Civilian control of the military							S	S
Predictable policymaking and implementation							S	S
Effective government oversight of the bureaucracy							P	S
Political institutions								
A parliamentary, not presidential, constitution					S	S	S	S
Institutionalized political parties	S				S		TS	S
Decentralization (devolution or federalism, strong local government)					S		S	S
Effective guarantees for the civil liberties of all ethnicities					S		S	S
Institutionalization itself							S	S
Contestation before inclusion		X	X					
An electoral system that balances representation and governability							S	S

Note: The letters in the right-hand columns denote the stage of democratization that each cause is thought to affect. P = preparation, T = transition, S = survival, X = any or all stages. Huntington (column D) specifies different causal processes for each wave of democracy. This column is blank because Huntington did not consider these causes useful for explaining waves of democracy.

Sources: A: Rustow (1970, 337–363). B: Dahl 1971, 203. I have omitted Dahl's well-known argument that transitions occur when the costs of repression exceed the costs of toleration. C: Huntington (1991, 37–38). In this passage, Huntington summarizes the conventional wisdom without endorsing it. He also mentioned internal democracy in political organizations. D: Huntington (1991, 106–107). In this passage, Huntington summarizes his own understanding of the causes of each of the three waves of democratization. E: Lipset (1994). F: Shin 1994, 135–170. G: Diamond, Linz, and Lipset (1995). The authors also list among their facilitating conditions the restriction of the military's role to national defense, an aggregative rather than representational party system, and mechanisms for recruiting and training leaders. H: Diamond 1999.

entities that change when a country becomes democratic. If institutions matter for any of the phases of democratization, therefore, it is for regime survival. The first example is political parties, whose existence and nature often transcend any specific regime. It has been argued that democratic transitions are more likely to succeed if institutionalized political parties are present in the streets and at the negotiation table (Levine 1973).

A second institution is the division of powers into separate bodies that are self-governing for certain issues or within subnational territories. Specific examples include federalism, regional autonomy, bicameralism, municipal autonomy, and consociationalism (Lijphart 1999, 243–257). Several of these institutions are believed to help manage social cleavages by allowing each group to govern itself on its own issues without imposing its will on other groups. In Table 4.3, I list as another institution Dahl's historical sequence of instituting contestation before inclusion. Although this sequence is not an institution per se, the reasoning behind it is that this sequence encourages the formation of institutions that help democracy survive. Dahl proposed that with this sequence, "the rules, the practices, and the culture of competitive politics developed first among a small elite, and the critical transition from nonparty politics to party competition also occurred initially within the restricted group.... Later, as additional social strata were admitted into politics they were more easily socialized into the norms and practices of competitive politics" (Dahl 1971, 36). These rules and practices and parties are all institutions, even when they are informal. Few other inventory takers have picked up Dahl's famous sequence for their lists (Huntington did, without endorsing it), but most of them do list the effective mutual guarantees and well-institutionalized, competitive political parties that theoretically result from this sequence.

Third, in the past decade, the liveliest debate about institutions and democratic survival has concerned the alleged advantages and disadvantages of parliamentary and presidential regimes. Juan Linz articulated the best-known and most comprehensive critique of presidentialism (Linz and Valenzuela 1994). He claimed that presidential democracies are prone to impasses between the president and congress that are likely to escalate into regime crises due in part to the psychologically aggrandizing impact of direct presidential elections. And once such a stalemate occurs, Linz reasoned, presidential constitutions provide no institutional mechanisms for resolving the crisis, and breakdown is therefore more likely. In a parliamentary system, there would be a vote of no confidence and the cabinet would fall or new elections would be held, all without risk to the regime. Other scholars have chipped away at this thesis ever since, claiming that it is true only in certain circumstances, that it is overstated, that it is a spurious association, or that it is true for reasons different from Linz's.[4] Nevertheless, the robust empirical association and the

---

[4] A good overview and critique of this literature is in Cheibub and Limongi (2002).

logic behind the argument have preserved the presidentialism thesis as a part of the conventional wisdom.

The most recent addition to theorizing about institutions and regime change calls attention to regime legacies (not listed in Table 4.3). Transitions from authoritarian regimes may be easier than transitions from totalitarian regimes; Linz and Stepan theorize further about transitions from posttotalitarian and sultanistic regimes (Linz and Stepan 1996). Others have claimed that dominant parties help authoritarian regimes survive (Brownlee 2003; Geddes 2003). Also, legislatures that exist in some authoritarian regimes may affect the prospects for a successful transition (Fish 2005; Schedler 2002).

International causes

The most recently developed family of hypotheses about the causes of democracy concerns international factors, which are listed in Table 4.4. Many scholars were fascinated by the dramatic third wave of democracy that washed over Southern Europe in the 1970s; Latin America from 1978 to 1990; and then Eastern Europe, Africa, and parts of Asia in the 1990s. This temporal and geographic clustering of transitions could not be a coincidence, the product of domestic forces working independently yet simultaneously; there had to be an international or transnational dimension to democratization (Huntington 1991; Starr 1991). This was a novel hypothesis in the early 1990s; Rustow did not even mention it in 1970, and Dahl in 1971 discussed only the most obvious international cause: postwar occupation of West Germany, Austria, and Japan by the Allies.

Although it is generally agreed that democracy diffuses internationally, it remains unclear how or why it diffuses. One of the most common hypotheses is that the idea or norm of democratic government spreads, perhaps through a process of historical learning. Many people questioned democracy in the wake of the Russian Revolution, during the rise of fascism in Europe, and in the Americas after the Cuban Revolution; and democracy regained favor as a standard for good government after the Allied victory in World War II, the fall of the Franco regime in Spain, and especially after the collapse of the Soviet Union. In some hard-to-specify way, democratization accelerates when its rival models of government are discredited.

There are, however, a few concrete hypotheses about how democracy spreads internationally. A few regional organizations – the European Union, the North Atlantic Treaty Organization, and the Organization of American States, among others – require member countries to be democratic. Countries

Table 4.4. International causes of democracy

Cause	Stages affected, according to each source							
International influences source	A	B	C	D	E	F	G	H
Demonstration effects, contagion, and snowballing			T	T3	T	T	T	TS
The demise of historic rivals to democracy				T2	T	T	TS	TS
Force, conquest, or weak or temporary occupation	T	T	T2	T			T	
Diplomatic or economic assistance, sanctions, or conditionality			T	T3		TS	TS	TS
British colonial past			X	T2	P		TS	no[a]
Membership in a regional organization, or desire to join				T3		TS	TS	TS
Diffusion of democratic values and models				T3	T		TS	TS
Transnational organizations and activities				T3		TS	TS	TS
External assistance to prodemocracy movements				T3		T	T	

Note: The letters in the right-hand columns denote the stage of democratization that each cause is thought to affect. P = preparation, T = transition, S = survival, X = any or all stages. Huntington (column D) specifies different causal processes for each wave of democracy. The numbers in this column refer to waves of democracy: T1 = first wave, T2 = second wave, and T3 = third wave.
[a] Diamond argues that a British colonial past has no effect.
Sources: A: Rustow (1970, 337–363). B: Dahl 1971, 203. C: Huntington (1991, 37–38). In this passage, Huntington summarizes the conventional wisdom without endorsing it. D: Huntington (1991, 106–107). In this passage, Huntington summarizes his own understanding of the causes of each of the three waves of democratization. He also mentions military defeats suffered by dictatorship, the breakup of the Soviet Union, and the shifts of the Catholic Church to a prodemocracy position. E: Lipset (1994). F: Shin 1994, 135–170. G: Diamond, Linz, and Lipset (1995). H: Diamond 1999.

that aspire to the benefits of membership therefore have an incentive to undergo a transition, and existing members have a disincentive to risk a breakdown (Pevehouse 2002b). In addition, transnational organizations such as party foundations, labor organizations, professional associations, and the Catholic Church sometimes exert international pressure on governments to become or remain democratic (Huntington 1991). Some national governments themselves have a policy of promoting democracy abroad, which they pursue by aiding parties and prodemocracy organizations, overseeing elections, mustering diplomatic pressure, and imposing economic sanctions. Few scholars believe that such efforts are the most powerful determinants of democratization, but many believe that international pressure can tip the balance toward democracy in close cases (Carothers 1999; Whitehead 1986).

One of the oldest international hypotheses is that a British colonial past favors later democratization. This idea came about as a way to account for the anomalous success of democracy in India and is sustained by the positive examples of the United States, Australia, New Zealand, Ireland, Canada, and the English-speaking Caribbean. It is also reinforced by the fact that the British often protected some political rights and allowed some colonists to elect representatives (although not governors-general) before independence. It is an increasingly controversial thesis, however, as some former British colonies are not notably successful democracies (Malaysia, Nigeria, Pakistan, Guyana, Ghana, Kenya, Zambia, Singapore, Sierra Leone, and Zimbabwe) and British colonial rule was harsh and exploitative in some respects. Nevertheless, it is common to read that British colonial rule favored eventual democratization in some countries, even if it was detrimental in others.

What checklists tell us

This is a condensed summary of most of the conventional wisdoms. All of these checklist items could be formulated differently, and most of them have nuances that I have glossed over, but this is a fairly comprehensive overview. Later chapters go into the details; for now, the important point is that there is a very large body of often-repeated propositions about democratization. It is surprising that these ideas are repeated so often when, as subsequent chapters show, these propositions come from such unsystematic and methodologically diverse sources.

Despite its unsound origins, checklist-based knowledge is appealing because it seems to work, roughly. It gives us an intuition about democratization that can actually make useful predictions. To illustrate this point, Annabella España Nájera compiled a small database to see whether such a checklist does a good job of predicting how democratic a country is. She classified a sample of seventeen countries on sixteen common checklist items for approximately the year 2000.[5] She then added up the ratings for each country and compared them with Freedom House scores for the same year. Her ratings are in Table 4.5. The checklist "worked" much better than most people

---

[5] I am grateful to the Department of Political Science of the University of Notre Dame for the research assistantship that made Annabella España Nájera's research possible. We worked together to choose variables on the basis of plausibility and data availability. I selected the countries. First, I chose Finland, Austria, Italy, France, Russia, and India, to ensure that some of the largest and best-known countries would be included. I then added eleven others taken from a random sample of forty, again favoring countries that would be relatively well known to readers. This is not, therefore, a random sample, but it is numerically representative of regions and was not deliberately designed to confirm or frustrate the checklist's predictions.

Table 4.5. Using a checklist to predict democracy in 2000

Conditions thought to favor democracy	Austria	Finland	Italy	France	Brazil	Nicaragua	Haiti	India	Peru	Tanzania	Nigeria	Russia	Indonesia	Ivory Coast	Thailand	Uganda	Iraq
Capitalist economy	•	•	•	•	•	•	•	•	•	•	•	•	•	•	•	•	
Separation of church and state	•	•	•	•	•	•	•	•	•	•	•	•		•		•	
Democratic neighbors	•	•	•	•	•	•	•		•	•	•	•	•	•			
Educated population	•	•	•	•	•	•			•			•	•		•		
High standard of living	•	•	•	•	•				•						•		•
No excluded minority	•	•	•	•	•		•		•								
Democratic political culture	•	•	•	•	•	•		•									
Elite belief in democracy	•	•	•	•	•	•	•	•									
Cooperative leadership	•	•	•	•	•		•	•									
Ethnic homogeneity	•	•	•							•							
National unity	•	•	•	•	•	•											
Former British colony								•		•	•					•	
Relatively equal distribution of wealth	•															•	
Competition before inclusion			•	•													
Imposition during postwar occupation	•																
Majority Protestant population		•															
Number of favorable conditions	13	12	12	11	10	7	6	6	6	5	4	4	3	3	3	3	1
FH combined score in 2000	14	14	13	13	10	10	5	11	9	8	8	6	9	5	11	5	2

Note: Each dot means that the condition was satisfied.

Source: Unpublished research by Annabella España Nájera, January 2003. Coding criteria and sources are described in the appendix to this chapter.

would expect: there is a definite positive relationship between the number of satisfied conditions and the Freedom House score for each country. This relationship has a correlation coefficient of 0.820 and the checklist tally explains 65 percent of freedom levels in a bivariate regression. This demonstration makes it easy to appreciate the appeal of the kind of knowledge that comes from checklists.

At the same time, it is important to understand the limitations of checklists. First, the predictions are not very precise. For example, in Table 4.5, satisfying six items on the checklist enables one to make predictions only within a wide range, from 5 to 11 on the Freedom House index. If there were more cases in this demonstration, the ranges would be more consistently wide. Second, as inspection of the table suggests, the predictions that one can make are more accurate at the "most likely" and "least likely" extremes. This is because only some of the conditions actually and consistently matter. Some conditions belong on the checklist, but others are spurious causes that should not be included. This is not a problem at the extremes. A relatively comprehensive checklist can efficiently discriminate between the countries that satisfy most of the true conditions for democracy and countries that satisfy few of them. It does not matter that the favored cases get credit for items that do not really belong on the checklist because they also get credit for the items that do matter; and it does not matter that the unfavored cases fail to get misleading credit because they also fail to get credit that should matter for democracy. But the intermediate cases, which satisfy the true conditions only partially, yield more uncertain predictions because they get some credit from true items and some from false items, and there is no way to tell which is which.

This is the third limitation of checklists: they do not tell us which items matter and which do not. If we interpret the checklist to mean that every item is necessary for democracy, then every democracy should satisfy every condition. If we interpret the checklist to mean that every item is sufficient for democracy, then no condition should be satisfied for any nondemocracy. But, in Table 4.5, no condition fits every democracy, some conditions fit nondemocracies, and no democracy satisfies every condition. Logically, these conditions cannot all matter in this strict sense. However, we might want to interpret checklists in a less rigid way. It may be that some conditions are powerful causes and others are weak causes. But a fourth limitation of checklists is that – as they are consumed and used by others, not necessarily as the original authors intended – they do not say how much any item matters; in effect, they assign all items equal weight. It is also possible that each item matters conditionally: that one cause matters only in the presence of another cause, or that the impact is reversed under some conditions, or that the causal process leading to democracy is distinct in different regions of the world. But if so, these are not relationships that a checklist typically conveys. The final limitation is therefore that in a checklist, every item is independent of the others. Checklists never tell us how the items on them should be used, alone or in combination, to explain or predict democratization.

Should we regard checklists as theory? By my criteria, we should not. Checklists are not general, in the sense that every proposition on them has been empirically confirmed in a large number of cases. As Barbara Geddes has observed:

Authors ... are frequently aware of the tentativeness of the evidence supporting their arguments and indicate their awareness in the caveats they attach to them. Readers, however, tend to ignore the caveats and give greater weight to unsystematic evidence than it deserves. Many studies in which authors have carefully hedged their explanatory claims are discussed in seminars, cited in literature reviews, and summarized in qualifying exams as though the tentative arguments advanced were actually supported by solid evidence. (Geddes 1997, 18)

Checklists are not really thick, either. They list a lot of propositions, but each proposition is stated in a very general way, devoid of the particularities of specific cases. And, as just argued, checklists do not integrate propositions. They are loose bundles of isolated, unrelated propositions. By these criteria, then, checklists are a pretheoretical kind of understanding. They are undeniably useful as reminders, and they may often make good predictions, but they are not theories.

Moving beyond checklists: Inductive theoretical frameworks

Because of these limitations of checklists, some scholars have sought to integrate a large but more modest number of propositions into a complex but coherent theoretical framework. The Johns Hopkins University Press published three books of this type that have been especially influential in democratization research: Linz and Stepan's *The Breakdown of Democratic Regimes* (1978); O'Donnell, Schmitter, and Whitehead's *Transitions from Authoritarian Rule* (1986); and Linz and Stepan's *Problems of Democratic Transition and Consolidation* (1996). These works all use chapter-length country studies (by the authors themselves in *Problems of Democratic Transition and Consolidation*, by other contributors in the other two works) to suggest reasons for the breakdowns, transitions, or consolidations in each case. The authors then synthesize a more general framework that classifies the actors and key steps in these processes, and they suggest conditions, relationships, and choices that tend to lead to one outcome or another. The result is a partially integrated body of inductively generated concepts and propositions that lies somewhere between a checklist and a theory. This section summarizes these three frameworks and some hypotheses that spring from them, explains why they have been influential, and clarifies their limitations as theories of democratization.

Linz: The Breakdown of Democratic Regimes

Linz and Stepan's *The Breakdown of Democratic Regimes* began with a short paper by Linz that laid out a basic model inspired by the cases of Spain, Weimar Germany, and Brazil. Linz and Stepan then commissioned case studies of breakdowns or reequilibrations of democracy in Finland, Italy, Germany, Spain, Austria, Portugal, Greece, Northern Ireland, Argentina, Brazil, Colombia, Peru, Venezuela, and Chile. Drawing on the insights of these studies, Linz then wrote a longer essay, which was published as a separate book (Linz 1978).

It is impossible to summarize Linz's long essay without omitting conditions, exceptions, and qualifications that he would consider crucial.[6] Nevertheless, the following skeletal version summarizes the Linzian model in a way that is faithful to its strengths and weaknesses. Democracies become vulnerable to a crisis when a very difficult problem arises. The difficult problem could be violence in the streets, ethnic conflict, or a deep economic crisis. The problem is also perceived as pressing; that is, many people believe that a solution must be found quickly. In addition, it becomes increasingly obvious that the democratic government is unable to provide an efficacious and effective solution in the short term. In the meantime, an irresponsible opposition promises an easy and quick solution. As a result, public opinion becomes polarized, with prodemocracy leaders increasingly isolated and semiloyal (or hidden disloyal) leaders gaining in support.

In some cases, according to Linz, either an extreme multiparty system or presidentialism worsens this polarization. Extreme multiparty systems have a centrifugal tendency that encourages irresponsibility and the politics of outbidding, culminating in the collapse of the center of the political spectrum

---

[6] Because Linz was my dissertation adviser, I can state this with some authority. I approach this section with trepidation because all of the authors reviewed here have been my professors, advisers, colleagues, or friends. I have tried to ignore these relationships to approach objectivity. If I have been too harsh, it is because I am trying too hard, and I ask for their understanding.

(Sartori 1976). Presidential, as opposed to parliamentary, systems promote zero-sum politics and therefore hinder accommodation and coalition building, thus ending in polarization. (This was a precursor to his later critique of presidentialism.) But in all countries, even without presidential constitutions or extreme multiparty systems, polarization is driven by any of six unwise choices by leaders. First, some choose to pursue an overly ambitious agenda, which inevitably and unnecessarily threatens those targeted by it and nevertheless disappoints its initial supporters. Second, some leaders practice vindictiveness toward the old regime. Third, some leaders choose to exclude old enemies from power. Fourth, some leaders refuse to work with the old state and therefore build up a new, parallel bureaucracy or military, which is costly and divisive. Fifth, some leaders unwisely alienate intellectuals. Sixth, some leaders pass responsibility for problem solving onto courts, the military, or other actors that lack a popular mandate. This choice is especially damaging when these other actors lack the capacity to solve the problem within the constraints imposed by a democratic regime.

Leaders who make these unwise choices find themselves increasingly isolated. When they reach the point of no return, the powerful opposition unites behind disloyal leaders to overthrow the isolated incumbent. This is not an inevitable outcome. If incumbents practice moderation, refrain from punishing their adversaries, share power with rivals and intellectuals, work with the existing state institutions, and take responsibility for solving problems themselves, then they can defuse the crisis and reequilibrate the democratic regime.

This is a very appealing framework for two basic reasons. First, it simplifies reality, but not too much, and in a way that promises to be useful. The framework outlines a process with a beginning (crisis), an end (breakdown or reequilibration), and a crucial turning point (the reaction of incumbents to irresponsible opposition). By identifying the beginning, Linz also specified the domain: the set of cases to which the framework applies. By identifying a turning point, he asserted that crises do not necessarily culminate in breakdown, which is intuitively plausible and focuses attention on pivotal moments in the process. The framework simplifies reality by identifying key actors: incumbents, loyal opposition, semiloyal opposition, and disloyal opposition. The fact that these actors are defined by their orientation to democracy practically guarantees that they are the relevant actors for understanding the fate of the regime. This attention to the actors assumes that individual leaders can make a decisive difference – an assumption that not all political scientists would share. But, at the same time, the framework places the leaders in a relationship with the mass public (which could become polarized) so it is not purely voluntaristic. The framework also places the leaders in a structural context, both institutional (the type of party system and constitution) and sociological (the unsolvable social, economic, or national problems they face), which influences their choices.

The second source of the framework's appeal is its flexibility, which allows it to be adapted to a variety of dissimilar situations. The nature of the initial crisis could concern economic decline, hyperinflation, national humiliation, terrorism, crime, irredentism, ethnic conflict, or other problems. Many different kinds of actors could fit into the categories of loyal, semiloyal, and disloyal opposition: political parties, armed services, business, labor, religious leaders, peasants, ethnic minorities, guerrillas, governors, and so on. These categories can be adapted to any of the groups found in any regime in crisis. The framework includes two variations on the basic process for presidential democracies and extreme multiparty systems. Finally, there are six different kinds of actions that leaders could take that would increase polarization.

This appealing framework also has two limitations. First, it leaves too much room for interpretation. How do we know, for example, whether on not there is an initial crisis? The multiplicity of relevant types of crisis actually makes this question harder to answer, for few societies in the world are problem-free in all these areas. Probably it is a matter of degree, but the framework does not specify how bad the problem must be to qualify as a crisis. It does say that many citizens must consider it a pressing problem that requires a quick solution. But this just restates the questions: How many citizens? How pressing? How quick? These unanswered questions leave room for scholars to disagree about the regimes to which the framework applies. The set of six actions that tend to increase polarization also invite interpretation. How many of these must the incumbent do to increase polarization – one, three, or all? What if the incumbent mixes wise and unwise actions, such as working with existing state institutions and having moderate ambitions but also alienating intellectuals (who may prefer a more ambitious agenda) and being vindictive toward the leaders of the old regime? The framework does not define what would happen in such cases, and this allows those applying the framework to interpret incumbent behavior selectively. Also, several key concepts are slippery – vaguely defined and therefore inconsistently applied – to the point of circularity. For example, opposition leaders who promise a quick, easy solution to an "unsolvable" problem are by definition "irresponsible." The trick is to know whether a problem is truly unsolvable; this is something that politicians and experts can debate forever. Another example: whether a leader is semiloyal is a highly consequential interpretation that is hard to make. This is doubly true for the hidden disloyal opposition Linz mentions.

If the framework does not provide clear criteria for classifying actors, we cannot use it to generate testable hypotheses. A final example: Linz argues that a breakdown happens when polarization passes a point of no return. But that point of no return is just a metaphor for the last chance to avoid a breakdown. Logically, once that point is passed, breakdown is unavoidable. This is a matter for post hoc judgment, not something that we can actually observe or measure, so it has no predictive utility.

The second limitation of Linz's framework is that it has not been confirmed as generally true. This is not a limitation with respect to his goals, which did not include systematic testing for general truth; it is only a limitation with respect to my rather idealistic standards for general theory. The *Breakdown* project included fourteen case studies, but they were fodder for Linz's inductive reasoning, not tests of generality. The authors in fact recognized that even their flexible framework did not fit all of the cases well. Linz and Stepan themselves presented their project as something less than a general theory: "Although we are concerned with middle-level generalizations, it is the editors' view that the historicity of macro-political processes precludes the highly abstract generalizing of ahistorical social scientific models of the type susceptible to computer simulations and applicable to all past and any future cases" (Linz 1978, ix). This is why I have chosen to call this project a theoretical framework rather than a theory.

O'Donnell and Schmitter: Transitions from Authoritarian Rule

The *Transitions from Authoritarian Rule* project sought to explain transitions rather than breakdowns but, in many other respects, it was very similar to the *Breakdown* project. Guided by an initial essay by O'Donnell, the editors commissioned thirteen European and Latin American case studies, which were published in a multivolume work (O'Donnell and Schmitter 1986). Unlike Linz and Stepan, the *Transitions* editors also commissioned seven comparative chapters that were published separately (O'Donnell et al. 1986). But, like Linz, O'Donnell and Schmitter wrote a summary volume that attempted to distill the case studies and comparisons into a single theoretical framework.

The parallels between the two projects extend to the content of the frameworks they developed. O'Donnell and Schmitter's framework simplified reality in ways very similar to Linz's framework. The *Transitions* authors pinpointed a beginning, a crucial turning point, and an end of the process; they defined the actors with respect to their orientation to democracy; and they placed the actors in a relationship with a mass public. The beginning of the process, according to O'Donnell and Schmitter, is always a division within the authoritarian leadership between hard-liners (*duros*), who favor continuing authoritarian rule, and soft-liners (*blandos*), who favor a more open regime. The soft-liners succeed in creating an opening (*abertura*) that allows for political liberalization. When prodemocracy opposition figures tentatively explore the new freedom without being punished, others become more courageous. Civil society undergoes a resurrection, which punctures the regime's facade of legitimacy and increasingly transfers authority to opposition leaders. Negotiations ensue among the hard-liners, the soft-liners, and the opposition over fundamental military, political, and economic questions. The turning point comes when the regime sets a date for elections. Before that point, the opposition could get out of hand, giving the hard-liners a pretext for a coup. After that point, the opposition needs the soft-liners to guarantee that the elections will actually be held, and the soft-liners need the opposition to behave moderately so as to vindicate the soft-liners' strategy of opening. Faced with this shared interest between soft-liners and the opposition, the hard-liners lose control of the process, which makes completion of some kind of transition increasingly likely.

Like Linz's *Breakdown* framework, the *Transitions* framework builds in several alternative paths. The most important is the urgency of the opening, which ranges from a speedy extrication to a painfully slow transition from above. When the military wants to extricate itself from responsibility for an economic or military calamity, the transition is faster and more certain, as in Argentina in 1982–1983. When a military government earns some legitimacy from successful governance, it can dictate the pace and the terms of the transition over a longer period of time, as in Brazil from 1974 to 1985. The *Transitions* framework also builds in flexibility by recognizing that some countries face far more difficult negotiation agendas than others. In some countries, negotiations must reconcile opposition demands for transitional justice with military officers' demands for immunity; in other countries, this is less of an issue. In some countries there are deep struggles over the constitution, the electoral law, and the rights of political parties, whereas in other countries there are few objections to restoring the pre-coup rules of the game. There are also many important decisions to make about the rules governing the relations among business, labor, and the state that vary from country to country. Finally, in some countries, some or all of these issues are temporarily decided in a formal, explicit pact, whereas in others no formal pact is signed, even though a pacted transition is always desirable, according to the authors.

In two respects, O'Donnell and Schmitter sought to distinguish their *Transitions* framework from the *Breakdown* framework, but the differences are more in style than substance. First, O'Donnell and Schmitter gave greater emphasis to uncertainty:

One of the basic arguments (which we share) of the Juan Linz and Alfred Stepan volume . . . is that none of those breakdowns was fatalistically bound to occur. . . . This, however, does not detract from the fact that crucial *personae* during the breakdown period seem in retrospect like actors in a Greek tragedy, anticipating their fate but fulfilling it to the bitter end. . . . What actors do and do not do seems much less tightly determined by "macro" structural factors during the transitions we study here than during the breakdown of democratic regimes. (O'Donnell and Schmitter 1986, 19)

I am not convinced that transitions are actually less certain than breakdowns. O'Donnell and Schmitter's claim may have been influenced by their vantage point, looking retrospectively at completed breakdowns and prospectively at ongoing transitions, and sympathetically seeing through the eyes of the losers in breakdowns and of the potential winners in transitions. Especially in comparison to the more macrocausal, structural theories, both frameworks stand out as unusually voluntaristic. Only game-theoretic explanations give greater weight to individual decision making and less to context. This emphasis is undoubtedly a consequence of the assumptions that were used, in both projects, to develop the framework. There is a danger of myopia – giving too much weight to microcauses and too little to macrocauses – whenever one pays close attention to cases. Admittedly, whether these frameworks give too much or too little weight to the choices made by leaders is an empirical question; it may be that scholars who adopt a structural perspective need bifocals. However, the fact that all of the cases included in the *Transitions* project ended up with successful transitions despite the many micro-level uncertainties suggests that structural or international factors should have been credited with greater weight (Mainwaring 1999).

O'Donnell and Schmitter were also more openly prescriptive. In fact, they saw themselves as writing a kind of manual for democratizers (O'Donnell and Schmitter 1986). Most of their advice urged the democratic opposition to strengthen the regime soft-liners in their struggle with the hard-liners until after the transition was complete, so that the friends of democracy would have powerful allies inside the regime. Therefore, the authors argued, opposition leaders should not encourage a popular upsurge that might provoke a backlash; they should be patient until elections are convoked; and they should do whatever is necessary, even collaborate in designing a biased electoral law, to ensure that parties of the right and center-right do well in the first elections.

This is not really very different from the aims of Linz and Stepan, however. They wrote:

Our problem formulation seeks to point out opportunities that democratic leaders might use to assure the consolidation, stability, persistence, and reequilibration of their regimes, as well as the pitfalls likely to be encountered in the process. We would hope that our knowledge will help them in their efforts, even though our insights, if valid, should also be useful to those who want to attend a "school for dictators." (Linz 1978, 5)

In view of the many similarities between the two projects, it is not surprising that the *Transitions* framework shares many of the limitations of the *Breakdown* framework. Slippery concepts that require judicious interpretation play a fundamental role in *Transitions from Authoritarian Rule*, most obviously in the terms *hard-liner*, *soft-liner*, and *opposition*. As with Linz and Stepan, these actors are defined by their objectives, not by any more objective characteristic. This is a problem because the framework cannot generate testable hypotheses unless there is some reliable way to identify these actors in specific situations. For example, the framework suggests that an opening happens when soft-liners gain ascendancy over the hard-liners but, empirically, what does this mean? If it means that there are some actors whom we could a priori identify as soft-liners, the framework does not tell us how to identify them (much less how to know when they become ascendant):

During these transitions, in many cases and around many themes, it is almost impossible to specify *ex ante* which classes, sectors, institutions, and other groups will take what role, opt for which issues, or support what alternative. Indeed, it may be that almost all one can say is that, during crucial moments and choices of the transition, most–if not all–of those "standard" actors are likely to be divided and hesitant about their interests and ideals and, hence, incapable of coherent collective action. (O'Donnell and Schmitter 1986, 4)

If it means that hard-liners become soft-liners, the framework begs the question of why they switched camps. Either way, it borders on circular reasoning: if there was an opening, the soft-liners must have become ascendant. O'Donnell and Schmitter recognized this problem but believed that it is impossible to employ "normal science methodology" because of the

high degree of indeterminacy embedded in situations where unexpected events (*fortuna*), insufficient information, hurried and audacious choices, confusion about motives and interests, plasticity, and even indefinition of political identities, as well as the talents of specific individuals (*virtù*), are frequently decisive in determining the outcomes. (O'Donnell and Schmitter 1986, 4–5)

Not surprisingly, these ideas that are so hard to test were not really tested, so the general applicability of the framework is an open question. Although many case studies were written for the project, they were not treated as tests but as examples (where they conformed to the framework) or alternate paths (where they did not). If the case studies had been used as tests, parts of the framework would not have fit well in some cases. Indeed, transitions as complex and unpredictable as O'Donnell and Schmitter claimed could hardly be expected to fit any framework well, except in being complex and unpredictable.

Linz and Stepan: Problems of Democratic Transition and Consolidation

In 1996, Linz and Stepan published another collaborative work on democratization, this time on transitions and consolidation rather than breakdowns (Linz and Stepan 1996). The later book also differs in being truly coauthored rather than edited, and in covering a more recent set of regime changes that extended their earlier Southern Europe–Latin America domain to Eastern Europe. Thus, *Problems of Democratic Transition and Consolidation* (henceforth referred to as *Problems*) was based on the authors' own case studies of Spain, Portugal, Greece, Uruguay, Brazil, Argentina, Chile, Poland, Hungary, Czechoslovakia, Bulgaria, Romania, Russia, Estonia, and Latvia. Because a more diverse set of cases was included, and probably because the authors analyzed the cases themselves, *Problems* yields a much more integrated set of propositions and gives greater weight to structural factors and less to the free will of individual leaders. It is, however, still a basically inductive approach.

The fundamental insight of Linz and Stepan is that the type of regime from which a country transits affects the transition paths it can take and the problems it must solve to become a consolidated democracy. They define four different types of nondemocratic regime – totalitarian, authoritarian, posttotalitarian, and sultanistic – and define each in terms of its degree or type of pluralism, ideology, mobilization, and leadership (Linz and Stepan 1996). Because each regime type has a different mix of actors and different relationships among them, certain transition paths are available to some regimes but not others. For example, the path of extrication from above by a hierarchical military is available for authoritarian regimes (if they have a hierarchical military), but not to the other regimes, because their armed forces are subordinated to or penetrated by the official party or the sultan's personalistic network (Linz and Stepan 1996). Similarly, because each regime type has many facets, any transition from one regime type to another (to democracy in all of these cases), is a transition on multiple fronts. Simply holding elections cannot change every aspect of the regime; it is also necessary to allow or create an active and independent civil society, encourage a variety of political ideologies, substitute participation for mobilization or demobilization, and install leaders who agree to be checked by the rule of law.

Furthermore, democratic consolidation is itself as complex as any regime type. According to Linz and Stepan, democracy is consolidated behaviorally, when no groups try to secede or overthrow the government by force; attitudinally, when most citizens are committed to democratic rules of the game; and constitutionally, when all groups expect to resolve conflicts within the rules recognized by the regime (Linz and Stepan 1996). The authors also reveal the causes that can produce this happy state of affairs: democratic consolidation happens, and continues, when five arenas reinforce one another. These arenas are civil society, political society (the party system and elections), economic society (business and labor and economic policy), the state apparatus, and the rule of law. Because each type of nondemocratic regime lacks one or more of these arenas, democratic consolidation faces a different set of problems, depending on the initial regime type. In this sense, Linz and Stepan propose a path-dependent model.[7]

It is not, however, a purely path-dependent model, for four other conditions can intervene to shape transitions and the prospects for consolidation (Linz and Stepan 1996). First, Linz and Stepan argue that stateness – agreement about territorial borders and citizenship rights – is a prerequisite for democratic consolidation. Second, international forces (foreign policies, the *Zeitgeist*, and diffusion) can influence transitions and consolidation. Third, domestic economic performance can affect democratization through its impact on the legitimacy of either predemocratic or democratic governments. Finally, the constitutional legacies that democratic governments inherit and the decisions they make about constitutional reform affect their ability to deal with emerging problems in ways that most citizens consider legitimate.

The *Problems* framework has great appeal for its ability to distinguish among the Southern European, Latin American, and Eastern European cases covered in the book, especially across these three regions. Why is it that the least successful regimes are found in the former Soviet republics and Eastern Europe, democratic but only partially consolidated regimes in Latin America, and consolidated democracies in Southern Europe? In Table 4.6, the most stable and democratic regimes are in the upper-left portion and the

---

[7] This is, in my opinion, the best path-dependent model anyone has yet devised. For that reason, I am tempted to discuss it alongside the comparative histories in Chapter 5. However, because it builds on the earlier Linz and Stepan and O'Donnell and Schmitter works and shares some traits with them, I am discussing it here.

Table 4.6. Basic distinctions made by the Linz and Stepan framework

<table>
<tr><td colspan="3" rowspan="2"></td><td colspan="2">Authoritarian</td><td colspan="4">Posttotalitarian</td><td rowspan="2">Totalitarian-cum-sultanistic</td></tr>
<tr><td>Stateness achieved</td><td>Stateness problems</td><td colspan="2">Mature</td><td>Frozen</td><td>Early</td></tr>
<tr><td rowspan="2">Economic Prosperity</td><td rowspan="4">Constitutional constraints</td><td>low</td><td>Greece</td><td>Spain</td><td colspan="4" rowspan="2"></td><td rowspan="2"></td></tr>
<tr><td>high</td><td>Portugal</td><td></td></tr>
<tr><td rowspan="2">Economic Decline</td><td>low</td><td>Uruguay
Argentina</td><td rowspan="2"></td><td colspan="4" rowspan="2"></td><td rowspan="2"></td></tr>
<tr><td>high</td><td>Brazil
Chile</td></tr>
<tr><td colspan="3" rowspan="3">Wrenching transformation from state socialist to capitalist economy</td><td rowspan="3">Poland</td><td rowspan="3"></td><td>Stateness achieved</td><td>Hungary</td><td></td><td>Bulgaria</td><td>Romania</td></tr>
<tr><td>Stateness problems</td><td></td><td>Czechoslovakia</td><td></td><td rowspan="2"></td></tr>
<tr><td colspan="4">Estonia, Latvia, Russia</td></tr>
</table>

least stable and democratic ones are clustered in the lower-right corner. As the table shows, two factors discriminate well between the Eastern and Western countries: prior regime type and political economy. All of the Eastern cases except Poland had nondemocratic regimes that were not authoritarian, and all suffered the truly wrenching adjustment from a state-socialist economy to capitalism. The Western cases had it relatively easy with transitions from classic authoritarian regimes and less traumatic economic transitions. Latin American economies had a rough time in the 1980s, to be sure, but not as difficult as those in the East; and the Southern European economies actually benefited economically during their transition years. The economic incentives also distinguish well between the Southern European and the Latin American cases. Spain, Portugal, and Greece could look forward to subsidies if they joined the European Union, which required democratization (Linz and Stepan 1996). For Latin America, however, democratic transitions coincided with the so-called lost decade of economic decline, stabilization, and structural adjustment programs.

The *Problems* framework also distinguishes to some extent among the more and less successful democracies within regions. In Latin America, the two most consolidated regimes, Uruguay and Argentina, restored their pre-coup constitutions, which were relatively legitimate. Brazilian consolidation was hampered by military interference in the constituent assembly; and Chile had to live with a constitution inherited from the Pinochet dictatorship. In the postcommunist states, there are two factors that sort out the more and less successful cases (Linz and Stepan 1996). First, the prior regimes differed enough to set these countries on different paths. At one end, Poland eventually had a basically authoritarian regime; at the other, Romania under Nicolae Ceauşescu had a totalitarian regime with some arbitrary and personalistic, sultanistic elements. The remaining cases were posttotalitarian, but some were more evolved than others. Posttotalitarianism was in the early stages in Bulgaria, "frozen" in Czechoslovakia, and "mature" in Hungary. Second, some of these states had to deal with challenges to the state – particularly the Soviet Union–Russia and its former republics – whereas Poland, Hungary, Bulgaria, and Romania had achieved stateness before 1989. Putting these two factors together, the more unified states that started from an authoritarian or mature posttotalitarian regime had an easier time of inaugurating and consolidating democracy than the states that had different regimes or stateness problems.

Despite its many virtues, this framework shares several limitations with the other inductive frameworks discussed in this chapter. One needs look no farther than the regime types themselves to find slippery concepts. The posttotalitarian regime type is defined very carefully, but the authors place a heavy explanatory burden on its three evolutionary degrees – the mature, frozen, and early posttotalitarian subtypes. The authors also make a convincing case for the distinctness of sultanistic regimes, yet the only case in this book with sultanistic characteristics (Romania) is classified as a totalitarian-cum-sultanistic regime. If these regime types were as useful as the authors claim, it should not be necessary to create ad hoc hybrids or subtypes to apply them.

In addition, the relationships among Linz and Stepan's explanatory factors are not completely clear. Table 4.6 actually makes these relationships appear to be clearer and simpler than they are in the book, but there are some puzzles even in the table. Why, for example, do constitutional constraints matter a great deal for the Southern European and Latin American cases but not for the postcommunist cases? And which matters more for the postcommunist cases, stateness or the degree of posttotalitarianism? If stateness matters more, then the relative success of Czech democracy is a puzzle; if the prior regime matters more, then Hungary's difficulties are puzzling. And, of course, the large empty white spaces in the table indicate areas in which the framework yields no predictions. Like a checklist, this framework does make useful predictions at the extremes, but for the mixed cases, its predictions are undefined. The authors seem to be free to refer to their explanatory factors selectively, as needed to explain any of their outcomes, but they do not commit themselves to any systematic correspondence between each possible set of causes and the possible outcomes. Actually, it would be very hard for them to do so, for there are more than one thousand possible combinations of causal conditions.[8] It is practically guaranteed, therefore, that Linz and Stepan could always identify something unique about each case that could account for its degree of success at democratic consolidation.

---

[8] I figure the combinations by multiplying the number of favorable or unfavorable values that each independent causal factor can take on. Stateness can be present or absent, so it has at least two values. According to *Problems*, Table 4.2, there are at least seventeen different available paths from the prior regimes to democracy. There are three kinds of international influences (foreign policies, *Zeitgeist*, and diffusion), and each can be at least favorable or unfavorable independently of the others, leading to $2^3 = 8$ combinations. Political economy can, at the very least, be favorable, unfavorable, or disastrous, to recognize the differing economic performance across the three regions and its impact on legitimacy. Finally, chapter 5 (Linz and Stepan 1996, 81–83) lists six different constitution-making environments. If each of these conditions is independent of the others, the number of combinations is obtained by multiplying them: $2 \times 17 \times 8 \times 3 \times 6 = 4,896$ possible sets of causal conditions. Even if we ignore Poland so that we can assume that prior regime type and paths are perfectly associated with the degree of economic decline, we get $2 \times 6 \times 8 \times 2 \times 6 + 2 \times 11 \times 8 \times 1 \times 6 = 1,680$ possible sets of causal conditions in the Linz and Stepan framework.

Finally, as in the *Breakdown* and *Transitions* projects, it is hard to know whether the propositions advanced in the *Problems* volume are generally true. These scholars move constantly back and forth between the cases and the framework they are constructing, always seeking to improve the fit between them. This may be the best way to produce propositions that are likely to survive rigorous testing later on, but because the framework is derived inductively from the cases, evaluating it by how well it fits these same cases is not a fair test. Nevertheless, the fit of the *Problems* framework is not perfect. If it were tested with the cases included in the volume, it would fail in a few respects. For example, most observers would agree that Greece has a less consolidated democracy than Spain or Portugal, but the framework suggests that it should be more consolidated. The prior regime was authoritarian like those of Spain and Portugal and it had the same positive economic and international incentives to democratize, yet unlike Spain it had achieved stateness, and unlike Portugal its constitution-making environment was unconstrained. Another example is the disparity between Russia and the Baltic republics. All are in the same cell of Table 4.6: posttotalitarian prior regimes with stateness problems and a wrenching economic transformation. Yet Russia has not achieved democracy, Lithuania has, and Estonia and Latvia are close. The differences are simple enough to explain by referring to the size of the territory, the level of economic development, the severity of the stateness problem, the length of totalitarian rule, the length of any pretotalitarian experience with democracy, or elite attitudes toward citizenship for ethnic Russians; and Linz and Stepan refer to all these to account for the disparity (Linz and Stepan 1996). The problem is that none of these explanatory factors are part of their theoretical framework. Rather, they are ad hoc arguments that are required to fill in the gaps between the framework and the reality. Such arguments do not strengthen the framework; on the contrary, they are evidence of its limitations.

Boolean analysis

Boolean analysis is a different method that shares some of the same strengths and weaknesses of frameworks.[9] It is a procedure that associates sets of explanatory conditions with outcomes that one wishes to explain. A Boolean

---

[9] What I am calling Boolean analysis here is more conventionally called crisp-set Boolean analysis, to distinguish it from fuzzy-set Boolean analysis, which I discuss in the next note and in Chapter 7.

analyst systematically codes each case as possessing (1) or not possessing (0) each hypothesized cause and as achieving (1) or not (0) the outcome to be explained, such as democratic survival.[10] A computer program then groups together all of the cases that have the same combination of causes and classifies them as positive confirmations (all causes = 1; outcome = 1), negative confirmations (all causes = 0; outcome = 0), contradictions (all causes = 1, outcome = 0, or vice versa), or mixed (some causes are 1; others 0). Unlike checklists and frameworks, therefore, Boolean analysis can be used to test individual propositions systematically using evidence that did not originally inspire the propositions.

In practice, scholars also use Boolean analysis in a more inductive way. Instead of counting only the all-1 causes as positive confirmations, only the all-0 causes as negative confirmations, and all other combinations as mixed, analysts can count some mixed combinations as noncontradictory, as long as all of the cases sharing the same causal combination had the same outcome. Software is available that can search systematically for all of the contradictory and noncontradictory combinations. The number of causal combinations can be large, and each one can be quite complex. For example, if there are five proposed causes, A–E, of democratic survival, then Boolean analysis can produce conclusions such as

IF : [(A and B and C) or (B and C and D) or (C and D and not A)] and not E,

THEN the democratic regime survives.

Boolean analysis can also produce reduced-form statements that boil down such complex formulas to the simplest expression that is not contradicted, such as (for the same example), "IF not E, THEN the democratic regime survives."

[10] Since 2002, software for Boolean analysis with polytomous variables, Tosmana, has been available, but so far it has very few users and no applications in democratization research as far as I know. Fuzzy-set QCA (fsQCA) has received more attention. It enables researchers to test and explore models in which there is some uncertainty about how cases should be categorized. Nevertheless, the number of users and publications is still quite small. In addition, a limitation of fuzzy sets is that they force gradations onto a single dimension – degrees of membership in a set – when often it would be more revealing and useful to work with gradations on more than one dimension. In the example of the two dimensions of polyarchy, for example, countries are scattered throughout the lower-right triangle of the plot, showing that some countries are less democratic because they limit contestation, and some are less democratic because they limit both contestation and inclusiveness. This could be a useful distinction but in fuzzy-set analysis, it would be lost because these distinct states would be merged into degrees of distance from the combination of high contestation and high inclusiveness. This fuzzy-set measurement would increase quantitative information but, ironically, decrease qualitative information compared to using a separate graded indicator of each dimension.

Charles Ragin, the best-known advocate of Boolean analysis, argues that it is more appropriate than conventional statistical methods for testing theories in comparative politics that involve multiple causal paths (Ragin 1987). Statistical analysis usually tries to fit the same model to every case, but Boolean analysis assumes that different countries can take different paths to the same outcome and can search for those different paths.[11] Boolean analysis can therefore be an inductive method for discovering how to integrate propositions. Boolean analysis, frameworks, and checklists overlap. Like frameworks but unlike checklists, Boolean analysis tries to integrate propositions and assumes that there are multiple causal paths. Like checklists but unlike frameworks, Boolean analysis reduces each proposition to a simple proposition and typically examines a relatively large number of such propositions.[12]

Boolean analysis is still rare in comparative politics. However, there is one very good example of it in the democratization literature that serves the useful purpose of summarizing the strengths and weaknesses of both checklists and frameworks. In 1994, Dirk Berg-Schlosser and Gisèle De Meur published a Boolean analysis of democratic survival hypotheses using sixteen countries in interwar Europe as the domain (Berg-Schlosser and De Meur 1994). The authors tested nine theories or theoretical frameworks elaborated by Lipset, Vanhanen, Moore (as amended by John Stephens), Luebbert, Hermens, Sani and Sartori, Dahl, and Linz. Between them, these works advanced nearly fifty different propositions about democratic survival, so this study amounts to a test of a quite extensive checklist, albeit in a medium-sized, geographically compact, and historically bounded sample.

This test illustrates well the characteristics of the kind of knowledge that we obtain from checklists and frameworks. First, it is revealing that different scholars trying to explain the same outcomes in subsets of the same countries in the same period came up with such different sets of propositions. The objectively true causes do not just leap out at anyone who looks at the historical record. Every scholar brings to these analyses his or her own worldviews, conceptual lenses, hunches, blinders, and biases, and therefore inevitably creates a selective and subjective version of events. This fact alone is sufficient to justify treating the propositions generated by inductive approaches as hypotheses, not confirmed theories.

---

[11] Although most statistical analyses do fit the same model to all cases, it is possible to use interaction terms to model multiple paths statistically. This practice has become increasingly common in quantitative democratization research, as we will see in Chapter 9.

[12] Even five propositions can be large in Boolean analysis because each additional one increases the complexity of the analysis exponentially.

Second, the frameworks do not work especially well when they are applied beyond their original domains. Berg-Schlosser and De Meur found that a few cases fit most of these frameworks quite well: seven of the nine theories correctly predicted democratic survival in Britain and breakdown in Italy, and six of the nine correctly predicted the breakdown in Spain. These cases were relatively easy to predict, even using quite different frameworks. The other thirteen countries, however, had a net confirmation rate of only 15 percent.[13] Furthermore, the average country was a mixed case in five of the nine frameworks, and the average framework classified 56 percent of the countries as mixed. These results are analogous to the tendency of checklists to predict well at the extremes but not in the middle.

Given the large number of mixed cases, none of the frameworks correctly predicted every outcome. Moreover, six of the nine frameworks were contradicted by at least one country when they did make a clear prediction. The most successful set of hypotheses was taken from Lipset's *Political Man*, which was positively or negatively confirmed in ten of sixteen cases and contradicted by one, for a predictive success rate of 56 percent $[(10 - 1)/16]$. No other framework predicted as many as half the cases correctly. In fact, the average net success rate for all nine frameworks was 28 percent. Berg-Schlosser and De Meur suggest that these frameworks tend to lack general empirical confirmation. Furthermore, although the frameworks make progress toward theoretical integration, they are not integrated enough to avoid a high proportion of undefined predictions, which makes them vulnerable to selective interpretation and application.

Berg-Schlosser and De Meur also carried out some exploratory inductive analysis, searching for reduced sets of propositions within each framework that did not result in contradictions. The simplest of these tended to be trivial. For example, Linz's proposition (as rendered by the authors) that "democracy survives where the anti-democratic upper classes do not intervene in politics" fits all of the cases perfectly but borders on circular reasoning (Berg-Schlosser and De Meur 1994, 243). Similarly, in the exploratory analysis of Dahl's propositions, the authors find that "when democratic legitimacy is strong and the military does not intervene, democracy survives," which they admit is "trivial or almost tautological" (Berg-Schlosser and De Meur 1994, 269). They also found several far more complex causal combinations. A good example comes from the section on Dahl, which concludes that democracies

---

[13] The net confirmation rate is the number of confirmations minus the number of contradictions, divided by the number of frameworks.

survive when (1) there are no antisystem parties and power resources are dispersed; or (2) there is an ethnolinguistic cleavage in a strongly egalitarian society; or (3) when there are segmented subcultures, and each subculture is organized and unified by strong leadership (Berg-Schlosser and De Meur 1994). These propositions "work," but they are hardly general.[14] The second combination in the preceding sentence, for example, applies only to Finland and Belgium, so we lack a solid basis for generalizing to the rest of the world.

The limitations of Boolean analysis stem directly from the tendency to increase the theoretical possibilities far beyond the number of available cases. The number of possible combinations of dichotomous variables is 2^x, where x is the number of variables being considered. In theory, with just 5 variables there are 32 possible causal combinations; with 10, there are 1,024; with 50, there are 1.13×10^{15}! A framework does not have to be very complex before every case has its own unique combination of causal factors, which then must coincide with only one outcome, and most other causal combinations have no cases and undefined outcomes. In practice, associations among variables prevent predictions from outstripping sample size quite so quickly, but it is still a real problem. In Berg-Schlosser and De Meur's analysis, the analyses of Dahl's and one of Linz's frameworks placed all but two countries in their own unique explanatory categories, and the second Linzian analysis had all the countries in unique categories.

This is a problem that is common to all inductive analyses; Boolean analysis merely exposes it more clearly.[15] One of the first things that students of comparative politics learn is that we suffer from the "many variables, small N" problem: too many possible causes, too few cases to test them all. What fewer have realized is that open-ended searches for combinations of variables augments the "many variables, small N" problem exponentially (or to be more accurate, factorially). Our task is not merely ruling out A and B and C; it is ruling out A, B, C, AB, AC, BC, and ABC. Checklists and frameworks are indispensable for reminding us about all the things that *may* matter, but they do not give reliable guidance about which things really *do* matter, how much, or in what combinations. Conventional wisdoms are more conventional than wise. To learn how much to trust the items on a checklist, we need strong theoretical guidance and rigorous empirical testing. The rest of this book

---

[14] Of course, propositions do not work when people make mistakes. Hungary actually contradicts part one of the preceding formula, according to table 7 on p. 268 of the Berg-Schlosser article.

[15] A more advanced form of Boolean analysis, fuzzy-set analysis (fs-QCA), is more appropriate for testing, although it suffers from some of the same limitations. This approach is discussed in Chapter 7.

critically examines how well the sources from which our checklist items sprang meet these theoretical and empirical requirements.

Appendix: Coding criteria and sources for checklist demonstration

Capitalist economy: Coded 1 if liberal capitalist principles are pursued by the government and economic elite (e.g., open markets, private property) (Department of State 2003).

Separation of church and state: Coded 1 if there is a clear separation of church (i.e., no official religion) and state, and freedom of religion (Banks 1999; Department of State 2003).

Democratic neighbors: Coded 1 if all of the country's closest neighbors, those that share a border, have a democratic government in place (if political rights + civil liberties < 5) (Freedom House 2003).

Ethnic homogeneity: Coded 0 if the effective number of ethnic groups (ENETH) exceeds 1.5; ENETH is the reciprocal of the sum of squared ethnic group shares of the population (Central Intelligence Agency 2003); for Italy and France (Cox 1997).

Educated population: Coded 1 if the country has a literacy rate equal to or above the median literacy rate of the sample (81 percent) (Department of State 2003).

High standard of living: Coded 1 if per capita gross domestic product exceeded or was equal to the sample median, $1,726 (International Labor Organization 2003).

No excluded minority: Coded 1 if there is respect for minorities, that is, an absence of a cultural majority that does not tolerate some ethnic minority group (Department of State 2003).

Democratic political culture: Coded 1 if challenges to government are forwarded through democratic channels, citizens have the right to organize and protest, and government and opposition work within the system in their dealings with one another and with citizens (this applies since the latest transition, attempted coup, or violent secessionist clash) (Department of State 2003).

Elite belief in democracy: Coded 1 if the elite generally believe in democratic principles and work according to them in their attempts to gain office and/or gain power. That is, there have been no recent coup attempts or antiestablishment strategies since the latest transition, attempted coup, or secessionist and violent clash (Department of State 2003).

Cooperative leadership: Coded 1 if the elite, despite differences, work within the system and with one another to achieve change and therefore maintain or achieve democracy. No serious attempts to discredit the opposition are made, beyond what would be considered negative campaigning examples. No political parties are banned (Department of State 2003; Human Rights Watch 2003).

National unity: Coded 0 if there are any terrorist activities against the government by nationals or violent secession movements (Central Intelligence Agency 2003; Department of State 2003; Human Rights Watch 2003).

Former British colony: Coded 1 if the country was under the control of the British Empire or a protectorate of the British Empire (Department of State 2003). We do not include Iraq because it was a League of Nations British mandate only briefly, from 1919 to 1932. However, if Iraq is coded as a former British colony, the correlation reported in the text is still 0.805.

Relatively equal distribution of wealth: Coded 1 if the Gini index was lower than 0.27 (World Bank 1999).

Competition before inclusion: Initial coding by Coppedge based on research assistance for Robert A. Dahl. This was revised in accordance with passages in Dahl (1971), and codings of European cases in Dirk Berg-Schlosser and Gisèle De Meur (1994). Note that France is coded 1 despite its being an example of simultaneous inclusion and contestation in polyarchy, based on the French Revolution. The Third and Fourth Republics afforded sufficient elite experience with democracy that is more relevant to today's French democracy.

Imposition during postwar occupation: Coded 1 if much of the country was occupied by the Allies during or after World War II (Department of State 2003).

Majority Protestant population: Self-explanatory (Department of State 2003).

Freedom House combined score in 2000: Using the Freedom House 2000–2001 ratings, FH = 16 − (political rights + civil liberties) (Freedom House 2003).

Case studies and comparative history

None of the inventories of the causes of democracy surveyed in Chapter 4 can be taken at face value because they summarize conclusions from disparate and poorly integrated sources of uneven rigor. Before giving credence to checklist items, it is essential to find out from where they came. The remainder of this book therefore evaluates the strengths and weaknesses of the methods and approaches employed by the scholars who have launched these propositions into our collective academic mind.

If there were a way to measure quantities of information, there would be no doubt that the bulk of our knowledge of democratization comes from histories and case studies. It is ironic that noncomparative research so dominates a field known as comparative politics, but this is an irony that is long-standing and well known. The huge number of books and articles about the birth, death, or survival of democracy in dozens of countries in the twentieth century alone is more than any one scholar can digest. In fact, anyone unlucky enough to be buried under this small mountain of printed matter would surely be suffocated and crushed. To be sure, this literature does not satisfy all of the criteria for good theory. I argue in this chapter that histories and case studies produce a kind of knowledge that is unsurpassed in its thickness yet lacking in generality and theoretical integration. In this chapter, I also survey and critique a smaller but still sizable body of literature that consists of comparative histories: detailed comparisons of the historical development of a (usually) small number of cases. Comparative history has enough characteristics in common with case studies and histories to warrant discussing them jointly. Comparative history is a methodological compromise that preserves some thickness while reaching out toward generality and theoretical integration. Those who value thickness would be better off with histories and case studies, those who value generality would be better off with large-sample approaches, and those who value theoretical integration would better focus their efforts on deductive theorizing. Comparative history combines the weaknesses of case studies and quantitative methods when it comes to testing the general truth of a theory. Nevertheless, it has some advantages when the goal is theory development.

Seeing these distinctions requires a clear understanding of inference. Inference is the process of using things we have observed to arrive at conclusions about what we have not observed or cannot observe. In practice, the term is often used, especially in quantitative research, to refer to statistical inference, which enables us to draw conclusions about a population from the characteristics of a sample of that population. Statistical inference can be either descriptive inference (What is the average level of democracy in the world?) or causal inference (Does increasing literacy tend to make countries more democratic?). But statistical inference is just one special type of inference. Drawing conclusions about whether a specific event caused a specific outcome (Did the attack on Pearl Harbor bring the United States into World War II?) is also inference – in fact, causal inference – because causation, ultimately, is not directly observable; we can only infer it. It is confusing that causal inference can refer to either statistical causal inference, which supports generalization, or the inference of specific causes, which does not. Yet this distinction is crucial for understanding the role of case studies, which are ideal for the latter but inappropriate for the former.

Histories and case studies

Histories (written by historians) and case studies (written by political scientists) are different genres with zealously policed boundaries.[1] In fact, one of my purposes in discussing them together is to highlight their differences. However, they also have two advantages in common. First, they are thick: multifaceted, detailed, conceptually rich, and multidimensional (see Chapter 3 for a fuller definition of thickness). Second, they analyze change over time in a way that makes especially solid causal inferences possible.[2]

Histories and case studies are the best examples of a thick approach. Both paint multifaceted, multidimensional portraits of countries and do so in rich detail. Studies of democratization in single countries, for example, are

---

[1] Some consider the definition of a case problematic. See Ragin and Becker (1992). I think that in practice and in context of a particular project, defining a case is not a problem. In the present book, a case is a country observed during a period of time.

[2] Any approach can be executed poorly or well. In this chapter, I have tried to focus on the best examples in the democratization literature, and my praises and criticisms are intended to apply to these best examples.

so richly detailed that they do not attempt to explain anything as grand as democratization. Instead, they explain a series of specific events that, taken together, amount to democratization. A typical history is R. K. Webb's *Modern England* (Webb 1980). England was clearly not a democracy at the book's opening in 1760 but had clearly become a (male) democracy 420 pages later in 1918. Yet no one event marks the democratization of England. Rather, democratization is the accumulation of small reforms: the separation of the bureaucracy from the king's household, the development of a prime minister as a first among equals, the toleration of other religions, the formation of principled political parties, the development of the principle of collective responsibility, the publication of parliamentary debates, the obligation of the monarch to appoint the ministers chosen by parliament, the elimination of the royal veto, the elimination of prior censorship of the press, the equal apportionment of electoral districts, the enfranchisements of middle- and working-class men, the responsibility of the cabinet to the House of Commons, and the diminution of the legislative powers of the House of Lords. Webb's story of these reforms makes them impossible to understand apart from the personalities of monarchs and politicians, personal rivalries and reputations, deaths of major figures, and the formation and dissolution of cabinets – all played against the backdrop of wars, economic crises, economic transformation, and social and technological change.

Similarly, a case study of the consolidation of democracy in Venezuela, Daniel Levine's *Crisis and Political Change in Venezuela*, recounts in detail crucial events of the first, short-lived, democratic regime of 1945–1948 and the first decade of the second democratic regime that began in 1958 (Levine 1973). It also analyzes the formation of party factions and the origins of party splits, explains negotiations over education and social policy, and characterizes the personalities of several key political leaders. As does a history, it reconstructs events; focuses attention on decisions made by individuals; and situates micro-level processes within macro-level institutional, economic, social, and international contexts. Both Webb's and Levine's books, and the histories and case studies they represent, deserve to be called thick in the best sense of the term.

Because they are thick and analyze change over time, histories and case studies share the ability to support powerful causal inferences. Causal inference – attributing causation of an outcome to some stimulus or stimuli – is hard. In fact, as Popper argued, we can never prove that a causal relationship exists; the best we can do is to disprove other hypothetical causal relationships: an indirect proof, at best (Popper 1968). What makes causal inference particularly hard in political science is the complexity of the political world. Recall the argument from Chapter 3 that politics is complex; events have many facets and outcomes are the product of a long and densely tangled chain of causation. This complex nature urges us to build complex, multifaceted explanations. But the more elements there are to an explanation, the greater the danger that some of them will be spurious or false, and the more difficult it becomes to disconfirm all of the possible explanations except the one we wish to prove, indirectly. (Chapter 7 will develop this argument further.)

Indirectly proving an argument about causes in politics therefore necessarily involves holding constant, or controlling for, as many alternative hypothetical causes as possible. Histories and case studies excel at this in two ways: by taking advantage of change over time in a single case and by intensively testing many theoretical implications. To take advantage of time, what they do in effect is compare each country to itself at an earlier time (Geddes 2003). This is a far more foolproof method than comparing one country to another, because every country has much more in common with itself in the recent past than it does with any other country at any time. The logic of inference is therefore that any feature that did not change from time 1 to time 2 cannot be a cause of an outcome observed at time 2. Because most features of a country do not change quickly, these static features can be ruled out as causes by this method and analysts can more confidently attribute causal force to the features that did change just before the outcome. The shorter the intervals between observations and the more finely the process is observed, the greater the confidence the inference inspires. A sweeping history of several centuries in one chapter probably inspires little confidence, but tracking events decade by decade begins to. Tracking them year by year or month by month is a vast improvement, and studies that manage to reconstruct events week by week or day by day begin to seem irrefutable. It becomes difficult to imagine an alternative story that would be consistent with all of the details.

This historical dimension grants histories and case studies of democratization their authority. For example, Levine's claim that moderating leadership helped consolidate Venezuelan democracy was bolstered by his accounts of attempts at radical mobilization that moderate party elites managed to isolate and defuse or marginalize (Levine 1973). Similarly, Webb can show that the Glorious Revolution of 1688, installing William and Mary as the monarchs of England, established the supremacy of Parliament over the king (Webb 1980). This kind of historical process tracing also enabled Alfred Stepan to show that President João Goulart's decision to mobilize landless peasants provoked Brazilian elites to conspire to overthrow him and that newspaper editorials helped legitimate the conspiracy (Stepan 1971). Comparisons within countries over time are the most powerful approach at our disposal for identifying the immediate causes of specific events.

Intensive testing of multiple implications also strengthens causal inferences. The thickness of case studies and comparative histories allows one to elaborate on a simple idea, such as economic development promotes democracy, so that it becomes a more complete story with actors, motives, stages, and causal mechanisms that move the plot along. For example, such a theory might hold that industrialization fosters the growth of working-class unions; that they ally with a better-educated middle class, including university students, to form associations or parties that demand the extension of the suffrage; and so on. This more elaborate theory then suggests many rich predictions that can each be compared against the rich evidence available to those who examine a case closely. How much did the working class grow during industrialization? Were unions successfully organized? Did middle-class groups agitate for democratization? Were students involved? Did unions and middle-class organizations form an alliance? Did it demand extension of the suffrage? The rigor of this kind of testing comes from the fact that the more different predictions one tests, the less likely it is that they could all be true while the theory is false. (Chapter 7 develops this point in greater detail.)

Of course, there are some important differences between histories and case studies. Two complementary differences come to mind. The first is simply a matter of degree: most histories are thicker than most case studies in political science. There are exceptions, such as Jared Diamond's sweeping history of humanity, *Guns, Germs, and Steel*, which is necessarily thinner because of its scope (Diamond 1997). And case studies can be unusually thick, such as the Graham Allison classic *Essence of Decision*, which reconstructs decision making during the Cuban Missile Crisis day by day, sometimes hour by hour (Allison 1971). Nevertheless, the general tendency is for histories, especially histories written by academics for academics, to be thicker than political science case studies. The latter may go into fine detail at points but tend to leap from crucial event to crucial event, and not necessarily in chronological order. They do not sustain a continuous, detailed narrative.

This is not the only difference between these two genres, however. If it were, we would have to conclude that case studies are merely inferior histories, as Juan Linz once implied in a remark to a convention audience: "If we do our work very well, we are *almost* historians."[3] The other difference is that case

---

[3] Author's personal observation at an American Political Science Association meeting in the mid-1990s. As a participant on a roundtable, Linz had been critical of some attempts at theorizing. The quoted

studies in comparative politics are more narrowly and explicitly focused on explanation. Political science case studies almost always explicitly identify the independent variables and put the causal process front and center. They are organized to advance and support an argument about what caused what. They also, whenever possible, embed their arguments in a larger theoretical framework. They self-consciously present the case as a specific instance of more general rules. Case studies are, by design, installments in the larger enterprise of theory building. Histories also seek to explain, but it is just one of their purposes, which include recounting the facts completely and accurately, interpreting what events meant to people at the time, and simply telling a good story. Historians vary in their mix of purposes. Some emphasize the scholarly recounting, some tell better stories, and some are more didactic than others. But none is as single-mindedly focused on demonstrating that the outcome was a necessary consequence of the explanatory factors. Histories generously grant more of a role to chance, whim, accidents, mistakes, coincidences, and miscalculations, which make for a more colorful story. These are exactly the elements that would render a theoretical explanation logically incomplete (see Chapter 3). As E. P. Thompson observed (even while defending the notion of a logic of history):

Historical concepts and rules . . . display extreme elasticity and allow for great irregularity; the historian appears to be evading rigour as he disappears into the largest generalisations at one moment, while at the next moment he disappears into the particularities of the qualifications in any special case. This provokes distrust, and even laughter, within other disciplines. (Thompson and Thompson 2001, 454)

Judged by the criteria of political science, histories are merely prolix, equivocating case studies.

By stereotyping histories as inferior case studies and case studies as inferior histories, I do not mean to imply that one is superior to the other; I merely mean to show that virtue in one discipline often appears to be a vice in another. The same is true for the vices that histories and case studies share when judged by the standards of other approaches in comparative politics. There are three shared vices in particular: myopia, an inability to generalize, and a tendency to capitalize on chance.

Myopia – already mentioned in Chapter 4 – is the tendency to exaggerate the impact of short-term microcauses. This tendency is practically inevitable

remark was his reply to an audience member who challenged him by asking, "Should we just give up on theory and become historians?"

in any approach that involves close examination of cases. Mom was right: squinting causes nearsightedness.[4] Looking at events in historical perspective, especially over closely spaced intervals of time, necessarily privileges causal factors that change over those intervals and discredits causal factors that remain unchanged throughout the period of observation. Case studies of democratization therefore tend to emphasize what is dynamic in the short term: leadership, natural disasters, economic crises, and wars. This tendency has already been noted, in Chapter 4, in the critique of inductive elite theories of democratization, but examples can be found in most case studies.

One good example is Malloy and Gamarra's *Revolution and Reaction: Bolivia, 1964–1985*, which analyzes Bolivian politics during the period from the breakdown of the revolutionary regime to the tortuous democratic transition of 1980–1982 (Malloy and Gamarra 1988). Although the authors (both political scientists) make it clear that chronic patrimonialism, corruption, human rights abuses, and an unsustainable development strategy undermined support for every government during this period, the factors that drive the narrative forward, from coup to election to coup to election, are specific short-term events: a hunger strike, a party split, an uprising by one or another military faction, pressure from the Carter administration, the failure of negotiations with Chile over an outlet to the Pacific Ocean, the power-hungry personality of General Hugo Bánzer, and popular reactions to repression by the Luis García Meza government. The authors conclude that "if [democracy] comes, it will be produced by serendipitous *salidas* [exit pacts] reflecting the pragmatic creativity of political elites and not grand solutions reflecting intellectual imports or architectural schemes" (Malloy and Gamarra 1988).

Another example – this time from a relatively stable case – is González and Gillespie's analysis of the impact of presidentialism on regimes in Uruguay (González and Gillespie 1994). Their goal is to attribute regime crises to the presidential features of the Uruguayan constitution, but the task is quite a challenge because Uruguay suffered only one coup (1973) and one semi-coup (1933) from 1918 to 1994, and presidentialism was a constant during that time. If a constant feature such as presidentialism caused breakdowns only twice in seventy-seven years, then the explanation must be incomplete. Something else must explain why coups happened in those years and not

---

[4] Actually, Mom had it backward as far as eyesight is concerned: squinting is caused by myopia (as I know well from personal experience). In comparative politics, whether a preference for micro-level explanations fosters a preference for case studies or the constraints of case studies encourage micro-level explanations, the approach and the findings are closely associated.

others. González and Gillespie therefore fill in the gaps with short-term, specific events and actions: the death of President Oscar Gestido in 1967, his replacement by the harder-line President Jorge Pacheco, a Tupamaro guerrilla offensive, repression of leftists, the loss of a governing majority in congress, Pacheco's selection of an unpopular successor, a pact between the two largest parties to support a crackdown, accusations of corruption, and the political isolation of the president (González and Gillespie 1994). If the authors were not determined to blame presidentialism, it probably would not figure in the explanation at all.[5]

In neither of these examples, nor in case studies generally, do scholars ignore or completely discount structural causes such as social structure, geography, constitutional design, or culture. Myopia is not a failure to see large, distant objects at all but rather an inability to see them in focus or (mixing metaphors) to give them their proper weight. Case studies and histories tend to give too much weight to the dynamic particulars they can portray clearly and too little weight to the large, immobile features of the landscape in the background that they take for granted.

The specificity of these approaches also interferes with generalization. This problem may appear to be of no concern to researchers who do not care to generalize; they only want to explain a specific case. However, no one can escape the need to generalize. Explanations of single cases cannot be entirely separate from general theory because they also rest on appeals to general laws. For example, in their case study of Bolivia, Malloy and Gamarra argue that President Jimmy Carter's human rights policy was one of the factors that prompted dictator Hugo Bánzer in July 1977 to call for elections (Malloy and Gamarra 1988). This is a specific cause of a specific outcome, but it cannot be persuasive without taking for granted the general causal principle that superpowers exercise significant sway over heads of state in their spheres of influence. To the extent that this principle is generally true, the authors' explanation is satisfying. To the extent that it is debatable, it raises further questions (Are all states equally susceptible to superpower pressure? Under what conditions is such pressure likely to be decisive?). Such questions can continue until they encounter reasons that are accepted as generally true.

---

[5] I would not allege that the authors were determined to blame presidentialism if I did not have personal knowledge of it. Both authors were advisees of Juan Linz, as I was, and all of us found his critique of presidentialism persuasive and saw evidence of its pernicious effects even in relatively successful presidential democracies such as Uruguay and Venezuela. This does not mean that we were biased and wrong. Tests of the critique of presidentialism are discussed in detail in Chapter 9.

Ultimately, the most satisfying explanations are true both in their particulars and in general.

The difficulties that case studies and histories encounter with generalization are conceptual, theoretical, and empirical. Conceptually, if one were to try to generalize about democratization from the case of England, for example, it would first be necessary to translate the particularities of the English process into concepts that usefully describe processes in other countries. Some of the small reforms listed at the beginning of this chapter do not match up easily with steps toward democracy in other countries. In particular, reforms that weakened the monarchy are irrelevant for countries that never had a monarch. One of the reforms that has the most traveling potential is the establishment of the responsibility of the cabinet to the Commons. If we substitute "lower or sole chamber of the national legislature" for "Commons," we have a reform that is comparable to similar reforms in most other parliamentary democracies. However, it is still irrelevant for the many presidential democracies, which permit the legislature to dismiss the executive only in extraordinary situations. If we hold fast to the exact concepts used in case studies and histories, it becomes difficult even to show that the concept of democracy has any useful and cross-nationally comparable meaning.

Theoretical specificity also hinders generalization. If concepts are too specific to travel, theories using those concepts do not travel well either. But even a theory expressed entirely in generally comparable concepts can be too specific for generalization if it combines a large number of propositions. Imagine, for example, a theory that predicts that democratic regimes will survive in countries that have a high standard of living, a small number of political parties, effective representation of business interests, have never been colonies, and are found on islands. Each proposition narrows the applicable domain of the hypothesis to an ever-more-limited set of cases. Many countries could satisfy the first three propositions, but ruling out former colonies excludes the United States, Australia, Canada, Iceland, and many others. Limiting the domain to islands shrinks the domain to Japan and Britain; and if we tack on the additional requirement of a homogeneous national identity, then only Japan is left (and even then, only if we ignore the Korean minority)! This happens even though all of the propositions are expressed in terms of general concepts.

General empirical confirmation is more difficult for the hypotheses that arise from case studies and histories because these studies involve implicit conceptual or theoretical specificity. The authors of the case studies may never have intended for their propositions to be generalized, but other scholars who try to generalize them find that the same propositions do not work as well when applied outside of their original context. For example, many scholars have noted that the survival of democracy in India is a puzzle because democracy rarely survives in other poor societies with deep ethno-religious-linguistic cleavages. To explain this paradox, scholars have repeatedly given some credit to British colonial rule, arguing that the British educated India's elite in its liberal values, created an efficient civil service, and gave Indians experience with limited self-government (Lipset 1994, 5; Weiner 1987, 20). Even scholars who are more critical of the British role argue that opposition to the British united Indians behind the Indian National Congress, which then neutralized many social cleavages for decades after independence, enabling democracy to survive. Although some version of this hypothesis works well for India and seems important for understanding the survival of democracy in the United States, Canada, Australia, New Zealand, and the English-speaking Caribbean, it does not help explain the failure of democracy in some other former British colonies such as Nigeria, Pakistan, Gambia, Zimbabwe, Ghana, Malaysia, Singapore, Kenya, and Zambia. The problem is conceptual: British colonial rule meant different things in different colonies. At a minimum, we must distinguish between colonies of settlement (as in North America and Australia) and colonies of conquest. There were also differences in the timing and length of colonization, degrees of self-government and exploitation, types of citizenship, and the nature of the independence struggle that may help resolve the Indian paradox (Lange 2009; Owolabi 2005). Applying watered-down versions of a proposition without its original contextual qualifiers amounts to concept stretching (Sartori 1970). We should not be surprised that hypotheses built from stretched concepts do not hold up when taken out of context.

Another illustration comes from case studies of oil producers arguing that dependence on oil exports either prevents democratization or undermines any democratic regime that comes into being.[6] This proposition gains support from nondemocracies in the Middle East and from fragile democracies such as Venezuela and Ecuador, but it founders on the shoals of Britain and Norway. One could conclude from this that the proposition is false, but it is more likely the case that it is true in some contexts but not others. Terry Karl has argued, for example, that dependence on oil exports is antithetical to democracy only where the oil industry developed before a bureaucratic state became consolidated; in Britain and Norway, an efficient state

---

[6] For an excellent summary and critique of this literature, see Michael L. Ross (2001).

bureaucracy (and democratic regime) developed long before oil was discovered in the North Sea (Karl 1997). Karl's argument, in effect, made an
implicitly specific theory explicitly specific, which made it clearer that it had
a limited domain. Propositions generated by case studies tend not to survive
attempts at generalization because they are, in reality, conditional on other
theoretical propositions that are taken for granted by scholars focusing on a
single case and, therefore, left implicit.

The three problems of generalization just described are all problems for
formulating theories or hypotheses that are likely to be generally true. Generalization, however, also concerns inference, in the statistical sense of drawing
general conclusions from limited evidence. Case studies and histories are
also handicapped for this task, for one can never infer that a proposition is
generally true because it is true in one case. Nevertheless, there have been
attempts to argue that although case studies cannot confirm a proposition,
they can disconfirm one. In 1975, Harry Eckstein argued that a single case
could disconfirm a general hypothesis if it was a crucial case, or one in which
the hypothesis must hold true if it is true for any case (Eckstein 1975).

Douglas Dion has used Bayesian conditional probability theory to show
that some hypotheses about necessary (but not sufficient) conditions could
be generally disconfirmed if they were falsified in a small number of cases,
sometimes even a single case. However, as Dion admits, this is true only
when one already knows that the condition of interest probably is necessary
and that any alternative explanations probably are not true (Dion 1998). In
other words, a single case is unlikely to tell us something general that we
do not already know. As noted in Chapter 3, reasoning about necessary or
sufficient conditions makes sense only if one believes that causal relationships
are simple and deterministic rather than complex and probabilistic (Sekhon
2004). Therefore, Lieberson's conclusions about the limits of small-sample
testing apply with special force to case studies: "Put bluntly, application of
Mill's methods to small-N situations does not allow for probabilistic theories,
interaction effects, measurement errors, or even the presence of more than
one cause" (Lieberson 1992).[7] Actually, Eckstein admitted as much in 1975;
he merely asserted that adequately measurable, deterministic, monocausal
relationships were not rare in comparative politics.

In all subsequent chapters of this book, I summarize the findings about
democratization uncovered by each approach. I do not do so with respect

[7] This critique emphatically does not apply to small-sample comparisons using Boolean or fuzzy-set
analysis, which are discussed in Chapters 4 and 7.

to histories and case studies, however, for the reason I have already given: they do not lend themselves to generalization. The conclusions of case studies of democratization in Britain, Ghana, Russia, Taiwan, Peru, or any other single case usually were not intended to be stated out of context. And even if some authors misguidedly present them as general lessons, we should not interpret them as such, because they could be taken as true only under implicit conditions that need to be made explicit. None of this should detract from the worth of case studies which, again, are the sources of our most rigorous explanations of the immediate causes of specific events. If you want to understand the birth or death of democracy in one country, read a case study. Better yet, read a history. But no one is now in a position to summarize the conclusions of these studies along with all of the contextual conditions attached to each conclusion that are needed to avoid overgeneralization. If someone were in a position to do this, we would have a better grasp of the nested general theory toward which we should strive, which is described in Chapter 3.

The third vice that case studies and histories share – in addition to myopia and an inability to generalize – is a tendency to capitalize on chance, that is, to confuse mere coincidences and spurious relationships with causal relationships. This kind of confusion is always a danger when alleged causal relationships are not tested with evidence different from the evidence that originally suggested the relationship. A good illustration is the claim made by some specialists on U.S. politics that the ingenious design of the U.S. Constitution is responsible for the long-standing success of democracy in the United States (Calabresi 2001; Diamond 1959). As long as attention is confined to the United States, it is very hard to challenge this notion, especially when it is easy to come up with examples of potentially regime-threatening conflicts that were resolved according to constitutional procedures. One way to rule out coincidences would be to carry out a truly comparative analysis. Including Latin American cases in the study would quickly cast doubt on the importance of the U.S. Constitution because most Latin American constitutions since the 1820s have incorporated most of its major features – presidentialism, bicameral legislature, supreme court, and in many cases federalism as well – yet Latin America is known for the instability of its democratic regimes. The constitution alone is clearly not a sufficient explanation (Riggs 1988).

Different evidence need not come from other countries. In principle, a scholar could base a hypothesis on one set of observations from one country and then test it with a different set of observations from the same country (King et al. 1994, 223–228). There are a great many within-case research designs, which the field of American politics exploits to the hilt – surveys, comparisons of states, analysis of time series, and so on – and all of these are available for case studies in comparative politics as well. Still, an insuperable problem arises when the outcome and its alleged cause are invariant. To test a hypothesis, the cause and the outcome must vary. This is the only way to tell whether they covary, and covariance is an essential attribute of causal relationships. If changes in Y do not correspond to changes in X, we can rule out a causal relationship; but if X and Y do not change, we can never be sure. Maybe Y would have happened without X; maybe Y could change even if X did not. Until X or Y changes, these possibilities are just hypothetical guesses. We can tell different stories – spin different theories – about their relationship, but it all remains hypothetical until we can observe actual change.[8]

Because every country has many relatively constant, unchanging features, and because academics are highly intelligent and creative people who can dream up causal connections among them without breaking a sweat, case studies and histories tend to identify ostensibly important invariant "causes" without providing us with any means for judging their relative importance or whether they are important at all. Why, for example, has Britain been a democracy without interruption for so long? Is it because it is an island separate from the European mainland, which lessened the need for a standing army that might also have been used to repress its own citizens? Is it because the English variety of feudalism and the early establishment of a limited monarchy created traditions and cultural expectations that quickly defeated attempts to encroach on democratic rule? Is it because England was the first country to industrialize? All of these characteristics were acquired so far in the past that today they are constants, so as long as democratic survival remains a constant as well, it is very difficult to show that they are or are not causes of British democracy. Other examples of invariant causes are geography, climate, and national character. Today, we rarely turn to them for our explanations, but all of these factors lead to the same problem.

The same problem arises in assessing explanations for the long-term absence of democracy in, for example, Egypt. Maybe it is the lack of any prior experience with democracy; maybe it is that Egypt has a majority Muslim society; maybe it is the Egyptian state's reliance on oil exports; maybe

---

[8] Hypothetical reasoning is unavoidable in any kind of research, even large-sample statistical comparisons (Fearon 1991). In regression, we must suppose that no omitted variables are correlated with the variables in the model. However, this strikes me as less fanciful than the supposition required in case studies: that there is an entirely new case that is just like the observed case save in one respect, and that we can know the consequences of this small difference.

it is Egypt's colonial past. Again, there is no way to be sure because neither these possible causes nor the lack of democracy vary in Egypt. Similar arguments have often been made about entire regions, not just countries: democracy is associated with Western Europe's feudal past, Christianity, or being in the core of the world economy, whereas weak or absent democracy is associated with non-European attributes such as Islam, Confucianism, or being at the periphery of the world economy (Wallerstein 1974; Huntington 1993). One could even extend this kind of reasoning to explain chronic regime instability in, for example, Peru. Democracy has rarely lasted long in Peru because it was an important part of the Spanish colonial empire (Palmer 1980), because a deep ethnic and linguistic cleavage divides the coast from the sierra, because a decades-long feud between the populist Alianza Popular Revolucionaria Americana (APRA) party and the armed forces was not resolved until 1980, or because El Niño periodically wreaks havoc with the economy and the environment.

Actually, hypotheses of this sort can be tested but only if we have variation of some sort. It could be variation among subnational regions, as in *Making Democracy Work* (Putnam et al. 1993); it could be variation over time, if a sufficiently large time span is considered; or it could be variation among individuals, if their opinions are relevant for the hypothesis and a survey can be done. It is also possible to break down the dependent variable to expose its inner clockwork – the causal mechanism – so that we can observe how its components move in synchrony. But these alternatives serve to reinforce the point that if cause and effect truly are static and unchanging, their relationship cannot be tested unless and until new evidence is found.

What can we say, then, about the kind of knowledge that we find in histories and case studies? First, they produce unparalleled descriptive knowledge in the form of concepts, facts, and narratives. Within the discipline, description is valued less than causal inference, but this is unjust. Good description is hard, it is an essential foundation for causal inference, and it is probably valued more by those outside the discipline than our attempts at building causal models (Schedler 2003). Furthermore, this descriptive knowledge tends to be custom made for each case and therefore fits exceptionally well. Second, histories and case studies also attempt to model causes, but they do so with three inherent limitations. Their causal arguments are biased in favor of short-term, micro-level causes; the arguments are unlikely to translate easily to other times and places; and any static causes remain at the level of hypotheses rather than tested propositions. Histories and case studies are great ways to develop ideas about things that *may* matter generally, but they cannot show that they *do* matter generally.

The weaknesses of histories and case studies do not imply that this approach is weaker than other approaches. After all, the core theme of this book is that each major approach has one strength and two weaknesses. And for case studies and histories, the strength – thickness – is crucial for good theory. Theories that are inspired by intimate familiarity with the phenomenon in question are much more likely to be true – that is, to survive rigorous testing – than theories that are deduced in an evidential vacuum. They are also more likely to pass the less strenuous test of being regarded as plausible before any rigorous testing has been done. For this reason, many of the most influential theories in comparative politics originated in case studies. The theory of social capital came from Putnam, Leonardi, and Nanetti's case study of Italy (Putnam et al. 1993); O'Donnell's theory of bureaucratic authoritarianism came from his case study of Argentina; modernization theory emerged from Lerner's case study of Turkey (Lerner 1958); Michels's iron law of oligarchy was inspired by his case study of the German Social Democratic Party (Sozialdemokratische Partei Deutschlands or SPD) in Germany (Michels 1962); and uncountable theories have come from studies of the United States. Some of our field's most innovative and influential ideas would never have come about if there had been such a strict division of labor that theorists did not also know a few cases well. Of course, theories can be influential without being correct, but gaining plausibility is a step in the right direction.

The nature of comparative histories

Comparative histories are intended to overcome the limitations of histories and case studies while retaining some of their advantages. By analyzing and comparing a few cases in some detail, comparative histories try to avoid myopia, move toward generalization, and test hypotheses against fresh data. Compared to most other approaches, comparative history is a method that employs relatively thick concepts and develops relatively thick theory, albeit not as thick as the concepts and theories in case studies or histories. Comparative historians tend to reject the goal of universality but strive to generalize within geographically and historically bounded domains. They often claim to be developing an integrated theory that is accumulating knowledge, as evidenced by a long tradition in which successive researchers address and revise the conclusions of their predecessors. Indeed, the roots of comparative history run so deep that it could be said to be the original approach of comparative politics. Comparative historians rightfully claim Tocqueville, Marx, Weber, and Durkheim as their ancestors; they would be equally justified in extending their lineage to Machiavelli (1988 [1513]). As structural functionalism and behavioralism rose in the 1960s, comparative history temporarily fell into disfavor. However, inspired by Barrington Moore's *The Social Origins of Dictatorship and Democracy* and joining in the reaction against structural-functionalism, comparative history resurged. Moore's thesis that privileged classes would maintain a nondemocratic regime unless they were swept away by a revolution was enthusiastically embraced by many scholars in the radical-ized intellectual environment of the late 1960s (Laitin 2007). Theda Skocpol, Charles Ragin, and others developed methodological justification for the approach in the 1980s (Ragin 1987; Skocpol 1984) and, by the 1990s, comparative history became a more self-conscious and vigorous approach (Evans et al. 1985; Ragin 1987).

Taking stock of comparative-historical analysis in 2003, James Mahoney and Dietrich Rueschemeyer defined the approach by stating that "all work in this tradition ... share[s] a concern with causal analysis, an emphasis on processes over time, and the use of systematic and contextualized comparison" (Mahoney and Rueschemeyer 2003, 10).[9] This definition differentiates comparative history from, respectively, descriptive histories, cross-sectional comparisons of static observations, and efforts to develop universalistic theories. This definition characterizes well a series of books on democratization and state building in Western Europe that took Moore's *Social Origins* (1966) as their starting point.[10] The major works in this series include Skocpol's *States and Social Revolutions* (1979), Luebbert's *Liberalism, Fascism, or Social Democracy* (1991), Downing's *The Military Revolution and Political Change* (1992), and Ertman's *Birth of the Leviathan* (1997). This literature spread to Latin America with Collier and Collier's *Shaping the Political Arena* (1991) and has since given rise to several important books that transcend any single region and focus more narrowly on democratization: Rueschemeyer, Stephens, and

---

[9] Their definition is useful, although they intend it to be broad enough to include statistical time-series analysis and cultural analysis, both of which I discuss in separate chapters because they raise distinct sets of methodological issues.

[10] Two important works in a similar vein are typically omitted from lists like this one: Reinhard Bendix (1964) and Charles Tilly (1975). This is a bit puzzling, but it could be argued that Bendix's work is more descriptive than causal and that Tilly's book is more concerned with state building than democratization. They tend to be classed with structural functionalism or modernization theory despite many arguments that are similar to those of Moore and his heirs.

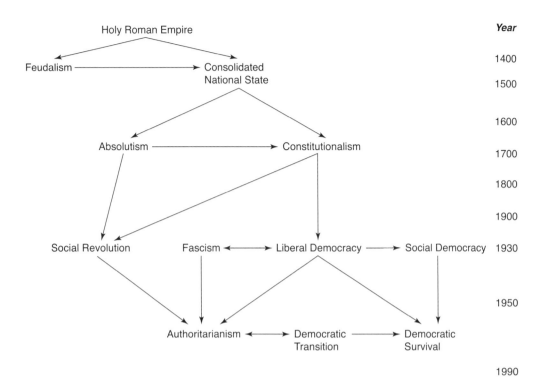

Figure 5.1   Major Historical Transitions

Stephens's *Capitalist Development and Democracy* (1992) and Ruth Collier's *Paths toward Democracy* (1999).

A superficial glance at the comparative-historical literature suggests that it has developed in a cumulative way, gradually elaborating and repeatedly test-ing a coherent theory of democratization that applies to an expanding set of countries. Figure 5.1 sketches out the major regime types and stages of regime building found in the Western European countries that have been the princi-pal focus of this literature and the time periods in which they predominated. The common starting point for all of them was the Holy Roman Empire, founded in A.D. 936. When the Holy Roman Empire began to disintegrate in the fifteenth century, it left behind many small feudal states. Some of these remained small feudal states for centuries; others were agglomerated into larger, consolidated national states. This is the first major division explained in this literature. The second bifurcation divided consolidated states that evolved into absolutist regimes in the seventeenth and eighteenth centuries from those that preserved a rough balance between crown and nobility, the rights of towns and guilds, and mutual obligations between landlords and peasants – a situation that Downing (1992) calls medieval constitutionalism. By the nineteenth and early twentieth centuries, these states parted ways a third time, either establishing the responsibility of the executive to parliament and expanding the suffrage to become liberal democracies or undergoing a social revolution. Many of the liberal democracies lasted only a short time before they became social democracies (in Luebbert's [1991] terminology) or fell prey to fascism. Finally, democratic regimes either survived or gave way to authoritarian regimes. In some countries, there were repeated cycles of democracy and authoritarianism. The Latin American countries covered in the works discussed here followed a different path until the twentieth century. All of them were originally European colonies, but when they became independent in the early nineteenth century, their consolidation as national states was delayed by several decades of civil war or dictatorship. However, the Latin American cases fit well into Figure 5.1 from about 1900 onward, as they have oscillated between democracy and authoritarianism.

Not all of the authors mentioned here claim that comparative histories constitute a cumulative research program, but defenders of comparative history as an approach have made that claim for them (Mahoney 2003; Mahoney and Rueschemeyer 2003). This claim is bolstered by the overlapping historical coverage of these works. Figure 5.2 superimposes on the framework of Figure 5.1 the domains covered by the eight comparative histories discussed in this chapter. Downing (1992) and Ertman (1997) cover approximately the same periods and propose answers to the same questions, such as, How did the remnants of the Holy Roman Empire become consolidated as states and why did some become absolutist regimes while others resisted absolutism? Moore (1966) and Skocpol (1979), although published earlier, study the later political transformations of either absolutism or constitutionalism into social revolution, fascism, or liberal democracy. Luebbert (1991) focuses on transitions from constitutional or protodemocratic regimes to liberal democracy, social democracy, or fascism, ignoring social revolution, which was missing in his exclusively interwar European sample. Collier and Collier (1991), in turn, omit social democracy and fascism (both missing from their Latin American sample) to focus on transitions between authoritarianism and democracy.[11] The most sweeping study is that by Rueschemeyer, Stephens, and Stephens (1992), which covers the gradual early democratization of Europe, recent

---

[11] Actually, the Colliers also include one case of social revolution – Mexico – but spend most of their time on the postrevolutionary period.

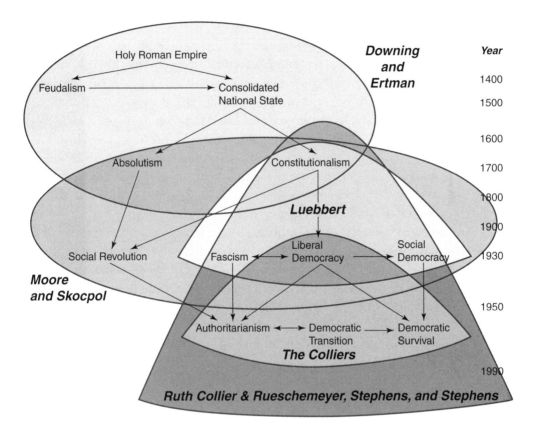

Figure 5.2   The Overlapping Temporal Domains of Comparative Histories

transitions in Latin America and the English-speaking Caribbean, and fascist interruptions of the early twentieth century. Therefore, although each study considers a different slice of history, collectively these comparative histories provide continuous coverage of the last half-millennium in Western Europe and Latin America.

Despite the considerable overlaps, these works contain too many fundamental differences to treat them as a fully integrated research program. Most fundamentally, they attempt to explain different outcomes. Obviously, only the works that extend into the years since about 1920 (when most European countries extended the suffrage to all adult males) really attempt to account for what we now consider democratic regimes. Moore and Skocpol barely reach this period, and only for some of their cases. Downing and Ertman seek to explain only institutions or traditions that were precursors to democracy, such as the balance between crown and nobility and the rights of towns and peasants. But the differences in outcomes are not due solely to different historical foci. Even authors dealing with the same period seek to explain different outcomes, and democracy is not always the outcome of chief interest. Whereas Downing is primarily concerned with representative assemblies and other institutions that predisposed Europe toward democracy, Ertman is equally interested in explaining the type of regime (constitutional or absolutist) and the type of state (bureaucratic or patrimonial). Moore was interested in three different kinds of revolutions: the bourgeois revolution, allegedly leading to democracy; the conservative revolution from above, leading to authoritarianism; and the peasant revolution, leading to communism. Skocpol was primarily interested in explaining social revolutions; democracy was for her just one of several possible outcomes in a residual category of nonrevolution. Of all the scholars of more recent periods, only Rueschemeyer, Stephens, and Stephens (1992) are exclusively interested in explaining democracy. Luebbert (1991) distinguished between liberal democracy and social democracy – economic systems as well as political regimes – and contrasted both with fascism. Collier and Collier, in *Shaping the Democratic Arena* (1991), are ultimately interested in explaining democratic survival (as an expected outcome of institutionalized party systems that incorporate labor in a peaceful way), but only in the final chapters. Along the way, they spend considerable effort explaining prior outcomes – the characteristics of parties, the mode of incorporation of labor, the nature of labor laws, and the strength of labor and the oligarchy. In her later (1999) book, Ruth Collier is actually interested in accounting for variations in the role of labor in democratization rather than for democratization per se.

Comparative histories have also disagreed about which actors matter. Skocpol took Moore to task for merely paying lip service to the notion of the state as an autonomous actor (Skocpol 1973). The same criticism could be made of Luebbert and perhaps Ruth Collier's (1999) book. Skocpol, Downing, Rueschemeyer and colleagues, and Ertman emphasize foreign states as important actors; Moore, Luebbert, and Collier and Collier do not. Similarly, authors disagree about the democratic orientations of key actors. Moore (like most of his predecessors and contemporaries) associated democracy with the interests of the bourgeoisie; if the bourgeoisie is defined to include the gentry and the urban middle class, Downing and Ertman would agree. Luebbert argued that only some of the middle class supported democracy, and only in some cases, because the outcome depended on the middle class's choice of allies. The central argument of Rueschemeyer and colleagues, however, is that the working class was a far more consistent friend of democracy than the middle class, except in South America. This dispute was the inspiration for Ruth Collier's book, which identified seven different roles played by labor in democratization, some of which were supportive and others not.

Comparative histories have varied most with respect to the set of explanatory factors or variables that they emphasize. The only factor shared by all of these works is the assumption that the economic interests of social classes played an important role. Barrington Moore's work is the purest expression of this; the others add other variables to social class. As noted before, Skocpol added state interests and international relations to the mix, initiating a tradition of centering comparative-historical analyses on class-class, class-state, and state-state relations (Mahoney 2003). Luebbert, however, went beyond the class cleavage to consider preindustrial religious, regional, linguistic, and urban-rural cleavages. Downing emphasized – in addition to class – medieval institutions and traditions, geography, military technology, trade, and colonial resources. The other works refer to a still richer variety of explanatory factors, including commodity specialization, immigration, leadership, modes of incorporation of labor, civil war, short-term economic performance, transnational political ideas and polarization, the nature of the antecedent regime, and coalition politics.

Although these works do not present a coherently integrated body of theory, they can be said to share a metatheory – a looser set of assumptions – as James Mahoney has noted (Mahoney 2003). All comparative-historical researchers make three fundamental assumptions, and a subgroup makes a few more. One fundamental assumption is that big events such as revolution, state building, and democratization can be explained. Not all social scientists agree with this. Barbara Geddes, for example, has argued that big events are too complex to explain and that we must focus on the microfoundations of politics if we are to make any progress (Geddes 1997). A related assumption is that big events have big (structural) causes. Most scholars who refer to structures mean class structure, but other social structures such as religious or ethnic cleavages can be included, and I would argue that other large-scale, slowly changing features such as physical geography, commodity specialization, and state capacity qualify as structures as well. Comparative historians do not claim that all causes are structural, but their belief that some causes are structural sets them apart from those who are exclusively interested in the effects of mutable institutions, culture, or strategic calculations of elites.

A third fundamental assumption is that it is meaningful and useful to treat social classes as actors. Some scholarly traditions long ago decided that class is not a useful concept except in the rare cases where a social class is conscious, cohesive, and conspiratorial (Parry 1969). Comparative historians tend to assume that members of classes do have a common economic interest, that they are aware of their shared interests, and that they collectively pursue their common interests. However, unlike primitive Marxists, comparative historians typically qualify these assumptions in two respects. First, they tend to divide classes into more precise and, therefore, more internally homogeneous, categories. Instead of writing about capitalists in general, they distinguish among agricultural landlords, industrialists, and bankers, and often among subcategories of these. Instead of the bourgeoisie, they distinguish among the rural middle class, urban professionals, merchants, civil servants, and so on, often to the point of reducing classes to a set of occupations. Second, comparative historians now tend not to assume that collective action in pursuit of common interests comes naturally. Therefore, important supplementary actors in their analyses are class-based organizations such as labor unions, political parties, and interest groups, which mobilize their members in the defense of the interests that they define on behalf of the class. These two modifications of the class-analytic approach do make it more useful. Taken to the extreme, it would become indistinguishable from the interest-group politics approach, but most comparative histories remain at a slightly more abstract level.

A subgroup of comparative historians shares several additional assumptions that help define the approach. After a long intellectual evolution from the Marxist dogma that the state is merely "a committee for managing the common affairs of the whole bourgeoisie," most contemporary comparative historians have adopted the French structural Marxist position that states are autonomous actors with interests of their own, independent from the interests of a dominant class (Marx and Engels 1932, 11; Poulantzas 1973).[12] States guard their territories from foreign encroachment and try to maintain public order, and to those ends they raise armies and revenues, staff bureaucracies, and gather information about their societies to make their task of governing easier and more efficient. This group also recognizes the impact on domestic politics of international forces such as war, trade, immigration, and revolutions in other countries. This international perspective may seem natural for scholars who take an expansive, long-term, structural view of politics, but it is not notable in the work of Barrington Moore or Gregory Luebbert, so it is most properly viewed as a subgroup characteristic.

---

[12] The intellectual evolution passed through a stage of holding that states are relatively autonomous – sometimes acting against capital to guarantee the continued existence of capital. See Nicos Poulantzas (1973).

The earlier comparative histories tended to employ John Stuart Mill's methods of similarity and difference to test or buttress their claims. Those using Mill's method of difference would choose cases that had as much as possible in common except for their differing outcomes, in effect holding the common characteristics relatively constant. These scholars could then argue that the different outcomes would be best explained by the remaining characteristics that differed. The method of similarity follows the opposite logic: choose cases that experienced similar outcomes despite being different from one another in as many respects as possible. Using the method of similarity, scholars argue that the similar outcomes must be attributed to the reduced set of remaining similarities. Somewhat confusingly, Mill's method of difference is the same as Przeworski and Teune's equally well-known most-similar-systems design, and his method of similarity is identical to their most-different-systems design (Przeworski and Teune 1970). Nevertheless, the logic is the same: differences explain differences, and similarities explain similarities. This was the common logic of most comparative histories before 1990.

Since about 1987 – the year of publication of Charles Ragin's *The Comparative Method* – comparative histories have preferred a path-dependent model of politics, which is incompatible with Millian comparative logic. Peter Hall has insightfully described this approach as one that sees "the world not as a terrain marked by the operation of timeless causal regularities, but as a branching tree whose tips represent the outcomes of events that unfold over time" (Hall 2003, 385). This approach is built around the key concepts of endogeneity and interactions. Comparative historians since 1990 have believed that outcomes occur in sequences; therefore, outcomes at one time become causes of other outcomes at later times. This is what it means for variables to be endogenous: they are both causes and effects. There are interactions when causes combine to produce an outcome; and because the effect of one cause depends on the presence of another cause, it is not useful to speak of the independent impact of either cause separately. Recent comparative histories emphasize both endogeneity and interactions (Pierson 2004). As Hall notes, "The prototypical contention is that the impact of *x* will depend on whether it occurs before or after *w*" (Hall 2003, 385).

This is a much more complex kind of model than a simple list of variables that lead to an outcome, and more complex than models with either endogeneity or interactions but not both. Figure 5.3 contrasts a path-dependent model with simpler models. Model 5.3a is a basic two-variable causal model in which continuous variables X and Z cause outcome Y. The same model could be written in equation form as $Y = X + Z$. (To avoid clutter,

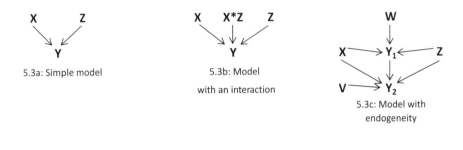

5.3a: Simple model

5.3b: Model
with an interaction

5.3c: Model with
endogeneity

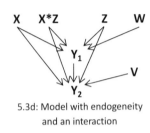

5.3d: Model with endogeneity
and an interaction

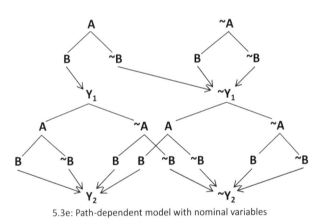

5.3e: Path-dependent model with nominal variables

Figure 5.3   Path-Dependent and Non-Path-Dependent Models

these examples assume that all explanatory variables have the same weight and therefore lack coefficients.) Model 5.3b contains an interaction between X and Z that helps cause Y; or, in equation form, $Y = X + Z + X \cdot Z$. Here, the full effect of X (i.e., $X + X \cdot Z$) depends in part on Z, and the full effect of Z (i.e., $Z + X \cdot Z$) depends in part on X. Each one conditions the other. Model 5.3c incorporates endogeneity by distinguishing between an initial outcome Y_1 and a subsequent outcome Y_2. (Typically, X and Z would vary with time as well.) Model 5.3c also incorporates the assumption that different variables matter at different stages. In this case, W helps cause Y_1 but not Y_2, and V helps cause Y_2 but not Y_1. Representing endogeneity algebraically requires a separate equation for each outcome: in this case, $Y1 = X + Z + W$ and $Y2 = Y1 + X + Z + V$. Model 5.3d combines the endogeneity of Model 5.3c with the interactions of Model 5.3b. It can be written as $Y1 = X + Z + X \cdot Z + W$ and $Y2 = Y1 + X + Z + X \cdot Z + V$.

Model 5.3d meets Hall's criteria for path dependence, but he made his definition so general that it included strategic bargaining models and some complex statistical models. To narrow the definition to the comparative histories discussed in this chapter, a further stipulation is necessary: the models must have nominal outcomes and at least one nominal cause; together, these produce a branching, path-dependent kind of model.[13] To represent this feature in Figure 5.3e, we must alter the notation. Therefore, Y_1 and Y_2 are no longer continuous variables but rather nominal (categorical) variables. The explanatory variables, A and B, are also nominal. Now B signifies that condition B is present, and $\sim$B signifies that condition B is absent; similarly for Y_1 and $\sim Y_1$ (not Y_1), for Y_2 and $\sim Y_2$, and A and $\sim$A.

In this example, Y_1 occurs only if A and B are both present in the first time period; if either A or B is absent ($\sim$A or $\sim$B), then the outcome is "not Y_1." The branching in Figure 5.3e that lacks arrows signifies every possible combination of A, $\sim$A, B, and $\sim$B. This is the nominal equivalent of the multiplicative interactions in other models. In the second time period, however, Y_2 is determined by a different rule. If Y_1 had already been achieved, then Y_2 occurs if either A or B is present; but if Y_1 had not been achieved, then Y_2 occurs only if both A and B are present. This argument can be expressed mathematically with Boolean logic:

If $[Y_1$ and (A or B)] or [not Y_1 and A and B], then Y_2;
If $[Y_1$ and not A and not B] or [not Y_1 and (not A or not B)], then not Y_2.

It is the qualitative nature of the variables that produces the branching trees typical of path-dependent models, as in Figure 5.3e. In such models, we cannot pin down a consistent effect of A, B, or AB on Y_2 because they may or

---

[13] Fuzzy-set qualitative comparative analysis (QCA), discussed in Chapter 7, accommodates variables that are not strictly nominal. I work with variables that are degrees of membership in sets. It seems to me that this is an appropriate kind of analysis when all of the noncategorical variance is understood to be a kind of measurement error. When variance reflects degrees on a meaningful continuum instead of degrees of membership in a discrete set, however, there are advantages to quantitative analysis.

may not be associated with Y_2, depending on whether or not Y_1 was previously achieved. Figure 5.1 implies a good example of a path-dependent argument: if a consolidated national state forms, then other conditions can eventually produce democracy there; but if there is no consolidated national state, then these other conditions do not produce the same democratic outcome. However, as in Figure 5.3e, outcomes need not branch away forever. In many path-dependent models, divergent paths can later converge. In this way, path-dependent models often identify multiple paths to a single outcome.

Evaluation of the comparative-historical approach

The preceding section described the nature of comparative history as an approach that is, by varying degrees, thinner than case studies and histories but thicker than most other approaches in comparative politics. It is also more theoretically integrated than most case studies, but only loosely integrated in the sense of sharing some metatheoretical assumptions; therefore, it is less integrated than approaches that derive propositions from a common well of formal theory or that repeatedly test the same hypotheses with slight modifications and different samples. Comparative history also aims for an intermediate level of generality, shunning both particularism and universalism in favor of the middle-range aspiration of generalizing about a century or two on a continent or two. Therefore, on all three criteria for a good theory – thickness, integration, and generality – comparative history is a methodological compromise. Its advocates claim that this makes the approach the best of all worlds, at least the best that we can actually achieve. As with any compromise, however, it is also possible that we are left with the worst of all worlds. A careful evaluation of the approach is therefore in order.

Comparative history is a very good approach for intensive testing: identifying and testing possible causes of specific events in specific cases. Unfortunately, it is not as rigorous in doing this as case studies and histories are, as they bring greater conceptual richness and much more evidence to bear on such questions. Comparative histories do have one advantage over case studies, however. They are less myopic, more likely to call attention to structural macrocauses.

However, comparative histories are less successful than sometimes claimed at moving beyond specific events to develop and test middle-range theories. They can also be criticized for not even attempting universality, as I have argued an ideal theory should. But even if we content ourselves with the lesser, more realistic, and practical goal of developing a multitiered conditional (or nested) theory (see Chapter 3) that unifies many middle-range theories, comparative histories are disappointing. In their attempt to generalize to the middle range, comparative histories typically encounter five problems. First, their concepts are slippery and inconsistently applied. Second, they do not adequately integrate the theories developed for small domains into a single theory for a larger domain. Third, the page limits on what presses will publish and what readers will read constrains the number of cases and the number of variables that any comparative historian can include. Fourth, comparative histories almost always end up with more variables than cases, thus rendering any testing indeterminate. Finally, comparative historians always amend their theories as they go along and never test the amended theory with different evidence, and this habit virtually guarantees capitalizing on chance. I discuss each problem as it manifests itself at three levels: in the typical work of comparative history, where the problems are often minor; in the collective body of comparative-historical research, where problems are most serious; and in the potential for comparative history as an approach.

The rich conceptualization that is typical of case studies and histories becomes a burden when scholars attempt to compare cases. It becomes impossible to respect the uniqueness of each case and necessary to work with simpler, less precise concepts. Comparative historians must write about the upper chamber of parliament instead of the British House of Lords; about the working class instead the nitrate miners of northern Chile. Moving up the ladder of abstraction is a tricky business that requires the scholar to define an umbrella concept that captures the common characteristics of diverse times and places without ignoring other characteristics that may be causally relevant. It is hard to do this well, so comparative historians often fall short in one of three ways. First, some define a concept vaguely and then use it even where it does not really fit, which Sartori (1970) called concept stretching. Ertman, for example, cites historical research showing that earlier comparative historians wrongly classified early modern England as a patrimonial state. In fact, England had a more highly developed bureaucracy than Prussia did (Ertman 1997). Second, some scholars define a concept in a much thinner, essentialist way but then tack on different causally relevant qualifications in some of their cases. In this situation, the concept hides important variations, thus creating an illusion of general applicability. For example, Brian Downing classified both France and Brandenburg-Prussia as having developed military-bureaucratic absolutism, but he also says that one reason that absolutism survived in Prussia while succumbing to revolution in

France was that France's absolutism was less absolute (Downing 1992). Third, some comparative historians simply use vague concepts, leaving it up to the reader to guess how they should be applied. Readers can search in vain for a concrete definition of concepts such as a rough balance between the crown and the nobility (Moore), economic dependence (Rueschemeyer et al. 1992), bureaucratic state (Ertman), bourgeoisie (Moore, Skocpol), labor-repressive agriculture (Moore), and solidarity of peasant communities (Skocpol), even though the truth of core arguments depends on how those concepts are defined.

This problem is found even in individual works, which we should expect to be internally consistent. There is quite a bit of variation in conceptual clarity in the genre. Ruth Collier's *Paths toward Democracy* (1999) stands out as unusually clear and consistent in its definitions, whereas Moore's *Social Origins* (1966) is frustratingly muddled.[14] However, the slippery or inconsistent use of concepts is much more of a problem for comparative history as a whole because of the lack of agreement among its practitioners. One need not take an outsider's word that this problem exists. Any comparative history selected at random will contain at least one lengthy discussion of concepts and classification that disputes the decisions made by other comparative historians. Thus, we find that Ruth Collier classifies Weimar Germany as an episode of successful democratization, whereas Moore, Luebbert, and Ertman consider it a case of rising fascism (Collier 1999). Skocpol considered Moore's concept of labor-repressive agriculture not to be useful and criticized Moore for using his key concept of the bourgeois impulse in inconsistent ways that glossed over important differences in the strength of the bourgeoisie (Skocpol 1973). And what are we to make of the fundamental disagreement between Ruth Collier and Rueschemeyer, Stephens, and Stephens? The latter argue that the working class was the primary actor advancing the cause of democracy in Western Europe, whereas Collier argues that labor organizations were not important actors in early democratization episodes in Greece, France, Portugal, Spain, Switzerland, Norway, and Italy (Collier 1999; Rueschemeyer et al. 1992). The difference is a conceptual disagreement about whether the inclusion of the working class must be accomplished before the outcome deserves to be called democratization. Rueschemeyer and colleagues believe

---

[14] As James Mahoney observes, "Moore's specific hypotheses were stated in a relatively vague manner that has made it difficult for subsequent scholars to evaluate his claims empirically.... [S]cholars have had difficulty summarizing *Social Origins*, leading to a rather diverse set of interpretations regarding the main arguments of the book" (Mahoney 2003, 137–138).

it must, so they disqualify early steps toward democracy that Collier considers relevant.

The second problem faced by comparative histories is the difficulty of integrating their findings with other comparative research. This problem affects both the integration of several comparative histories into a larger, cumulative, comparative-historical research program and the integration of the findings from each case into a single work of comparative history. The integration problem at the level of the research program can be understood as a difficulty in drawing a sample that is comparable to the larger population of cases; in other words, as a problem of sample selection. If the cases selected for comparison are comparable to all of the relevant cases that could have been chosen, then one would be justified in treating the findings of the comparison as complete, finished hypotheses ready for application to other cases in the larger population. But, if the selected cases are systematically different from the larger population in any relevant way, then the comparisons will suffer from selection bias. In a large sample with cases selected at random (in a public opinion survey, for example), this is not a problem because the sample differs only randomly, not systematically, from the population. The noncomparable aspects of the sample can be assumed to cancel out one another so that, on average, the sample is representative of the population from which it was drawn. Unfortunately, a few dozen cases are needed for the benefits of randomization to be realized, so this solution is not available to comparative historians (King et al. 1994). For them, selection bias is unavoidable. This should be especially obvious with regard to comparative histories that focus (as most do) on a particular geographic region or a particular period of history precisely because it is systematically different (Geddes 2003). There is a price to pay for the advantages of middle-range theory.

Fortunately, selection bias is – in principle – correctable, but only if we know the nature of the bias. There are several possibilities. First, the selected cases may have some fixed advantage or disadvantage in achieving the out-come; for example, Latin American countries since the mid-1970s tend to be more democratic than non–Latin American countries at the same level of socioeconomic development in the period (Coppedge 2005). If we know why these countries have this bonus or penalty, we can add an extra wrinkle to the theory to take it into account. But even if the reason is unknown, it is better to know and acknowledge such systematic differences than to pretend that they do not exist. Taking these differences into account makes the sample comparable to the population, at least in this respect. Another kind of bias occurs when the same cause has a more powerful or a weaker effect in the selected cases than it does in other cases. A good example is the belief that U.S. foreign policy has a more powerful impact on Central America than it does on the Southern Cone of South America. Again, if we knew the reason for this varying effect – say, the size and distance of each country from the United States – then we would have an improved theory that would travel more easily beyond the region. Even lacking a good explanation, it is better to state that a process is different in this region than in that one. This leaves us with a multiple-paths kind of theory that applies equally well to both regions.[15] Finally, it is possible that the selected cases are harder or easier to explain than the ones not selected: the outcomes just vary more. The more apparently random variation there is in the outcomes, the more likely it is that the impact of a cause will get lost in the noise, leading scholars to conclude, falsely, that the cause has no effect. In such situations, the appropriate correction is to adjust the standards for each set of cases so that a big change in the less predictable cases is treated as equivalent to a small change in the more predictable cases. For some purposes, for example, a failed coup attempt in Northern Europe could be equivalent (i.e., as traumatic, as severe a regime crisis) to a successful coup in sub-Saharan Africa.

In all of these situations, what must be done is to identify explicitly how the cases selected for a comparative history differ systematically from the rest of the world. When this is done, then we have some guidance about how to integrate the findings of one comparative history with the findings of other comparative histories. Failure to do so biases the conclusions of a study in unpredictable ways, rendering effects more or less optimistic than they would be in a larger sample, causes more or less powerful, and confidence in conclusions either inflated or deflated. Without a large sample, there is no way to estimate the degree of the bias or the required correction, but we must at least specify the nature and direction of the probable bias.[16]

Without the explicit guidance needed to make the different sets of countries comparable, the best we can do is circumscribe the relevance of the findings to only the times and places actually studied. Although this is enough to satisfy most comparativists today, it is important to keep in mind how far it falls short of the covering-law model of explanation, which requires universal laws. If an explanation is limited to particular times and places for arbitrary

---

[15] Actually, as noted earlier in this chapter, multiple paths are required only when the condition on which the effect depends is conceived of in categorical terms. If it is thought of as a continuum, then an interaction between two variables is a more precise model.

[16] The issues encountered here are the same as those that arise in regression analysis of observational data. For a discussion of matching and other strategies for dealing with selection bias, see Chapter 9.

(i.e., unspecified) reasons, then it is an incomplete explanation, at best. Of course, it is unrealistic to expect comparative politics, still in its infancy as a science, to produce complete explanations. Producing incomplete explanations that work well for certain middle-range regions and periods is without doubt a useful first step along the road to complete and therefore universal nested theories, as described in Chapter 3. In one influential view, what we learn by testing is not so much whether a theory is true or false but rather "how much of the world the theory can help us explain" (King et al. 1994, 101).

However, even at this early stage, it is essential for comparative historians to make explicit the reasons for their selection decisions. Otherwise, even the smallest differences in case selection make it impossible to cumulate knowledge in a coherent research program. We have already seen that the major comparative-historical works involving democratization have used different, although overlapping, sets of cases. This makes it all the more important for every author to point out how the selection might have influenced the results. Downing (1992, 18) is a good model for others to follow. He explicitly identifies many differences between Europe and other regions:

To say that European social, political, and economic history is markedly different from that of the rest of the world is to say nothing new. The West was the first to develop innovative agricultural techniques, large-scale capitalist production, and a system of states. Europe was also the first – and, unfortunately, virtually the last – to develop democratic political systems that featured institutional checks on political monopoly, varying but frequently increasing degrees of political representation, chartered rights of citizenship, and the rule of law. (Downing 1992)

He then offers brief case studies of Russia, Japan, and China to show that these non-Western countries "never developed constitutional government as found in late medieval Europe. Structural configurations conducive to constitutionalism in the West, rough balance between crown and noble, contractual-feudal military organization, and lord-peasant dynamics were absent or weak" (Downing 1992, 53). Moore limited his conclusions to large, powerful states to the exclusion of smaller, dependent states on the grounds that "the decisive causes of their politics lie outside their own boundaries" (Moore 1966, xiii). This is brief and dubious, but at least he addressed the issue.

Many other authors discuss this issue in only the most cursory ways, if they address it at all. Collier and Collier (1991, 5), for example, merely note, "The present study parallels the concerns of various analysts of Europe who have viewed the incorporation of the working class as a pivotal transition within this larger process of societal change," without identifying the differences between the European and Latin American experiences. All of their discussion of case selection deals with selection within Latin America. Skocpol (1979) includes a section titled, "Why France, Russia, and China?" but does not address external validity. She defends the selection of these three cases from different regions and periods against charges that they are not comparable to one another but neglects to address how they might not be comparable with other cases. Elsewhere, she does recognize that "there always are unexamined contextual features of the historical cases that interact with the causes being explicitly examined in ways the comparative-historical analysis either does not reveal, or must simply assume to be irrelevant" (Skocpol 1979, 39) but does not attempt to identify these features in her analysis. Given the vague and inconsistent justifications for case selection, we cannot assume that different comparative histories study comparable sets of cases. This is an obstacle to the accumulation of findings in the comparative-historical research program.

Achieving comparability across temporal domains is as important as comparability across spatial domains. Comparative historians should tell us not only what is systematically different about the territories they study but also what is different about the historical period. This kind of guidance is necessary for unifying theories inspired by different waves of democratization. For example, it probably matters a great deal that first-wave democratization in Britain took place without a model to follow (until 1776). Democracy was not a familiar goal to achieve rather but a set of evolving institutions and practices that people invented as they went along. Transitions after World War II had many models to emulate, and this is probably an important reason that transitions are much faster now.

Individual works of comparative history must also demonstrate the comparability of the cases they include. Because cases in one region during one period are relatively similar, this is usually less difficult than ensuring the comparability of one set of cases to all other sets of cases. However, because comparative historians are primarily interested in accounting for the differences among the cases they have selected, they do a much better job of addressing this problem. Perhaps comparative historians could be faulted for not accounting exhaustively for the differences among their cases. In practice, they present a simple set of explanatory factors that most efficiently sorts the cases into the possible outcomes. An exhaustive analysis would identify all of the differences among cases and would leave us with multiple, sometimes competing, explanations. However, this would be expecting each comparative history to do all of the work required of the entire collective comparative-historical research program over a long period of time; it is expecting too much.

Nevertheless, contemplating the demands of rising to this challenge exposes the third problem that comparative historians encounter: the practical limits to the complexity of any analysis. Even if a scholar or teams of scholars were interested in coming closer to exhaustive explanations of differences among a larger number of cases, no press would publish their massive write-up. And even if a press would publish it, few readers would actually read it. There is therefore an unavoidable trade-off between the thickness of an analysis and the size of the domain it can cover. We can see this trade-off in the works discussed in this chapter. Using crude indicators of domain size (e.g., the number of countries studied) and thickness (e.g., pages per country), we find *Shaping the Political Arena* at one extreme, with 877 pages for eight countries, or an average of 110 pages per country. (Case studies, of course, are even thicker: several hundred book pages per country.) Skocpol and Moore are also at the high end, with six to eight countries and about seventy pages per country. With eleven to thirteen cases, Luebbert and Ertman slip to twenty-eight to thirty-eight pages per country.[17] At the low extreme, Ruth Collier's set of twenty-two countries and Rueschemeyer, Stephens, and Stephens's set of thirty-four countries weigh in at only about eleven pages per country. The larger the domain, the thinner is the analysis.

The fourth problem of comparative history is indeterminacy. In a single-case study, many variables are held constant over time, and the only variables necessary are those that explain variation within that case. In a comparative history, more variables are needed to account for cross-national differences. Comparative histories face the real danger of having more variables than cases – the problem of many variables, small N problem. This is a problem because it virtually guarantees capitalizing on chance – that is, mistaking spurious or coincidental associations for causal relationships. The relationships can be tested, but any extensive tests would yield indeterminate conclusions.

If the cases had been selected at random (an important qualifier to which I return herein), the probability that the finding of a comparative-historical analysis could have been produced by chance could be checked with Fisher's exact test.[18] I have done this test for most of the works discussed in this chapter by summarizing their findings in tables, which are in the appendix to this chapter. Table 5.1 presents the results of the Fisher tests for the major comparative histories. Only two of them – Ertman and Luebbert – satisfied

---

[17] Here, I count the Papal States and the twenty German territorial states as single entities because Ertman always discusses them as undifferentiated blocs. This gives him a total of thirteen cases.

[18] The more familiar chi-square test is actually a large-sample approximation of this test. Some readers will be familiar with the Fisher test in 2×2 tables. The same test, although computationally difficult, can be performed with larger tables.

Table 5.1. Fisher tests of comparative-historical models

Author	Number of cases	Explanatory categories (rows)	Outcome categories (columns)	Cases per cell	Probability of a chance result
Skocpol	6	6	2	0.50	.933
Collier and Collier (Heritage period)	8	4	2	0.67	.393
Rueschemeyer, Stephens, and Stephens (timing of initial democratization in Latin America)	10	6	4	0.42	.271
Moore	7	6	4	0.29	.188
Rueschemeyer, Stephens, and Stephens (rise of authoritarianism in Europe)	10	6	2	0.83	.164
Downing	7	5	3	0.47	.077
Ertman (simple version)	13	4	4	0.81	.001
Luebbert	15	4	4	0.94	.000

Note: The table form of each author's model is in the appendix to this chapter. Ruth Collier's (1999) model of the impact of labor on democratization considers several hypotheses but does not integrate them into a single model. The probabilities of a chance result must be calculated for each specific table.

the conventional $p < .05$ criterion for statistical significance, mostly because the other tables were sparsely populated, as indicated in the cases-per-cell column. Chance results are harder to rule out when the table is large (i.e., when there are complex explanations for complex outcomes), the cases are few, or there are many exceptions to the pattern. Therefore, comparative histories, which tend to have complex explanations for few cases, are prone to chance results.

Table 5.1 suggests that even if the cases were chosen at random, it would not be possible to distinguish results this strong from sheer coincidence. But, of course, comparative historians do not select their cases at random; random selection is inappropriate when the sample is small. There are various alternative criteria for selecting cases for testing when the sample is small – some better than others. According to King, Keohane, and Verba (1994), "The most egregious error is to select observations in which the explanatory and dependent variables vary together in ways that are known to be consistent with the hypothesis that the research purports to test." There are two ways to do this: selecting cases to fit the hypothesis, and selecting a hypothesis to fit the cases. I doubt that many comparativists deliberately select cases to fit a hypothesis and then present the comparison as a test; if they did, it would be research fraud. However, I think it is likely that some comparativists unconsciously select cases to fit their hypothesis. The temptation to present confirming evidence and sweep inconvenient cases under the rug is difficult to resist (Goldthorpe 1991). Moreover, it is fine to do this as long as such evidence is presented as an illustration of how a hypothesis might work and not as a test.

Comparative historians do, however, deliberately select hypotheses to fit their cases. In fact, not only do they do it; they admit it and praise it as methodological virtue itself. Mahoney and Rueschemeyer (2003, 13), for example, write that comparative historians can "move comfortably back and forth between theory and history in many iterations of analysis as they formulate new concepts, discover novel explanations, and refine preexisting theoretical expectations in light of detailed case evidence." Actually, there is methodological virtue in selecting hypotheses to fit cases, but it is a virtue for building theory and generating hypotheses. Staying close to cases is probably the most efficient way to develop explanations that work well for the cases being studied. But selecting hypotheses to fit cases is not a virtue for testing. As far as testing is concerned, it is a corrupt practice. To the extent that scholars deliberately select hypotheses to fit their cases or unconsciously select cases to fit their hypotheses, Fisher tests, which assume random selection, inflate the significance of the comparative evidence for comparative-historical theories. In this light, the strong significance levels for the Ertman and Luebbert models in Table 5.1 are not meaningful. Comparative historians should drop the pretense that there is any truly cross-national testing going on in their work.

Some will object that there is plenty of testing in comparative histories. In fact, I have already argued that comparative histories share the advantage of case studies in testing hypotheses about the immediate causes of specific events. *Designing Social Inquiry* admonishes us to multiply observable implications, to search for evidence that might disconfirm any of the many things that must be true if the theory is true (King et al. 1994), and I agree that comparative histories have a home-court advantage in this respect, even if case studies and histories have an even greater advantage. But this is testing of hypotheses about each case. What is missing is extensive comparative testing of more general propositions that apply not to just one case but rather to all of the cases in the sample and to the larger population that the sample represents.

The only solution to this problem is to test the propositions that emerge from a comparative history with a different set of cases. In principle, it would be possible for a comparative historian or a team of comparative historians to work out a model in one sample and then test its implications in a different, sufficiently large, and fairly selected sample. A few comparative histories seem to do this, including Moore (1966), Skocpol (1979), and Rueschemeyer and colleagues (1992). However, the fifth and final problem with comparative history is that its practitioners keep amending the theory while the testing is going on. If the theory building never stops, the testing cannot begin. *Capitalist Development and Democracy*, for example, could be said to develop its hypotheses in Western Europe and then test them in Latin America and the Caribbean. However, the authors modify their core thesis when applying it to South America, where, it turns out, the middle class sometimes played a more important role in democratization than the working class did. By making this amendment, the authors used the South American cases to develop new theory instead of testing the theory they already had. One of the better comparative-testing efforts is Ruth Collier's *Paths toward Democracy* (1999), most of which is an out-of-sample test of the Rueschemeyer, Stephens, and Stephens (1992) thesis that the working class played a leading role in democratization. She finds the thesis wrong in a great many cases, and this is a fine test. However, this is the exception that proves the rule because Collier then proceeds as do other comparative historians: she amends the hypothesis drastically by defining seven distinct patterns of democratization, speculates about their possible causes, and never tests them all systematically or with different cases.

The logic of comparison for extensive testing is weak in comparative histories. Most of their value for testing lies in the individual case studies, and even these are inferior to case studies and histories. As a method for generating hunches and building theory, comparative history may well be the best of both worlds. But with respect to extensive testing, it is the worst of both worlds.

Nevertheless, comparative histories have made many contributions to the study of democratization. They have unearthed relevant descriptive information, or at least brought it to the attention of nonhistorians. They have developed highly plausible explanations for the unique democratization paths taken by major countries. They have called attention to macro or structural factors, such as class conflict, technological change, international events, and war, that case study authors may have downplayed or taken for granted. They have cumulatively developed a framework or metatheory in which the material interests of rising social classes spur conflict that culminates in the achievement of democracy. Comparative histories may have left the extensive testing to others, but they have played a leading role in theory building.

Appendix

This appendix summarizes the arguments and outcomes of the major comparative-historical studies of democratization in tabular form. Each column of a table corresponds to one of the outcomes being explained; each row corresponds to the combination of explanatory factors that allegedly explain the outcome in a case or set of cases. The counts of the number of cases in each cell were used to calculate the probabilities in Table 5.1. Fisher's test sums the probabilities associated with all of the other possible tables with the same dimensions and the same number of cases that show a stronger association between the causes and effects. Conventionally, if this sum of probabilities is less than 0.05, we can feel confident in rejecting the possibility that the apparent association was a chance result.

Table 5A.1. Summary of arguments and outcomes in Skocpol (1979)

Causal conditions	Social revolution	No social revolution	N
ULBCAtrISMV	France		1
UlBCAtrISMV	Russia		1
ULBCatrISmv		China (by 1911)	1
UlBCATRiSMv		Prussia (west of Elbe)	1
UlBCATRismv		Prussia (east of Elbe)	
UlBcAtrIsmv		Japan	1
ULbcATRIsmv		England	1
N	2	4	6

Note: Capital letters indicate the condition was present; lower-case letters indicate the condition was absent.

U: There was a powerful, landed upper class.

L: The upper class had leverage over the state.

B: The state was semi- or highly bureaucratic.

C: The state was centralized.

A: Agricultural productivity was increasing.

T: There was a transition to capitalist agriculture.

R: The transition to capitalist agriculture included core regions.

I: International pressures were at least moderate.

S: Smallholding peasants own at least 30 percent of the land.

M: There is a strong peasant community.

V: Villages are fairly autonomous from central control.

Source: Skocpol (1979), parts A and B of table 1, pp. 155–156.

Table 5A.2. Summary of arguments and outcomes about the timing of initial democratization in Latin America in Rueschemeyer, Stephens, and Stephens (1992)

Causal conditions	None	Early	Medium	Late	N
No export expansion, labor-intensive agriculture, state incorporation, late industrialization	Paraguay				1
Export expansion into labor-intensive agriculture, state incorporation, medium timing of industrialization			Brazil		1
Export expansion into labor-intensive agriculture, incorporation by clientelistic parties, late industrialization			Colombia	Ecuador	2
Export expansion into non-labor-intensive agriculture, incorporation by clientelistic parties, early industrialization		Argentina, Uruguay			2
Mineral exports, incorporation by radical mass parties, medium timing of industrialization		Chile			1
Mineral exports, incorporation by radical mass parties, late industrialization			Peru, Venezuela	Bolivia	3
Mineral exports, revolution, early industrialization	Mexico				1
N	2	3	4	2	11

Source: Author's interpretation of Rueschemeyer, Stephens, and Stephens (1992), table 5.1, p. 164, and the surrounding text.

Table 5A.3. Summary of arguments and outcomes about Europe in Rueschemeyer, Stephens, and Stephens (1992)

Causal conditions	Authoritarian breakdown	Democratic survival	N
LABDr	Germany, Austria		2
LAbdr	Italy	Australia	2
LABdr	Spain		1
LAbdR		United States	1
LabdR		Britain	1
labdR		France	1
labdr		Small European countries, Canada, New Zealand	3
N	4	7	11

Note: Capital letters indicate the condition was present; lower-case letters indicate the condition was absent.

L: The landed upper class was politically very significant.

A: The landed upper class was historically engaged in labor-repressive agriculture.

B: The bourgeoisie was strong enough to be politically very significant but not more powerful than the landed upper class.

D: The bourgeoisie was the dependent partner in the coalition.

R: There was a revolutionary break from the past.

For the Fisher test, I treated the small European countries as a single case because the authors do not differentiate them.

Source: Rueschemeyer, Stephens, and Stephens (1992), table 4.4, p. 144.

Table 5A.4. Summary of the impact of party system types on coups from Collier and Collier (1991)

Type of party system	Coup	No coup	N
Integrative	Mexico, Venezuela		2
Electorally stable but socially conflictual	Colombia	Uruguay	2
Stalemated		Peru, Argentina	2
Multiparty polarizing		Brazil, Chile	2
N	3	5	8

Note: This is just one argument from Collier and Collier's (1991) analysis of the Heritage period, but it is the one that is most relevant for democratization. Their work advances many other arguments about the Heritage period and the preceding Reform, Incorporation, and Aftermath periods.

Table 5A.5. Summary of arguments and outcomes from Downing (1992)

Causal conditions	Military-bureaucratic absolutism	Loss of sovereignty	Preservation of constitutionalism	N
High warfare, high domestic military mobilization	Brandenburg-Prussia, France			2
High warfare, low domestic military mobilization		Poland		1
Low warfare, low domestic military mobilization			England to 1648	1
High warfare, medium domestic military mobilization aided by wealth, alliances, and geography			England 1688–1713, the Netherlands	2
High warfare, low military mobilization but aided by access to foreign resources			Sweden	1
N	2	1	4	7

Source: Downing (1992), table 2, p. 242.

Table 5A.6. Summary of arguments and outcomes in Ertman (1997)

Causal conditions	Patrimonial absolutism	Bureaucratic constitutionalism	Bureaucratic absolutism	Patrimonial constitutionalism	N
Geopolitical competition before 1450, administrative local government	France, Spain, Portugal, Naples, Tuscany, Savoy, and Papal States				7
Geopolitical competition before 1450, participatory local government, active parliament		Britain			1
Geopolitical competition after 1450, administrative local government			German states		1
Geopolitical competition after 1450, participatory local government		Sweden	Denmark	Hungary and Poland	4
N	7	2	2	2	13

Source: This is the simple model presented early in the introduction to Ertman's (1997) book. By the end of the chapter, however, Ertman revised the model by distinguishing among parliaments that were weak (Denmark), parliaments that were initially strong but later weakened (Sweden), and parliaments that were strong and remained strong (Hungary and Poland). This change associated each set of causal conditions with a unique outcome. However, expanding the table from 4×4 to 7×4 cells does not improve the significance of the "test."

Table 5A.7. Summary of arguments and outcomes in Luebbert (1987)

Causal conditions	Pluralist democracy	Social democracy	Traditional dictatorship	Fascism	N
Early industrialization, dominant liberal parties, Liberal-Labor coalitions, and mass support for democracy	Britain, France, Switzerland				3
Late industrialization, greater Socialist Party success, previously mobilized agricultural sector		the Netherlands, Belgium, Denmark, Sweden, Norway, Czechoslovakia			6
Late industrialization, greater Socialist Party success, socialist recruitment of agricultural proletariat, united bourgeois parties			Austria, Finland, Hungary		3
Late industrialization, greater Socialist Party success, socialist recruitment of agricultural proletariat, divided bourgeois parties				Germany, Italy, Spain	3
N	3	6	3	3	15

Source: Author's synthesis of arguments in Luebbert (1987, 1991).

Table 5A.8. Summary of arguments and outcomes in Moore (1966)

Causal conditions	Democracy	Fascism	Communism	Peaceful change	N
Commercialized agriculture, strong bourgeoisie allied with reformist landed upper class, peasantry weakened	Britain				1
Commercialized agriculture, strong bourgeois impulse, peasants sweep aside landed upper class	France				1
Commercialized agriculture, strong bourgeois impulse, no peasantry	United States				1
Commercialized agriculture, moderately powerful bourgeoisie allied with landed upper class		Japan			1
Commercialized agriculture, weak bourgeoisie, landed upper class swept away by peasant revolution			Russia, China		2
Little commercialization of agriculture				India	1
N	3	1	2	1	7

Note: Because there have been many conflicting interpretations of Moore's arguments, I relied on his own simple summary in the preface: Moore (1966). I excluded Germany because Moore devotes no separate chapter to it and included India because there is a chapter on it. Chi-square results for this table would be significant if the first three rows were collapsed into one. I did not do this because Moore takes care to differentiate the British, French, and American paths; he would not be comfortable lumping them all together as similar cases of commercialized agriculture with a strong bourgeois impulse, ignoring the role of the peasantry.

6 Formal models and theories

The approaches discussed in previous chapters – checklists, frameworks, case studies, and comparative history – can generate theory. However, they do so in a mostly inductive way, by generalizing from observations. Scholars working inductively stay close to what they observe whether they are defining concepts, developing theories, laying out a framework, generating hypotheses, or performing tests. The alternative is to work deductively, starting from fundamental axioms and using logic or mathematics to derive hypotheses (which can then be subjected to tests). Deduction and induction sound like opposites in principle, but in practice any attempt at theorizing must do some of both. Observation is impossible without a preexisting set of concepts, a rudimentary theory that tells one what to observe; and deductive theories are always inspired to some extent by real-world cases. Nevertheless, scholars differ in the importance they attribute to the deductive and inductive stages of the theory-building process. Those who emphasize the deductive stages can be said to work with formal models and theories.[1]

Some formal theorists are critical of the more inductive approaches. In fact, some – probably a minority – claim that only deductive theories qualify as theory at all; they demote other general propositions to the lesser status of atheoretical empirical generalizations (Green and Shapiro 1994, quoting Riker, Bueno de Mesquita, and Achen and Snidal). This stance inflates the value of deduction and devalues the inductive processes required for building any good theory. However, formal models have two characteristics that make them different from, if not better than, other sorts of theory. First, formal models have clear and explicit assumptions. They have to; without premises, it would be impossible to derive implications. Stating assumptions explicitly makes it possible for other scholars to see the relationship between one study and another as a sort of tree diagram. The assumptions they share locate their origins on the same trunk or branch; the different assumptions they

---

[1] The distinction between theories and models is developed more in Chapter 3.

make push them out onto different branches and twigs. Explicit assumptions therefore provide a way to achieve theoretical integration. Lacking this guidance, the more inductive approaches are harder to integrate. They end up with conclusions that are confined to provisionally bounded temporal-spatial domains that rarely coincide perfectly with the domains of other studies. Second, formal models also have a heuristic: a hypothesis-generating procedure that is logically rigorous, or truth preserving. It allows the theorist to say with perfect confidence what must be true if the model is true. It is invaluable for generating hypotheses for testing the model.

Rational-choice theory – a subset of formal theory, but a dominant subset among formal theories in comparative politics[2] – has the additional characteristic of focusing on the intentions of actors. Defenders of rational-choice theory often argue that politics is an inherently goal-driven activity. Therefore, only theories that call attention to actors and their goals – the microfoundations of politics – can possibly capture the essence of politics. My own view is that any political theory that ignores intentional actors is merely incomplete, not entirely wrong, just as any political theory that ignores culture or institutions is incomplete.[3] But it is true that no approach pays as much attention to actors and their intentions as rational-choice theory.

Integration

The most distinctive methodological virtue of formal modeling is its emphasis on theoretical integration: making necessary connections among the propositions constituting a theory (Lalman et al. 1993). We have already seen that checklists have no integration, frameworks are only partially integrated, and case studies and comparative histories are only very loosely and uncertainly integrated. In Chapter 9, we will see that the large-sample, statistical approach does not demand that the hypotheses it tests come from a well integrated theory. However, whether formal modeling is actually an integrated approach depends on whether one is referring to one theorist's model or the approach as a collective effort. The propositions of each model are indeed well

---

[2] Agent-based modeling is one example of formal theorizing that is not rational-choice theory (Miller 2007). There are few applications to democratization research, however.

[3] Advocates of microfoundational theory may object that they can offer a complete, albeit trivial, explanation because all of the causal forces are ultimately channeled through the choices of individuals. But my definition of thickness in Chapter 3 includes depth: tracing the chain of causation far back from its eventual effect. By that standard, a purely microfoundational explanation is far from complete.

Moderates ally with:

		Radical opposition	Reformist rulers
Reformist rulers ally with:	Hard-liners	Existing authoritarianism 2, 1	Authoritarianism with concessions 4, 2
	Moderate opposition	Democracy without guarantees to old regime 1, 4	Democracy with guarantees 3, 3

Figure 6.1   Przeworski's Extrication Game. *Source:* Adapted from Przeworski (1991), table 2.1, p. 69.

integrated, but only a few models are integrated with other models. These models are icebergs floating in a sea of theory.

There are important benefits in the integration of the propositions in a single model. Formal models achieve internal integration by using game theory, logic, or other mathematics to derive predictions from their initial assumptions. A good example of game theory is Przeworski's analysis of strategizing by a moderate opposition and some reformers within an authoritarian regime (Przeworski 1991, 67–79). Przeworski assumes that each actor could ally only with an adjacent actor – the reformers with either the hard-liners or the moderate opposition, and the moderate opposition with either the radical opposition or the reformers in the regime. The regime outcomes associated with each choice, and the associated payoffs for each actor, are shown in Figure 6.1. In the conventions of strategic-form games, the first payoff in each cell is for the row player (reformist rulers) and the second is for the column player (moderate opposition). Which payoff each player receives is determined by the choices they both make.

Assuming full information ("everyone knows everything and everyone knows the same") (Przeworski 1991, 62) and an unrepeatable game of simultaneous moves without communication, Przeworski derives the conclusion that both actors would rationally choose the upper-right outcome – authoritarianism with concessions. The moderates anticipate that if they ally with the radicals, hoping for their highest payoff (4), the reformers would ally with the

hard-liners, improving their payoff from 1 to 2. However, the reformers anticipate that if they ally with the hard-liners, hoping for the authoritarianism-
with-concessions payoff (4), the moderates will not prefer an alliance with
the radicals because this would reduce their payoff from 2 to 1. Of course, the
moderates would be better off with democracy with guarantees (3), but as
long as the reformers ally with the hard-liners, this option is not available to
the moderates. The moderates know that the reformers could make authoritarianism with concessions stick, and the reformers know that the moderates
know that they could make it stick, so both actors settle on authoritarianism
with concessions. Therefore, Przeworski concludes, there will be no transition
given these players' rankings of the regime outcomes and payoffs associated
with them.

Acemoglu and Robinson's *Economic Origins of Dictatorship and Democracy*
(2001) is a good example of mathematical deduction. They write equations in
which the incomes of the elite and the poor are functions of taxation, transfer
payments, the degree of inequality, the growth rate, and other variables. Taxes
represent a net gain for the poor because taxes fund transfer payments that
are distributed equally to all, and for the same reason taxes are a net loss for
the rich. When the poor govern (i.e., a democracy), they set the tax rate high;
the elite could lead a coup to take over the government, but a coup is costly
and risky. When the elite govern (i.e., a nondemocracy), they keep taxes low;
the poor could lead a revolution, but a revolution is also costly and risky. The
expected gains and losses from coups and revolutions enter into each actor's
calculations. This allows Acemoglu and Robinson to predict that the poor will
lead a democratic revolution against a nondemocracy when (simplifying a bit)
the economic benefits of expropriating the elite, raising taxes, and increasing
transfer payments outweigh the expected costs of carrying out a revolution.
The elite will lead a coup against the poor when the economic benefits of
lowering taxes and preventing further expropriations outweigh the expected
costs of a coup. The theory also links the marginal probability of transitions
and breakdowns to observable conditions by making these costs and benefits
depend on growth rates, degrees of inequality, and other economic factors.

There is a big difference, however, between the degree of integration
achieved within models and the degree achieved among models. Rational-
choice theory as a whole is far less integrated than the models that constitute
it. Nevertheless, this approach is the democratization literature's best illustration of the process of constructing an integrated theory. An integrated theory
begins with a set of simplifying assumptions that (to some scholars, at least)
seem to be insights into some fundamental truths about politics. A group of

scholars dedicates itself to exploring the implications of these assumptions for some political phenomenon of interest. The number of propositions entertained in this emerging approach grows in three different ways. First, some scholars elaborate pure theory: they progressively relax some of the overly simple assumptions and then rigorously derive the implications of this more complex set of axioms. This activity builds the core of the theory, and it does so in a "truth-preserving" way that guarantees strict integration. The core theory is often still simplistic and not testable. Nevertheless, theory development continues in the hope that eventually, when the core theory becomes sufficiently complex, it will become a reasonable approximation of reality.

Second, theory grows by what I call modeling: attempts to build bridges between the core theory and reality. Modelers selectively interpret real-world cases so that the theory seems to apply to them, and they add to or revise propositions in the theory so that it does a better job of fitting the case or cases at hand. Modeling helps develop propositions in the periphery of the theory that are tentatively plausible under certain circumstances. Modeling also lends credibility to the core theory by confirming the pure theorists' faith that the approach possesses the potential to approximate reality.

Third, theory cumulates as a result of systematic testing. Scholars derive testable hypotheses from their theories – things that must be true if the theory is true – and systematically gather and analyze evidence to see whether or not the hypotheses are consistent with the evidence. If the evidence is consistent, it strengthens scholars' confidence in the theoretical propositions from which the hypothesis was derived. If the evidence is inconsistent, it weakens confidence in the theory and spurs a new round of theoretical innovation.

Have formal theories and models of democratization developed into a well-integrated body of theory? Beyond the shared traits that make them formal – clear definitions of the actors, their goals, the choices they face, and the use of deductive logic (Geddes 2003) – formal models of democratization are surprisingly disjointed. In other areas, such as models of legislative behavior, formal theory is actually well integrated, but for models of democratization, integration is still a mostly unrealized goal, and some think it always will be:

The greatest achievement of rational choice theory has been to provide tools for studying political outcomes in stable institutional settings. But in moments of transition, rules are ill-defined and symbols, emotions, and rhetoric seem to count for more than do interests, calculations, and guile. . . . Political transitions seem to defy rational forms of analysis. (Bates et al. 1998, 604–5)

To be fair, formal models of democracy are in their infancy: the first serious effort was published only in 1991. It is possible that one of the early efforts discussed in this chapter will blossom into a dominant theory that will subsume or marginalize all the others, leaving us with a well-integrated core theory. For this to happen, such a theory would have to provide an explanation for events that were not well explained by other theories, in addition to explaining all of the events that other theories had covered well. In fact, I argue here that theories descended from Carles Boix's *Democracy and Redistribution* (2003) and Acemoglu and Robinson's *Economic Origins of Dictatorship and Democracy* (2006) are likely to become dominant in this approach, although more testing is certainly needed.

Rational-choice models are elaborate arguments from analogy: they assert a fundamental similarity between a simple, abstract formal model and real-world political or economic situations. These models are vulnerable to the weakness of all analogies: for those who do not perceive the similarities and therefore reject the analogy, the entire analysis is irrelevant. This quality of rational choice has divided many political scientists into two camps – those who accept such models as similar enough to reality to be useful versus those who do not. The two camps have been surprisingly uninterested in debating whether the formal analogies are apt. Those who propose models tend to feel that accurate description is not the point, and critics tend to see no point in engaging with models that strike them as inherently wrongheaded. This is a tragic situation because all models, formal or not, are based on analogies and share this vulnerability. It is incumbent on everyone to persuade others that their models are the appropriate ones for each application.

My view is that this is partly an empirical task because it is a matter of establishing that the assumptions of one's model are reasonable simplifications, as discussed in Chapter 3. Doing this may be harder for formal models because the assumptions are starkly simple and therefore farther removed from messy reality. But whether these models capture the features of the situation that best predict outcomes is an empirical question. It is desirable for assumptions to be plausible. In economics, David Kreps notes, "game theory has succeeded when it begins from a common-sense observation and takes a few small steps further along" (Kreps 1990, 88). If the assumptions are not plausible, then it is all the more important to gather evidence to make sure that they are not false. Who are the powerful actors and what are their motives? What kinds of choices face them? How much information do they have? Do they choose simultaneously or sequentially? Once or repeatedly? These are fair questions. If the model is descriptively false, it makes no difference whether or not it predicts correctly. If it is a reasonable approximation of the situation, then further testing is required to see whether its predictions are true. The big question about this approach, then, is whether formal models and theories of democratization make reasonable assumptions and accurate predictions.

There are two schools of formal theory about democratization.[4] Each makes a different assumption about the kinds of actors that struggle to define the regime and what their goals are. The first is what I call the positional school. It assumes that the actors think about political regimes as ends in themselves. They usually rank the possible regime types in a preference ordering, and their preferences and position in the existing regime defines who they are – hard-liners, soft-liners, opposition, and so forth. The second school I call the economic school. It defines the actors according to their economic resources – usually a wealthy elite versus poor nonelite – and assumes that the actors ultimately want to defend or improve their economic interests. Political regimes are assumed to affect economic interests in various ways, so actors prefer the regime that best serves their economic interests. The crucial difference with positional models is that this regime preference is merely instrumental: a means to the actor's ultimate economic ends. Both approaches grew out of earlier, nonformal theories of democratization. The positional school formalizes and extends many of the arguments made first in the O'Donnell and Schmitter volume of the *Transitions from Authoritarian Rule* project (O'Donnell et al. 1986). The economic school elaborates on Dahl's argument in *Polyarchy* that polyarchy arises when the costs of repression exceed the costs of toleration (Dahl 1971). Dahl may not have intended these costs to have been literal economic costs, but it is understandable that some scholars would interpret them that way.

It is tempting to view these as models of different processes: economic models concerned with the long-term trends that include preparation, transition, and survival, and positional models concerned only with the short-term transition phase. Indeed, the examples that these authors adduce suggest this distinction. However, there is nothing in the economic models themselves that restricts their applicability to the long term because they do not distinguish between stages of democratization. I therefore treat them as having the same purpose.

---

[4] There are many other possible ways to categorize works in this approach – by the kind of game being played, the number of actors, the options available to them, the stage of democratization, the nature of rationality, the degree of formalization, and so on. I have chosen the nature of the actors and their goals as the most fundamental divide because it is the most substantively interesting difference and because it groups together the best-integrated set of works – those assuming that economic interests are at stake.

I find the economic theories to be only marginally plausible. It is not at all clear, for example, that democracies are actually better at redistributing wealth; if there is a difference, it is a marginal or conditional one. I see democratization as a struggle over power: the power to set tax rates and become wealthy, to be sure, but also the power to start or end wars, to govern oneself, to choose competent and trustworthy leaders, to be free of arbitrary punishments, to live with respect and dignity and without fear. Distribution policy is, in my view, an important but small piece of what is at stake in democratization. In this sense, my view of the world comes closer to the positional school. However, I am not willing to dismiss the economic theories as false. They are in the ballpark of reasonable simplifications, but whether they are the best of all possible reasonable simplifications must be decided by the accuracy of their predictions. The conclusion of this chapter is that the economic models work better than I would have expected but that more testing is needed.

The following sections of this chapter give an overview of the assumptions and conclusions of the most similar subschools within these two main schools. In the positional school, I discuss models of liberalization and then models of transition and/or survival, which I subdivide according to the number of actors involved. Following these long sections, I summarize the economic school, which makes more uniform assumptions about the number of actors and the stage of democratization to be explained. Table 6.1 outlines the relationships among these submodels and sub-submodels and identifies the major works in each one. The chapter concludes with a critique of the benefits and limitations of formal theory for understanding democratization and some speculation about the future prospects for this approach.

Positional models of liberalization

Although formal models in the positional school do not always explicitly acknowledge their debt to *Transitions from Authoritarian Rule* (O'Donnell and Schmitter 1986), the shared concepts, assumptions, and arguments make their intellectual lineage unmistakable. Like O'Donnell and Schmitter, almost all of these theorists assume that political liberalization must precede democratization; that liberalization becomes possible only when a split develops between the hard-line rulers who favor continued nondemocratic rule and soft-line rulers who do not want democracy but favor a more open nondemocratic regime; that members of an opposition must decide whether to

Table 6.1. Formal models of democratization

I. The positional school
  A. Models of liberalization
  (Crescenzi 1999; Kuran 1989, 1991; Lohmann 1994; Marks 1992; Przeworski 1986;
  Przeworski 1991; Zielinski 1995)
  B. Models of transition and survival
    1. Unitary rulers versus unitary opposition
    (Sutter 1995; Swaminathan 1999)
      a. With a foreign actor: (Sutter 1995)
    2. With one actor subdivided
      a. Unitary opposition vs. divided rulers
        (1) Hard-liners, soft-liners, opposition: (Crescenzi 1999; Zielinski 1999)
      b. Unitary rulers versus divided opposition
        (1) Defender, challenger, mass public: (Casper and Taylor 1996)
        (2) Sovereign, citizens A, citizens B: (Weingast 1997)
    3. With both actors subdivided
      a. Hard-liners, reformers, radicals, moderates: (Przeworski 1991)
      b. Radical and moderate factions of hard-liners, soft-liners, and opposition:
      (Colomer 1991, 2000)
II. The economic school
  A. About breakdown, involving radical and moderate factions of left and right:
  (Cohen 1994)
  B. All about transitions and/or survival, all involving two actors, rich and poor:
  (Acemoglu and Robinson 2001; Acemoglu and Robinson 2006; Boix 2003; Feng and Zak
  1999; Gould and Maggio 2007; Rosendorff 2001; Zak and Feng 2003)
    1. With a third actor (a middle class) and consideration of capital mobility: (Boix 2003)

collaborate with the rulers or protest their rule; and that the rulers must decide whether to open up the regime or repress the opposition. Also, in almost all of these models, strategic choices must be made by both sides: the rulers' choice depends on whether repression would end the protests, and the opposition's decision to protest depends in part on what impact the protests would have on regime change. The difference between O'Donnell and Schmitter's analysis and the formal models of liberalization is that O'Donnell and Schmitter opened the door to so many complex and dynamic possibilities that it became impossible for them to reach a definite conclusion. Their framework was wonderfully descriptive, even poetic at times, but it led them to conclude that transitions were full of uncertainty and inherently unpredictable. Formal theorists simplify more radically, permitting fewer possibilities, so that they can derive definite predictions.

Each model focuses on one of two submodels, or both: a submodel between hard-line and soft-line rulers and a submodel within the opposition. Typically, they then bring these analyses together in a metagame to deduce what the rulers would do given the most likely choice of the opposition, and what the opposition would do given the most likely choice of the rulers. If rulers and opposition would agree on the same combination of opening or repression and cooperation or protest, then the metagame has an equilibrium. The equilibrium is the expected outcome, according to these models.

The models of liberalization make different assumptions about the submodels that lead to different answers to a key question: Why would authoritarian rulers ever initiate a political opening? In the rulers' submodel, the simplest assumption is made by Crescenzi (1999), who states that Nature chooses (i.e., the players inherit a state of affairs they cannot influence) whether the regime is a hard-line regime that will repress or a soft-line regime that will tolerate opposition protests. There is no strategy involved in this submodel, which does not derive an answer so much as assume one. Przeworski (1991) has the soft-liners (i.e., liberalizers) decide whether to ally with the hard-liners or to open toward the opposition. In this strategic situation, Przeworski argues, the soft-liners would not lead an opening unless they knew that the opposition would accept their goal, a broadened dictatorship. Marks (1992), which is so faithful to O'Donnell and Schmitter's volume that it can be considered a formalization of the *Transitions* framework, models the bargaining between hard-liners and soft-liners as a game of "chicken". Because disagreements between armed forces can be fatal, both factions would prefer mutual agreement to any disagreement. The prediction of this model is that if the hard-liners are stronger or have more intense preferences, the soft-liners will go along with repression; but, if the soft-liners are stronger or have more intense preferences, the hard-liners will go along with toleration.

The central question of the opposition submodel is: Why would citizens ever protest during authoritarian rule, even in response to what seems to be an opening? Most of the theorists deal with this as a collective-action problem: How can each citizen know whether enough other citizens will join the protest to ensure safety in numbers? Przeworski argues that citizens would not protest until some sort of signal occurred that increased their confidence that many others would protest and that protest would not be successfully repressed. He gives examples of such signals (the imminent death of a dictator, a looming economic crisis, or strong foreign pressures), but his model leaves it up to the historical context to determine the kind of signal that would be effective (Przeworski 1986). Marks (1992) provides a more specific, although not more helpful, answer: the signal is a critical number of protesters. If protests (presumably by unusually daring citizens who are not acting rationally) reach a critical mass, it becomes rational for all citizens to join them. However, Marks also argues that if a higher critical threshold were reached, the protests would provoke a backlash from the regime, in which case it would be rational for everyone to stay at home. Not knowing what these critical thresholds are, it is hard for us to make a prediction. Lohmann (1994), analyzing turnout in East German protests in 1953 and 1989–1990, provides a more helpful answer.[5] She recasts the opposition submodel as a signaling game in which every citizen was both a sender and a receiver of messages about the depth of discontent with the regime. She argues that the signal is not aggregate turnout but rather the gap between actual and expected turnout and the kind of citizens who turn out. Citizens discount protests that appear to be organized or that involve people who are likely to protest with little provocation. They take more seriously any protest by those who are less likely to protest, especially when it seems to happen spontaneously. Early spontaneous turnout of moderates sends a strong signal that discontent is widespread, and this encourages others to join.

In the metagame, Przeworski (1991) lays out an extended-form (sequential) game in which (1) the soft-liners liberalize (or not); (2) the opposition cooperates with broadened dictatorship or mobilizes in protest; and, if the opposition mobilizes, then (3) the soft-liners either repress (successfully or not) or become prodemocratic reformers (Figure 6.2). He argues that because the soft-liners would not sponsor an opening if it was likely to lead to democracy, a transition is possible only if the soft-liners miscalculate (about the opposition's willingness to acquiesce in a broadened dictatorship or about the rulers' chances of repressing successfully) or secretly are, or subsequently become, sincere advocates of full democracy (in which case they were not, or ceased to be, liberalizers).[6] Marks (1992) reaches a more optimistic conclusion than Przeworski's in which liberalization can happen without an accident or a change of heart. First, he finds that there are some nonstrategic situations in which the rulers would always tolerate or always repress, regardless of how the opposition behaves. Second, he identifies three strategic situations

---

[5] Lohmann's model is similar to a more influential and somewhat earlier model by Timur Kuran (1989, 1991).

[6] In a somewhat different analysis, Zielinski (1999) applied reasoning like Przeworski's to different actors: the Soviet Union and a government, instead of hard-liners and soft-liners. This was probably a useful shift in focus for understanding his case – Poland in the 1980s. His conclusion was that the less likely a Soviet intervention was, the more likely an opening became.

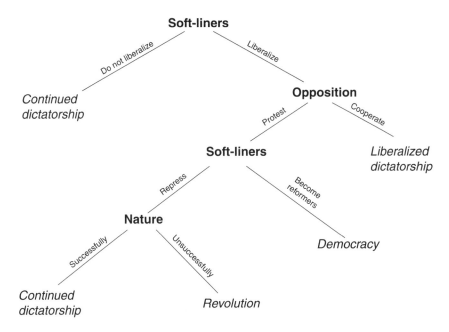

Figure 6.2   Przeworski's Extended-Form Game of Liberalization

in which the rulers would eventually decide to tolerate rather than repress. In one of these situations, the opposition's determination to resist repression leads the ruler to tolerate. In the second situation, the ruler's willingness to answer protest with repression persuades the opposition to acquiesce to a liberalized dictatorship. The third situation is a prisoner's dilemma that would normally lead to violence. However, if both actors foresee a long struggle and value liberalization much more than violence, they can both compromise on a liberalized dictatorship.

Models of liberalization provide answers that are interesting but not entirely satisfying. For example, why does a split develop between hard-liners and soft-liners? Crescenzi assumes an answer, Przeworski all but proves that any liberalization would contradict his model, and Zielinski (1995) appeals to a deus ex machina – the Soviet Union. Marks's chicken game is the most sophisticated answer, but even this answer starts from the assumption that hard-liners and soft-liners already exist and have different goals, so the origins and the nature of the split are assumed, not explained. And what makes it rational for citizens to protest against a dictatorship? The notion of a signal is intuitively appealing, but Przeworski's ideas about signaling are vague, Marks's are circular, and Lohmann's cannot be applied beyond the now-extinct East Germany without additional interpretive effort. However, it would be too harsh to dismiss these efforts. Every model is incomplete in some way, and every deductive theory has to start with assumptions of some kind. These models tell us when a hard-liner and soft-liner split would lead to liberalization and when it would lead to more repression. The job of explaining how the split arises can be left to other works and other scholars. This upstream integration has not yet been done for models of liberalization. However, as the following section shows, there has been downstream integration linking models of liberalization to models of transition and survival.

Positional models of transition and survival

In the positional school, the existing models of transition and survival appear to be integrated in an upstream-downstream hierarchy. Farthest upstream are the simple models with just two actors – a ruler and the opposition. Downstream there are more complex models with a ruler facing two opposition subactors, some with a single opposition facing two ruling subactors (the familiar hard-liners and soft-liners), and a couple of models with ruling subactors facing opposition subactors. The logic of the hierarchy, then, is that the downstream models relax the assumption that one of the upstream actors is unitary. This allows the downstream model to explore a submodel within the opposition or ruling camp, bringing each downstream model progressively closer to the complexity of real-world politics. However, this hierarchy is interrupted. The links among models are broken by the idiosyncratic assumptions made in each model that remove it from the most direct line of descent. The genealogy linking these formal models lacks direct parent-child relationships; instead, it is a spotty genealogy containing only great-aunts, third cousins, and other distant relations.

The basic sequential game is the same in the two-actor models (Sutter 1995; Swaminathan 1999). A unitary opposition either challenges the ruler or acquiesces in nondemocratic rule. If the opposition challenges, the ruler can either surrender or repress. If the ruler represses, there is some probability (a lottery, in formal-theory jargon) that the opposition will win and a transition will happen; otherwise, nondemocratic rule continues.[7]

---

[7] Although the logic is the same, the authors use different terminologies. Sutter (1995) calls the ruler the dictator, defines his choices as fighting or abdicating, and allows the opposition to rebel or accept dictatorship. Swaminathan (1999) calls the ruler the government, defines his choices as negotiating or not, and allows the opposition to mobilize or not.

At this point, each model adds wrinkles that make it unique. Swaminathan (1999) assumes that the power of the ruler is constantly declining and that of the opposition is constantly increasing. Given this assumption, a transition is inevitable. The only questions are when it will happen and whether or not it will be peaceful. In Sutter's (1995) model, the opposition can choose to negotiate rather than challenge or acquiesce, and the crucial consideration is not risk aversion but rather how generous a deal the opposition can offer the ruler in exchange for abdication. If the ruler would prefer such a deal to losing a costly struggle to stay in power, he or she will negotiate the terms of abdication. The possibility of the ruler retaking power after abdication helps ensure that the opposition will honor the terms of the deal. Sutter also introduces a third actor, a foreign power, which can offer the ruler asylum in case of abdication. He finds that the possibility of asylum would improve the chances of a transition if the ruler would accept it. However, the foreign power has little reason not to renege on the offer, so the dictator is less likely to accept, which in effect narrows the opposition's choices to negotiating or fighting. The conclusions of these models hinge crucially on the extra assumptions they make, which prevent us from integrating them into a single theory. Without deriving new models, we cannot say whether Sutter's conclusions depend on the actors' tolerance of risk or how Swaminathan's ruler would respond to the prospects of going into exile or getting a share of the former opposition's spoils of office. This is less integration than one would expect from formal theory.

Moving downstream, we encounter some three-actor games involving the opposition and two ruling subactors: the hard-liners and soft-liners.[8] The crucial element in both games is how various actors cope with uncertainty about how other actors are likely to respond. Crescenzi (1999) focuses on the opposition's uncertainty about whether it is dealing with a hard-line or soft-line regime (which is determined by Nature, as mentioned previously). The opposition updates its beliefs about whether hard-liners or soft-liners are in control based on any liberalization that is adopted. Without liberalization, the opposition will conclude that the rulers are hard-liners and will acquiesce. However, a pacted transition can occur if the rulers liberalize, the opposition negotiates with them, and the rulers turn out to be soft-liners. A revolutionary transition can occur if the rulers liberalize, the opposition tries to negotiate but is rebuffed, and then the opposition radicalizes and (if it is strong enough) wins a violent struggle. Zielinski (1999) models a negotiation between the

---

[8] If I were to push the genealogy analogy, these models would be cousins of a nephew of the Sutter and Swaminathan models.

soft-liners and the opposition over the degree of reform, on a continuum ranging from the status quo through liberalization to transition. In his model, it is the soft-liners who are uncertain: in this case, about whether the hard-liners will ratify a deal struck with the opposition or intervene to reimpose a dictatorship. As long as the soft-liners accurately gauge the limits of the hard-liners' tolerance, they can use the threat of a hard-liner intervention to induce the opposition to support a soft-liner degree of reform. But if the soft-liners misjudge the hard-liners' intentions, their reform agreement will be overturned and dictatorship will continue.[9]

A different path downstream leads to models that retain a unitary ruler but subdivide the opposition. However, these authors subdivide the opposition in different ways. Casper and Taylor (1996) have the rulers (i.e., the defender) face off against a challenger and the mass public, whereas Weingast (1997) pits the ruler (i.e., the sovereign) against two undifferentiated groups of citizens, A and B. Because neither group can be equated with Casper and Taylor's challenger or their mass public, the two models are not really integrated with each other; all they have in common is the assumption that the ruler is unitary and the opposition is not.

In Casper and Taylor's model, there is a familiar process in which the opposition either challenges or backs down and the rulers either give in or repress.[10] The chief difference of this model is that within the opposition there is a mass public that mediates the contest between the rulers and the challenger. The more the mass public signals its support for democracy, the greater the bargaining leverage the challenger can wield. On the basis of this mass public reaction, the rulers and challenger update their perceptions of their strength and a new round of negotiation begins. This stage ends when either rulers and challenger agree or one of them ends negotiations to pursue a violent solution. Transition becomes unlikely when the rulers repress early on, silencing the mass public's cues. Transition is possible when strengths are initially evenly matched. The rulers recognize early on that they cannot stop the mass public from supporting the challenger, so they compromise, negotiating rules to protect themselves after the transition. These are success-ful transitions, but according to Casper and Taylor, they have trouble with consolidation. Transition is also possible when there are initially diverging

---

[9] Zielinski does not allow for the opposition to prevail in a violent struggle, so this model rules out revolutionary transitions.

[10] Casper and Taylor's model is only loosely formalized. They present diagrams that resemble extended-form games, but they never present an actual game with payoffs or preference orderings or sophisticated strategies. Some of their fundamental assumptions remain implicit.

preferences that make the rulers overconfident and the challenger uncertain. But the mass public consistently supports the challenger, so perceptions of strength shift. Eventually, the rulers lose their ability to impose protective rules, so the transition is more complete and consolidation is more successful.

In Weingast's (1997) model, the rulers (i.e., the sovereign) deal with two groups of citizens (A and B) of relatively equal status – unlike the unequal challenger and mass public in Casper and Taylor's model.[11] Nondemocratic rule lasts as long as the rulers can divide and conquer the citizens, co-opting a large enough group to prevent a successful revolt by the other. Transition (to limited government, not necessarily democracy) becomes possible only when A and B coordinate their resistance to the rulers' transgressions against citizens. Limited government is consolidated when A and B find a self-enforcing solution to their coordination dilemma. The self-enforcing solution is a pact that commits both groups to resist any transgression by the rulers against any citizen. This pact is self-enforcing because either group can credibly threaten to help the rulers punish the other group if that group shirks its responsibilities under the pact. Again, these models are cousins (distinct in more than one respect) rather than siblings, so we cannot say for certain why their conclusions differ. Nevertheless, it seems likely that the coordination dilemma that Weingast considered so central is an artifact of his assumption that the two opposition actors are of equal status and act simultaneously. Casper and Taylor's more hierarchical and sequential model does not pose this dilemma. Readers must decide for themselves which set of assumptions is more realistic.

Finally, another set of theorists works a bit farther downstream, where both rulers and opposition are subdivided. In their models, there are more actors, but they usually interact in pairs. The outcome of the game is determined by which pair of actors is involved. These models do not tell us how some of the possible pairs are selected or how to know which pair is relevant in a specific case; this is left up to the skill of the analyst who wishes to apply the models. These models are therefore less complex and less complete than they appear.

The seminal model of this type comes from a later section of Przeworski's *Democracy and the Market* (1991). The essence of his model is that there are four actors, arrayed on a democracy-dictatorship continuum as follows. At the most democratic pole are the radical opposition (which Przeworski calls

---

[11] Weingast claims more general applicability of his model, but because he claims that it reveals the critical nature of pacts in transitions and defines democratic consolidation as the achievement of the kind of coordination he describes, it is appropriate to discuss it in this section.

the radicals), followed by the moderate opposition (moderates), then the soft-liners (reformers), and finally the hard-liners. Although there are four actors, there are only two players, the moderate opposition and the soft-liners. Each chooses which adjacent player to ally with, and their choices determine the outcome. Four outcomes are possible. First, if the soft-liners stick with the hard-liners and the moderate opposition remains allied with the radical opposition, then the old authoritarian regime survives unchanged. Second, if the soft-liners stick with the hard-liners but the moderate opposition tries to ally with the soft-liners, then the soft-liners are able to persuade the hard-liners to accept a liberalized authoritarian regime. Third, if the moderate opposition tries to ally with the soft-liners and the soft-liners reciprocate, then there is a transition to a democratic regime that includes some immunities for the outgoing authoritarian rulers and each actor is able to persuade its more extreme counterpart to accept this deal. Fourth, if the soft-liners wish to ally with the moderate opposition but the moderate opposition sticks with the radical opposition, then there is a democratic regime without guarantees for the outgoing rulers.

The two pivotal actors choose their alliances strategically, in a simultaneous one-shot game (Przeworski 1986). The moderate opposition knows that if it allies with the radical opposition, the soft-liners would always be better off sticking with the hard-liners, thus resulting in the opposition's worst-case scenario: survival of the authoritarian regime. Therefore, the moderate opposition takes the risk-averse course of seeking an alliance with the soft-liners. The payoffs to the soft-liners, however, depend on whether they remain united with the hard-liners or can act independently. If they are united, then the soft-liners stay with the hard-liners, which produces authoritarianism with concessions. It is only when there is a division between hard-liners and soft-liners that the soft-liners are better off allying with the moderate opposition, leading to democracy with immunities.[12]

Although this model has been influential, it is not the best example of formal theorizing because some of its assumptions are implicit and some of its logic is not fully developed. Przeworski does a good job of defending his assumption that this is a one-shot game, but it is not clear why the actors must choose simultaneously. Extensive-form games give the analyst opportunities to fine-tune assumptions about the sequence of moves, the information available

---

[12] Przeworski later describes a consolidation game in which the incumbent must decide whether or not to accept an election loss. He argues that this choice depends on constitutional rules that affect the incumbent's chances of returning to power.

to each player, and bargaining with threats and promises. Przeworski's game does not say much about these issues. Also, it is unnecessarily restrictive to assume that the two centrist actors are pivotal and that they can ally only with adjacent actors. Indeed, at one point Przeworski equivocates on this by speculating about how the outcomes could differ if the moderate opposition allied with the hard-liners or the soft-liners allied with the radical opposition (Przeworski 1991). In effect, it becomes a three-player game when the soft-liners' payoffs depend on whether or not there is unity with the hard-liners. But Przeworski never tells us what would happen if the radical opposition spurned an alliance proffered by the moderate opposition. Finally, what is least clear and most crucial is the association of regime outcomes with the actors' choices. Would democracy always result if the moderate actors allied? Would united rulers always defeat a united opposition? We have to take Przeworski's word for it.

Josep Colomer (1991 and 2000) builds a model around six actors, obtained by subdividing the hard-liners and soft-liners into moderate and radical factions. As in Przeworski's model, only two or three actors participate in any one game, and the outcome of the game is determined by which actors are included. However, unlike Przeworski, Colomer makes explicit assumptions about the connections between regime outcomes and actors' choices. His actors are defined by their preference ordering over the same three transition options: democratic rupture (D), intermediate reform (I), and non-democratic continuity (N). (Intermediate reform could be either Przeworski's authoritarianism with concessions or his democracy with guarantees.) Each actor also has a unique ordering of preferences over all of the collective outcomes that would result from the choices made by pairs of actors: DD, DI, II, DN, IN, and NN. Colomer uses these preference orderings to assign payoffs to each actor, and these payoffs allow him to solve for the equilibria (if any) of all the possible games. When both actors agree (DD, II, or NN), the outcome is stable – democracy, an intermediate regime, or nondemocracy, respectively. When the actors disagree (DI, DN, or IN), the outcome is conflict.

What is distinctive about Colomer's model is its open-endedness. The fifteen two-player and three three-player games that he discusses can lead to any of the possible outcomes, depending on which actors are in the game. If there were a reliable way to know which actors are relevant in any given situation, this would be a very useful (or at least testable) model. But the model does not tell us how to know which actors are relevant. Also, the assumption that only two or three actors of the six possible ones are ever relevant in any given situation strains credulity.

All of these regime-preference models share an additional problem with the O'Donnell-Schmitter-Whitehead framework that originally inspired them: the near circularity of defining actors in terms of their regime preferences. As discussed in Chapter 4, it is difficult to identify these actors in actual situations if they are not defined in terms of their institutional role or social class.[13] Furthermore, if actors are allowed to change their preferences during the process, as both Przeworski (1991) and Colomer (2000) contemplate in some passages, the model loses all explanatory traction. It may seem that this is a soluble problem, but it is actually inherent in the fundamental assumptions of the positional school. Actors could be allowed to choose which type of actor they are, prodemocracy or prodictatorship, depending on expected payoffs. But how would those payoffs be defined? If they get higher payoffs for one kind of regime and lower payoffs for another kind of regime, we are back to defining actors' preference in terms of regime outcomes. If we define their payoffs instrumentally (how much would this regime increase, for example, my income, security, life prospects), then we find ourselves in the economic school. The next school of formal theorizing avoids this problem.

Economic models of transition and survival

With one small exception, formal models of democratization that assume that actors value regimes only as a means to economic ends are better integrated. The family relationships are easier to trace because they have so many more assumptions in common. Almost all assume that there are just two actors, an elite and the poor; all define democracy as a regime in which the poor make economic policy and nondemocracy as a regime in which the elite make policy; all deal with policies such as tax rates and distribution of the economic surplus; and all propose that actors choose the regime that maximizes their economic returns. These models sometimes arrive at opposite conclusions as a result of other assumptions that are different, but the resemblances are so strong that any reader of these articles will encounter much that is familiar.

The one small exception is Youssef Cohen's game-theoretic explanation of the breakdown of democracy in Brazil (1964) and Chile (1973) (Cohen 1994). Cohen defines the actors as the extreme left, the moderate left, the moderate right, and the extreme right. He argues that the moderate left faces a prisoner's dilemma when deciding whether to break with the extreme left,

---

[13] Boix (2003, 9) makes the same point, but I arrived at this conclusion independently.

and the moderates and extremists on the right face the same dilemma. One would think that the two moderates would choose to cooperate in supporting a program of moderate economic reform. Unfortunately, Cohen argues, the moderate left fears that the moderate right would betray it and the moderate right fears that the moderate left would betray it, leading to their least-preferred outcomes. Therefore, both prefer solidarity with their respective extremists. This results in polarization and deadlock, which Cohen equates with the breakdown of the democratic regime. The literature on the prisoner's dilemma has found that such outcomes can be avoided if the actors expect to play the game indefinitely and do not discount the future (Fudenberg and Maskin 1986). Cohen, however, like Przeworski, argues that regime-transition decisions are nonrepeatable one-shot games.

The other economic models that developed after Cohen's book start from scratch, with very different assumptions. Whether or not they acknowledge their pedigree, all develop Dahl's 1971 argument that transitions occur when the costs of repression exceed the costs of toleration (Dahl 1971). The first formalization of this model was by Feng and Zak (1999), who translated the costs of repression as spending on the police, and the costs of toleration as the tax rate. However, they complicated the model much more than this. The ruler (i.e., autocrat) could not only vary the tax rate and spending on the police; he could also vary levels of spending on education. For its part, the opposition (i.e., agents) could decide how many hours to work productively and how many hours to spend demonstrating against the ruler. Ultimately, agents seek to maximize their lifetime consumption. Because demonstrations destroy assets, they shrink the tax base and undermine the ruler's ability to pay for police. Feng and Zak argue that a transition happens when "antigovernment demonstrations overwhelm the autocrat's ability to maintain public order" (1999, 169). After some complex derivations, they conclude that (1) a transition will happen . . . immediately if most agents are rich, (2) . . . quickly if the economy grows and there is a large number of agents just below the threshold at which it becomes profitable to demonstrate, or (3) . . . slowly if there is such great inequality that most people are far below the threshold and the economy is not growing, (4) . . . transitions are also more likely when the government invests in education (which boosts productivity and therefore assets) or police (because it prevents demonstrations) and (5) . . . when people have a "preference for democracy."[14] The model is very

---

[14] The model predicts that overspending on education or police would hurt growth and therefore slow democratization, but the authors claim to have shown elsewhere that governments generally

simple, but the fact that most of its predictions coincide with the known empirical relationships is encouraging.

Rosendorff (2001) made three modifications to Feng and Zak's model. First, whoever is ruling (the elite in an autocracy, the median worker in a democracy) distributes lump-sum shares of collected taxes to all, equally. (As in most of these models, democracy – rule by many – necessarily implies a higher tax rate.[15]) Second, if the elites lose control, they will be expropriated entirely and the proceeds will be distributed equally. (Rosendorff also assumed that the elite has the option of investing its capital abroad rather than in the domestic economy. The elite can use this as leverage to keep the tax rate below 100 percent, even in a democracy. He also says that the elite can spend on maintaining control rather than on education and police, specifically.) These modifications provide extra incentives for workers to demonstrate and for the elite to spend more on security. Rosendorff's conclusions, like Feng and Zak's, focus on the impact of inequality and economic growth. He finds that as inequality worsens, both sides spend more on protecting or contesting the autocracy. But if equality increases beyond a certain threshold, then the elite's costs of maintaining the regime exceed their expected losses from redistribution, so they agree to a transition. Transitions are therefore likely when the income distribution becomes flatter, the growth rate is low, or the size of the workforce decreases.

Acemoglu and Robinson (2001) published a still more elaborate version of this basic model. One major difference in their assumptions, however, is that both actors rely on carrots more than sticks. In their model, an autocratic elite government does not normally prevent a democratic revolution by investing in repression but rather by redistributing tax receipts more generously, and a democratic government prevents an authoritarian coup by lowering the tax rate enough to pacify the wealthy elite. Various economic conditions impinge on the probability of democratic transitions. Other things being equal, transitions to democracy are more likely when a severe recession denies the elite the resources it needs to prevent a revolution, and also when inequality is high.[16] Transitions are less likely when the economy is growing fast or when the elite

---

underspend on both. In other words, typically spending more on police would spur growth and therefore accelerate democratization.

[15] The original inspirations for these models, however, appear to be economic models of redistribution such as Alesina and Rodrik (1994) or Persson and Tabellini (1994), which were not intended to explain regime change.

[16] They reached the opposite conclusion on this point in their subsequent book (Acemoglu and Robinson 2006).

invests in repression, especially when inequality is high. Once established, a democratic regime is more likely to survive when the ruling poor keep taxes low; they may even constitutionally limit the tax rate to reassure the elite. Such reassurance is especially welcome when recessions are frequent. Democratic stability is also favored when the economy depends on investments that pay off only as long as democracy survives. Acemoglu and Robinson also propose that a relatively equal distribution of assets would enhance democracy's survival prospects, although they are aware that the threat of massive redistribution to attain this level of equality could well provoke an elite coup. Curiously, one of their conclusions is that there should be no association between average wealth and democracy unless wealth is associated with economic volatility or the power of the poor.

Gould and Maggio (2007) develop a similar, but simpler, model that proposes an explanation for an empirical finding of Przeworski and colleagues (2000): wealth does more to help countries remain democratic than it does to help them become democratic. They assume, in the spirit of the works just discussed, that (1) in a dictatorship, elites maximize earnings but risk a costly revolution; (2) nonelites would earn more in a democracy, but a democratic revolution would be costly to them; (3) in a democracy, elites earn less but face no risk of regime change; and (4) nonelites in a democracy earn more but face the risk of a coup. Using Kahneman and Tversky's prospect theory, Gould and Maggio argue that both actors are loss-averse (Kahneman and Tversky 1979). That is, elites would tolerate democracy to avoid the losses associated with an unsuccessful coup, and nonelites would take the risk of opposing a coup to avoid the losses they would suffer under dictatorship. This model predicts that democracy is stickier as countries become wealthier because the loss aversion is more pronounced when the stakes are higher.

Zak and Feng (2003) – building explicitly on their own 1999 article – Acemoglu and Robinson (2001), Lohmann (1994), and several other contributions, generate even more plausible predictions by emphasizing the distinction between income and assets. As in their 1999 article, citizens choose a mix of productive work and destructive demonstration that will maximize their lifetime consumption, and an autocrat chooses a mix of taxation, investment in public goods, and paying for police that will maximize the economic growth rate. And, as in their 1999 model, transitions occur when the autocrat cannot raise police spending enough to prevent demonstrations.

These assumptions are still a gross simplification of reality. Nevertheless, the predictions that flow from them mirror empirical relationships faithfully in a surprising range of respects. Zak and Feng's central distinction is between a wealth effect (wealthier citizens demanding civil liberties when the economy is growing) and an income effect (middle-class citizens protesting low incomes resulting from economic contraction). The authors find that the citizens who will spend more time on demonstrations are those with large assets but low wages, such as the middle class and students. Transitions happen when either the economy is growing so rapidly that the wealth effect dominates the income effect, or there is such a deep recession that the income effect dominates the wealth effect. In either situation, demonstrations outstrip the police protection that the autocrat can afford. In contrast, slow, positive growth retards transitions. Zak and Feng also find that unequal wages inhibit transitions but unequal wealth hastens transitions, provided that the autocrat spends too little to prevent his overthrow.

Already there is a noticeable trend: the early models in this school were overly simplistic, but the more complex ones began to approximate recognizable tendencies in the real world. An economic model that approximates reality in a very wide range of respects is that of Carles Boix (2003), which not only brings together the best insights of its rational-choice predecessors but also formalizes several ideas from modernization theory and comparative historical research on democratization. This theoretical synthesis is an impressive achievement. His efforts to test hypotheses from the model (which are evaluated in Chapter 9) make it even more impressive. Acemoglu and Robinson's subsequent book (2006) proposes a very similar and equally if not more impressive theory but contains very little extensive testing, so this chapter focuses on Boix's work.

As do other economic theorists, Boix assumes that the wealthy rule in an authoritarian regime and the poor in a democracy, that governments make decisions about taxes and spending on repression, that taxes are redistributive, that inequality and growth rates affect these decisions, that violence is costly, that elite assets are confiscated after a revolution, that assets pay dividends, and that actors prefer the regime that best serves their economic interests. However, Boix makes several assumptions that are distinct from those made by other theorists in the economic school. The key one is that assets vary in their specificity: some assets, such as agricultural land or oil fields, are specific to a country whereas others, such as labor, technology, and commercial goods, are mobile across national borders. This distinction is highly consequential, as we shall see. Boix also adopts the important distinction between income and assets, which only Acemoglu and Robinson (2001) and Zak and Feng (2003) also make. This useful assumption also helps distinguish between democratic and communist regimes, which most other works in this school fail to do.

A third distinct assumption is informational asymmetry: the wealthy know how much repression costs them but the poor do not, yet the poor are better informed about how well organized they are and, therefore, about their ability to revolt successfully. Boix argues that sudden shifts in the distribution of information about the chances of successful repression or revolt explain the timing of regime changes. Finally, Boix relaxes the assumption that there are only two classes (as Acemoglu and Robinson do in their 2006 book). After developing a basic two-class model, he adds a middle class, which introduces two more possible regime outcomes (limited democracy and a milder revolutionary regime, in addition to democracy, right-wing authoritarianism, communism, and civil war) and opens up the possibility of class alliances.

The variety of predictions that Boix derives from his model, and their correspondences with at least some empirical cases, make this model quite promising. He predicts that capital mobility forces even democratic governments to keep taxes low, which helps the wealthy make peace with democracy. This is why, he claims, economic development favors democracy: it is not so much that incomes rise as that wealth shifts from highly specific investments in land to more mobile investments in industry, commerce, finance, and technology.[17] This reasoning also eliminates the paradox of premodern democracy in societies with relatively low levels of development, such as ancient Athens and the nineteenth-century United States (Boix 2003). It is also consistent with the lack of democratization in wealthy oil-exporting countries, which have highly specific assets. Economic development can also favor democracy if it reduces inequality because the more equal the society, the less a democratic government would need to raise taxes to redistribute wealth, and the less the wealthy would prefer to install an authoritarian regime. Boix argues that European transitions coincided roughly with periods of growing equality in the United Kingdom, Denmark, Norway, and Spain (2003). Boix's assumptions about the impact of working-class organization on the costs of repression help explain the timing of Western European transitions in the first decades of the twentieth century, when unions and leftist parties began to form (Boix 2003). Also, his emphasis on asset specificity allows him to model situations in which large landowners would oppose democracy whereas the urban bourgeoisie would favor it, much as Barrington Moore proposed (Moore 1966).

---

[17] In an appendix, Boix (2003, 63–64) develops two alternative reasons for the association between development and democracy. It may be that a democratic government would keep taxes low to prevent taxation from dampening productivity, or it may be that taxation is subjectively less onerous to the wealthy at higher levels of income. However, he places more emphasis on the role of asset specificity.

Whether these correspondences between theory and facts are systematically true or merely selective examples is discussed in Chapter 9. The most relevant conclusion for the present chapter, however, is that Boix's model is the best illustration of the distinctive potential of formal theory to achieve theoretical integration, which is a necessary characteristic of good theorizing.

Evaluating formal theories and models

Although formal theory has been part of political science since the 1950s, it has been applied to democratization only since the early 1990s. It would be unfair to judge an entire approach based solely on the record of one of its youngest applications, so I base my evaluations on tendencies that are typical of formal theorizing on topics that have a longer track record, and I do this in a spirit of charity and hopefulness. In brief, formal theory does a relatively good job of producing integrated theory but a relatively poor job of producing thick theory that is empirically general. I emphasize *relatively* in this conclusion because formal models of democratization are neither well integrated nor completely devoid of thickness or general confirmation; they are merely better integrated, thinner, and less well tested than other approaches. Furthermore, within the formal approach, some of the economic models are better integrated, thicker, and better tested than the positional models.

Thickness

Formal models are sometimes criticized for oversimplifying reality. To be fair, we must be clear: all models simplify reality. Models select certain features of reality to highlight while ignoring other features (Morton 1999). A reasonable simplification is one that calls attention to the most important features of a process while ignoring less important features. However, some models oversimplify, by which I mean that they neglect the most important parts of the story as they focus on factors that are less important.[18] Some other models try to pass off contradictions of the real story as simplifications. It is a reasonable simplification to say that Al Gore lost the U.S. 2000 presidential election because it was so close to a tie that the imprecision of Florida's

---

[18] Researchers may and should analyze the less important factors but, while doing so, they must not lose sight of more important factors.

balloting system created legal challenges that allowed the U.S. Supreme Court to decide the election. To say that he lost because of the butterfly ballot or Ralph Nader's candidacy is an oversimplification because these factors would not have mattered if it had not been such a close race. To say that he lost because he wanted George W. Bush to win is simply false.

The concepts and propositions of formal models of democratization are extraordinarily thin. Some positional models refer to the rulers (Swaminathan 1999; Zielinski 1995) or sovereign (Weingast 1997), the opposition (Marks 1992; Sutter 1995), or the mass public (Casper and Taylor 1996) as monolithic, undifferentiated blocs, ignoring differences between hard-liners and soft-liners, unions and parties, left and right, that are likely to be consequential. Of course, some other positional models break down these actors a bit: Colomer (1991, 2000) goes the farthest, theorizing about six actors. But even in the case of Colomer, the six actors are defined purely by their rank ordering of just three permissible "strategic preferences for a greater or lesser degree of discontinuity with the existing regime" (Colomer 2000, 33) – democratic rupture, intermediate reform, or nondemocratic continuity. This tells us nothing about the actors' positions on an economic left-right continuum, their popular support, the charisma of their leaders, their internal unity, or how well organized they are. Defining actors solely in terms of regime preferences amounts to an assertion that these other qualities do not matter for democratization.

Among economic models, the most disturbing thin concept is democracy itself. Most of these models define democracy as a regime in which the poor (or the median voter, who is poor) make economic policy, including setting tax rates and redistributing assets. Acemoglu and Robinson (2001, 941–942) do not distinguish between a democratic transition (which they call a revolution) and a utopian communist revolution: "After a revolution, poor agents expropriate an additional fraction . . . of the asset stock of the economy. . . . We also assume that the rich lose everything after a revolution." This bears almost no resemblance to the regimes that we refer to as democracies. Boix comes closer to reality by distinguishing between communism, in which "the poor rule after expropriating all the wealthy's capital," and democracy, in which "property is preserved and everybody votes on the tax rate" (Boix 2003, 23). However, this definition of democracy fails to mention civil liberties, political rights, representative institutions, or any other procedures; it alludes only vaguely to some kind of election. Boix reduces democracy to the number of economic classes that participate in setting the tax rate. Given the complexity of regime transitions, the concepts used in any analysis must be somewhat thin, but it should not be hard to do better than these examples.

These thin concepts become the building blocks of thin theories. The positional models are thin in the sense that they limit their attention to the final moment of a transition, when everything but the outcome has been decided. The actors have been selected, the choices available to them are identified, their preference orderings are defined, their time horizons and access to information are known – all they have to do is strategize and reach a decision. Given these highly structured situations, these models can make a prediction. But these models do not tell us how these actors, out of all the many possible actors in a society, came to be the ones making the final decision; why the choices offered them are the only ones available; why they prefer some outcomes to others; or other important details about how the game is structured. A thick theory would address these other issues, if only by speculating about what the boundary conditions of the model are.

In some ways, the economic models are thicker. Unlike the positional models, which tend to take shape as simple 2×2 strategic-form games with discrete choices and ordinal payoffs, the economic models are written as algebraic utility functions for each actor. These functions allow the payoffs to vary continuously in response to tax rates, economic growth, the rate of return on investment, and other variables. Furthermore, each player's utility can be calculated at any point in time, not just at the moment of decision. So these models are structured less rigidly and are therefore less narrow. The better models also approach thickness by taking into consideration a richer variety of economic variables. Zak and Feng (2003), for example, incorporate into their model wages, assets, returns on investment, the rate of economic growth, tax rates, tax receipts, redistribution, spending on education, spending on police, the effectiveness of spending on police, productivity, time devoted to productive work, time devoted to destructive protests, wage inequality, and asset inequality. Boix (2003) adds to this mix capital mobility, which enables him to distinguish among economic sectors within the wealthy class; unionization; and cross-class coalitions. Nevertheless, these models are still thin in their exclusive focus on economics. They ignore traditions, institutions, noneconomic values, demonstration effects, and noneconomic power resources such as moral authority (although Boix also considers mass organization and access to information). Because of this theoretical thinness, the positional and economic models of democratization are incompatible with each other. Positional models claim that actors value regimes as ends in themselves, whereas economic models assert that actors value regimes only as means to economic ends. Only one of these can be a reasonable simplification; the other must logically be an oversimplification. Combining economic and noneconomic motivations would be a move toward thickness, but so far formal models have avoided assuming that actors have conflicting motives.

Thickening these thin models would make them more realistic and change their premises from oversimplifications or contradictions of fact into reasonable simplifications. However, it is too much to expect any single model to approach a realistic degree of complexity all by itself; it must build on simpler and therefore less realistic models worked out by others – the kind we have now. There is hope that eventually formal models will reach this degree of sophistication. But simply increasing the number of models is not enough; rather, they must be integrated so that each model improves on the ones that came before it.

Integration

Deductive theorizing is supposed to aid in the creation of a cumulative science of politics (Lalman et al. 1993). Cumulation actually involves two processes: building a structure of logically integrated propositions, and dismantling and rebuilding parts of that structure in the light of empirical findings. The empirical aspects of this process, which are more demanding, are discussed here. In research outside the study of democratization, rational-choice theory has indeed cumulated theory in the narrow sense of integrating propositions in the absence of evidence, with regard to voting theory, game theory, the collective-action problem, and other topics. Unfortunately, however, this level of integration has not been achieved so far in models of democratization. If we treat all formal theorizing about democratization as a single theory, the purely theoretical core is very small – only the assumption that actors are rational. There are no universally shared assumptions about how many rational actors there are, what their goals are, what choices they face, or even what kind of rationality they practice. However, if we consider the positional models and economic models separate theories, their cores become a bit more elaborate. The positional models assume that actors are defined by their regime preferences, that some actors are in the regime and some in the opposition, that a regime change involves a loss of power for the rulers and a gain in power for at least some in the opposition, and that liberalization precedes democratization. Beyond this, all those modeling liberalization share some additional assumptions, and all those modeling transitions or survival share some other additional assumptions. However, few theorists in this school agree on the number of actors, the alliances available to them, the choices available to them, or which game they are playing. Nevertheless, despite the different assumptions, the positional models tend to conclude that (1) the outcome of the game depends heavily on the regime-preference orderings of the people who happen to be leading the regime and the opposition in a given country; (2) hard-liners will not liberalize if they know it will lead to democracy; (3) some kind of signal is necessary to embolden the opposition to challenge the regime; (4) if the odds of success shift in favor of the opposition, a transition eventually becomes inevitable; and (5) the actor with better information has a better chance of imposing his or her preferred regime. This may not be perfect integration, but it is enough to constitute an interesting school of thought.

In the economic school, there is an even larger body of core theory, already described here. Still, it is not complete integration: each article adds wrinkles that others ignore. Only Feng and Zak (1999; Zak and Feng 2003) suppose that protesters destroy productive assets; only Acemoglu and Robinson (2001) consider whether commitments to lower taxes are credible; only Gould and Maggio (2007) use prospect theory; only Rosendorff (2001), Boix (2003), and Acemoglu and Robinson (2006) take capital mobility into account; and Boix never cites Zak or Feng. Despite these different assumptions, the economic models tend to agree that (1) democracy is more likely to be born and survive in egalitarian societies, (2) democracy is more likely to survive when elites can shift their assets abroad, and (3) regime change is a rare event because challenging a regime is costly and risky.

Generality

Formal theory may seem to be general because it is expressed in universalistic terms. However, this universalism is almost entirely an aspiration rather than a reality. This approach employs concepts defined at a high level of generality, such as soft-liner and the poor, and (aside from the models of particular cases) it tends not to circumscribe its domain of applicability. The work with the most extreme generality of aspiration, Barry Weingast's article on democracy and the rule of law, claims to shed light not only on the English Glorious Revolution of 1688 but also on social capital in regions of Italy, consociationalism in divided societies, the Salvadoran peace accords, and the Missouri Compromise of 1820 (Weingast 1997). But, to be truly general, these models must not only be cast in general terms; they also must be empirically general. That is, they must be consistent with all of the known evidence in their domain of applicability and not restrict their domain arbitrarily. Few formal models even come close to meeting this standard.

Working toward empirical generality requires testing. However, there is disagreement about what should be tested. Some defenders of rational-choice theory urge others to test the predictions but not to test the assumptions. This stance is certainly not shared by all who use formal models, particularly not those who do applied research, but some formal modelers are quite adamant on the point (Lave and March 1993). The first line of defense for this advice is the claim that many of the assumptions of formal theories are unobservable, such as the subjective value of payoffs and the strategic reasoning of the actors. This would be an airtight defense if not for the fact that some assumptions of these theories are in fact observable. We can know how many actors are parties to negotiations over regime change, whether it is realistic to say that the median voter sets tax policy, whether authoritarian regimes have lower tax rates than democracies, and so on. When these assumptions can be tested, they should be.

The second line of defense that some modelers offer for not testing assumptions is that the worth of a model is better gauged by the accuracy of its predictions than by the accuracy of its descriptions; all theories simplify and therefore do not describe reality with great accuracy. Here, it is important once again to distinguish between reasonable simplifications and assumptions that are simply false. If we know that an assumption is strictly false, we should go no further because a conclusion derived from a false premise is logically false even if it is empirically true. But often the only way to know whether an assumption is true is to test it. Sometimes false assumptions can yield predictions that are consistent with one set of evidence (particularly when a researcher, consciously or not, designs the model to fit some familiar evidence), but false assumptions are not likely to be consistent with new evidence. Predictions for new observations are more likely to be correct, and the goal of generalization best served, when the assumptions of a model are accurate descriptions, or at least reasonable simplifications. From this different perspective, both assumptions (when they are observable) and predictions are fair game for testing.

The need for testing is exacerbated by the unfortunate emphasis that some rational-choice advocates place on their ability to generate nonobvious hypotheses (Lave and March 1993; Geddes 2003). It is easy to understand why they do this. On the one hand, a capacity to generate obvious or trivial hypotheses is of little value. On the other hand, the great breakthroughs in other sciences involve ideas that were not obvious before, such as the insights that Earth is spherical, that all life evolved from primitive organisms, and that time slows down as one approaches the speed of light. But the fact that great scientific breakthroughs were not obvious does not logically imply that all nonobvious propositions are breakthroughs. (One would think that scholars who place so much emphasis on logic would recognize this.) In fact, breakthroughs are breakthroughs not because they were not obvious but because they fit a great deal of evidence despite initial expectations that they would not (Kuhn 1996; Lakatos 1970, 1978). Common sense dictates that the less obvious an idea is, the more evidence is required to support it. As Carl Sagan was fond of saying, "Extraordinary claims require extraordinary evidence" (Sagan 1980). Sometimes an implausible idea improves after many revisions and eventually becomes an insight. But until that happens, counterintuitive propositions that do not fit the available evidence should be regarded as highly tentative and provisional. The exception to this is that counterintuitive propositions that are rigorously derived from propositions that are known to be true should be seriously entertained until evidence can be gathered to test them. This exception applies to mathematics and some natural sciences that have developed many laws that are known to be true. It does not apply to formal models in political science, which are derived from propositions that are usually oversimplified or false (Clarke and Primo 2007).

It is therefore especially tragic that the approach that tends to generate hypotheses most in need of testing has done so little testing and has done that little so poorly, as Green and Shapiro (1994) have argued. However, as Green and Shapiro recognize, it takes time for a new body of formal theory to develop to a point at which it is ready for testing. Their critique was directed at areas of rational-choice theorizing that have been active for several decades. Formal models of democratization are relatively new, so it is premature to expect much testing. Perhaps the fairest judgment is that no one should be surprised that the testing in this area has been inadequate.

Much of the theorizing in this approach uses such general concepts that no real-world cases can satisfy the highly restrictive assumptions. Understood properly, these models predict something like "If there is one rich ruling actor and one poor actor, and if the ruler sets the tax rate and distributes assets, and if the poor would confiscate all the assets of the rich in a democracy, and if [...], then the greater inequality is, the less likely a democratic transition is." If we could find a case that satisfied all of the if clauses, we could test the prediction fairly. But if there are three rich actors or fifteen poor actors or two middle classes or the tax rate is sticky or the poor would not confiscate many assets, and so on, then the model makes no prediction that is relevant in the real world: it cannot be tested. The modeler could permit a test with imperfectly fitting cases on the grounds that the model makes only reasonable simplifications, so real-world cases match the model's premises well enough. But if the model were to fail the test, the modeler would be justified in objecting that a test using those cases was not fair after all. Whether or not a test is fair hinges on whether the assumptions of the model were reasonable simplifications or oversimplifications. And this, in turn, hinges on whether or not the model captures the most important features, which is the empirical question that the test is supposed to answer (Morton 1999). It thus becomes very hard to say whether a model failed a test because the test was inappropriate or because the model was oversimplified or wrong. By the same token, if a model passes an empirical test, it is hard to know whether the test really confirms the model or the modeler simply got lucky (abetted by unrigorous testing) (Clarke and Primo 2007).[19]

Chapter 7 lays out more comprehensive criteria for rigorous testing. However, the inadequacy of testing of formal models is obvious in several ways that need not wait for the next chapter. First, some of the works in question are purely theoretical; they do not even attempt tests. The pure, untested models include those by Marks (1992), Sutter (1995), Acemoglu and Robinson (2001, 2006), and Zak and Feng (2003). Some of these authors rarely even mention specific countries or events.

Second, most of the works that do refer to cases and evidence do so selectively, using the evidence to illustrate the model rather than to test it. This is a tendency in comparative history and case studies as well; less so in quantitative research; and hardly at all in survey research, where representative random samples from a well-defined population are the norm. The positional school has relied more on modeling specific cases as it has grown. Colomer modeled Spain (1991) and several postcommunist cases (2000); Zielinski modeled Poland (1995) and Poland and Hungary (1999); Lohmann (1994) modeled East Germany; Weingast (1997) modeled the Glorious Revolution in England; Crescenzi (1999) modeled Hungary and Brazil; and Przeworski (1991) was obviously, if not always explicitly, attuned to transitions in Eastern Europe. These models have served to increase the plausibility of the approach but have not been well integrated. The economic school relies more on general

---

[19] This problem is present in other approaches to some degree, and the only solution is more rigorous testing. But a prerequisite for rigorous testing is being able to define a relevant universe of cases. If this cannot be done, it is hard to know where to begin.

theories than models of cases, with the exception of Cohen (1994) on Brazil and Chile and Rosendorff (2001) on South Africa. In some respects, one suspects that Feng and Zak's (1999) model may have been inspired by East Asian experiences such as those of South Korea and Taiwan, given the important role attributed to student protests, and that Boix (2003) drew on the exceptional experiences of both the Middle East and his native Catalonian region of Spain; but, for the most part, the economic school has been devoted to the development of general theory rather than applying it to specific cases.

A serious test would systematically gather evidence for all of the cases that satisfy the assumptions of the model, or at least a representative sample of them, thereby creating the risk that some of the evidence might turn out to be inconsistent with the predictions of the model. Selection of only cases that are consistent with the model, and that therefore are useful as illustrations, thwarts the goal of testing. Works in this category include Przeworski (1991) and Weingast (1997). Those who model specific events do essentially the same thing because there is virtually no chance that their model will not fit their case – or, at least, the details of the case that they choose to present. For these models, the examination of evidence is no more testing than the presentation of evidence in comparative histories; in fact, it is less rigorous because the evidence presented is far thinner and therefore more selective.[20]

The third inadequacy of testing in this approach in democratization research is that the small number of formal studies that do analyze systematic evidence tend to subject the evidence only to unchallenging tests. This is probably a function of the relatively late application of formal modeling to democratization, as rigorous testing of formal models applied to voting behavior, legislative behavior, and other topics is common. In democratization applications, often the scholar tests just one prediction of the model, even when the model yields other potentially testable implications and bases the test on indicators that are only very indirect measures of the concepts in the model. Such tests neither confirm other predictions of the model nor disconfirm any competing hypotheses that are consistent with the same evidence. Swaminathan (1999), for example, makes predictions that depend on how risk acceptant government and opposition are, how high the costs of conflict are, how much each actor discounts the future, and other factors. But his test merely confirms that the association between the incidence of

[20] Casper and Taylor (1996) belong in this category as well despite their large sample (twenty-four countries) because ten of these cases had to be assigned to some alternate path that differed from the original model. They adjusted the model to fit the cases.

democratic transitions and a rather crude indicator of power parity between government and opposition is not attributable to chance.

Crescenzi (1999) develops an elaborate model in which, after the regime liberalizes, the opposition must decide whether to cooperate, negotiate, or radicalize. The outcome could be a pacted transition, narrowed authoritarianism, or a revolutionary transition, depending on whether hard-liners or soft-liners dominate the regime and the regime's ability to prevail in a conflict with the opposition. Lacking adequate data to model all of the possible paths, Crescenzi abandoned the details of his model's predictions and settled for testing the proposition that when the regime's recent acts of liberalization outnumber its acts of repression, the opposition is more likely to engage in peaceful protest (which he confirmed for Hungary 1948–1982 but failed to confirm for Brazil 1964–1982). Feng and Zak (1999) claim that their model is confirmed after they show that in fifty-nine developing countries from 1970 to 1992, transitions to democracy are more likely in countries with higher income equality and either a high per capita gross domestic product (GDP) or a high level of education. Needless to say, these same results are compatible with many theories. In some respects, the most rigorous testing is the experimentation by Gould and Maggio (2007). However, the relevance of their experiments to regime change is debatable because the subjects were U.S. college students who were asked to make decisions about monetary payoffs; the connection between these small payoffs and much larger economic stakes, and between economics and regime preferences, was simply assumed.

The most thorough testing of a formal model has been done by Carles Boix in his *Democracy and Redistribution* (Boix 2003). His tests, which cover between 12 and 20 countries from 1950 to 1990 and 208 states that existed at any time from 1850 to 1980, equivalent to approximately 6,500 country-years, are as general as available data permit. They include tests of not one hypothesis from his model but rather several: that equality favors democracy, that oil producers tend to be less democratic, and that it was industrialization rather than per capita GDP that drove the first wave of democratization. He controls for several competing explanations in addition to vindicating the predictions of his own model and tests thick implications of his model with process-tracing over centuries of Swiss and U.S. history. Chapter 9 examines the rigor of some of Boix's tests in more detail, but for now it suffices to say that *Democracy and Redistribution* is a resounding exception to the rule that formal models have not been tested.

It is natural to hope that as formal models come to be tested more frequently and thoroughly, their kinks will be progressively straightened out until they jibe with common sense and generate predictions that are not only unexpected but also consistent with most of the available evidence. However, there is nothing about repeated encounters between this theory (or any theory) and evidence that guarantees such an outcome. The sobering reality is that inconsistent evidence offers no guidance about where the theory went wrong or which proposition should be modified to make it right (the Duhem-Quine hypothesis).[21] However, because scholars have faith in the potential of their approach, they tend to revise only the peripheral assumptions of the theory, not to question its core.

Formal theory's emphasis on integration therefore works against empirical generality in several ways. While the core theory is being developed, it is insulated from potentially disconfirming evidence, which is considered irrelevant until the theory becomes complex enough to approximate reality. Modeling begins to bridge the gaps between theory and reality but with the goal of vindicating core assumptions rather than questioning them. And when the theory eventually confronts systematic disconfirming evidence, the core theory is still safeguarded; only peripheral assumptions come under fire. It is only when a great deal of evidence inconsistent with a theory accumulates and a more promising alternative approach emerges that scholars begin to question the core assumptions rather than the peripheral propositions, and the theory is replaced in a scientific revolution or paradigm shift (Kuhn 1996). In this, they obey the first rule of wing walking (on biplanes): don't let go of one thing until you've got a hold on another. Even then, according to Kuhn, few scholars change their minds. A paradigm dies when its adherents retire and are replaced by the followers of a different paradigm. Integration is an essential quality of good theory, but it forces a steep trade-off with generality.

Conclusion

The value of the theorizing in formal models of democratization has not been integration so much as posing new questions. By using strict logic or mathematics to derive implications, they reveal the fallacies and non sequiturs in nonformal theories. Formal theory has repeatedly identified problematic assumptions that cannot be taken for granted. Several of these issues are

---

[21] Diermeier (1996, 63) states the Duhem-Quine hypothesis as "(1) A theory is accepted or rejected as a whole, not through the acceptance or rejection of particular components of the theory. (2) A rejection of a theory based on a critical experiment is impossible."

relevant for democratization. For example, several approaches treat democratization as though it were a nonstrategic process. This is especially true of approaches without actors, such as those that emphasize socioeconomic modernization, mass political culture, or economic crisis, and of some approaches that blame breakdowns on divided societies or credit international diffusion for transitions.[22] Even when these approaches refer to actors, their choices are treated as reflexive responses: involuntary reactions to objective conditions. Rational-choice theory focuses attention on the intentions of actors who have choices. What these actors choose, and why, becomes a central part of the explanation for the outcome. In a sense, their choices are completely determined by the situation in which they find themselves; but because the "correct" choices are not obvious, a theory is needed to explain why actors choose as they do. Nonformal models tend to overlook such issues.

Formal models of democratization constitute a distinctive approach because they do a relatively good job of satisfying one criterion for good theory. They come closer to achieving some degree of theoretical integration than checklists, case studies, comparative histories, or (as we will see later) statistical analyses. The degree of integration is less than one would hope; in fact, there are two completely distinct schools of theory within this approach, one of which (the positional school) is not integrated well internally. Nevertheless, there is more integration here than elsewhere. But, like the other approaches – small-sample qualitative analyses and large-sample quantitative analyses – formal theory does a relatively poor job of satisfying two criteria for good theory. This approach is perhaps the thinnest of all, and most of it (Boix 2003 excepted) cannot claim to approach generality.

---

[22] There are examples of each of these approaches that would not fit this characterization, such as Lijphart's work on consociational democracy and Huntington's attribution of the third wave of democratization partially to the Catholic Church's support for democracy (Lijphart 1977; Huntington 1991). However, the majority of the work in these approaches either alludes to vague actors, such as fuzzily defined social classes, or glosses over actors entirely. An example of the latter is my own work on democratic diffusion (Brinks and Coppedge 1999).

7 Rigor in extensive and intensive testing

Chapters 3–6 developed criteria for a good theory and surveyed many of the strategies used to develop theories of democratization. Chapters 8 and 9 survey the results of theory testing. This chapter introduces these tests by laying out criteria for rigor in testing. How to test rigorously occupies most of the chapter because it is the most complex issue. Many discussions of rigorous testing are confined to statistical testing. My perspective gives equal weight to qualitative methods, which support rigorous testing of a different kind. I argue that there are two fundamentally different kinds of testing that serve different but complementary purposes. The first is extensive testing, which helps establish that a causal relationship is generally true, on average, in a large sample. The second is intensive testing, which reveals which of several competing explanations best explains a specific outcome in a single case. Ultimately, a good theory should make predictions that survive both extensive and intensive testing.

Before developing these arguments, there are three preliminary questions that must be answered: Why is testing necessary? When is a theory ready to be tested? And what about the theory should be tested? The prevalence of untested propositions in comparative politics (such as most of those discussed in Chapters 4–6) suggests that a justification of testing is needed. Testing is necessary because many propositions that seem obviously, incontrovertibly true turn out to be false when exposed to evidence. Why do they seem to be true? There are several reasons. First, some propositions are intuitively appealing; that is, they are consistent with other ideas that we do not question. The problems with intuition are that (1) it does not require any systematic comparison of the consistency of the new ideas with the old ones, and (2) the old ideas that have gone unquestioned may themselves be false. A good example is the common assumption of Washington policy makers and pundits that democracy and free-market capitalism are mutually reinforcing.

The catchphrase "open markets, open societies" is widely accepted,[1] but mostly because it conforms to the prevailing liberal individualist ideology, which conveniently overlooks promarket dictatorships and statist or protectionist democracies.

Other propositions come to be accepted as true because they were derived in a rigorously truth-preserving way, using logic or mathematics. Unfortunately, logical truth does not guarantee empirical confirmation. A deductive approach does preserve the truth of the initial assumptions, but it also preserves (and may even magnify) their error, to the extent that the assumptions are oversimplified or false. Of course, it is not necessary for all theories to be tested immediately. We must make allowances for early stages of theorizing, which entertain overly simplistic assumptions until the model can become more realistic. But, eventually, every theory must be tested if it is to avoid becoming a sterile intellectual irrelevance.

Both of these tendencies are reflections of human nature: human beings often believe – in fact, often cannot help believing – whatever they need to believe, whether or not there is any evidence for the belief. The best example of this tendency is the globally widespread acceptance of comforting religious doctrines that cannot be tested and may even be inconsistent with known facts. Although every religion has defenders who attempt to justify it with arguments of various kinds, ultimately all religions rest on faith. The point here is not that any religion is right or wrong but rather that the fact of widespread religious belief shows how willing human beings are to believe things without evidence. This tendency is less common in science, which teaches skepticism toward propositions that are not supported by evidence. Nevertheless, credulity creeps into the sciences as well. We fall easily into excessive faith in the universality of our theories, the objectivity of our judgments, the validity of our indicators, the representativeness of a few cases, the truth of our "facts," and the completeness of our models. We are not naturally inclined to entertain the possibility that things we worked hard to discover, that are consistent with our other beliefs, that we need to believe may be false. We need the discipline of testing to save us from our naturally error-prone selves.

When to test is a relevant question because some theories are not ready for testing. To be tested, a theory must be falsifiable; that is, we must be able to imagine some hypothetical evidence that would reveal the theory to be false.

---

[1] See, e.g., Strobe Talbott (deputy secretary of state in the Clinton administration), "Securing and Promoting Open Markets and Societies in the Americas," transcript of speech in Panama, *U.S. Department of State Dispatch*, June 10, 1996; and Daniel T. Griswold, "Trading Tyranny for Freedom: How Open Markets Till the Soil for Democracy," Cato Institute, January 2004.

Unfortunately, falsifiability cannot be taken for granted. In fact, some influential theories have not been falsifiable. Nonfalsifiability can arise if, as in the case of some formal theories, the assumptions are not concrete enough to make it possible for the researcher to identify cases that would constitute a fair test. A more common problem in small-sample research is a lack of clarity about what the theory predicts. For example, the checklists surveyed in Chapter 4 each list a dozen or more factors that favor democracy. These checklists make a clear prediction when all of the favorable factors are present or absent but not when some are present but others are not. Most cases are usually in this mixed category. Until a theory defines a clear correspondence between outcomes and the conditions that lead to them, it cannot be falsified. Finally, some non-falsifiable theories unconsciously employ circular logic. For example, Higley and Burton argued that democratic regimes are stable when the elite is united and break down when elites are divided (Higley and Burton 1989). But the authors also judged whether or not elites were united in part by whether the regime broke down, which reduced their theory to a near tautology.

What should be tested raises the question of whether we should test theoretical assumptions themselves or merely the predictions that flow from the theory. As mentioned in Chapter 6, one justification for not testing theoretical assumptions is that they are unobservable.[2] The unobservable nature of theoretical assumptions has been asserted with such force and frequency to justify the rational-choice approach that it has become an article of faith for some that all theoretical assumptions are unobservable. However, we must distinguish between assumptions that are inherently impossible to observe and those that are merely difficult to observe. Few theoretical propositions in political science are inherently impossible to observe; they are probably limited to past events of which there is no record and mental processes that the actors themselves understand poorly. (However, psychological research using fast magnetic-resonance-imaging technology is beginning to break down even the latter boundary [Amodio et al. 2007; Kanai et al. 2011]). Most of the allegedly unobservable processes are merely difficult to observe. Barbara Geddes writes, for example, "To gather the necessary detailed information about the internal politics of a large number of authoritarian regimes would require learning many languages and traveling to many places.... In situations like this, one must rely on tests of the *implications* of the argument, which

---

[2] We need not get into the philosophical issue of whether or not theoretical terms are inherently unobservable; for our purposes, if a theoretical term can be reliably operationalized in the context at hand, I consider it observable; see Hempel (1965).

can sometimes be done with less detailed information than would be needed to test the argument itself" (Geddes 2003, 64–65). My position is that many of these things can be observed, given sufficient ingenuity, time, and funding; and that when scholars overcome these obstacles, their efforts are recognized as pathbreaking. Another example: most theorists would be satisfied to say that the type of rationality that actors practice must be assumed rather than demonstrated. But when Kahnemann and Tversky carried out an experiment that demonstrated risk aversion, they won a Nobel Prize for it (Kahneman and Tversky 1979). Similar (although less prestigious) recognition has been won by Putnam and his collaborators for measuring the responsiveness of regional governments in Italy, by Stepan for gaining access to promotion records in Brazil's closed military, by Keck and Sikkink for concretely describing the ties binding transnational issue networks, and by many comparative historians for their painstaking archival work to reconstruct the past (Putnam et al. 1993; Keck and Sikkink 1998; Stepan 1971). Surveys – both elite and mass – are invaluable because they help us get inside the heads of individual actors. In principle, then, when assumptions can be tested, they should be.[3]

There are scholars who argue that as a matter of principle we should test only the predictions of a theory, not its assumptions. Their rationale is that predictive accuracy matters far more than descriptive accuracy, especially because all theories are selective simplifications of reality and are therefore, by definition, descriptively inaccurate. The extreme version of this argument, most notoriously championed by the economist Milton Friedman, concludes that realistic assumptions should not be expected; only the truth of the predictions matters (Friedman 1953). Lave and March take the less extreme position that assumptions can be tested but that the cost of doing so is "reject[ing] potentially fruitful ideas too rapidly." They caution that "leaping to test assumptions is likely to keep you from trying to figure out what derivations the model has. Learn to exercise the model before you start testing it" (Lave and March 1993). Of course, taking the time to derive implications from unrealistic assumptions is a gamble: the effort may yield good predictions, but it could also be a waste of time. Lave and March clearly believe that the risk is worth taking.

Ultimately, however, we cannot reconcile Friedman's instrumentalist view with the covering-law model of explanation, which requires that the

---

[3] Some propositions are unobservable because the concepts from which they are built lack clear empirical referents. These should be clarified and operationalized; otherwise, they are not really useful concepts.

fundamental laws from which other theoretical propositions are derived be both general and empirically accurate (Green and Shapiro 1994). Adopting Friedman's purely instrumental view of theory would reduce theory to the status of empirical regularity. Such theories would be no more than patterns that recur for unknown reasons, that is, for reasons that are different from the false ones assumed by the theory. We should have a higher standard than this for theory, to guard against spurious associations and "mere flights of intellectual fancy" (Green and Shapiro 1994, 31) and to boost confidence that our theories will explain outcomes that we have not yet observed. This is just as important in quantitative analyses that posit dubious causal mechanisms to account for empirical regularities as it is in rational-choice theories built on unrealistic assumptions.

It matters a great deal whether theoretical assumptions are reasonable simplifications, oversimplifications, or false assumptions. A reasonable simplification selectively calls attention to the most important causes while ignoring the lesser ones. An oversimplification ignores the most important causes in favor of less important ones. A false assumption is simply inconsistent with the evidence. For example, I could tell my wife that I will be home late every Monday evening during the fall because I teach an evening graduate class. This explanation would do a good job of predicting my arrival times on Mondays throughout the fall. But if the truth is that I am hanging out in a bar after work watching *Monday Night Football*, the explanation I offered is false no matter how well it predicts my behavior. My wife's quickest path to the truth would be to test the theory itself by, for example, checking the course schedule, showing up at my classroom, or interviewing my students, rather than testing the prediction that I will be home late. Elements of social science theories can also be tested by similar fact-checking. A theory that predicts well but is descriptively false is only a clever lie.[4]

What should be tested is a theory's (or its predictions') consistency with fresh evidence. The freshness of the evidence is crucial to testing. *Freshness* does not mean that the evidence was recently collected, about recent events, or that it was collected in some new way. It only means that the scholar did not have this particular evidence in mind when he or she formulated the theory. In comparative politics, we often assume that this entails building a theory inspired by one country and then testing it with respect to other countries. However, there are many other strategies that also qualify as testing.

---

[4] This does not mean that everyone must test assumptions in every project. To the extent that theory cumulates, it is sufficient if someone tests assumptions sometime, when this is possible.

For example, one could formulate a theory based on some evidence from one country and then test it using other evidence from the same country – similar evidence from different periods (if the domain of the theory permits), related evidence at different levels of analysis (if the theory has implications at multiple levels), or qualitatively different evidence from the same period (if the theory is thick enough to generate a variety of observable implications). The same possibilities obtain when a theory was inspired by the comparison of a small number of countries: such theories can be tested by selecting still other countries, by examining different time periods in the same countries, by gathering evidence at the group or individual level of analysis rather than national aggregates, or by analyzing a different kind of evidence that is also relevant for the theory. Of course, if a theory was deductively derived rather than inductively inspired, any relevant evidence is fresh. Chapter 6 suggests, however, that many formal models of democratization have been inspired by actual cases, whether or not the sources of inspiration are explicitly acknowledged.

Using fresh evidence is not a high standard for rigorous testing. In fact, it is the lowest, most basic standard. Without fresh evidence, there is no test; there is at best an illustration, a redescription of what was already known, or at worst, an effort to shield one's hypothesis from even the possibility that it could be disconfirmed because the "findings" are known in advance.

By this standard, some of the research that is called testing is not testing but instead theory development or concept refinement. For example, Chapter 5 shows that most comparative historians modify their theories when they apply them to additional cases. This practice uses the new cases inductively to inspire an improved theory, but it does not test the improved theory with fresh evidence. Some scholars have extended this false claim of testing to any situation in which a scholar moves back and forth between theory and evidence, incrementally adjusting the theory to fit the evidence. These approaches include constructivism and interpretative studies, which concentrate on getting the theoretical concepts right without necessarily bothering with a causal theory, and some studies of path dependence that abandon the goal of building general theories in favor of simply describing complex sequences of events properly (Hall 2003). If this is testing, the test takers are cheating: they peek at the answers before answering the question.[5] The problem with this procedure is that such "tests" do little to increase our confidence

---

[5] Quantitative researchers who engage in specification searches, also known as curve fitting or data dredging, are cheating in the same sense.

that the theory is correct; that is, that the theorist really understands the politics. The theory may fit this evidence, but there is little reason to believe that it will fit the next set of evidence. This is why fresh evidence is so crucial.

The minimal goal of testing is to confirm that a hypothesis is consistent with evidence. However, some tests are more rigorous than others. In a loose sense, the more evidence a hypothesis is consistent with, the more rigorous the test is. With sufficiently rigorous testing, theories that are based on false assumptions can usually be shown to be false. To return to the Monday-night example, if my wife tested some of the implications of my teaching-a-course explanation – that I am in a classroom at that hour, that I can report credibly about what happened in class, that I do not stink of beer and cigarette smoke – then she would soon know that I had lied. My explanation was consistent only with the evidence about the time I would come home. But this is the least rigorous form of testing: a demonstration that the explanation is consistent with some evidence. More rigorous testing examines whether the explanation is consistent with many different kinds of evidence.

Of course, not all evidence is relevant for testing. There is no need to confirm that my explanation is consistent with planetary motion or microbial reproduction rates in the Amazon. Rather, the theory must be consistent with the evidence identified by all of the implications of the theory. Even so, this richer, thicker testing is still not the most rigorous kind. The most rigorous testing demonstrates that the evidence is consistent with *this* theory and *only* this theory. In other words, rigorous testing disconfirms all of the alternative explanations in addition to confirming the ones we favor. The explanations we favor will probably be complex and multivariate, and they may often be confirmed partially, other things being equal, by holding other parts of the explanation constant. But no matter how complex the confirmed explanation is, there are always false alternatives that must be disconfirmed. This standard is consistent with a Popperian view of science in which we social scientists never prove anything, not even with our most sophisticated methods. Popper argued that the goal of science is not to prove a theory but rather to disconfirm alternative hypotheses (Popper 1968).[6] Disconfirmation

---

[6] Of course, we also need to demonstrate that our hypotheses do fit the evidence. This is not always easy, but it is easier than ruling out all of the other possibilities, so I emphasize disconfirmation here. One of the alternative hypotheses is that any association we discover is due to chance. For this reason, some scholars encourage us to avoid procedures that increase the probability of false positives, such as testing a hypothesis with the same sample that suggested it or engaging in exploratory specification searches or mere curve fitting. Some even find methodological virtue in procedures that are more likely to generate hypotheses that are wrong, that is, logical deduction of the implications of simplistic assumptions. I consider this stance an overreaction to the danger of chance associations.

of alternatives is arguably more important for the social sciences than it is for the natural sciences.

Experimental methods aim to create situations in which only the variables of interest vary: other variables are literally held constant and cannot influence the outcome. But comparative politics (with increasing exceptions) is an observational rather than an experimental science (Collier et al. 2004a). Controlled situations do not occur naturally, so we have to go to greater lengths to justify the assumption that the omitted variables do not determine the outcomes we observe. Some methods in political science, such as survey research, practice random sampling to justify the assumption that omitted variables cancel one another out. This is what makes it possible to use a sample to make inferences about a population. But, in comparative politics, random sampling (aside from surveys) is usually not feasible, so it is especially important to identify what the alternative explanations are and gather evidence about their implications to disconfirm them.

Unfortunately, comparative politics is so complex that it is impossible to gather sufficient evidence to disconfirm all of the alternative hypotheses. It is commonly supposed that it is the number of variables that makes comparative political relationships complex. Having a large number of variables certainly exacerbates the problem, but extreme complexity can arise even in a simple three-variable model. If one assumes that (1) any of the three variables may have a causal impact on any of the other two, (2) any of the three variables may be partly a product of its past values, and (3) any of the three variables may be caused in part by an interaction between the other two, then 4,577 different models are possible![7] Introducing more variables increases the number of possible models fantastically. And these calculations do not even factor in nonlinear relationships, fixed effects, spatial lags,

---

The counterintuitiveness of a hypothesis should increase our skepticism and our insistence on thorough testing, not our confidence in thinly documented associations. There are better ways to guard against false positives: enlarging the sample, replication using different indicators, and testing other observable implications of the hypothesis.

[7] This calculation was done as follows. First, I listed all of the twelve fully combinable elements possible in the three-variable model described in the text: three lagged variables, six causal pairs, and three causal interactions. I then calculated all of the possible combinations of these, taken twelve at a time, eleven at a time, ten at a time, and so on, down to none at a time. These sum to 4,096 models. But there are also many restricted models, in which one variable is not caused by either of the other variables. Because there are still six other elements it could be combined with, this leads to 128 more models. And this total must be tripled to 384 because there would be parallel models for the other two variables. In addition, there would be 96 additional models with two variables restricted, and 1 unique model in which none of the three variables is caused by either of the others or by any interactions among them. These all add up to $4,096 + 384 + 96 + 1 = 4,577$ possible models.

heteroscedasticity, and other phenomena frequently encountered in statistical modeling. The best way to address such complexity is to be guided by strong theory, as discussed in Chapter 6. But, in comparative politics, our theories are rarely strong enough to justify focusing on a small number of variables, much less just one model specification. Therefore, even if we have a strong theory, and even if few variables are involved, it is still important to rule out alternatives.[8] This is the essence of rigor. In a strict sense, our goal is to disconfirm *all* of the alternative hypotheses. But no serious social scientist requires proof that, for example, space aliens have not been destabilizing democracies by poisoning their water supplies. In practice, therefore, we are content to disconfirm only the alternative hypotheses that are conventionally considered plausible by other social scientists (Shadish et al. 2001). (Of course, if implausible hypotheses become plausible later, we are obliged to try to disconfirm them as well.) This convention lightens our burden tremendously because the vast majority of the hypotheses an imaginative person could dream up are implausible. But it leaves room for a still-overwhelming number of alternatives, for two reasons. First, different people find different things plausible. Some people are convinced by intimate personal knowledge of a case, others by sophisticated statistical tests, still others by strict logical deduction. Second, as Lakatos argued, disconfirmation is no simple yes-or-no exercise. Every hypothesis is embedded in a web of theories, not the least of which is the interpretive theory used to gather evidence for the test (Lakatos 1978). If a hypothesis fails a test, we need not (and tend not to) abandon the whole theory that generated it. Rather, we tinker with our control variables, question the sample and boundary conditions, search for better indicators, or tweak marginal assumptions in the model. And the more we revise these peripheral features of the theory, the more plausible alternatives there are for us to disconfirm.

To recapitulate the argument so far:

1. Why? Testing is necessary because we are naturally inclined to believe a great many things that are false.

---

[8] Motivated partly by this daunting complexity, Christopher Achen has argued for "a rule of three" (ART): "A statistical specification with more than three explanatory variables is meaningless," because with more than three explanatory variables, it is highly unlikely that the researcher will have taken the trouble to ensure that the model is properly specified and that all the assumptions of the model are justified (Achen 2002, 446). In my opinion, this rule is excessively strict. Convention and intuition play an important, and defensible, role in our evaluations of which models are sufficiently better than previous work to be considered publishable advances.

2. When? Theories must be falsifiable – concrete, internally complete, and noncircular – before they can be tested.
3. What? We should test both assumptions and predictions, when possible, by examining their consistency with fresh evidence.
4. How? There are different levels of rigor in testing, ranging from the use of evidence to illustrate the potential of a theory to energetic attempts to discredit all of the plausible alternatives.

There is much more to be said in answer to the how question, but this much is already sobering. Because the world is complex, plausibility is subjective, disconfirmation is not simple, and there are more alternative explanations than we can realistically manage, our grasp of the truth must be probabilistic, partial, conditional, and provisional. Those who will be satisfied only with deterministic, complete, universal, or final understanding should devote themselves to some other field of inquiry.[9]

Our understanding is probabilistic because it is partial and partial because it is probabilistic: there will always be some aspects of these complex processes that we will not be able to model; consequently, our predictions and explanations can be accurate only some of the time, for some of the cases. Nevertheless, we can hope to identify the most important causes so that we are right most of the time, about most of the cases, and our errors can be dismissed as random noise. Our understanding is conditional because there are probably very few, if any, laws of politics that would hold for all times and places; otherwise, we would have discovered them by now! It is also conditional because of the practical difficulty of studying all of the political systems on Earth, much less all of human history. Practicality forces us to develop our understanding incrementally – one country, one period, one region at a time. The conclusions of these middle-range studies are geographically and historically bounded and therefore, in effect, conditional. It may turn out that when we are able to generalize about larger samples, we can relax some of the conditions but, in the meantime, our knowledge must be treated as conditional.[10] In this sense, our understanding is also provisional:

---

[9] Physics, perhaps? Albert Einstein once remarked that "politics is more difficult than physics" (Clark 1955, 24).

[10] There is no contradiction between aspiring to universal theory and conceding that our theories must be conditional. A general theory can contain subtheories that apply under special conditions, provided that these conditions are aspects of some universalistic criterion. For example, Duverger's law was not the simple statement that majoritarian elections tend to produce two-party systems, and proportional elections tend to produce multiparty systems. Duverger himself inserted a condition: that the election have a single round. For two-ballot elections, he predicted that majoritarian rules

it is the best we can do today, with the understanding that it will be revised and improved tomorrow. It is also provisional in the sense that tomorrow our understanding may become not only more universal but also less partial and more certain.

Degrees and kinds of rigor

The discussion of orders of complexity in Chapter 3 underscores how challenging testing is in comparative politics. I argued in that chapter that there are five basic parameters in any model: a level of analysis, dependent variables, independent variables, units (e.g., countries), and a time period. I defined the order of complexity as the number of relationships among parameters that a model assumes. Even this rough survey of complexity suggested that the number of possible alternative models was very large and that existing research on democratization has found some evidence in support of models at all orders of complexity. But this overview only hinted at the complexities involved, for within each order of complexity there are many, many possible models. Earlier in this chapter, I calculated that there are more than 4,500 different models even when one limits the number of variables to three. And this estimate did not take into account temporal or spatial heterogeneity (unless they were captured by one of the three variables), alternative ways of measuring the concepts, or any kind of heteroscedasticity. So it seems safe to conclude that there are thousands of models that are potential alternatives to any model that interests us. Testing to rule out all of the alternatives is clearly impossible. Theory and convention, not testing, do most of the elimination of alternatives for us, by focusing attention on models backed by a theory and those that are considered plausible by some community of scholars. Convention also helps us lower our standards by allowing publication of research that may be flawed, as long as it is an improvement on previously published research. This is far from an infallible way to proceed, but because conventional theories can be completely off-base and the next test may invalidate the previous one, it is defensible on the grounds that it is provisional: the best we can do for now.

would produce multiparty systems (Duverger 1972). Further research added other conditions: that the law holds at the district level but not necessarily for national aggregates (Cox 1997), that proportional representation leads to multipartism only in plural societies (Ordeshook and Shvetsova 1994), and so on. Furthermore, all these nested propositions should be prefaced by more fundamental conditions, such as that the elections be conducted fairly, that elections be held, and so on. See Chapter 3 for elaboration.

Although the models we actually test are only a tiny subset of all of the possible models, it is still normal to have multiple competing models and therefore to need testing to choose among them. Because there are so many alternatives, most of them undreamt of, no one kind of test can lead us to the final, complete truth, and no one kind of test is always the most effective test for taking us as close to the truth as is feasible. Nevertheless, all approaches have some value because the truth lies at the confluence of independent streams of evidence.[11] This perspective suggests a practical and realistic standard for evaluating the utility of competing methodologies. It is not enough for a method to document isolated empirical associations or regularities; and it is asking too much to expect incontrovertible proof of anything. The question that should be asked is, rather, what are the strengths and weaknesses of each approach in helping us render alternative hypotheses more plausible or less? What follows in this chapter is an evaluation of the degree and kind of rigor in testing of two broad approaches – case studies and small-sample comparisons, on the one hand, and large-sample statistical comparisons, on the other.

There are two fundamentally different kinds of testing, which can be called extensive testing and intensive testing. These two kinds of testing have different goals that are analogous to the goals of wholesalers and retailers, respectively. Retailers are interested in matching specific products with specific customers. Similarly, the goal of intensive testing is to confirm that a given model is the best explanation for a given case. Wholesalers are not interested in matching a specific good with an individual consumer; they just want to maximize overall sales volume and profits. Similarly, extensive testing has the goal of confirming that a given model approximately fits a large number of cases, on average. Intensive testing is typical of case studies and small-sample comparisons, whereas extensive testing is typical of large-sample statistical research. Each kind of testing asks a different question about the fit between theory and evidence. Extensive testing uses large-sample statistics to ask whether this model is the best approximate general explanation for some class of events; intensive testing uses case studies and small-sample comparisons to ask whether this model is the best specific explanation for a specific event.

Both kinds of testing are legitimate and essential for good theory, but they are different and have complementary strengths and weaknesses. Extensive testing overlooks the imperfect fit of the model with particular cases. There

---

[11] This saying has been attributed to Karl Deutsch, but it is a common saying in many branches of science.

is no expectation that any single case will conform exactly to the model's predictions: all of the cases deviate from the predictions to some degree. Large-sample tests tolerate these deviations as long as the cases fit the model on average, the deviations are normally distributed and random, a certain proportion of the variance is explained, and so on. Intensive testing emphasizes getting each case right rather than generalizing beyond the case or small sample. Each kind of testing is good at what it tries to do but poor at doing the other's job. Extensive tests sacrifice an exact fit for generality, whereas intensive tests sacrifice generality in favor of an exact fit. Innovative kinds of testing are emerging that combine some of the advantages of both, and these are described at the end of the chapter. But because most research to this point emphasizes one or the other goal, the following section discusses them separately and emphasizes the trade-offs.

Trade-offs between extensive and intensive testing

Extensive testing is the most familiar kind of testing: the kind accomplished with statistical hypothesis testing, such as regression and its variants. In fact, for many scholars, statistical analysis is synonymous with testing. Nevertheless, statistical tests are useful for drawing only certain kinds of conclusions; they cannot answer all of the questions we ask when we want to know whether a model or a theory is true.

Although researchers often use statistical analyses to help them decide what the model is, this is, strictly speaking, an abuse of statistical methods. In principle, the analyst should assume a model before beginning. Then, given the model, ordinary-least-squares regression (the most typical procedure) tells us three basic things: (1) how much of a change in the dependent variable is, on average, associated with a unit change each independent variable, other things being equal; (2) how confident we can be that this impact is distinguishable from no impact at all, given the imprecision of the estimated impact; and (3) how much of the variation in the dependent variable can be explained by the variation in all of the independent variables together. All of these parameters could be different if a different model were specified. These are, to be sure, extremely valuable pieces of information to have. It is difficult to imagine tests of causal hypotheses that do not require some of this information, and some of it can be acquired only with statistics.

Nevertheless, it has its limits. First, it is conditional on the sample that was used to come up with these estimates. The data that are used for extensive testing may be truly extensive, such as thousands of country-years covering most countries over several decades; but they may also be confined to one country, as with time-series data for one country or some onetime observations of a large number of subnational units or actors. The generalizations that may be inferred from these analyses are therefore bounded: they are not valid beyond the universe that was sampled by the dataset. Thus, an extensive test could yield conclusions about something as extensive as the post–World War II globe or something as limited as South Korea in 1998.[12]

Second, regression estimates are valid only to the extent that the rather strict assumptions of the regression model are justified, and they rarely are. For example, regression analysis is based on the assumption that all of the variance that is not explained by the variables in the model is random noise. In effect, this means that the model omits no variables that are correlated with the explanatory variables that *are* in the model. But because data are scarce, many variables that are probably quite important are always omitted, and the chance that all of these are uncorrelated with the variables in the model is virtually zero. If this assumption is violated, then estimates of the impact of the explanatory variables are biased and inefficient, which means that judgments about whether their impacts are large or small, negative or positive, clear or cloudy, may be wrong (Fearon 1991).[13] This and other problems are addressed in more detail in Chapter 9.

On first thought, one might say that complex hypotheses cannot be tested extensively at all using small-sample methods because of the "many variables, small N" dilemma. The more complex the hypothesis, the more variables are involved; therefore, a case study or paired comparison seems to provide too few degrees of freedom to mount a respectable test. This cynicism is not fair, however, because in a case study or small-sample comparison, the units of analysis are not necessarily whole countries. Hypotheses about democratization do not have to be tested by examining associations between structural

---

[12] The logic of experiments is also about generalizing about a sample of test subjects, even though the sample can be small. For this reason, one of the most powerful criticisms of experimental methods is their lack of external validity. For example, it is questionable whether findings based on experiments with college students in a laboratory apply to the general population. Because almost all research on democratization is observational rather than experimental, I do not discuss experimental methods in detail.

[13] Other assumptions of ordinary least squares are often violated as well, but this is not a distinctive weakness of large-sample quantitative analysis vis-à-vis small-sample methods, which cannot even address such issues. The idea of a normal distribution and equal variances is difficult to handle without mathematical tools. A discussion of how best to detect and correct for violations of the statistical model is best handled in technical statistical references and does not belong in this comparison of large- and small-N methods of testing.

causes and macro-outcomes. If one is working with a thick theory that has many implications, then it is usually possible to say what the theory predicts at a lower level of analysis, for smaller and more numerous actors, or about a process developing over time. If so, we are still doing a large-sample analysis; but the observations are no longer countries or country-years but rather groups or individuals, who may be observed at shorter intervals such as months, weeks, or days. If the evidence is quantifiable, statistical methods can be used; if not, we can sometimes analyze qualitative evidence using the same logic as that employed in statistics.

In fact, the longitudinal case study is the best research design available for testing hypotheses about the causes of events within a case. A case study does the best job of documenting the sequence of events, which is crucial for establishing the direction of causal influence. Moreover, it is unsurpassed in providing quasi-experimental control because conditions that do not change from time 1 to time 2 are held constant, and every case is always far more similar to itself at a different time than it is to any other case. A longitudinal case study is the ultimate most-similar-systems design. The closer together the time periods are, the tighter the control. In a study of a single case that examines change from month to month, week to week, or day to day, almost everything is held constant and scholars can often have great confidence in inferring causation between the small number of conditions that do change around the same time. Such a procedure is still extensive testing because one is generalizing about many actors or time points. However, it is a poor cousin of cross-national extensive testing because its conclusions are still limited to the one or few cases that were studied.

Valuable though regression analysis is, it does not provide an exact fit between the cases and the model. In fact, it does not even attempt to fit cases exactly. Built into regression is the assumption that the model fits each case only approximately. Every case is presumed to have a residual, which is the vertical distance between the case and the regression line on a scatterplot. Ordinary least squares minimizes these residuals – actually, it minimizes the sum of the squared residuals, hence the name *least squares* – but the residuals are a necessary part of the method. Regression estimates cannot test how many cases the model fits exactly, and they do not aim to test whether a given model is the best model for a given case. (Regression can be used to identify how large the residual is for any case, but because its purpose is not to fit any case exactly, the chances of a perfect fit for any single case are minuscule.) Statistical testing is useful only for extensive testing, not for intensive testing. Using an approach that assumes that the model will not fit any case perfectly

	Y	X1	X2	X3	X4	X5	X6	X7	Xj
Obs 1	1	1	1	1	1	1	0	0	0
Obs 2	1	0							
Obs 3	0	0							
Obs 4	0	0							
Obs 5	1	1							
Obs 6	0	0							
Obs 7	0	0							
Obs i	0	0							

Figure 7.1   Data Used in Intensive and Extensive Testing

is inimical to the goal of ensuring that *this* model is the best explanation for this case.

Case studies and small-sample comparisons afford greater leverage for intensive testing, that is, for confirming that a model is the best specific explanation for a specific event. Figure 7.1 illustrates the logical difference between the two testing goals. It displays the typical configuration of a data set, with variables across the columns and observations down the rows. Here, Y is the dependent variable and the X's are the independent variables. Extensive testing makes use of the i observations on Y and X_1. It asks whether, on average, we can confidently infer that a unit change in X_1 produces an average change of a certain magnitude in Y; or (in logit or probit) that a shift in X_1 from 0 to 1 increases the probability of Y taking on the value of 1. This same logic is used in extensive testing whether the observations come from a large number of countries or a large number of within-case units. (In practice, there is usually more than one independent variable, but to heighten the contrast between thin and thick theories, I have limited the large sample to one independent variable.) In a case study (rather than a small-sample comparison, again to heighten the contrast) used for intensive rather than extensive testing, we have only one observation for each of many variables, $X_1 - X_j$ and Y. Using the logic of generalization, it is absurd to think that any inference could be drawn from such evidence. But the logic of intensive testing is different. It starts from King, Keohane, and Verba's (1994) injunction to maximize the number of observable implications of the theory. That is, we brainstorm about things that must be true if our theory is true in this case, and systematically confirm or disconfirm them. Here, our hypothetical theory predicts that a value of 1 on Y will be associated with a value of 1 on X_1–X_5; that is, that Y is true if X_1–X_5 are true.[14] We can test five different predictions of the theory this way rather than the one prediction for which we had large-sample data.

In Figure 7.1, all five predictions are confirmed for the hypothetical case. This is pattern matching: the pattern in the data matches the pattern predicted by the theory. But how does this increase our confidence in the theory? If our goal were to be confident that the theory is generally true, it wouldn't. But our goal is to increase confidence that our theory is the best explanation for a single case, observation 1. Here, our confidence is increased by the number of predictions that are confirmed, not by the number of observations for which any of them is confirmed. More precisely, there is some probability that any one of these conditions, X_1–X_5, is true, which can be denoted as $P(X_1)$, $P(X_2)$, and so on to $P(X5)$. There is a necessarily smaller probability, $P(X_1 \cap X_2 \cap X_3 \cap X_4 \cap X_5)$, that all five conditions are true. The probability that the theory that identified these conditions is true for this case is the probability that Y is true, given that X_1–X_5 are true. This becomes

$$P(Y|X_1 \cap X_2 \cap X_3 \cap X_4 \cap X_5),$$

which is solved as

$$P(Y \cap X_1 \cap X_2 \cap X_3 \cap X_4 \cap X_5)/P(X_1 \cap X_2 \cap X_3 \cap X_4 \cap X_5)$$

or, in plain English, the probability that predictions X_1–X_5 are confirmed when conditions X_1–X_5 are all true. The logic behind intensive testing, therefore, is that the more predictions one makes, the less likely it is that they will all be confirmed and the more the theory is exposed to possible falsification; but if the predictions are confirmed, this boosts our confidence that the theory that generated the predictions explains the case well. We would have much more confidence in this theory as an explanation for this case than in alternative theories that predicted X_6–X_j, which are false.

Figure 7.2 illustrates this principle visually. Suppose we have a theory that democracies break down (Y) when corruption (A), which may have been tolerated for decades, suddenly becomes intolerable in the midst of an economic stabilization shock program (B), and opposition-party leaders are willing to knock on the barracks doors, requesting military intervention (C). This theory generates a three-part thick hypothesis: if A, B, and C are true, then

---

[14] I am assuming, for simplicity's sake, that in this example we are aiming for jointly necessary and sufficient conditions.

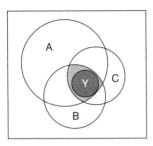

Figure 7.2   The Logic of Intensive Testing

the democracy breaks down. In the figure, the area of each circle represents the probability of each condition, and their intersections represent their joint probabilities. None of these hypotheses, by itself, would explain much. The probability of a breakdown, given corruption alone, is not high, according to the ratio of the area of Y to the area of A; and the other probabilities, taken separately, are not high, either. But the probability of a breakdown at the intersection of A, B, and C is quite large. The power of this test comes from the fact that Y was not necessarily to be found at the intersection; that is, some of the predictions could have been false. The more predictions a theory makes – that is, the more we take advantage of its thickness – the less likely it is to be confirmed, and the more confident we become that the theory is true if its complex and multifaceted predictions are confirmed in a particular case.

Unfortunately, it is not likely that any of the probabilities discussed here can be quantified. If they could be, we would have sufficient information to conduct an extensive test as well and be in the best of both worlds. In our actual world, where data are often scarce, it is not feasible to calculate the exact degree of confidence in a theory that an intensive test should inspire. Nevertheless, the logic of the test stands: the more predictions a theory makes, the easier it is to falsify, and when the predictions are confirmed, the more confident we can become that this theory explains a particular case well. This is rigorous testing even if we cannot quantify how rigorous it is.

The rich variety of information available to comparativists with an area specialization makes intensive testing ideal for them. In fact, it is what they do best (Brady and Collier 2004; George and Bennett 2005; Gerring 2001). For example, a scholar who suspects that Salvador Allende was overthrown in large part because he was a socialist can gather evidence to show that Allende claimed to be a socialist; that he proposed socialist policies; that these policies became law; that these laws adversely affected the economic interests of certain powerful actors; that some of these actors moved into opposition immediately after certain quintessentially socialist policies were announced or enacted; that Allende's rhetoric disturbed other actors; that these actors issued explicit public and private complaints about the socialist government and its policies; that representatives of some of these actors conspired together to overthrow the government; that actors who shared the president's socialist orientation did not participate in the conspiracy; that the opponents publicly and privately cheered the defeat of socialism after the overthrow; and so on. Much of this evidence could also disconfirm alternative hypotheses, such as the idea that Allende was overthrown because of U.S. pressure despite strong domestic support. If it turns out that all of these observable implications are true, then the scholar could be quite confident of the truth of the hypothesis in this case. In fact, the scholar would be justified in remaining confident of it even if an extensive test showed that most elected socialist governments have not been overthrown, because she has already gathered superior intensive evidence that confirmed the hypothesis in this case and disconfirmed known alternatives.

Harry Eckstein's advocacy of crucial case studies sustained hope that some generalizations could be based on a single case. He argued that there are sometimes cases in which a hypothesis must be true if the theory is true; if the hypothesis is false in such a case, then it is generally false (Eckstein 1975). But this claim would hold only in a simple monocausal world in which the impact of one factor did not depend on any other factor. Such a situation must be demonstrated, not assumed. In a world of complex contingent causality, we must presume that there are no absolutely crucial cases, only suggestive ones: cases that would be crucial if there were no unspecified preconditions or intervening variables. Crucial cases may therefore be quite useful for wounding the general plausibility of a hypothesis, but they cannot deliver a death blow. Douglas Dion's (1998) argument that small-sample studies can be quite useful for identifying or ruling out necessary conditions is mathematically sound but not very practical. First, it does not help at all with sufficient conditions (or combinations of conditions), which we cannot afford to neglect. Second, it applies only when one already knows that the condition of interest probably is necessary and that any alternative explanations are probably not true. Given the diversity of the political world, few conditions can be close to necessary, and the chances that one of the thousands of alternative explanations is true are very high. Therefore, such an approach is not likely to yield any general knowledge that we do not already have, and it is most likely that it will tell us nothing at all.

These are the virtues of intensive testing in principle. In practice, four problems are common. The first is indeterminacy, the classic "many variables, small N" problem. In this situation, different, incompatible explanations can fit the available evidence equally well; there is no way to rule some of them out, so they all seem to matter. This tends to be more of a problem when the evidence is not as thick as it should be, so that even in a within-case comparison, there are more variables than observations. In practice, how do scholars deal with this problem? Sometimes they interpret the evidence selectively, presenting the confirming evidence that they prefer for ideological or extraneous reasons. In the worst cases, they may even suppress disconfirming evidence, consciously or not. These practices amount to weak tests that may be rigorous enough to rule out some explanations but not to leave only one explanation standing. (It is only fair to acknowledge that this problem is equally prevalent in large-sample statistical research.)

But let us suppose that the scholar is honest and doing her best to be objective. When the evidence supports her theory, she keeps it; when it contradicts the theory, she modifies the theory to bring theory and evidence into agreement. She does this many times, iteratively, until she has a rich, plausible theory that fits the available evidence perfectly. And let us suppose that she has gathered such thick evidence that there is only one plausible theory that fits all of the available evidence. Even in this ideal small-sample, intensive testing situation, methodological problems two through four are still likely. The second problem is overfitting the model, also known as capitalizing on chance, or data dredging. It is illustrated by the anecdote about a visitor to a medieval shire who noticed that dozens of trees had archery targets painted on them, and each target had an arrow in its bull's eye. Much impressed, he asked who the master archer was, only to be told that a prankster had shot the arrows first and then painted the targets around them. In comparative politics, it is dangerously easy for a clever researcher to paint a theoretical target around any intriguing factual arrow, so we must not allow ourselves to be greatly impressed when theories are developed, or modified, to fit evidence that is already known. Just as fair archery contests place the targets before the archers draw their strings, fair testing requires fresh evidence; that is, evidence that the researcher did not have in mind when the theory was last developed or modified.

The third problem is that the focus on one country exaggerates the importance of factors that happened to change during that period in that country. These tend to be explanatory factors that vary within countries over time in the short run, such as leadership, personality, weather and natural disasters, short-term economic crises, and so on. The fourth problem is that the focus on one country blinds the researcher to other factors that did not vary, or changed very slowly, even if they might be important explanations of cross-national differences or historical change. Together, these biased estimates of importance could be called myopia: focusing attention on what is small, close, and quick at the expense of what is large, distant, and slow.

Toward testing that is extensive and intensive

The ideal testing procedure would be both extensive and intensive: it would tell us whether the model is the best model for each case and would also assess how generally applicable the model is. No such method exists. However, there are various modifications of the basic case-study and the standard regression model that take us closer to this ideal. Comparative histories apply case-study methods to a more extensive set of cases. Boolean analysis achieves even greater extension without sacrificing exact fits. Several regression variants approach the ideal from the other direction by tailoring large-sample statistical models more closely to groups of cases. Finally, various nested analysis strategies provide ways to integrate the results of statistical analyses and case studies.

Small-sample comparisons claim an advantage over single-case studies in principle but, in practice, they tend to be worse as a method for testing. One alleged advantage of these comparisons is that they call attention to causal factors that are taken for granted when examining a single case. However, every additional case requires a repetition of the same meticulous process tracing and data collection that were performed in the original case. To complicate matters further, the researcher usually becomes aware of other conditions that were taken for granted in the first case and must be examined systematically in all additional cases. Comparison therefore introduces new complexity and increases the data demands factorially, making comparative case studies unwieldy.

Another alleged advantage is that tests can be run with new data that did not originally suggest the hypotheses. However, this advantage is lost every time the researcher modifies the theory in the light of new evidence. It is difficult to resist the temptation to salvage a theory by noting that it works differently under X circumstances. Every modification requires fresh evidence for a new test, so the many variables soon outstrip the small sample once again.

But let us suppose the researcher manages to collect as much evidence in each of a dozen cases that was originally collected in a good case study. Is the problem of myopia avoided? Not completely. Within-region comparison is sometimes defended as (or assumed to be) a way of controlling for factors that the countries of the region have in common, but this practice deserves a closer look (Mainwaring and Pérez-Liñán 2005). Such "controls" would be effective if there were no variation on these common factors. But, in many cases, there is, in reality, quite significant variation on these factors within the region. Latin American countries, for example, were penetrated by colonial powers to different degrees, they were settled in different ways, their standards of living vary by a factor of ten, their social structures are quite distinct, many aspects of their political culture are unique, their relations with the United States and their neighbors are very different, they have evolved a great diversity of party systems, and there is a wide range in the strength of secondary associations and the rule of law. Bolivia and Guatemala should not be assumed to be comparable in each of these respects to Chile and Uruguay, yet this is exactly the assumption that the defenders of within-region comparisons make if they do not control directly for all of these differences. Therefore, limiting a sample to Latin America – much less any other region – does not really control for these allegedly common factors very well.

Another problem is that there may not be enough variation in any of these factors to make controlling for them feasible in a regional sample. Although there is variation, it is often variation within a smaller range than could be found in a global sample, and this may make it impossible to detect relationships. That is, in a truncated range, variance is higher relative to the range of the independent variable, which makes significance levels lower. Some important relationships with democracy are probably observable only over a global range. For an illustration of this, see Figure 7.3. There is definitely a relationship between the log of per capita gross domestic product and contestation that can be perceived on a global scale but that does not necessarily hold up within the narrower range of variation of both wealth and democracy that is found in Western Europe or sub-Saharan Africa but is evident in the most diverse region, Asia and the Pacific. What is large, distant, and slow moving is barely perceptible within some regions.

Ultimately, therefore, small-sample testing turns the "many variables, small-N" problem to its advantage for intensive testing but has no solution when it comes to generalization. At its best – when carried out with all the attention to detail and process found in case studies – a small-sample comparison is an accumulation of intensive tests. This is an improvement in

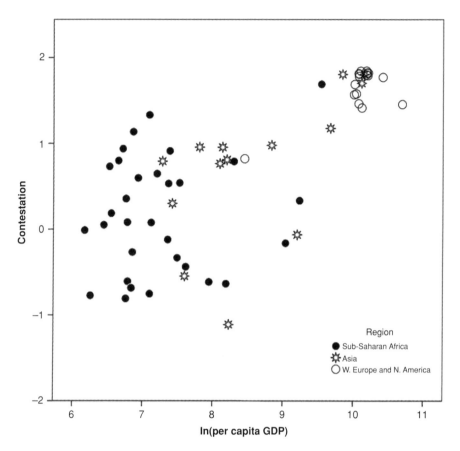

Figure 7.3   Contestation and Income by Region. *Note:* Contestation is from Coppedge et al. (2008); per capita gross domestic product is from the Penn World Tables 6.1. All observations are for 2000.

the sense that understanding several cases well is better than understanding one case well. But it is simply not feasible to carry out intensive testing for a large enough set of cases to justify inferences to a larger population. This would require several dozen case studies, and chances are that the model would be revised long before the studies were complete, thus necessitating fresh evidence from all of the cases in the sample. And, in practice, as argued in Chapter 5, the more cases are included in a qualitative comparison, the thinner the evidence from each one becomes. So, small-sample comparisons can just as easily be the worst of both worlds rather than the best. They tend to sacrifice some of their intensiveness without gaining enough extensiveness to achieve generality. And even when such testing is done honestly, meticulously, and thoroughly, inferences to any larger sample are inevitably biased toward causes that vary within the sample and biased against causes that vary only outside the sample. Nevertheless, such studies are valuable if the purpose is to generate or modify theory rather than to test it.

At present, the more promising path toward testing that is both intensive and extensive aims to test increasingly complex models statistically, with large cross-national datasets, which provide the degrees of freedom necessary to handle complex relationships with many variables. The only real solution to the "many variables, small N" problem (given that focusing on few variables would amount to burying our heads in the sand) is "many variables, large N." Chapter 9 discusses these methods in detail, but they can be described briefly here. Ordinary-least-squares (OLS) regression can be fairly complex by itself, especially when it includes a long list of independent variables. Some progress toward fitting each case well can be made, and most often has been made, by adding different variables to models, measuring concepts more accurately, and so on. But often even a long list of variables does not do a good job of explaining individual cases well. It is increasingly evident that one-size-fits-all models rarely fit well in comparative politics, especially in the large cross-regional samples that are needed when striving for generalization, and that what is needed is conditional theory that allows different models to fit different sets of cases.

Another approach that is gaining currency is Boolean analysis, which is discussed in more detail in Chapter 4. Crisp-set Boolean analysis is based on a deterministic and categorical logic in which a model either fits a case or does not. By categorizing all of the variables as binary yes-no items, crisp-set Boolean analysis enables scholars to handle large, multicountry samples and to use the Boolean logic of necessary and sufficient conditions to confirm or disconfirm whether certain combinations of conditions are uniquely associated with outcomes (Ragin 1987). Unfortunately, dichotomizing all of the variables sacrifices useful information and introduces arbitrary placement of classification cut points that can influence the conclusions (Elkins 2000). Dichotomizing also makes it difficult to handle the "how much" questions implied by the logic of means, deviations, and the goal of explaining variance.[15] It also dispenses with probability and tests of statistical significance, which are very useful for ruling out weak hypotheses and essential for excluding the possibility that some findings are due to chance. Another weakness of Boolean analysis is that it greatly increases the risk of chance

---

[15] It is not completely impossible to deal with some of these questions in a qualitative framework. Charles Ragin has pioneered the application of fuzzy sets to comparative politics (Ragin 2000). However, it is not clear that referring to a degree of being in a qualitative category is fundamentally different from measuring the same quality quantitatively.

associations, which exacerbate its tendency to turn up many equally well-fitting explanations for any outcome and no good way to choose among them (Berg-Schlosser and De Meur 1994).

Fuzzy-set analysis (fs-QCA), also pioneered by Ragin, is a promising improvement over plain Boolean analysis (Ragin 2008). Fuzzy-set logic was designed to handle situations in which cases only partially satisfy the defining criteria for a concept. It therefore releases qualitative researchers from the obligation to dichotomize their variables strictly. For example, a country could be treated as having fractional membership in the set of "democracies" if it satisfies only some criteria for democracy. In fuzzy-set analysis, there is no empirical difference between definitional relationships and causal relationships: both are understood in terms of necessary or sufficient conditions and degrees thereof. Whether a relationship is treated as definitional or causal is up to the researcher. Therefore, the same logic that applies to definitions and measurement also applies to causal testing. This approach leads to two kinds of inference. First, it yields information about consistency: the degree to which a proposition holds true where it is expected to be true. This inference about necessity, according to Ragin, is the analogue of statistical significance in correlational analysis. Second, fuzzy-set analysis yields information about coverage: the fraction of the cases that are explained by a proposition. This inference about sufficiency, he holds, is similar to the strength of a relationship or how empirically relevant it is (Ragin 2008).

Fuzzy-set analysis is only beginning to be applied in comparative politics (Goertz and Mahoney 2005). In democratization research, a good example is Schneider and Wagemann's attempt to explain democratic consolidation in a medium-sized sample of countries in Eastern Europe and South America (Schneider and Wagemann 2006). The advantage over simple Boolean analysis is that fs-QCA tells them not only which propositions fit the evidence but also how well they fit. Some of the drawbacks of Boolean analysis remain, however. Fuzzy-set analysis is just as likely to turn up a bewildering variety of hypotheses that work well, and to have insufficient evidence (i.e., limited diversity) to test many logically possible combinations of hypotheses (i.e., logical remainders) (Schneider and Wagemann 2006). Schneider and Wagemann propose coping with these problems by imposing a distinction between proximate and distant factors – a two-level theory. This is an encouraging step in the direction of nested theorizing, but it is a theoretical move that could be tested with a variety of methods other than fs-QCA.

There are quantitative methods that can easily handle categorical or ordinal data alongside continuous variables, and complex interactions as well, so there would be little reason to prefer qualitative methods if quantitative data were available and sound. This is a conclusion with which Ragin should agree, as his principal argument against statistical approximation of Boolean analysis is that "most data sets used by comparativists place serious constraints on statistical sophistication" (Ragin 1987, 67). He is correct to point out that regression estimates might not be possible or meaningful if one were to specify all of the permutations of interaction terms, as Boolean analysis does (Ragin 1987). However, it is not clear that being able to obtain many rough answers, an unknown number of which are produced by chance, is an improvement over admitting that no answer is obtainable. Besides, social scientists should not be testing every possible interaction in the first place; they should only test those that seem plausible in the light of theory. "Testing" them all without theoretical guidance is the definition of capitalizing on chance. Many large-N studies today have enough observations to handle dozens of variables and interactions with ease. The only truly satisfactory solution is to improve the quality and quantity of data across the board.

It is natural to wonder whether there are ways to combine the advantages of small-sample intensive testing and large-sample extensive testing. After all, we would ideally (in my view, at least) like our theories both to be generally true and to explain individual cases. A variety of multimethod strategies are emerging that integrate intensive and extensive testing. Evan Lieberman has usefully synthesized these options into a menu of possibilities that he calls nested analysis (Lieberman 2005). Nested analysis becomes possible when one has both large-sample thin data and thicker case-study evidence. Lieberman recommends always beginning with a preliminary large-sample analysis (LNA). If this preliminary test yields robust and satisfactory results, then one can conduct a model-testing small-N analysis (Mt-SNA), which is equivalent to the intensive testing described in this chapter. The preliminary LNA is also useful for selecting cases for intensive testing and for framing the puzzles that one takes on in the intensive testing (Coppedge 2005). If the intensive testing confirms the original model from the LNA, then the analysis is done. But if the original model fails the intensive testing, one must examine why it failed. It may be that the intensive testing used a truly odd case; if so, the intensive testing can be repeated with a more typical case. But if the model failed because of real theoretical flaws, then the next step would be to undertake what Lieberman calls model-building small-N analysis (Mb-SNA), which is the practice of moving back and forth between theory and evidence, iteratively modifying the theory until it fits. (One could also begin Mb-SNA if the preliminary LNA did not yield robust and satisfactory results.) This step would remove us temporarily from testing and, therefore, beyond the scope of this chapter. However, once this model-building effort yields a new, coherent model, one could then return to testing it with a new, less preliminary large-N analysis. The basic idea, then, is that it is wise to insist that a model pass both extensive and intensive testing before it is accepted; and if it cannot, small-sample analysis can be helpful for identifying a model that has a better chance of surviving both kinds of test.

Prospects

These multimethod approaches are still in their infancy. The bulk of testing in comparative political research continues to be conducted in ways that would be easy to classify as either intensive or extensive. Although better methods will probably become more common in the future, what is being done now, and what has been done for decades, is still valuable. However, it is always important to remember that the findings of this research – indeed, of any scientific research – are provisional. The theory that survives extensive testing should be regarded as provisional, pending more rigorous tests using fuller specifications that better approximate the uniqueness of each case. The results of intensive testing are also provisional, pending generalization to other times and places, perhaps conditioned by factors that had escaped attention due to myopia.

In the meantime, it is essential for comparativists to build bridges between small- and large-sample research and between these two methods and formal theory. If scholars in both camps communicated better, we could achieve a more efficient division of labor that would accelerate social-scientific progress. Large-sample researchers should continue to specialize in explaining the large, most obvious variations found in big samples. These explanations would define the normal expected relationships, which would serve as a standard for identifying the smaller but more intriguing deviations from the norm – the outliers. Specialists in case studies and small-N comparisons can intensively test models in confirming cases or improve theory by studying the outliers. Both tasks require specialized, labor-intensive, qualitative evidence sifting that is feasible only in small samples. Formal theorists could work to make assumptions increasingly realistic so that they can connect with the kinds of propositions used in more empirical work.

This is merely a call for each approach to do what it does best – large-N to sketch the big picture, small-N to fill in the details; some to imagine how the final picture will look, others to look through all of the jigsaw-puzzle pieces searching for corner and side pieces for the frame, and still others to fit together the pieces with similar colors and patterns. Perhaps a division of labor is an unfortunate metaphor because if large- and small-sample scholars are truly divided, we cannot learn from each other. Instead of a division of labor, what we need is overlapping labors, which require some scholars who do research of both types – perhaps not cutting edge on either side, but valuable as a bridge.

8 Political culture and survey research

This chapter begins the survey of empirical testing of theories of the creation and survival of democratic regimes. Chapter 9 surveys the impact of institutions, socioeconomic development and performance, and other factors, all of which emphasize forces external to individuals. In noncultural approaches, individuals are in a sense interchangeable: their political behavior is determined by their social class, their occupation, their role in an institutional context, and so forth. In cultural approaches, people are not interchangeable: they are different inside and therefore respond differently to the same external forces. Those who study political culture believe that we cannot discover useful theories without getting inside the heads of political actors.

Political culture is not a distinct methodological approach like case studies and comparative history, formal modeling, or quantitative testing. In fact, culture is studied using a variety of methods ranging from the qualitative extreme found in anthropological research to highly technical quantitative analysis using survey data and experiments. It has its own chapter here because the debate about approaches to the study of culture illustrates well the trade-offs that are the central theme of this book and because it is a large, complex, and fascinating literature in its own right.

Any discussion of political culture must begin by defining it. I begin this chapter by siding with the dominant behavioral understanding of culture while acknowledging that it tends to be thin. I then critique macro-macro comparisons, which are tantalizing but superficial, and argue that the causal pathways linking individual attitudes to regime outcomes must be more clearly specified. This principle frames the subsequent section, which takes stock of the micro-level evidence that is relevant for each causal linkage in mass-led transitions or survival.

Versions of political culture

The notion of political culture came to U.S. political science from German sociology, where it had a long and diverse lineage by the early twentieth century. The German tradition did not coalesce into a single coherent definition of culture; rather, different authors emphasized different characteristics of culture: as the sum total of all societal norms and practices, a legacy of history, norms or accepted ways of thinking and acting, a set of psychological orientations, a system that organizes society, or something that humans create and pass along to the next generation (Lane and Ersson 2005). This holistic understanding of political culture resonated well with the national and ethnic stereotypes and racism that were widespread in the West in the first decades of the century, and it was common at the time for U.S. political scientists to use "national character" as an explanation: the French act one way, the English another, and so on. Cultural theories have fallen out of favor more than once since World War II – partly because of their dalliances with racism and ethnocentrism – but reformulated versions have been proposed periodically.

Today, a variety of cultural approaches can be found in political science. The dominant version of political culture since the 1960s has been a behavioral approach that borrows from psychology and uses survey research and experiments. Nevertheless, other kinds of cultural theories survive that owe more to anthropology and the earlier German tradition. I contrast the approaches by first describing the ideal-type poles of a continuum running from the anthropological pole to the psychological pole. These ideal types are useful for highlighting the methodological trade-offs encountered in different ways of studying culture even though actual research tends to combine some of the advantages of each approach.

The anthropological view, most famously described by Clifford Geertz (Geertz 1973), holds that culture is a property of a whole society, or subgroups in society, but in any case not of individuals (Elkins and Simeon 1979). Culture consists of both attitudes and behaviors, especially those that have become stable, routine, and unquestioned. Culture therefore is relatively static, in this view. Culture is also rich and complex: there are many attitudes and behaviors. Furthermore, these cultural elements cohere, united by their own internal logic. In this view, individuals may deviate from cultural norms, but the culture exerts pressure on them to conform. For this reason, individuals cannot be fully understood apart from the culture in which they live. This approach calls for *verstehen*, which in German simply means "understanding" (Schedler 2004), but in English-language academic circles has come to mean an empathic, deep understanding of the culture by a perceptive scholar who knows it intimately enough to see it through the eyes of its members. This approach emphasizes the meaning of words and actions to the actors themselves. Several authors have claimed to describe cultures that are distinctively favorable or unfavorable for democracy. For example, Howard Wiarda has repeatedly argued that Latin American societies have a corporatist culture influenced by the teachings of St. Thomas Aquinas and the hierarchical organization of the Catholic Church (Wiarda 2004). This corporatist culture carries values antithetical to individualism, pluralism, and capitalism, all of which have been associated with political democracy. Another example is Lucian Pye's *Asian Political Culture*, which derives various orientations to political authority – some compatible with democracy, others not – from anthropological descriptions of family structure and child-rearing practices in seventeen Asian countries (Pye 1985).

One common criticism of this anthropological approach, or at least of its extreme stereotype, is that it exaggerates the homogeneity of a society. Societies, especially large ones on the scale of nations, always contain subgroups with their own subcultures, and these often contain individual dissenters (Knight and Camp 2001; Dalton 2002). Another common criticism is that although a static version of culture may be very useful for explaining political stability, it provides no leverage for explaining political change.[1] A third weakness is that this approach forces the social-scientific community to trust the subjective judgment of expert interpreters of a culture because it would be difficult or impossible for other researchers to replicate the expert's field experience, even if they had access to extensive documentation. Nevertheless, this approach probably yields more detailed, accurate, and insightful portraits of a culture than a battery of survey questions can. A recent reformulation, inspired by later work in critical anthropology, rectifies some of the drawbacks. The semiotic-practices approach does not assume that cultures are uniform or static or internally coherent. Rather, culture is the ongoing process in which individuals make meaning by engaging in political activity

---

[1] Harry Eckstein argued that even a relatively static concept of culture can make a few testable predictions about political change: in response to external shocks, cultures will change slowly while preserving some essential characteristics, and if the external shock is overwhelming, cultures will go through a period of formlessness before new cultural patterns emerge (Eckstein 1988). Note, however, that all of these predictions concern the impact of other things on culture, not the impact of culture on other phenomena such as democratization.

(Wedeen 2002). In this view, culture becomes a hive of constantly evolving activity that means different things to different participants. This approach strives for even finer-grained and exhaustive descriptions of a culture, which demand even more skill and effort to collect and analyze texts, conversations, and practices.

At the opposite extreme lies the behavioral approach to culture, inspired by psychology. In this approach, culture is merely the aggregation of individuals' attitudes and (in some applications) behaviors. Culture does not exist except in the minds of individuals, although for some purposes it may be useful to describe the culture of a group, society, or nation by referring to the distribution of attitudes or an average attitude in a society. This approach takes as little as possible for granted concerning the uniformity, stability, and coherence of attitudes. It may be that certain attitudes are dominant, that various attitudes go together because they are constrained by underlying value orientations, and that these patterns are stable or slowly changing; but in this approach, these are hypotheses to be tested, not features that can be safely assumed or asserted, even after extensive "soaking and poking" by an insightful expert. The best way to understand culture, according to this approach, is to conduct rigorous survey research. Sometimes researchers also conduct psychological experiments. One early example of this approach with relevance for democratization was *The Authoritarian Personality*, a project that began as a study of anti-Semitism in 1943 but eventually led to a scale measuring a right-wing authoritarian personality presumed to be supportive of fascist regimes (Adorno et al. 1950; Altemeyer 1981; Stone et al. 1992). On the democratic side, the landmark study was *The Civic Culture*, which used public opinion surveys in five countries to identify a cluster of attitudes that the authors believed to be most propitious for stable democracy (Almond and Verba 1965). Both studies suffered fierce criticism on methodological grounds, much of which was justified (Verba and Almond 1980). However, because their mistakes inspired others to do better, they founded what is a vast body of survey research on political culture and democratization.

These are, again, only ideal types. Actual research on culture rarely conforms to these extreme stereotypes. In comparative politics, most relatively anthropological research recognizes subcultures, is careful not to generalize beyond the small communities it studies, and does not assume that beliefs and norms are coherently structured and stable (Banfield 1958; Ross 1997; Scott 1976). The relatively psychological research does not really reduce culture to an aggregation of individual beliefs, norms, and attitudes; rather, it views these as imperfect individual expressions of a collective culture. It also holds that culture is embedded in socializing institutions such as churches and schools that reinforce some coherence, uniformity, and stability (Almond and Powell 1966; Putnam et al. 1993). Some research uses such diverse materials and is so open to many sorts of interesting relationships that it is hard to classify on this continuum (Laitin 1986). Nevertheless, the continuum I have described is useful for understanding methodological trade-offs. To the degree that research on culture approaches the anthropological pole, it has the virtues of thickness and the limitations of lacking generality and integration. To the degree that it approaches the psychological pole, it contributes to generalization (usually within countries but increasingly across countries as well) but tends to be thin and unintegrated with other theory.

Whether an anthropological or a psychological approach is better therefore depends on one's purpose. If the goal is to provide a rich, thick description of a small, relatively homogeneous community, then the prolonged immersion that anthropological approaches require is likely to lead to better insights. But if one's goal is to develop and test fairly general ideas about the impact of political culture on democratization, then survey research and statistical analysis are indispensable. Because the goal of this book is to summarize and critique what we know about general theories of democratization, I must devote the bulk of my attention in this chapter to survey research. But, in some respects, the distinction between these approaches is not absolute. Anthropological researchers must get to know a range of community members well to make any claim that their portrait represents the entire community, and a survey questionnaire is useless if it forces respondents to choose among answers that mean nothing to them. A well-designed survey implements *verstehen*: it anticipates all of the likely answers and offers respondents choices that they can agree with wholeheartedly.[2]

For the study of democratization, which involves processes that transcend small, homogeneous communities, the psychological approach is superior overall to any anthropological approach. By making questionnaires more comprehensive and more in tune with how people really think, survey research can approach thick description; but survey research has valuable advantages that anthropological approaches can never equal. Only survey research takes samples that are demonstrably representative of a population, thus eliminating the need to rely on the authority of one observer. Only survey research can reveal how a population is distributed among different attitudes – a great

---

[2] This statement paraphrases a remark by Juan Linz at a dinner in his honor in Philadelphia, September 2, 2006.

improvement over asserting that the culture is homogeneous or admitting that it is heterogeneous without revealing the sizes of the subgroups. Only survey research can rigorously test a claim that certain attitudes cohere in a more fundamental structure. Only survey research can tell us whether certain attitudes or patterns really are stable. And only survey research, in combination with probability theory and statistics, can estimate how confident we can be that a sample is representative, a subgroup is of a certain size, an underlying cultural dimension exists, or attitudes are changing or stable.

In my view, statistical concepts provide the best way of thinking about, describing, and analyzing the role of political culture in large-scale processes such as democratization, provided that a survey captures individual attitudes validly and reliably. Statistics make it possible to describe the average (or median or modal) opinions, perceptions, beliefs, and norms of the collective without ignoring the dispersion of individuals around the group's central tendency. Any useful generalization about the culture of a group must pay attention to both the central tendency and the dispersion. For example, an anthropological article once described Venezuela's political culture in elaborate and fascinating detail (Coronil and Skurski 1991). It claimed that Venezuelans do not feel responsible for their own prosperity; rather, they believe that the "magical state" should provide for them by distributing the proceeds from oil exports equally among all citizens. Furthermore, the state should be headed by a strong leader with a direct, unmediated relationship with "the people," and who punishes any dishonest politicians who seize more than their share of the wealth. This description has the ring of truth, and it seems to explain the popularity of President Hugo Chávez Frías (1999–present). Survey research, however, shows that this portrait is a caricature that simplifies and exaggerates reality. According to the 2004 LatinoBarómetro, 47 percent of Venezuelans rejected "iron fist" (*mano dura*) leadership. Venezuela was also the Latin American country with the highest percentage of people who felt that they, rather than the government, were responsible for their own well-being (LatinoBarómetro 2004)! Coronil and Skurski's characterization of Venezuelan political culture was useful for highlighting some tendencies that were probably stronger in Venezuela than in some other societies, but it underplayed Venezuelan subcultures. Ignoring these discrepancies would make it impossible to understand why President Chávez ever faced any opposition. Survey research would not obscure absolute unanimity on a broad set of attitudes, if it existed. But the lack of such findings suggests that interpretive approaches lead to necessarily inaccurate, oversimplified distortions of reality.

Statistics are also essential for testing claims about the internal coherence of a culture. Because a culture is not just any jumbled mix of beliefs and norms, it is important for cultural analysts to find out whether there really are underlying cultural orientations that structure a larger set of attitudes. More concretely, this means that certain attitudes are closely associated with one another and with some underlying dimension or dimensions. One can test for associations among attitudes by cross-tabulating or correlating indicators of those attitudes. Factor analysis is often used to determine whether these relationships are structured by a common underlying dimension. For example, Ronald Inglehart and Christian Welzel have shown that a dimension ranging from a focus on physical survival to an emphasis on self-expression meaningfully structures forty or more attitudes across dozens of countries (Inglehart and Welzel 2005; but see Davis and Davenport 1999).

The fundamental difference between the anthropological and psychological or statistical approaches to political culture is that the latter holds that the attributes of a culture should not be asserted by an authority or merely assumed; rather, they should be demonstrated with evidence. This principle applies to descriptions of individual attitudes, claims about the structuring of attitudes, relationships between attitudes and behavior, and claims that any aspect of a culture is dynamic or static. Before the 1990s, lack of data made it practically impossible to demonstrate trends or stability in political culture beyond a handful of countries and topics. However, repeated waves of surveys – especially the U.S. National Election Studies, the EuroBarometer, and the World Values Surveys – have begun to make such generalizations possible. These studies cast doubt on the alleged stasis of political culture. In fact, much of this research has been devoted to explaining patterns of change such as the decline of institutional trust and the emergence of postmaterialist values.

Macro-macro studies

The kind of political culture research that is most obviously relevant for democratization examines associations between national averages of individual-level attitudes, on the one hand, and levels of democracy, the duration of democratic regimes, or the probability of regime transitions, on the other hand. Almond and Verba's *The Civic Culture* inaugurated this line of research (Almond and Verba 1965). This study of the United States,

Britain, Germany, Italy, and Mexico argued that democracy was most likely to thrive and survive where citizens possess a civic culture. Such a culture is a balance of participant traits, which incline citizens to take an interest in politics and participate in elections and other activities that make democracy work, and subject traits, which incline citizens to respect the law and the authority of the state and the government. Because this was the first cross-national survey project, it was pathbreaking for its time but amateurish by today's standards. Critics pounced on it for using unrepresentative samples, asking invalid questions, overestimating the stability of attitudes and underestimating the impact of short-term political events, and drawing unwarranted connections between cultural patterns and regimes – in general, for reaching conclusions not justified by the evidence. But it hinted at what would be possible if such research were done more rigorously, and therefore it inspired innumerable other studies (Verba and Almond 1980).

In subsequent decades, comparative survey research became much more rigorous and abundant. Consequently, social scientists gained the ability to describe attitudes, trends, and relationships with much greater confidence. And, as knowledge of political culture improved and trends became evident, theories about the impact of culture on democratization evolved considerably. In *The Crisis of Democracy*, Crozier, Huntington, and Watanuki argued that slow economic growth and high inflation were eroding the capacity of governments in the United States, Western Europe, and Japan at the same time that citizen demands on government were increasing. They predicted that the growing gap between expectations and performance would eventually undermine confidence in leaders, institutions, and democracy itself (Crozier et al. 1975). Some scholars predicted that many advanced democracies would fail within a few decades (Putnam et al. 2000). One of these predictions did come true: confidence in institutions did decline, even outside wealthy Western countries. In most countries, confidence or trust in government, legislatures, courts, politicians, civil service, armed services, police, and especially political parties fell from the 1970s to the 1990s (Putnam et al. 2000). There were signs of widespread deterioration in other symptoms of civic culture as well: electoral turnout, party membership, generalized social trust, and face-to-face participation in voluntary associations (Putnam 1995).

Nevertheless, Western democracies did not fail, and support for democracy is strong, if not stronger than before. It has been suggested that this paradox can be explained by the moderation of inflation and by the conservatism of the 1980s, which lowered expectations of government (Putnam et al. 2000). But these reasons are incompatible with declining trust in institutions.

Two other arguments are more convincing. First, Rose, Mishler, and Haerpfer's comparisons of post-Soviet countries (some of which did become less democratic after 1991) suggest that no matter how unpopular politicians, parties, and democratic institutions become, democracy will not break down unless some alternative regime has greater legitimacy (Rose et al. 1998). If true, this means that in the West, support for democracy remains strong partly because the collapse of communism left it without a rival. Second – and contrary to Almond and Verba's embrace of some degree of the subject orientation and the *Crisis of Democracy* school's fear of disorder – there is a growing consensus that a certain amount of distrust in government is actually healthy for democracy. The growing numbers of critical citizens who question elite authority; shun traditional forms of participation; and invent new ways to associate, act collectively, and make their demands heard may be improving the quality of democracy by making representatives more responsive and accountable to the public (Inglehart and Welzel 2005; Norris 1999a; Putnam et al. 1993).[3] This explanation is also consistent with the fact that many formal democracies in the third world are "illiberal" or "hollow" (Diamond 1999) because, being less economically developed, they have fewer critical citizens.

The culmination of research in this vein is Inglehart and Welzel's *Modernization, Cultural Change, and Democracy: The Human Development Sequence* (Inglehart and Welzel 2005).[4] This ambitious book proposes a sweeping theory of cultural change and democratization, based on a quarter-million survey interviews in up to eighty-one countries from 1981 to 2001. Using factor analysis, Inglehart and Welzel identify two fundamental dimensions that structure national-average attitudes across countries. The first is the preference for traditional (especially religious) authority versus secular-rational authority. The second is an emancipative values dimension ranging from concern with basic economic or physical survival to an emphasis on elite-challenging self-expression. The authors also confirm the existence of various civilizations, defined by religion and colonial heritage, which tend to occupy distinct positions on these two dimensions. For example, Confucian national cultures tend to be relatively secular and survival oriented, Islamic national cultures tend to be traditional and survival oriented, English-speaking national cultures tend

---

[3] This line of thought is appealing, although it may be too optimistic. It is probably too soon to be confident that increased individual autonomy and less-institutionalized forms of participation will be compatible with stable, well-functioning representative democracy in the long run.

[4] This book modifies the conclusions of Inglehart's voluminous earlier work on postmaterialism, which I do not discuss in detail here because Inglehart and Welzel's book is more rigorous and is based on much additional data and therefore entirely supersedes the earlier research.

to be relatively traditional and oriented to self-expression, and Protestant European national cultures tend to be secular and oriented to self-expression. Societal values shift along both dimensions in response to economic transformations, in two phases. First, industrialization shifts the source of authority from religion and tradition to secular states, science, and technology. But often before this cultural shift is complete, postindustrial transformations (particularly the growth of the service sector) halt secularization and promote the questioning of authority of any type. Any country's average position today in this two-dimensional cultural space, the authors contend, is a function of which civilization it started from and how far industrial and postindustrial transformations have shifted its values toward secular-rational authority and self-expression values.

Contrary to the modernization theory of the 1960s, Inglehart and Welzel argue that secularization has nothing to do with democratization: secular culture is as compatible with communism and fascism as it is with liberal democracy. Instead, the cultural tendency that really matters is the level of self-expression values. There is a logical connection between, on the one hand, having a large proportion of citizens who value self-expression – who feel economically secure, independent from elite domination, and claim "the ability to make decisions and actions based on autonomous choices" (Inglehart and Welzel 2005, 47) – and, on the other hand, the probability of a country having a democratic regime in which representatives respect citizens' demands. Inglehart and Welzel argue explicitly that the Linz-O'Donnell-Schmitter elite-bargaining frameworks for understanding regime change underestimated the impact of political culture:

Democracy is not simply the result of clever elite bargaining and constitutional engineering. It depends on deep-rooted orientations among the people themselves. These orientations motivate them to press for freedom, effective civil and political rights, and genuinely responsive government – and to exert continual vigilance to ensure that the governing elites remain responsive to them. (Inglehart and Welzel 2005, 300)

Inglehart and Welzel present massive evidence and sophisticated analyses to support most of their key arguments. Their two fundamental dimensions are robust; that is, they appear even when different sets of countries and different sets of variables are used. They show that the traditional-secular-rational dimension is associated more strongly with the degree of industrialization and the dimension of survival and self-expression more with the degree of postindustrial transformation (in a contemporary cross section). They show that cultural zones cannot be reduced to economics or regime experience. They show that wealthier countries have tended to experience value shifts in the same direction and that these shifts are associated with increases in elite-challenging political activity. They distinguish between formal democracy and effective democracy, which incorporates information about elite integrity. They go to great lengths to show that self-expression values cause stable democracy but stable democracy does not cause self-expression values while controlling for a variety of competing causes (more about this later).

Nevertheless, the analysis is not airtight. Macro-macro comparisons are vulnerable to several criticisms. Inglehart and Welzel's book partially overcomes some of them, but not all, so it is still useful to evaluate their contribution while discussing five problems frequently encountered in other macro-macro analyses.

One of the biggest challenges in cross-national survey research is achieving conceptual validity. When surveys must be administered in different languages and different cultural contexts, in which the meaning of words and symbols can vary in subtle ways, designing questionnaires that can measure what is demonstrably the same concept across many countries requires care, experience, and trial and error. *The Civic Culture* was harshly criticized for its failure to do this, for example in its mishandling of the difficult-to-translate standard U.S. question, "Do you think that quite a few of the people running the government are a little crooked, not very many are, or do you think hardly any of them are crooked at all?" One common tactic for dealing with this problem is simply to keep trying a variety of questions until a consensus develops that it validly measures what it purports to measure. A question is more likely to be valid to the extent that it elicits the answers that were expected from respondents, it is strongly correlated with questions designed to measure the same concept, and it is strongly correlated with factors that were expected to cause it and with phenomena that it was expected to cause.[5] Another tactic, which has become very common in survey research, is to use factor analysis to create an index that measures a fundamental dimension captured imperfectly by multiple survey questions. Each question can be thought of as a reflection of both the concept that one wishes to measure and one or more contaminating ideas. The more questions one has that capture the concept of interest, even if each one is quite contaminated, the more feasible it is to isolate the variation in each one that reflects the concept from the contaminants, which

---

[5] Concept validation is discussed in much greater depth in Adcock and Collier (Adcock and Collier 2001).

reflect extraneous information. Factor analysis (or a common variant of it, principal-component analysis) is simply a statistical technique that reveals whether it is useful to reduce multiple questions or variables to a simpler set of underlying dimensions. The factor analyst still must use subjective judgment to interpret what the underlying dimensions are, but factor analysis is extremely useful for identifying how many dimensions there are and which variables reflect which ones.

Inglehart and Welzel's two dimensions are indices constructed from just this kind of factor analysis. Because interpreting dimensions requires as much art as science, they remain subject to challenge, especially when an analyst claims to have identified universal values that have the same meaning in all countries. For example, it is not obvious that all of the variables included in the index of self-expression values really belong there. Is rejection of science really part of self-expression? Toleration of homosexuality? A preference for female leaders? Describing one's own health as good (Inglehart and Welzel 2005)? More generally, is "self-expression" the best label for the commonality in all these attitudes? Are "elite-challenging values," "individual autonomy," and "human development," different labels Inglehart and Welzel often attach to this same dimension, really interchangeable? Are all of these the same as "post-materialism," the label that Inglehart favored for more than twenty years before revising and reinterpreting his index? If not, why did the interpretation change? The dimensions Inglehart and Welzel identify are robust enough that there is little doubt that they are real, but there is some fuzziness around the edges of the interpretation that has been imposed on them.

A second common problem in macro-macro comparisons is that it is hard to disentangle the impact of culture from that of other static or slowly changing country characteristics, such as institutions, geography, level of economic development (within a short time-frame), world-system position, or particular historical legacies. This problem is strictly insuperable when the data are cross-sectional: a snapshot of many countries at one instant in time. Unfortunately, for many years, all comparative survey research was cross-sectional because there were no repeat surveys for large numbers of countries (Inglehart 1977; Muller and Seligson 1994; Diamond 1999). But even though public-opinion time-series are available for many countries, it is still difficult to distinguish the impact of cultural characteristics that change slowly from the impact of fixed effects or gradual trends that tend to move in a consistent direction. If many countries are simultaneously becoming more democratic, more prosperous, and shifting toward self-expression, then it is very hard to say with confidence whether it is the economy or culture that is driving democratization. One of the great strengths of Inglehart and Welzel's study is that it is the first to take advantage of the three waves of World Values Survey data from 1981 to 2001. This span of time is long enough to contain some dramatic cultural shifts and to contain changes in democracy and economic performance that do not necessarily parallel changes in culture. This makes it possible for the first time to estimate the relative impacts of culture and economic development on democratization. By the standards of more advanced time-series research – for example, analyses of presidential approval ratings month by month over many years, which make strong causal inferences possible – Inglehart and Welzel's research design is still primitive. It does not go beyond examining the impact of a change in culture (and control variables) in one period on changes in democracy in one subsequent period, across anywhere from nineteen to eighty-one countries. It is still much more a cross-sectional analysis than a dynamic analysis. Nevertheless, it is a clear advance over other cross-national cultural research on democratization in this respect.

A third weakness of cross-sectional research designs is that they often reveal nothing about the direction of causation. Even if culture and regimes are strongly associated, cross-sectional analyses leave open the possibility that regimes shape culture rather than culture shaping regimes. Indeed, this was a contentious issue in cultural research on democratization as long as studies were cross-sectional, and some of the most rigorous analyses persuaded many political scientists that a democratic culture was a by-product, not a cause, of democracy (Przeworski 1986; Muller and Seligson 1994). However, Inglehart and Welzel report a fairly sophisticated series of tests to show that the causal order is as they claim: economic transformations cause shifts in values, which then make countries become more democratic and remain so. More specifically, they rely on the notion (standard in quantitative analysis) of Granger causality, which holds that one can infer causation when (1) the cause temporally precedes the effect, (2) one controls for any factor that might affect both the cause and the effect, and (3) one also controls for past values of the effect (Granger 1969). In their most rigorous test, Inglehart and Welzel demonstrate that self-expression in the early 1990s has a significant impact on average levels of democracy in the period 1997–2002, controlling for socioeconomic resources and average levels of democracy in 1981–1986; but average levels of democracy in 1981–1986 have no significant impact on self-expression in the early 1990s, controlling for socioeconomic resources and self-expression values in 1981 (Inglehart and Welzel 2005, 180–186). I regard this evidence as inconclusive because the before and after samples that Inglehart and Welzel used were quite different. To test the impact of self-expression on democracy, they used a large, diverse sample of sixty-one countries; but to test the impact of democracy on self-expression, they had to use a smaller, more homogeneous sample of just the nineteen countries in the 1981 wave of the World Values Survey. Purely because of the difference in sample sizes and diversity, we should expect the coefficients for the impact of democracy on values to be smaller and less significant than the coefficients for the impact of values on democracy. This biases the analysis in favor of the authors' hypothesis. Nevertheless, Inglehart and Welzel raised the standard for demonstrating that influence flows from culture to regime.[6]

Studies that associate regimes with highly aggregated indicators of attitudes often suffer from a fourth problem. It is usually called the ecological fallacy, or the error of assuming that a relationship between variables at a higher level of analysis also holds at a lower level of analysis. The classic example is the positive association between the size of the black population in Southern U.S. congressional districts in the 1950s and the share of the vote won by segregationist candidates: the positive association at the district level does not mean that blacks were voting for segregationists (Robinson 1950). One may also commit the opposite, individualistic fallacy of believing that a relationship among individuals must hold when aggregated to districts, states, nations, or any higher level of analysis. For example, the fact that observant Muslim citizens of countries on the periphery of the Middle East tend to support democracy more than nonobservant Muslims should not lead us to predict that Islamic countries tend to be democratic (Tessler 2002). The simple fact is that a relationship at the national level says nothing about the relationship at the individual level, and vice versa. This is a paradox, but Figure 8.1 shows how it works. Each of the three lines in each of the nine figures shows a hypothetical relationship between two variables at a lower level of analysis, such as a relationship among individuals in a country. The relationship across the

---

[6] Inglehart and Welzel (2005, 186–206) report other analyses of the direction of causation. One model of self-expression in the early 1990s substitutes the mean self-expression level of each country's regional culture in the same period for prior levels of self-expression in the same country. A model of effective (rather than formal) democracy in 2000–2002 substitutes the number of years of democracy before 1995 for the prior democracy control. A series of models reject six additional social and economic control variables, but one at a time rather than in combination. There is also an interesting test of Eckstein's congruence hypothesis, showing that "the more the cultural demand for freedom exceeded its institutional supply around 1986, the greater were the subsequent moves toward more democracy, from 1987 to 2002" (Inglehart and Welzel 2005, 189–190). These additional tests lend support to Inglehart and Welzel's claims, although one has to wonder whether, out of the many tests that their data made possible, the authors chose to present the confirming ones and omit any that undermined their thesis.

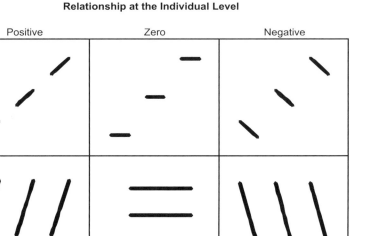

Each line represents the individual-level relationship within one country.

Figure 8.1   Illustration of the Ecological Paradox

three lines in each of the nine figures shows the relationship at a higher level of analysis, such as relationships across countries. Every kind of relationship – positive, negative, or null – is possible at each level, independently of the relationship at the other level. This could be called the ecological paradox: one can never assume that it is safe to make cross-level inferences.

Some of Inglehart's harshest critics have accused him of committing the ecological fallacy. Davis and Davenport, for example, claim that the post-materialism dimension does not exist at the individual level (because some of its components do not covary), and that it cannot be valid at the cross-national level if it is invalid at the individual level (Davis and Davenport 1999). Seligson similarly argues that the apparent cross-national relationship between mean national self-expression values and democracy is spurious because there is no corresponding relationship between self-expression and support for democracy at the individual level (Muller and Seligson 1994;

Seligson 2001). Inglehart mounts two somewhat contradictory defenses against these charges (Inglehart and Welzel 2005, chapter 10). On the one hand, he insists that political culture is a system-level (national) phenomenon whose relationship with democracy is appropriately studied at the system level. Critics who demand confirmation of the relationship at the individual level are committing the individualistic fallacy, he contends. On the other hand, he goes out of his way to report that some of the relationships he identifies at the system level also exist at the individual level, although much less strongly (Inglehart and Welzel 2005, 51). If the relationship were purely a system-level phenomenon, this evidence would be irrelevant. Furthermore, his expositions of the theory behind these relationships frequently refer to the motives and behavior of individuals (Inglehart and Welzel 2005, 25–46). In summary, Inglehart and Welzel present strong empirical evidence that countries with a high percentage of the population with self-expression values are very likely to be democracies, but the evidence prohibits them from claiming that there is a powerful dimension of survival versus self-expression values at the individual level within many countries, or that individuals who value self-expression do more, on average, to produce or sustain democracy than their fellow citizens who care more about mere survival. Why the relationship exists cross-nationally therefore remains a mystery, which I discuss further in the following section.

Finally, there is a related but subtler problem in these macro-macro comparisons that has attracted little notice. Cross-national comparisons of means sacrifice information about variability within each case and therefore exaggerate the size and significance of the relationship. In effect, they ask us to believe that all respondents hold the national mean attitude. To deal with this problem and the previous one, it would be advisable for scholars to use pooled cross-national data when estimating the relationship between individual attitudes and macro-level democracy variables. If there is any variation in democracy within countries, it would be best either to obtain separate estimates for each national sample or to interact country dummies with the attitudinal variables in a pooled sample (which is often the exact equivalent) (Franseze 2005). It would be even better if researchers were to develop and test a good theory to resolve the ecological paradox.

A comprehensive framework

This critique of macro-macro comparisons suggests that a fundamental problem with cultural theories of democratization is that the alleged cause and the effect are on different levels of analysis. Culture (understood as individual attitudes) is a micro-level phenomenon, but democratization is necessarily a macro-level phenomenon. Attempts to bring the two together in an explanation casually shift the level of analysis of either the cause or the effect. As we will see, micro-micro studies translate regime change or survival into individual level actions or attitudes, such as protest, voting, strikes, tolerance, trust, or regime support. The macro-macro studies aggregate individual attitudes into a national mean attitude. The latter is a defensible move, but it is certainly not the only way, and probably not the best way, to shift levels, as agent-based modeling suggests (Granovetter 1978). It is the best way only if theory says that (1) the impact of culture is a matter of degree – the larger the proportion of the population that has the attitude in question, the greater is the impact on democratization; and (2) it does not matter which citizens have the relevant attitude – generals and beggars are interchangeable. Even if a theory made these assumptions explicit and justified them, it would be incomplete because it would not tell us how clusters of attitudes translate into behavior by certain actors to bring about the regime outcome.

To avoid shifting levels, or even to know how best to shift levels, it is essential to develop theories that specify the causal mechanism linking culture to regime survival and regime change. At present, we do not have such a theory, but we can describe several of its elements. First, a cultural theory of democratization would have to connect attitudes to behavior. Which attitudes produce which kinds of actions? How reliably? Under what conditions? Without an understanding of this linkage, we are left to imagine a population magically willing a regime into existence or oblivion. Second, a theory must identify which citizens are in a position to have a significant impact on the regime. The attitudes and actions of military officers, politicians, judges, police, guerrillas, and union leaders are clearly more consequential than those of ordinary citizens, especially if the latter are not politically active. Therefore, an adequate theory should focus attention on the actors whose subculture really matters. But the set of actors who are influential depends on the institutional context. So, third, a cultural theory of democratization should be conditioned on the initial regime and the direction of the regime transition. More actors, especially mass actors, are relevant for the survival or breakdown of democracy than for the survival or breakdown of nondemocratic regimes. For the study of transitions to democracy, one would want to pay more attention to the official party if the initial regime is totalitarian, to the military if it is a military authoritarian regime, to the ruling family in a traditional monarchy, to parties and the legislature if it is an electoral authoritarian regime, and to the dictator's cronies if it is a sultanistic regime (Linz and Stepan 1996). Each context requires a distinct variant of the theory, depending on who the most directly relevant actor is. Fourth, there are various pathways to regime change (or consolidation) in each context. A democracy can break down by military coup; presidential coup; civil war; revolution; or a subtler slide into human rights violations, party proscriptions, manipulated elections, or other illiberal practices. Different actors and behaviors are relevant for each one. Fifth, a theory should also distinguish among phases of a transition. Mass actors can play a leading role in a regime breakdown and their pacific behavior is essential for its survival, but only elites can create the institutions of a new regime (O'Donnell and Schmitter 1986). A theory of the impact of culture on regimes should therefore be highly conditional. Each kind of transition requires a different variant of the theory for different contexts that focuses attention on different actors, behaviors, and attitudes.

Specifying the conditions under which culture could matter for regime change would be a substantial improvement, but an adequate theory should also tell us more about the dynamics of culture. The most common criticism of theories of political culture has been that culture is too static to explain political change. This criticism is directed more against the anthropological understanding of culture than against the individualistic behavioral view. But a behavioral understanding of culture is entirely compatible with a more dynamic and powerful causal role for attitudes. Breakdowns should be associated with declines in support for democracy among key actors; transitions to democracy should be associated with increasing support for democracy at least among some actors; and democratic consolidation requires, by definition, the spread and strengthening of regime support. An adequate cultural theory of regime change should incorporate and explain these attitudinal changes.

Such a theory would ideally show how the attitudes of the most directly relevant actor are influenced by the attitudes of other, indirectly relevant actors.[7] In some cases, for example, the most directly relevant actor is the military. Why do some top military officers sometimes reject democracy and carry out a coup? They are not completely isolated from the rest of society, so it would be good to know to what extent they are responding to, or anticipating, a rejection of the democratic regime by business elites, foreign powers, the

---

[7] Even if we assume that all actors have equal influence, merely allowing behavior to be contingent on the number of other actors who have taken action leads to complex theories that can often make counterintuitive and unstable predictions (Granovetter 1978).

middle class, or the church. Or, if the armed forces decide not to initiate a coup despite difficult structural conditions, it may be that they are constrained by the attitudes of these other groups in society. Theories of regime change that focus exclusively on elites may give culture too little credit if they ignore the broader cultural environment that influences elite actions. Influence can flow in both directions, however. The phenomenon known as leadership can be understood as elite influence on mass attitudes. For democratization, therefore, it would be useful to know to what extent the positions of elites (e.g., executive, party leaders, business leaders, the military, leaders of ethnic or religious groups) move mass opinion for or against democracy.

It is also important to understand how different kinds of attitudes are interrelated. Certain attitudes seem to be closely connected to behaviors that would affect regime change and stability, such as support for the incumbent regime and government or the rejection of violence. But other attitudes, such as moderation, political trust, social trust, tolerance, and evaluations of government performance, may affect these attitudes and gradually move them toward a threshold of regime change. A good cultural theory should make these connections explicit. It should also identify nonattitudinal factors that directly affect attitudes that are relevant for regime change. These could include generation-defining events such as the Great Depression, wars, Watergate, and the September 11 attacks; learning; crime; and corruption scandals. Whose attitudes are affected? Which attitudes are affected? How quickly? How long do these effects last? All of these questions are relevant for a cultural theory of democratization.

No one has ever surveyed enough actors at sufficiently frequent intervals to test such a complete theory. However, a simulation (posted online at http://www.nd.edu/~mcoppedg/crd/Simulation.htm) can reveal the kinds of patterns for which we should be looking. Suppose that we have four elite actors – the executive, the legislature, the courts, and the military. Suppose further that each one has an orientation toward the regime that ranges from 1 (prodemocracy) to 0 (antidemocracy).[8] Let us also assume that there is a mass public that has a variety of attitudes, also ranging from 0 to 1. Some are political support attitudes, from the very general and abstract to the

---

[8] In this example, I do not attempt to connect elite or mass attitudes to regime outcomes. However, it would not be hard to make these connections in a loose way: military coup when the military opposes democracy, presidential coup when the executive and military oppose democracy but the courts and legislature support it, consolidation when all actors move toward unanimous support for democracy, and so on.

very specific. These include support for democracy as an abstract principle, for the actual democratic regime, for the government, for government leaders, and for government policies (which could be further broken down, if necessary). The mass public also has other attitudes that may be related to democracy, such as trust, tolerance, and moderation. Finally, the simulation lumps together all of the nonattitudinal factors as a single variable that we will call performance. It stands for economic performance, maintenance of public order, war, corruption scandals, and every other event that might influence elite or mass attitudes. Again, this variable could be broken up into a variety of variables to make the simulation more realistic, but this is not necessary to identify the fundamental patterns that interest us here.

I have programmed a spreadsheet simulation that incorporates all of these actors and attitudes and also allows one to define how much of an impact each element has on each other element (i.e., how much each elite's support for democracy is responsive to or constrained by mass attitudes and performance, how much mass attitudes are influenced by elite leadership, and how the various mass attitudes are interconnected and influenced by performance).[9] These impacts are repeated in any number of iterations until all of the attitudes converge on an equilibrium. The simulation therefore reflects all of the elements of an ideal framework for understanding the impact of culture on democratization. It is a framework rather than a theory, however, because it is completely open-ended. Its flexibility makes it compatible with an infinite variety of different theories. Its usefulness lies in its ability to derive the eventual consequences of any combination of these simple assumptions about culture and democratization.

The patterns of convergence reveal which actors, and which attitudes, are most important in each scenario. If one specifies purely top-down influence (elite positions shape mass attitudes, but elites are not constrained by mass attitudes) and if performance is neutral, then mass attitudes eventually converge on the average position of the elite actors. If one specifies purely bottom-up influence (the mass public constrains elites, who exercise no leadership over the mass public), then elite positions converge on the average mass position. If influence flows in both directions, then the simulation reveals vicious or virtuous circles that spiral toward the positions of the most influential actors. Such scenarios are completely endogenous: every element

---

[9] This spreadsheet, which includes color graphs that cannot be reproduced here, is available from the author on request.

is both a cause and an effect. If elites have more influence over the mass public than the mass public has over elites, then positions converge toward elite positions faster than they do toward the mass public's positions. If the patterns of influence are more bottom up than top down, then convergence is faster toward the mass public's positions. However, if any element is exogenous – a cause but not an effect – then all of the endogenous elements converge toward its position. For example, if performance has a prolonged and consistently positive impact (without being influenced itself by mass attitudes or elite positions) and is the only exogenous element, then eventually the elite and the mass public converge toward prodemocratic attitudes. In the same way, negative performance leads to antidemocratic attitudes.

In practice, performance (or whatever the relevant exogenous forces are) is rarely so consistently and uniformly positive or negative in the long term; it is variable, so attitudes may never converge. Nevertheless, this simulation suggests an agenda for research on political culture and democratization. First, the most important question is whether any elements in the system are exogenous because they will drive the whole process in the long run. Second, we must specify which elements are endogenous because they will tend to vary together. Third, it would be very interesting to know whether the patterns of influence are more bottom up or more top down. The answer has obvious implications for democratic theory, as well as for understanding democratic breakdown and consolidation.

Cross-national survey research has been growing explosively, but it is still not adequate for answering these questions (Norris 2004). This framework would require surveying not only the mass public but also any elite groups whose behavior may be relevant for regime change or consolidation. Furthermore, all of these surveys would have to be repeated frequently, at intervals of weeks or months, to be able to detect patterns of convergence. It may be impossible to carry out such research, especially in nondemocratic regimes where elites refuse to grant interviews. Nevertheless, we can take stock of the research that has been possible by comparing it with this framework's ideals. Which pieces of this big picture have been filled in and which remain blank?

Political culture and mass-led regime change or consolidation

The best place to begin taking stock of the literature is with the pathways to regime change or survival in which the mass public takes the leading role. These are only a minority of the pathways because usually elite involvement is necessary and the mass public plays only the indirect role of pushing or constraining elite attitudes and actions:

These institutions do not emerge spontaneously by a group of demonstrators courageously confronting Communist police with the chant, "We are the people." The chant was a challenge to the authority of an undemocratic regime; it was not a draft constitution for a new democracy. . . . [E]lites propose, the masses dispose. (Rose et al. 1998, 8)

But the mass public can play the most direct role in democratic consolidation and regime-threatening disturbances such as rioting, civil war or insurgency, and massive peaceful demonstrations calling for regime change (in either direction).

Many scholars reject the notion of democratic consolidation because it presupposes a situation in which it is no longer possible for a democratic regime to break down. However, consolidation can be interpreted in a less categorical way, to mean that a breakdown is very unlikely in the near future, while recognizing that in the distant future all bets are off. In this sense, democratic consolidation is not a regime attribute that can be observed; rather, it is a prediction that can be made if one has a sound understanding of the warning signs of imminent regime breakdown. Linz and Stepan propose a conception of democratic consolidation based on this kind of understanding (Linz and Stepan 1996). They propose that there are three dimensions of consolidation – behavioral, attitudinal, and constitutional – and that consolidation is achieved when civil society, political society, economic society, the state, and the rule of law all reinforce one another. This complex framework is discussed more fully in Chapter 4. Here, the important point is that, according to Linz and Stepan, attitudes are by definition an essential aspect of democratic consolidation; specifically, most citizens must be committed to democratic rules of the game and expect to resolve conflicts within the rules of the game recognized by the regime.

Violent mass disturbances such as rioting and civil war can initiate a transition from either democracy or nondemocracy. Although such disturbances cannot complete a transition to a new regime without elites taking a leading role, they can be sufficient first steps and they should be examined here because mass attitudes presumably help cause them. Peaceful demonstrations can similarly start but not finish a transition, although they involve different attitudes and actions.

The bulk of survey research on public opinion and regime stability or change can be situated under the heading of mass attitudes that either signify the acceptance of democracy or presumably contribute to mass actions that could conceivably undermine it. I have carefully hedged this heading ("presumably," "conceivably") because the research in question rarely states explicitly, much less tests, how its findings are relevant for regime change. Therefore, I discuss it as an isolated body of research in this section and discuss research on its linkage to regime outcomes in subsequent sections. The aspects of culture that have been most studied in this regard are support for democracy, political trust, interpersonal trust, tolerance, moderation, and self-expression values. Later, I discuss some indirectly relevant aspects of culture such as religion, ethnicity, and social capital, which may influence these more directly relevant attitudes.

Support for democracy and democratic institutions

One would expect that if any attitude is closely associated with democracy, it would be support for democracy as the best form of government. This is not the case, however: an index of four democracy-support variables is correlated at only 0.351 with Freedom House scores for 1995 and at 0.506 with average Freedom House scores for 1981–2000 (Inglehart 2003). Clearly, there are many countries that are not democratic despite strong popular support for it and many countries that are democratic despite weaker support. Democracy does not come about simply because many people want it or fail whenever they become disillusioned with it. There are several reasons for the weak correlation. First, there is surprisingly little variation in support for democracy in principle (Norris 1999b). Questions that ask whether respondents support something called democracy tend to find high and stable support almost everywhere. In the World Values Surveys in thirty-eight countries in the mid-1990s, for example, the percentages of people who agreed relatively strongly with the statements, "Democracy may have many problems but it's better than any other form of government" and "Having a democratic system" is a very good or fairly good "way of governing this country" averaged 90 percent in Western Europe and 81 to 86 percent in the six other regions, falling below 71 percent in no country except Russia, where it was 51 percent (Klingemann and Norris 1999). Using a different question,[10] the regional barometers found lower but still majority support: an average of 80 percent in Western Europe,

---

[10] "Which of these three statements is closest to your own opinion? (A) Democracy is preferable to any other form of government; (B) In certain situations, a non-democratic government can be preferable; or (C) To people like me, it doesn't matter what form of government we have" (Mattes and Bratton 2003, 3).

70 percent in twelve relatively democratic African countries, 59 percent in Latin America, and 56 percent in East Asia (Mattes and Bratton 2003, 4). Furthermore, there does not seem to be a trend in any direction since the 1970s, when systematic cross-national survey research began (Norris 1999b, 9–13).

A second reason for the weak correlations is that simply asking people whether they support democracy probably does not tell us what we want to know about culture and democratization. For one thing, it is important to gauge the levels of relative support for democracy compared to alternative regimes. Rose, Mishler, and Haerpfer argue that the Churchillian hypothesis applies well to Eastern Europe and Russia: we should expect democracy to survive despite low support when citizens believe it is the worst form of government except for all the rest (Rose, Mishler, and Haerpfer 1998, chap. 5). Mattes and Bratton (2003) confirm this argument in Africa. It is also reasonable to suppose that high support for democracy could coexist with nondemocracy if the nondemocratic regime had even higher support. For another thing, correlations between support for democracy and indicators of democracy such as the Freedom House index or Polity may underestimate the association because the democracy indicators were not designed to capture differences in the quality of democracy. If we had more sensitive indicators at the high end of democracy, we might find that societies with a very high level of support for democracy are, in fact, more democratic than societies with only a moderately high level of support.[11] Many of the new democracies are not very democratic, and there is some evidence that their citizens tend to be less supportive of democracy (Diamond 1999). As long as we use indicators that make all democracies appear equally democratic, the observed relationship appears weak.

But the most important reason for the weak correlation is that democracy means different things to different people. For example, summarizing survey research in three Latin American countries in 1999, Roderic Camp reports, "First, among Latin Americans there is no consensus on what democracy means. Second, only Costa Ricans see democracy in largely political terms, very similar in content to the view professed by North Americans. Third, the Mexicans and Chileans . . . view democracy in social and economic, not political, terms" (Camp 2001, 15–16). Because of these divergent interpretations,

---

[11] Inglehart and Welzel (2005, 191–196) show that self-expression values are more strongly correlated with "effective democracy" (an interaction of the Freedom House index and the World Bank's control-of-corruption variable) than they are with formal democracy.

asking people whether they support democracy is, in effect, asking them whether they support whatever democracy means to them. Because democracy has become practically synonymous with good government, it is not surprising that support is so high virtually everywhere. The best example of this is Venezuela. The 2005 Latin Barometer reported that support for democracy was higher in Venezuela than in any other Latin American country except Uruguay, at a time when Freedom House and many international observers were lamenting the rise of the illiberal, less democratic regime of Hugo Chávez.[12] In reality, Venezuelans were bitterly divided over their regime. Chávez's supporters believed that their leader had replaced a corrupt, elitist regime with the country's first true democracy, whereas his opponents believed that Chávez was destroying a fairly successful liberal political democracy. They all agreed that democracy was good, but they had entirely incompatible understandings of the word. For this reason, Mitchell Seligson has said, "If you want to measure support for democracy, the one thing you should never do is use the word 'democracy' in the question."[13]

There is some debate about whether this is good advice because there has long been a divide between idealists, for whom "meaning for the analyst has taken priority over meaning for the participants" and a phenomenological approach, which respects subjective meaning more (Welch 1993, 9). Several research projects have sought to describe what democracy means to the citizens themselves (Schaffer 2000; Pérez Liñán 1998; Camp 2001; Beetham et al. 2002). This can be fascinating work that furthers the goal of thick understanding. However, it must not tempt political scientists into concept stretching. If we are interested in the nature, causes, or consequences of what *we* mean by democracy, we cannot surrender the authority to define the concept to our research subjects. It is important not to confuse concepts with words. One book that makes this mistake is Schaffer's *Democracy in Translation*, which reveals that in Senegal, the Wolof word *demokaraasi* connotes evenhandedness, mutuality, and consensus more than competition (Schaffer 2000). This is an interesting finding, but its lesson for those who wish to measure support for Western-style liberal political democracy in Senegal is that the Wolof cognate *demokaraasi* would be a poor translation for the English word *democracy*. We must define our concepts on our own terms and design questions that ask respondents about their support for *our* version of democracy.

---

[12] Seventy-six percent of Venezuelans agreed with the statement, "Democracy is preferable to any other form of government," compared to 77 percent in Uruguay and 53 percent in the average Latin American country (LatinoBarómetro 2005).

[13] Oral communication, circa 2004.

Because respondents cannot help but interpret the word *democracy* in their own ways, it is more useful to examine survey questions that refer to institutions and practices that we mean by democracy rather than to some undefined version of democracy (Norris 1999b; Levi and Stoker 2000).[14] Some surveys ask whether it would be preferable to let the army rule or to have "a strong leader who does not have to bother with parliament and elections" (Moreno 2001). The most common questions of this sort ask how much confidence or trust respondents have in various institutions, some of which are inseparable from liberal democracy, such as elections, political parties, and the legislature. Although confidence in the political community and the principle of democracy tends to be high, confidence in specific democratic institutions tended to decline from the 1960s to the 1990s in older democracies and was very low in most of the newer democracies (Norris 1999a; Levi and Stoker 2000; Newton and Norris 2000). Engagement with parties declined in seventeen of nineteen wealthy democracies; confidence in parliament declined in eleven of fourteen countries; and in twelve of thirteen countries, growing numbers of citizens agreed that "politicians are only interested in votes," "MPs are out of touch," politicians and government "don't care about people like me," "politicians are untrustworthy," and "there are many dishonest politicians" (Putnam et al. 2000, 3–19). In Latin America by 2005, confidence had sunk to an average of 31 percent in the courts, 28 percent in congress, and 19 percent in political parties (LatinoBarómetro 2005, 55).

As noted earlier, the fear that this trend presaged the breakdown of even established democracies was not fulfilled by the first decade of the twenty-first century, and some came to believe that it is healthy for citizens to distrust their representatives. This optimistic view makes sense in the wealthy, older democracies, at least in the medium term. Individuals who distrust democratic institutions tend to be if anything more, not less, supportive of democratic principles. But it is hard to discount the possibility that distrust of institutions will eventually metastasize into a rejection of democracy in principle (Norris 1999a, 261–4). As Putnam, Pharr, and Dalton note, "If the decline in public confidence is justified (because of growing corruption, for example), then we might applaud citizens' ire but not its cause, just as we would be glad to have discovered a child's fever without being glad that her temperature was high" (Putnam et al. 2000, 22). I share with Norris "a nagging concern that where regimes are not widely believed to be

---

[14] Levi and Stoker go farther, exhorting researchers to ask questions about trust in whom, to do what (2000, 496–500). Vague questions about trust in government yield little useful information.

legitimate then public opinion will not act as an effective deterrent against anti-democratic forces" (Norris 1999a, 268). This is especially plausible in the newer democracies. In Peru and Venezuela, voters elected antiparty presidents who dissolved congress or rendered it irrelevant, and in Ecuador, Bolivia, and Honduras, congresses and courts removed presidents in semiconstitutional maneuvers. The public in all of these cases had little confidence in parties or congress, but more information is required before we can make a solid connection between culture and these regime changes. When majorities voted for antiparty politicians, did they intend to give a mandate to weaken liberal democratic institutions, or were their intentions betrayed? When legislatures removed presidents, was public opinion mostly supportive, or merely powerless to prevent it? These are the kind of questions that would be answered if studies of culture and regime change were refocused on specific causal pathways.

Other mass attitudes

But it may be that attitudes that are not explicitly about democracy or democratic institutions may have a greater impact on the birth and survival of democracy. The related attitude that has been most studied is generalized interpersonal trust, sometimes called simply social trust, to distinguish it from political trust in politicians and political institutions. Interpersonal trust was one of the components (along with political efficacy and pride in institutions) of Almond and Verba's civic culture, which they believed to favor stable democracy in the United States and Britain, compared to West Germany, Italy, and Mexico (Almond and Verba 1965). Other scholars fleshed out the reasons for this hypothetical connection (Sullivan and Transue 1999). Inglehart was best known for emphasizing the cultural shift to postmaterialism, but he also argued that interpersonal trust (combined with subjective well-being) lowers the stakes in politics, which favors democratic legitimacy and stability. Putnam and colleagues (1993, 177–181) added that social trust – a natural by-product of face-to-face participation in secondary associations – is self-reinforcing because if society is generally trusting, it becomes rational for individuals to be trusting as well and unwise to be distrustful. This virtuous circle encourages public officials to be responsive, which improves the quality of democracy, and presumably high-quality democracies tend to be more stable. Putnam's finding that trust and social capital are on the decline in the United States raised concerns that the quality of democracy, and eventually its survival, was in jeopardy (Putnam 1995).

The evidence is mixed, however, for any general decline of trust or for a strong impact of social trust on democracy. Generalized trust has declined in some democracies but not in others (Stolle and Hooghe 2004). The evidence for a causal relationship has been mixed. For example, one study using World Values Survey data for seventeen countries reports that there is an association among social trust and trust in the police, civil service, and parliament at the aggregate, cross-national level but not at the individual level (Newton and Norris 2000). This is probably because there tends to be much less cultural variation within countries than between them (Inglehart and Welzel 2005, 69), which may make it impossible to detect this kind of weak relationship except in cross-national samples, where the variation on both variables is wider. This interpretation is consistent with a study of three Latin American countries in which social trust at the individual level is weakly related to support for democracy only when the model includes no country dummies, which capture more general cross-national differences (Seligson 2001). When actual democracy, rather than support for democracy, is the dependent variable, the most extensive and rigorous study finds that interpersonal trust explains only 15 percent of effective democracy and has no significant impact on formal democracy (Freedom House), even in a simple cross-sectional model with only one control variable (Inglehart and Welzel 2005, 252). As Inglehart and Welzel conclude, the cultural variable that has the most direct and important impact on democracy is probably not interpersonal trust.

What is the centrally important variable, then? Over the years, various scholars have pointed to tolerance (Inglehart and Welzel 2005, 245–72), moderation or consensus (McClosky 1964, 1983), and subjective well-being (Inglehart 1977). But, again, the most extensive and rigorous study – Inglehart and Welzel's – concludes that all other attitudes take a back seat to self-expression values. In a comparison of approximately sixty countries, the average level of self-expression in the early 1990s explains 32 percent of the variance in formal democracy and 55 percent of the variance in effective democracy, averaged for 2000–2002 (Inglehart and Welzel 2005, 252). Political trust, overt preference for democracy, obedience, and other values are significantly related to democracy only to the extent that they are correlated with self-expression, for their coefficients fail to reach conventional significance levels when models control for self-expression (Inglehart and Welzel 2005, 255). There are many reasons to reserve some skepticism about their finding: the available samples limit the analysis of change to just the impact of values in the early 1990s on average levels of democracy in 2000–2002, their models fail to control for anything except prior democratic experience, the causal pathways and relevant actors are undefined, and there is still some doubt about how to interpret self-expression values (which in the section in question are confusingly redubbed "liberty aspirations" [258–263]). But the best evidence available at this point suggests that the aspect of culture that is most closely associated with democracy cross-nationally and over time is something like self-expression.

Culture and behavior

Inglehart and Welzel spin an elaborate and plausible theory about the causal pathway that links self-expression values to democratic transitions (Inglehart and Welzel 2005, 224–228). They argue that transitions happen when and where self-expression values increase the numbers of civil rights activists and dissidents. As these changes swell the ranks of civil rights movements and back them up with greater mass support, it becomes more likely that liberal elites will endorse regime change. When prodemocracy activists eventually take the initiative, these elites are less likely to attempt to repress them.

These are excellent hypotheses that suggest possible causal connections in several stages, and Inglehart and Welzel produce empirical evidence in support of two links in their chain. They demonstrate that elites (those with education) almost always value self-expression more than society in general does (Inglehart and Welzel 2005, 220). They also show that self-expression in the early 1990s is strongly associated with Anheier and colleagues' Civil Society Index for 2000 in thirty-one countries ($r = 0.81$) (Anheier et al. 2005, 229). They also refer to several confirming case studies.[15] Unfortunately, this evidence tells us nothing about several of the other links in the hypothesized chain. Are the individuals who value self-expression the same individuals who are politically active? Do societies that value self-expression more also consider civil rights and other movements more legitimate? Does the growth of self-expression increase the probability that elites will support democracy and refrain from repressing prodemocracy activists? Is this true for the elites who can actually make a difference? We must look elsewhere to find out whether all of the elements of this plausible theory are empirically true.

---

[15] Inglehart and Welzel also examine the relationship between self-expression and the fate of potentially transitional authoritarian regimes (Inglehart and Welzel 2005, 227–229). Unfortunately, they report average self-expression for each category of outcome rather than the probability of each regime outcome based on levels of self-expression. This switches the dependent and independent variables, rendering the analysis meaningless, despite the fact that self-expression was measured for an earlier year than the outcomes.

Thorough testing is essential because there are compelling competing arguments suggesting that mass culture does not have an important impact on transitions to democracy. One strain of theorizing holds that attitudes and behaviors that we usually think of as antithetical to democracy may actually help spur transitions, or at least not harm them. Nancy Bermeo argues that moderation is not required for transitions to democracy (Bermeo 1997). She points out that Portuguese democracy emerged from a socialist revolution and Spanish democracy has coexisted with Basque terrorism. She also calls attention to successful transitions in Brazil, Chile, Ecuador, South Korea, Peru, and the Philippines despite high strike rates. Echoing Barrington Moore, who argued that violence was necessary to break the power of conservative antidemocratic classes, Elisabeth Wood makes the case that armed insurgencies in South Africa and El Salvador brought authoritarian elites to the bargaining table (Moore 1966; Wood 2001). In these cases, the economic costs of violence were necessary to persuade business, political, and military leaders that it was time to share power.

These arguments do not contradict Inglehart and Welzel's finding of an association between culture and transitions to democracy as much as it might appear at first glance, for two reasons. First, Bermeo's brief is with moderation, which is not one of Inglehart and Welzel's self-expression values. In fact, extremism and perhaps even violence may have more in common with the qualities that Inglehart and Welzel emphasize: challenging elite authority and being critical rather than passive citizens. Second, extremism and violence are usually characteristics of a minority, not the majority culture. It is perfectly possible for the majority to be moderate and peaceful even where there is an extreme or violent minority, and the existence of such a minority may in fact make authoritarians more eager to transfer power to moderates. Such a situation would resemble formal theories that focus on pacts or alliances between soft-liners and moderates: in effect, a "good cop, bad cop" routine acted out on an immense stage. A synthesis of these two theories would suggest that a good combination for transitions to democracy may be two subcultures: one radical, violent, but minority; the other moderate, peaceful, and majority. But, at this point, this is mostly speculation, tested in only a handful of case studies.

It is also possible that mass culture has no impact on transitions. One of the most prominent students of culture and democracy, Larry Diamond, has stated that "[d]emocratic culture is certainly not a precondition for the initiation of democracy" because elites and activists usually have decisive influence at this stage, as opposed to during consolidation (Diamond 1993a, 423).

It could also be that a democratic mass culture has only indirect influence. Mass support for democracy (or moderation, tolerance, or trust) may percolate up through society, either inducing elites to change their minds or replacing authoritarian elites with new leaders who are more in sync with attitudes of the majority culture.

There are opposing points of view about the impact of political culture on the survival of democracy. On the one hand, Linz and Stepan (1996, 5) argue that belief in democracy as "the only game in town," the only legitimate means for resolving conflict, is one of the defining aspects of democratic consolidation; and democratic consolidation, in turn, means a low probability of breakdown. To complete what could be called the Tinkerbell syllogism,[16] the more people believe in democracy, the less likely democracy is to die and the more likely it is to survive. In Linz and Stepan's definition of consolidation, supportive mass attitudes and behavior are absolutely required: citizens who want political change must shun violent means in favor of peaceful, constitutional activity (Linz and Stepan 1996, 6). They accept fundamental democratic rules and comply with the law; if they protest, they do so peacefully. Ideally, they vote, and they do not vote for antisystem parties or leaders. Inglehart and Welzel argue that the rise of self-expression values similarly helps existing democracies survive. The more citizens value self-expression, the more social-movement activists there are, the more legitimate nonactivists consider them to be, and the more likely elites are to be responsive to mass demands. Such democracies are more effective and therefore more likely to survive (see Diamond 1999, 239–250, for a discussion of twelve ways in which social movements can contribute to the survival of democracy).

On the other hand, there are many reasons to question any tight linkage of democratic survival and mass culture. First, now that public opinion surveys have become common in new democracies, we know that democratic regimes can often survive for years even when the public has little confidence in political parties, legislatures, courts, elections, and other democratic institutions. Rose, Mishler, and Haerpfer (1998) have pointed out that we should not expect disillusionment to turn citizens against democracy unless they believe that some alternative regime is preferable. In the absence of a more legitimate alternative, democratic regimes can hobble along without enthusiastic support for a long time. Second, Putnam's thesis has come in for heavy criticism. It is not clear that participation in voluntary associations promotes trust and

---

[16] In *Peter Pan*, fairies die if children do not believe in them. Audiences are asked to clap to show their belief in fairies so that Tinkerbell can be restored to good health (Barrie 1991).

cooperation; at the very least, such effects depend on the type of association. One would not expect salutary consequences unless citizens have face-to-face contact, the group is more horizontal than hierarchical, and it reaches out into the community rather than bonding members into a united front against outsiders. Weimar Germany was full of associations that did not stop, and may have aided, the rise of Nazism. Third, it is anything but clear how participation in clubs, social movements, and other secondary associations affects major outcomes such as regime change. There has been considerable research on social movements, but it has mostly focused on their causes rather than their consequences. It seems clear, for example, that democracy favors the formation of social movements, but whether social movements favor democracy remains an open question.[17]

Fourth, much of what we do know suggests that elite opinion matters much more than mass culture. Democracies can fail despite a broad popular preference for democracy. In *Ordinary People in Extraordinary Times*, Nancy Bermeo advances the provocative argument that mass public opinion almost never favors authoritarianism (Bermeo 2003). Rather, elites – the executive, party leaders, parts of the armed forces – mistakenly interpret the demands of antidemocratic minorities as representative of the majority and overreact. Sometimes elites install a right- or left-wing nondemocratic regime in the mistaken belief that the majority wants it, and sometimes they lead a coup to prevent what they falsely perceive as a revolution from taking place. Bermeo's thesis may contradict the naive assumption of political-culture theorists that regimes express mass preferences, but it is quite plausible from a layperson's understanding of politics: the squeaky wheel gets the grease and silent majorities tend to be ignored. Her brief cases studies of the failed democracies of interwar Europe lack the public opinion evidence necessary to make her case convincingly; it is always possible that elites judged, and responded to, mass opinion correctly, even if it was not fully expressed by votes, membership, or the other available indicators of behavior. However, her more detailed analysis of four more recent South American cases – Brazil in 1964, Uruguay in 1973, Chile in 1973, and Argentina in 1976 – have the benefit of public opinion data, which does establish that these right-wing military authoritarian regimes were not a fulfillment of the wishes of the majority. In Brazil, although there was majority support for land reform, which conservatives and the military considered threatening, the majority never wavered in its

---

[17] Nevertheless, Marco Giugni has laid out an interesting agenda for how to proceed to study the consequences of social movements (Giugni 1999).

preference for democracy. In Uruguay, majorities wanted the military to remove President Bordaberry but only to restore democracy; the military assumed power despite massive popular opposition and resistance (Bermeo 2003, 135–37). In Chile, there was polarization that was dangerous for democracy, but only among party elites, not among the mass of voters (Bermeo 2003, chap. 5). Most Argentines in 1976 may have been exhausted by violence and strikes and grateful for the military removal of Isabel Perón, but there is little evidence that they preferred prolonged military rule (Bermeo 2003, chap. 6). Bermeo's argument is convincing for these cases in the narrow sense that popular majorities appear not to have turned against democracy per se or to have been polarized to the point of having more people at the extremes than in the center.

However, while making her case, Bermeo also demonstrates that there is sometimes majority support for military coups (when the majority believes that the interruption would be brief) and does not exclude the possibility that nonmajority levels of polarization may sometimes lead to disruptions of political order that make it difficult for democracy to survive, even if relatively few desire that outcome. Her evidence is therefore compatible with the possibility that mass, although not necessarily majority, attitudes make an indirect contribution to the breakdown of democracy. Overall, however, her analysis reinforces the conclusion that the search for cultural explanations of regime change should focus not on the mean or modal attitudes of the undifferentiated mass of ordinary people but rather on the attitudes of smaller groups in society who are in a position to effect change, whether they are extremist social movements, political party leaders, or military officers.

A fifth counterargument is that elite leadership shapes culture rather than culture constraining elite attitudes and actions. Most of the research on this question has examined the relationship between U.S. members of Congress and their constituents, regarding policy, not regime choice, so the implications of this relationship for regime change are virtually unexplored, although they remain worth exploring rigorously. The one exception to this is the attention paid to ethnic violence. In this line of research, few scholars believe that violence (which obviously can undermine democracy) is an automatic expression of deep, primordial hatreds. Rather, contemporary emphasis is on political "entrepreneurs" (leaders), who reinforce latent religious, ethnic, racial, linguistic, and national identities and exploit them to maximize their own political power. It has also been shown that leaders sometimes have the ability to prevent violence where it otherwise would be expected to break out (Varshney 2003).

Sixth, it has often been argued that culture is epiphenomenal: it has little direct, independent impact once one controls for the forces and events that shape both culture and the outcomes that it supposedly causes. Welch calls this the phenomenon of the retreating cause: the closer one comes to understanding when, where, and why culture matters, the more it appears that culture is only a mask for the forces that really matter (Welch 1993). On this point, however, I find Inglehart and Welzel's arguments more convincing than the alternative. Empirically, there are more differences across countries than within countries; structural factors move countries from their cultural starting points; and culture is inertial, slowing or dampening the impact of other forces. But more rigorous testing would be desirable.

There is another way that mass culture might affect the survival of democracy. Democracy may die not with a bang but a whimper: apathy, withdrawal from participation, abstention, delegitimation of institutions and leaders. Perhaps democracy will die not because citizens care too much but because they care too little. This seems to be the motivating assumption behind the large literature on political culture and turnout, party membership, group membership, and voting behavior (van Deth and Scarborough 1995; Norris 2002). We should obviously be concerned about declines in these forms of participation if they signal the slow death of democracy, but it is hard to list many countries that have gone this far.

Conclusion

The history of cultural research on democratization is a history of conceptual refinement. The early ways of thinking about culture were far too simplistic, but as research has become more empirical, it has also become much more nuanced and precise. Furthermore, as research has broadened from close examination of small societies to generalizations about many diverse societies, the complexity of what has been found has progressively driven toward conceptual and theoretical refinement. Therefore, if this approach teaches us anything, it is that there is no unanimity in any political culture.

The central problem is how to connect individual-level characteristics to regime outcomes at the macro level. Scholars have had trouble keeping everything in focus at once. Some study national aggregates and show us cross-national variation but lose sight of subcultures and causal mechanisms. Others confine their attention to the individual level and turn up many interesting relationships but lose sight of how and why relationships at this level may matter at the macro level. The only solution is to specify the causal mechanisms that bridge levels of analysis and test them appropriately. But research in this vein is more of a promise than an accomplishment.

Another problem is the fact that the research agenda has been distorted by the availability of data. There has been much more research on the impact of attitudes on the survival or breakdown of democracy than on transitions to democracy simply because it is easier to do surveys in democracies and because democracies are more likely to have the means to pay for surveys. However, this is beginning to change. Oddly enough, there has been much more effort devoted to polling samples of hundreds or thousands of ordinary citizens – whose impact on regimes is questionable – than to surveys of party leaders, military officers, business leaders, or other elites whose opinions are much more likely to be consequential for regime change. Elite surveys are hardly unknown, but because each one is custom designed for a particular project, it is difficult for them to cumulate into a coherent body of knowledge. And, if we are ever going to understand the relative influence of elites on masses and masses on elites, we would have to survey both in repeated, simultaneous waves. This has never been done in research on regime change.

What we have at present is a collection of tantalizing pieces but not a whole picture. We have many more questions than answers. But before we can prioritize our questions, we need to devote more attention to an overall theory that would suggest how to link the macro and micro levels of analysis: which groups matter, for what kind of regime change, following which scenario, under what conditions, and how do these groups influence one another?

9 Quantitative testing

In Chapter 3, I argued that the three fundamental goals of research are generality, integration, and thickness and that each of the three main approaches accomplishes one of these goals well and two of them poorly. In Chapter 5, I argued that case studies maximize thickness but do little for generality or integration. In Chapter 6, I argued that formal models and theories pursue theoretical integration, but often at the expense of thickness and generality. In this chapter, I argue that quantitative research achieves generality better than other approaches but tends to be thin and poorly integrated.

More specifically, the goal of quantitative analysis is to estimate the strength and significance of the average impact of one or more independent variables on a dependent variable while holding other variables constant. This kind of analysis is most appropriate for extensive testing, as described in Chapter 7. For example, it is appropriate if one wants to know how much more likely a presidential democracy is to break down than a parliamentary democracy, on average, controlling for level of economic development; how much more democratic one would expect a rich country to be than a poor one, on average, after holding colonial heritage and ethnic fragmentation constant; or whether the typical Latin American country is more democratic than the typical Asian country, other things being equal. Quantitative research is not, however, appropriate for intensive testing, which has the very different goal of determining which theory best explains a single outcome or small set of outcomes. In quantitative analysis, it is accepted that many cases will not be well explained, and this is not considered a problem so long as the average tendency can be estimated well.

This chapter makes five key arguments. First, quantitative analyses of democratization routinely violate one or more of the fundamental assumptions of statistical analysis. These assumptions, developed over more than a century, are well established and clear – more so than in case studies and comparative history, and more elaborate than in formal theories. The following section discusses the basic principles that apply to measurement, inference, specification, and estimation. Some scholars focus on these violations to dismiss the entire approach, but a more balanced conclusion is that its findings are tentative and provisional, as all scientific findings are. The development of these methodological principles makes violations easier to detect, and because scholars have been increasingly aware of these problems, they have also developed many techniques for dealing with them. However, these innovations have been picked up and applied unsystematically, thus leaving the findings less integrated than one would hope.

Second, quantification encourages the use of thin concepts and theories, which widen the gap between theories and evidence. It is normal to test observable implications of the theory rather than the theory itself. There is always, in any test, a gap between our theoretical understanding of the workings of a complex causal process and the evidence that we can examine to ascertain whether our understanding is correct. But when quantitative analysis reduces complex concepts to numeric indicators and complex theories to simple interchangeable propositions, the gap is especially wide. As a result, many empirical findings are consistent with multiple theories. This approach tends to uncover as many puzzles as it answers: it tells us that certain factors are associated but not why. It encourages a tendency to crunch first and ask questions later.

Third, as the quantitative approach has evolved, concepts and theories have become thicker – more complex and multifaceted. One sign of this is the proliferation of dependent variables. Scholars are no longer focused exclusively on *how democratic* countries are; they also seek to explain *changes* in levels of democracy, the probability of *being* a democracy, the probability of *becoming* a democracy, and the probability of *remaining* a democracy. Another sign is the now-crucial distinction between the static (cross-national) and dynamic (within-country) components of democratization, each of which implies a different causal process. In addition, some scholars are beginning to test more complex theories involving conditional relationships, causal sequences, and selection processes. The strictures of statistical analysis no longer prevent testing of complex theories, although data limitations still do.

Fourth, the most thoroughly explored relationship is that between democracy and economic development. This large literature illustrates well all of the foregoing tendencies. First, in studies based on correlations, democracy and economic development were just two of many strands of modernization. Then, as regression became a standard tool of political science, attention narrowed to per capita gross domestic product (GDP; or its log) as an independent variable causing cross-national levels of democracy. Now that time-series data are abundant – a revolutionary development for this research area – there is a debate about whether income plays a causal role at all. Some say that it has a long-term effect and perhaps a different short-term effect; some say that income does not cause countries to become more democratic, although it does help democracies survive; and some say that the relationship between income and democracy is spurious. We know that democracy and income are associated, but we do not know why.

Finally, few other explanatory variables have been convincingly ruled in or out. There are so many dependent variables and so many plausible independent variables that few combinations have been tested repeatedly. Some intriguing propositions have survived one test but have not been replicated. Many of the variables that have survived repeated testing, such as past democracy and dummy variables for regions or historical periods, have ambiguous interpretations. And tests of many of the most interesting hypotheses are, so far, inconclusive because different tests yield different results, and it is not clear whether differences in the concepts, the samples, the models, or the estimators are responsible. It would be an exaggeration to say that this approach is still in its infancy fifty years after Lipset's seminal article (1959), but it is still a toddler, capable of taking a few unsteady steps while lurching from one stance to another.

Assumptions of quantitative analysis

The statisticians, economists, and other social scientists who have developed quantitative methods have made core assumptions about measurements, inferences, and model specification and estimation. This section discusses each of these aspects of research design.

Measurement

All quantitative analysis presumes adequate measurement. Concepts do not have to be measured perfectly; in fact, statistical analysis was developed in part to deal with measurement error and does so quite well. But concepts must be measured validly, without systematic bias, and reliably. These assumptions can be violated in multiple ways. Invalid indicators are biased or in other ways measure something other than the concept they are supposed to measure. Unreliable indicators measure the correct concept, but with large, possibly random errors that make the measurements imprecise. Truncated indicators ignore one or both extremes of a continuum.[1] All of these problems are familiar in democratization research. Arguments about what democracy is and how to measure it validly have never ceased (Collier and Levitsky 1997). Debates about whether democracy has one dimension or many are debates about validity (Bollen and Grandjean 1981; Coppedge, Alvarez, and Maldonado 2008; Coppedge and Reinicke 1990). Most indicators of democracy are reliable enough to make only rough distinctions between levels or degrees of democracy (Pemstein et al. 2008). The Freedom House, Polity, and other indicators appear to be truncated at the upper extreme; that is, they do not reflect degrees of democracy beyond a certain threshold (Brinks and Coppedge 2006; Pemstein et al. 2010; Treier and Jackman 2008). Only better measurement can eliminate these problems. But, in the meantime, statistical analysis can tell us how much of a problem they are and, to some extent, enable us to compensate for poor measurement.

Inference

I have argued that the main strength of quantitative analysis is that it supports generalization. Quantitative researchers often write (even if they do not state this explicitly) as though their analysis of a sample supported inferences about the entire population from which the sample was drawn. Valid inferences about a population, however, require us to define the entire relevant universe so that we can either study that whole universe or take a random sample from it. This is, oddly enough, rarely done in comparative research. One could treat nonrandom samples as a problem of sample bias. But an alternative is more common: most research, in effect, generalizes only to the sample rather than the whole population.

It is tempting to believe that any finding that stands up to a test with a thousand or so observations could not be contradicted by adding a thousand more. It would be wonderful if that were true, but the fact is that the generality of every statistical inference is bounded. In the optimal situation, one works with a large random sample of an extensive yet causally homogeneous population. In this best-possible situation, the magic of sampling theory does indeed justify generalizing the findings from the sample to the whole population. However, even a very extensive population is not

---

[1] Interval, ordinal, and nominal data can also be viewed as violations of a default assumption of ratio data, which assumes an absolute zero, equal intervals, and rank ordering. However, techniques for analyzing nonratio data are so much part of mainstream quantitative analysis that I do not discuss them separately here.

universal. A sample of all countries from 1800 to the present is as extensive as most democratization researchers could possibly expect, but it still excludes all countries before 1800. The sample would not support generalizations to countries before 1800 unless they were already part of the population from which the sample was drawn and were in no way systematically different from the countries that were selected. This is highly unlikely. In fact, many would object that countries before approximately 1800 were so different as to be incomparable to present-day countries. If one goes back a few hundred years, there were not even recognizable nation-states or regimes that match the types that are familiar to us today. One could reasonably conclude that those cases belong to an entirely different population. This is an excellent reason for bounding the generalizations from the sample; nevertheless, it remains a bounded sample. Similarly, future cases could exceed the range of variation found in the sample. For example, in the future, a state may grant suffrage to resident aliens and citizens age fourteen or older, achieving a more extensive suffrage than any existing country. Our sample provides no basis for generalizing to this out-of-sample extreme unless we have strong reasons for believing that the relationships found in the limited-range sample can be extrapolated to more extreme values. We may have persuasive theoretical reasons for believing this but, ultimately, we cannot trust that belief until it is tested, and it cannot be tested with the limited-range sample. Therefore, generalizations beyond the sample are always subject to challenge.

All general causal inferences rest on the causal homogeneity assumption: the same cause can be expected to have the same effect in each observed case, other things being equal (Collier et al. 2004b; King et al. 1994). If relationships were different before 1800, or if relationships will be different in the future, generalizations from the sample are not supported. In the same way, relationships could also be heterogeneous within the population that we have sampled. In other words, the assumption that the population is homogeneous may not be justified, and our generalizations within the sample therefore have limited value. For example, a study of voting behavior may have a national random sample of U.S. citizens, but it may not be reasonable to assume that blacks and whites respond to the same influences in the same ways. The study would still identify the average tendency, but it would be misleading because, in reality, it would be a weighted average of different tendencies in these distinct ethnic groups.

The foregoing assumes that one has a truly random sample. Inferences are more limited when – as is common in comparative politics – we use nonrandom samples. In fact, the most common way to select a sample is to assemble a dataset of all the country-years for which variables have been measured and to omit observations simply because data are missing. And, it is common for the sample to vary from one analysis to another within one book or article because researchers typically allow cases to be dropped whenever they are missing data on a relevant variable. Because such samples make no claims to randomness, they do not support generalization to any larger population. They do support inferences to the average tendency within that sample, however, and are in this way more radically, and somewhat arbitrarily, bounded.

Quantitative researchers are increasingly aware of this limitation and are beginning to use special techniques to correct for selection bias so that it is safer to generalize to a larger population (Brinks and Coppedge 2006; Heckman 1979; Przeworski et al. 2000). One of these techniques, matching, is gaining acceptance. The intuition behind it is that researchers can select treatment and control samples from a larger population in a way that statistically approximates random assignment. In the most literal form of matching, the researcher chooses cases that have nearly identical values on several matching variables. The more matching variables there are, the harder it becomes to find matching cases. In the face of this difficulty, some researchers opt for propensity-score matching, in which cases are matched according to their overall probability of receiving the treatment, as estimated by a model that can analyze many variables. It is difficult to do this well because a good matching model requires very large samples and treatment and control groups that overlap thoroughly in propensity. Furthermore, rather than solving the omitted variables problem, matching passes it along to the selection model stage: if one cannot model the selection process well, significant selection bias can still be present (Sekhon 2009; Shadish et al. 2001).[2] The safest course, therefore, is to treat each finding as a generalization about the sample on which it was based. This, of course, makes it much harder to cumulate the findings of analyses that use different samples, but it is the most conservative way to proceed under the circumstances.[3]

With the understanding that statistical generalization in comparative politics tends to be generalization to the sample rather than to a larger population, it makes sense to speak of generalization to a single country, which can consist of many observations within a single case, such as a long time-series from

---

[2] Moreover, any dataset used to correct for selection bias is itself a sample from a larger population, so ultimately there is no perfect solution.

[3] For this reason, it is very helpful if researchers replicate their findings using the same samples used by other researchers.

one country or a survey of many individuals in one country. Quantitative methods are used to analyze such data, and the goal of doing so is the same: to generalize about the average tendency in that large sample. It is extensive, not intensive, testing, even though the generalization is to a more radically bounded population.

The possibilities for extensive testing have exploded as datasets have grown to include more countries, years, and variables. Before 1990, it was rare for a sample to have two hundred or more observations; since then, they typically have had several thousand. Most propositions can now be tested with samples that cover practically every country in the world, annually, from 1950 to nearly the present, and some testing has been done going back to 1850 or even 1500 (Acemoglu et al. 2008; Boix 2003). This is practically the whole domain that one would want to use for democratization studies because national, representative, full-adult-suffrage democracy barely existed before 1920 (Dahl 1989). Nevertheless, extending a sample to years before 1950 radically restricts the variety of independent variables that can be tested.

Specification

Quantitative methods provide surprisingly little guidance about specification, which requires answers to questions such as: Which variables are included? Are they dependent or independent? Endogenous or exogenous? Should they be added or multiplied? Is it safe to assume causal homogeneity? What is the functional form of each relationship? Should we include invariant factors? Therefore, this guidance has to come mostly from theory.[4] In practice, many researchers do test many variables, discarding those that have no significant impact and retaining those that "work," and they end up presenting the most significant variables as the best explanatory model. Unfortunately, the estimates produced by, say, a regression, are correct only if the model is correct. Quantitative analyses do not tell us which variables matter; rather, they tell us that *if* the model is correctly specified, then we can have a certain degree of confidence that this variable has this much of an impact on that one. Comparing the estimates of different models tends to boost the researcher's confidence in one model or another, but it can do so falsely. Strictly speaking, there is only one correct model; or, more practically, there is one best approximation of the true model, and that best model may not be one of the

---

[4] Statistical techniques such as F-tests and Hausman tests can provide some limited guidance when one needs to choose between two specific models. No test, however, can tell us whether a given model is the best approximation of the true model.

models that one is able to test. Tempting though it is to settle on the model that explains the most variance or the one that has the most significant coefficients or the one that is most robust to slightly different specifications and estimators, we cannot rule out the possibility that the best approximation of the true model would yield very different estimates and therefore might not be the most robust, most powerful, or most significant one among those that we are able to test. The testable models may "work" deceptively well for the wrong reasons: because of omitted variables, spurious relationships, reversed causal arrows, autocorrelation, selection bias, or other conditions.

One defense of engaging in specification searches to see which model works best is that we have to do the best we can with the data we have; we do not have the luxury of waiting for the variables that would be needed to test the best approximate model before we get any estimates. The best we can do, according to this defense, is to produce an inferior approximation of the best model and hope that future research will improve on it. All scientific findings are provisional, after all. The problem with this reasoning is that this is not the best we can do. In our best efforts, the choice of which model to estimate is guided by theory rather than an open-ended search for a good empirical fit. And, ideally, this theoretical guidance would be both thick and integrated: based on a complex and nuanced understanding of political processes, and logically connected to a body of theoretical propositions that are, as much as possible, tried and true. This is not to say that theory should always override empirical findings. What it means is that our best efforts to discover the truth are informed by both theory and empirical research.

Estimation

Another set of limitations is well defined by the assumptions of ordinary least squares (OLS) regression. These assumptions are necessary because linear equations never fit actual data perfectly. Rather, regression equations describe the best average fit, from which actual observations deviate, some by more, some by less.[5] Deviations from the true model using data from the whole population are called errors and are not observable. Deviations of

---

[5] To recapitulate some basic algebra: any straight line can be described by the equation $Y = mX + b$, where Y is the dependent variable, X is the independent (explanatory) variable, m is the slope (the ratio of change in Y to change in X: "the rise over the run"), and b is the intercept (the value of Y when $X = 0$). The regression equation that best fits the data in a scatterplot adds an error term, e_i, to the right-hand side of the equation to represent the vertical distance between each point and the line of best fit.

sample data from any model that is intended to approximate the true model are called residuals or disturbances. Because of this imperfect fit, there is no single equation that describes the straight line that fits the data. However, the Gauss-Markov theorem has proved that OLS is the best linear unbiased estimator (BLUE) of such a line *if* certain assumptions hold true.[6]

First, OLS assumes that the relationship between the dependent variable and each independent variable is linear; that is, that a straight line describes their relationship better than any sort of curve. If this assumption is false, then OLS gives a biased (too large or too small) estimate of the impact of the independent variable (the slope). Fortunately, this problem is usually easily solved by transforming the independent variable (e.g., logging it, squaring it), although there is often inadequate theoretical guidance about which trans-formation to choose.

Second, OLS assumes that the explanatory variables that are included in the model are not correlated with any omitted explanatory factors. This is the greatest weakness of regression analysis because this assumption is difficult to satisfy and the consequences of violating it can be severe. It is satisfied well only in well-designed experiments, in which randomization makes it possible to assume that omitted variables cancel one another out. Unfortunately, in comparative politics, most regressions are run on observational data, which are not selected at random. This places a burden on the researcher to prove that either the model is fully and correctly specified (there are no relevant omitted or endogenous variables) or no omitted variables are correlated with the variables that the model does specify. If the researcher's claims are not convincing, then the estimated impacts of the independent variables must be assumed to be biased, and the standard errors – which tell us how confident we can be that the estimated impacts are significant – are wrong. For these reasons, regression results often provoke debate about whether the model controlled for this or that omitted variable and whether the model is correctly specified in other respects.

A third assumption of OLS is that there is no correlation between the disturbances in any pair of observations; that is, there is no reason to expect

---

[6] There are many different lists of the Gauss-Markov assumptions that are required for OLS to be BLUE. Some list three assumptions, some list seven, and although many lists overlap, few are exactly the same. Here, I gloss over assumptions that are obvious or substantively trivial – that no independent variable is a constant, that no independent variables are a linear combination of one another, that independent variables are measured precisely, that the independent variables have finite variances, that the sum of the disturbances is zero – so that I can focus on the five assumptions that are most relevant for actual research.

any sets of observations to be systematically over- or underpredicted. When this assumption is not satisfied, there is autocorrelation, which can take many forms. When current prediction errors depend on past prediction errors, there is serial autocorrelation; when they depend on the errors in nearby units (e.g., countries), there is spatial autocorrelation. Autocorrelation can also arise when units are clustered with similar units, survey respondents influence one another, and so on. It is difficult to satisfy the requirement that there is no pattern of any kind in the residuals – that they are completely random. Yet, when there is autocorrelation, we are likely to misjudge how confident we can be that slope coefficients are significantly different from zero.

A fourth OLS assumption is that the variance of the residuals is the same for all values of the explanatory variables. In other words, the dependent variable is equally well (or poorly) explained within all intervals along its range. If this is false, then there is heteroscedasticity, which also makes us likely to over- or underestimate how confident we can be that a coefficient is significant.

A final assumption is that the errors are distributed normally; that is, that their frequency distribution approximates a bell curve, with many small over- or underpredictions and relatively few large ones.[7] There are statistical tests to determine how good an approximation of normality one has but, in practice, the most common violations of this assumption are extreme outliers – cases very poorly predicted by the model – which can bias slopes and wreak havoc with significance tests. Practitioners deal with outliers differently, depending on their purpose. Those who work in an experimental paradigm and believe that they are doing regression on a sample to make inferences about a larger population tend to delete extreme outliers because this makes the sample more representative of the population. Those who work with observational data and have no ambition to generalize beyond their sample have more respect for what the outliers can reveal, and therefore tend to add variables to the model to explain the outliers. Some researchers do both.

Quantitative methodologists are well aware of all of these limitations. In fact, the purists among them dismiss regressions using observational data as hopelessly flawed and therefore meaningless; they prefer randomized experiments and the rare natural experiments and matching models that

---

[7] Some writers are careful to point out that this assumption is not necessary for OLS to be the best estimator, in the strict sense that it is not included in proofs of the Gauss-Markov theorem. However, it is necessary for using OLS estimates to generate probabilities and confidence intervals without resorting to resampling techniques. In a practical sense, therefore, it is a standard assumption of regression analysis (Hanushek and Jackson 1977).

approximate randomization well (Rodrik 2005; Seawright 2007; Sekhon 2009; Summers 1991). This is an extreme stance that exalts unbiased causal inference over the legitimate research goal of generalization because experiments are almost always limited to small, unrepresentative populations and therefore tend to lack external validity. It also ignores the collective and provisional nature of scientific research: no one experiment will demonstrate unchanging truth; rather, many streams of research collectively modify our beliefs, which always remain bounded and somewhat uncertain (Gerring 2011).

Other quantitative methodologists, however, spend their time diagnosing problems and devising corrections for them. Over many decades, sophisticated statistical techniques have been developed to deal with nonlinear relationships, omitted variable bias, nonrandom selection, heteroscedasticity, various types of autocorrelation, nonnormally distributed errors, and many other problems. These techniques often strike the uninitiated as arcane and excessive, especially given the poor quality of much of the data political scientists have. This is exactly the wrong conclusion to draw, however, for it is the problematic data that make the intimidating methods necessary. If we had abundant valid, reliable data generated by experiments or selected at random, very simple methods would suffice. It is because the political data available to us are problematic that complicated statistical fixes, imperfect though they may be, are necessary.

With these caveats, however, quantitative analysis is uniquely useful for the parts of the research process that require knowing whether we can generalize (within certain bounds) about average tendencies. It is also the only method that can tell us how confident we can be that the magnitude of an impact is within a certain range. For example, it allows us to make statements such as, "If the largest party wins at least 70 percent of the seats in the legislature, then we can be 95 percent confident that the country's Freedom House score (on a 2–14 scale) is less than 9." This is a kind of knowledge that is very useful and meaningful to all but those who want a purely categorical, qualitative understanding of politics.

The following sections of this chapter survey the development of quantitative research on democratization. I believe that one should not take researchers' conclusions at face value. They are often misleading or overstated because there are strong professional incentives to exaggerate the quality of the data, treat ambiguous evidence as proof, and extend the implications of any findings far beyond their actual empirical scope. The prudent way to read this research is to pay attention to the empirical findings, interpreting the evidence literally: What do these two indicators actually measure, and what does this relationship between them actually mean? Readers should believe the findings that are often replicated, doubt the ones that have not been replicated, and think creatively about what they may mean (i.e., about which theorized causal process is most likely to have produced the reported empirical relationships). I therefore structure this chapter around the empirical findings and discount the lofty theoretical inferences that authors claim to make. I ignore the distinction between variables of interest and control variables; it is an artificial construct anyway: the statistics don't care which variables we're interested in. This attitude may strike the researchers and my readers as strangely atheoretical, but it is true to the nature of quantitative research. It is a body of empirical generalizations in search of theories.

The survey begins with cross-sectional analyses and then proceeds to the more recent and rigorous time-series cross-sectional tests. Both of these sections deal primarily with hypotheses about modernization or (more narrowly) per capita GDP, which have been central to this literature for a half-century, and which allow me to illustrate the consequences of methodological choices. The survey then continues by examining the proliferation of dependent variables and the more limited testing of a variety of additional independent variables. It ends with an inventory of what we know so far, how well we know it, and what remains to be done.

Tests with cross-sectional data

Efforts to measure democracy quantitatively were very limited before the 1960s.[8] There were, of course, classifications of countries into regime types, but these remained at the nominal or, at best, ordinal level of measurement. In his seminal 1959 article, Seymour Martin Lipset distilled these conventional understandings into his classification of European and Latin American countries.[9] Similarly, James Coleman classified sixty-six countries or territories in Asia, Africa, and Latin America as competitive, semicompetitive, or authoritarian (Coleman and Almond 1960). A more extensive and specific set

---

[8] The principal exception is Russell Fitzgibbon's poll of experts to assess levels of democracy in Latin America, which he began in 1945 and that has been repeated every five years since, with direction of the project passing to Kenneth Johnson, then Phillip Kelly, and now Joseph Klesner (Fitzgibbon 1951).

[9] Unfortunately, Lipset divided the European countries into stable democracies versus unstable democracies and dictatorships, and the Latin American countries into democracies and unstable dictatorships versus stable dictatorships, thus conflating the level and stability of democracy and using inconsistent cut points in his two regions (Lipset 1960).

Table 9.1. Democracy and British colonial rule, 2000

	Ever a British colony?	
	No	Yes
Democracies	35	28
	54%	50%
Dictatorships	30	28
	46%	50%
Total	65	56
	100%	100%

Notes: $\chi^2(121,1) = .178$, $p = .673$; Somers' D $= .038$; gamma $= .077$; tau-c $= .001$; lambda $= 0$.
Source: Author's analysis of ACLP and Cheibub and Gandhi (2004) data.

of cross-regional measurements was Banks and Textor's *Cross-Polity Survey* (Banks and Textor 1963). This was a disaggregated set of mostly ordinal variables with rather vague coding criteria. Nevertheless, they covered up to 141 countries in the 1960–1963 period (when decolonization was rapidly increasing the number of independent countries), and several scholars quickly used them or adapted them for their own cross-sectional analyses. One of the best known was an ordinal classification of polyarchies circa 1969 by Mary Frase Williams and Richard Norling, working for Robert Dahl (Dahl 1971). Banks and a series of his collaborators have continued to revise and update these series until the present, gradually accumulating a monumental collection of data on democracy, political stability, and other political phenomena. However, other scholars have continued to construct their own democracy indicators, many of them cross-sectional (Adelman and Morris 1965; Adelman and Morris 1967; Bollen 1980; Coppedge and Reinicke 1990; Cutright 1963; Hadenius 1992; Jackman 1973; Neubauer 1967).

The development of indicators of democracy made it possible for the first time to examine systematically the relationship between kinds or levels of democracy and many socioeconomic indicators that had already been developed. One can analyze even nominal and ordinal data in simple quantitative ways. If all of the variables are discrete, variables can be cross-tabulated to show how many cases fall into each of the possible combinations of values. For example, Table 9.1 uses cross-tabulation to examine the relationship between regime type and British colonial rule. The dependent variable is the Cheibub and Gandhi (2004) update of the Alvarez, Cheibub, Limongi, and Przeworski

(ACLP) classification of countries into dictatorships or democracies, the sample includes all former colonies as of the year 2000, and the explanatory variable is whether or not the country had ever been a British colony. Table 9.1 suggests that countries that had been British colonies were slightly less likely to be democracies in 2000 (50 percent) than countries that had never been British colonies (54 percent). The statistics beside the table, however, also indicate that this relationship is weak (all are much closer to zero than to one) and that there is a 67 percent chance that democracy and the British legacy are statistically independent. The appropriate conclusion, therefore, is that there was no significant relationship in 2000. Cross-tabulation was typical of the analyses reported in Dahl's *Polyarchy* (1971). It has also been used to test Linz's hypothesis that presidential democracies are less stable than parliamentary democracies (Stepan and Skach 1993) and other hypotheses involving categorical explanatory variables.

Another simple quantitative analysis sometimes found in the literature is the *t*-test for difference of means, which is used when the dependent variable is continuous but the explanatory variable is discrete. Substituting the Contestation Index (the first principal component of many democracy indicators, described in Chapter 2) for the ACLP dichotomy, for example, the average level of contestation in 2000 was 0.25 for former British colonies and 0.39 – a bit more democratic – for other countries but, again, this difference in means is not statistically significant.[10] The lack of significance is not surprising considering that contestation ranges from -1.5 to nearly 2.0 in this sample; thus, the difference in means is comparatively small. This kind of analysis is relatively rare (Diamond 1999; Huntington 1991) because having a continuous dependent variable makes it possible to run regression, which is more informative and flexible. Both cross-tabs and *t*-tests tend to be used for bivariate analyses – those with only one explanatory variable – which are rarely published nowadays.[11]

What was learned from these analyses was at first constrained by the level of measurement achieved by the available indicators and the technical sophistication of the researcher. In his famed 1959 analysis, Lipset had dichotomous indicators of regime stability and continuous socioeconomic indicators (Lipset 1959). He therefore chose to compare the average values of the socioeconomic indicators for stable democracies versus unstable

---

[10] Independent samples t-test: $N = 125$, $t = .912$, $p = .364$ with 123 degrees of freedom.
[11] Multiple explanatory variables can be used, but they make the analysis and interpretation unwieldy, so more straightforward kinds of analysis are preferred.

democracies or dictatorships (in Europe), and for democracies and unstable dictatorships versus stable dictatorships (in Latin America). Unfortunately, this kind of analysis was inappropriate for determining the impact of socio-economic development on democracy because it held the regime categories constant and then allowed the development indicators to vary. It would have been appropriate for investigating the impact of regimes on development, but that was not his purpose. James Coleman made the same mistake a year later with a larger sample (Coleman and Almond 1960). A logit or probit analysis would have been a better choice, but few political scientists were familiar with these techniques before 1975.[12] However, if one is not concerned about causal direction, both analyses demonstrated positive bivariate associations between democracy and many aspects of development – wealth (per capita gross national product, or GNP; number of persons per doctor, vehicle, telephone, radio, or newspaper); industrialization (per capita energy consumption, population in unions); urbanization; and education (literacy and school enrollment). Fortunately, appropriate reanalysis of Lipset's and Coleman's data yields results that are consistent with their conclusion that economic development has a positive impact on stable democracy.

When relatively continuous indicators of democracy became available, social scientists in the 1960s made use of correlation and regression. Daniel Lerner found positive associations among urbanization, literacy, media participation, and electoral turnout in fifty-four to seventy-three countries (Lerner 1958).[13] Phillips Cutright, far ahead of his time, published the first recognizable regression analysis on this topic (Cutright 1963). He found that education, urbanization, economic growth, labor-force characteristics, and especially communications development accounted for about two-thirds of the variance in national political development in seventy-seven countries.[14] Adelman and Morris – also far ahead of their time – found that their indicator of political Westernization, which they constructed using factor analysis, was associated with per capita GNP in a nonlinear fashion (Adelman and Morris 1965). A bit later, Robert Jackman identified this relationship as specifically

---

[12] Probit was invented in 1934, logit in 1944, but they were not immediately adopted by political scientists (Aldrich and Cnudde 1975).

[13] Lerner's analysis was multivariate and directional, but he reported only the multiple correlation coefficient (the square root of the R^2 more familiar today) without any slope coefficients.

[14] Cutright's "national political development" was a combination of Cross-Polity Survey variables. It was a credible indicator of the stability of formal democracy from 1940 to 1960. His analysis stands out for reporting slope coefficients and the R^2, imputing missing values, plotting the regression line and its confidence interval on a scatterplot, and analyzing outliers. Unfortunately, he also predicted that the outliers would regress to the line of fit. This exaggerated the implications of his estimates.

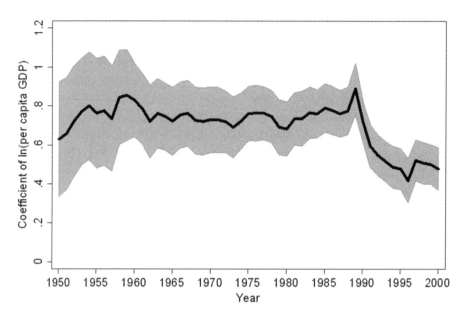

Figure 9.1   Impact of Income on Contestation by Year: Cross-Sectional Estimates with 95 Percent Confidence Intervals

logarithmic (Jackman 1973).[15] This finding has turned out to be probably the single most robust empirical association in comparative politics. Figure 9.1 reports the coefficient of the log of per capita GDP as a predictor of contestation, and 95 percent confidence intervals, in annual cross-sections for every year from 1950 to 2000. Although the association became markedly less strong after 1989 (a puzzle that deserves further exploration!), the coefficient has been consistently positive and significant for a half-century in any cross-sectional sample that covers most of the globe.[16] Most of the exceptions have used smaller samples, such as developing just countries or just one region (Hadenius 1992; Mainwaring and Pérez-Liñán 2003).

[15] Logging per capita GDP also tends to eliminate heteroscedasticity: in this case, the tendency for per capita GDP to explain high levels of democracy better than it explains nondemocracy. Diagnosis and correction of heteroscedasticity would have been possible with cross-sectional data and probably would have increased confidence in this relationship. However, because Jackman identified this logarithmic relationship before many comparative scholars were aware of heteroscedasticity, correcting it never became a standard practice as long as cross-sectional analysis was the norm.

[16] The diminished coefficient indicates that there is now less of a difference between rich and poor countries with respect to democracy than there was before 1989. This is more because of relatively poor countries – specifically postcommunist and African countries – becoming more democratic than because of wealthy countries becoming less democratic. However, this begs the question of how it became possible for poor countries to improve their level of democracy.

But before attention narrowed to per capita energy consumption, GNP, or GDP as the most powerful and robust predictor, these scholars came to the conclusion that all of these processes – industrialization, growing wealth, rising levels of education and literacy, urbanization, and democratization – constituted a single syndrome, which they called modernization. All of these processes moved in parallel, which made it impossible, and perhaps (making a virtue of necessity) undesirable, to determine which process was the cause and which was the effect. As Frank Adelman poetically observed,

> ... The warp of the social tapestry,
> The weave of the nation's polity,
> And the economic woof do intertwine
> When threads one tries to separate,
> To characterize and differentiate,
> The strands become entangled in a froth.
> This intersocietal napery
> Is made into a drapery
> Of pure, untrammeled, integrated cloth!
> (Adelman and Morris 1967)

The conclusion that it was impossible to disentangle cause and effect was inevitable as long as scholars had to work with cross-sectional data, which continued to be used into the 1990s. The most comprehensive cross-sectional analysis was *Democracy and Development*, by Axel Hadenius, which employed a sample of 130 developing countries and tested a great variety of predictors concerned with economic and social modernization, trade, oil exports, and the state (Hadenius 1992). At this point, however, this line of research hit a wall as a result of several limitations of cross-sectional analysis. First, it assumes that differences across countries are equivalent to changes within countries. This is a risky assumption because countries at the same level of socioeconomic modernization are likely to be at different levels of democracy because of factors other than modernization. This makes it unsafe to assume that, for example, Mozambique would be as democratic as Austria if it had an equally high per capita income; there are many other cross-national differences that may matter. One can control for some of these other factors but, if we are honest, we must admit that our models are rarely fully and correctly specified, even though OLS assumes that they are. Failure to control for everything that matters is a concern in all quantitative analysis (and even more so for much qualitative analysis), but it is a much greater problem for cross-sectional analysis than it is when analyzing change within countries. Nevertheless, this problem is less severe when the phenomena being studied are themselves fairly static. Therefore, cross-sectional analysis can be an adequate way to test hypotheses about relatively fixed determinants such as culture, geography, ethnicity and ethnic divisions, colonial legacies, and even the general level of economic development. This is a very relevant consideration in the analysis of political regimes, most of which do not change dramatically or often. For instance, 75 percent of Freedom House scores do not change from one year to the next. Similarly, the absolute average annual change in contestation for all countries, 1950–2000, is only 0.11, in a range from -1.84 to 1.96 ($n = 7,363$). This makes it likely that the findings of the most carefully controlled cross-sectional analyses will often hold when tested with time-series data.

The second limitation of cross-sectional analysis is that it provides no basis for generalizing its findings to other years. The nature of causal relationships may evolve, strengthen, or weaken; it is possible that an association exists in one year but dissipates in others, as Figure 9.1 confirms. It is also possible that a relationship discovered in one cross-section could be spuriously related to some temporary global event or trend. Once again, this is less of a risk for relatively static phenomena.

A third limitation is that cross-sectional estimates can be sensitive to the composition of the sample. In an earlier work, I found that which modernization variables mattered and whether their effects were positive or negative could vary greatly depending on which regions of the world were included in the sample (Coppedge 1997). Biased sample composition was more of a problem in the early years of quantitative democratization research, when data tended to be available only for the more privileged countries – the poorest countries, smallest countries, communist countries, and Middle Eastern countries tended to be excluded. But even when data became more abundant, Hadenius included only developing countries, which probably biased his results against finding a significant impact of per capita GDP (Hadenius 1992).

Finally, as noted already, in cross-sectional analysis, it is often impossible to disentangle the effects of variables that are strongly correlated with one another. This problem is called multicollinearity. It could be argued that multicollinearity gave rise to the very concept of modernization, the essence of which was parallel change in a large number of collinear variables. Today, the preferred technique for dealing with this dilemma is to use factor analysis or structural equation modeling to reduce the commonalities in several collinear variables into a smaller set of latent variables. In the early days, these techniques were practically unknown (although Adelman and Morris used them in 1965!), so it became the norm to use the easier but cruder solution of letting one variable stand for all of the rest. Per capita GDP was the most robust of the modernization variables (Diamond 1992). This is how the thicker hypotheses of modernization research on democracy came to be narrowly represented by per capita GDP in today's testing. If we are interested in thickening the concepts and theories we test, however, it would be wise to return to the practice of using multiple variables to represent modernization.

The complications and advantages of time-series cross-sectional data

Beginning in the 1980s, some scholars developed democratization data sets that contained observations on multiple countries and multiple years (Arat 1988; Gasiorowski 1995; Gonick and Rosh 1988; Hannan and Carroll 1981; Helliwell 1994; Starr 1991). This practice expanded in the 1990s with increasing use of the Polity and Freedom House indexes and the Alvarez and colleagues' classification (Burkhart 1997; Burkhart and Lewis-Beck 1994; Londregan and Poole 1996; Przeworski and Limongi 1997; Przeworski et al. 2000).[17] The development of time-series cross-sectional (TSCS) data on democracy and relevant predictors of it revolutionized this line of research. The findings of cross-sectional analyses became almost completely irrelevant because the same hypotheses could then be tested with superior TSCS data. Since about 2000, almost all quantitative analyses of democratization published in leading journals have used TSCS data.

These datasets made it possible to study short-term change separately from long-term differences rather than assuming that cross-national differences were equivalent to change. However, this potential was not realized at first because taking advantage of the variation over both space and time that is contained in the data requires more advanced statistical techniques. Without those techniques, the cross-national differences and changes within countries are simply pooled together as undifferentiated variance to be explained. If there is more variation across countries than there is within them – which is *always* the case when democracy is the dependent variable – then a regression with a simple pooled sample still explains cross-sectional variation in levels of democracy more than it explains change.

---

[17] An intermediate stage of simple time-series analysis was skipped because when time-series data became available for any country, they became available for many countries. Therefore, research proceeded directly from cross-sections to time-series cross-sectional analysis.

Gradually, comparativists recognized that TSCS data presented them with complications that were ignored and intractable in cross-sectional analysis. All the complications stem from violations of the OLS assumption that there is no pattern in the residuals. If our samples were randomly selected from a universe of independent cases, this would be a safe assumption. But when our dataset consists of repeated observations from the same countries in the same span of years, prudence requires us to assume that there are patterns in the residuals. It is likely that democracy is systematically over- or underpredicted in certain countries or years (fixed effects); that the impact of some variables is different in some times or places (causal or cluster heterogeneity); and that democracy is easier or harder to predict in some countries or years (heteroscedasticity). It is also likely that countries influence one another's level of democracy (spatial autocorrelation) and that how democratic a country is in one year depends on how democratic it was the year before (serial autocorrelation). Unfortunately, these complications are unavoidable in TSCS data; fortunately, there are ways of dealing with them that can actually reveal useful information about empirical relationships.

In democratization research, dependent variables and models have evolved to exploit the advantages of the increasingly abundant data. These modeling choices have conceptual and theoretical implications. To a degree that has not been sufficiently appreciated, scholars are testing fundamentally different questions about democratization because of their choices of dependent variables and estimation methods. I illustrate this point by using examples from research on the impact of per capita GDP (or, more broadly, modernization). Later sections of this chapter survey tests of other hypotheses.

The most basic choice made possible by greater data availability has been the differentiation of between-country and within-country estimates. Time-series cross-sectional data make it possible for researchers examining the relationship between democracy and per capita GDP to estimate either one or both, and this decision leads to dramatically different estimates and interpretations. Those who estimate between-country effects test the hypothesis that the higher the average income a country has compared to other countries, the higher its average level of democracy is. This is nearly the same as the hypothesis implied by estimates with cross-sectional data. Both hypotheses are consistent with (among other processes) a long-term process in which new social actors arise, become educated and politically active, and experience prodemocratic cultural change. The effect of these processes would be observable in the long term and across countries but would not necessarily manifest itself in the short term, within countries. Both models focus on explaining differences between countries rather than changes within countries. Figure 9.2a shows the kind of relationship these models estimate.

In contrast, those who estimate within-country effects (with fixed-effects regression) – a seemingly minor change in the estimating technique – test a radically different hypothesis, that the richer a country is this year compared to itself in other years, the more democratic it is relative to itself in other years. Such a process could be called micro-modernization, or modernization writ small: the hypothesis that small changes in national income cause small, immediate changes in the level of democracy. The estimators of this relationship transform the data so that each country's deviations from its mean income explain each country's deviations from its mean democracy score. This implies a quite different process than modernization writ large. We would have to understand it as a different process that would not allow enough time for the creation of new social actors, the growth of an educated populace, or cultural change. Instead, it would have to be a short-term process that quickly empowered prodemocracy actors who already existed, perhaps by putting organizational resources, information, or technology in their hands that made coordinated action possible. Micro-modernization would also have a large cumulative cross-national effect in the long term, but it differs from the between-country model in that it would also necessarily be detectable in the short term, within countries. Figure 9.2b shows just how distinct this relationship is. If one did not know that both plots were generated from the same variables, it would seem that they had nothing to do with each other.

The published estimates are also quite different. Between-country estimates almost always show a significant and positive effect of income on democracy, but within-country estimates are far from robust. Some scholars using fixed effects have found a significant, positive effect (Brinks and Coppedge 2006); some a significant, negative effect (Rudra 2005); and some no significant effect at all (Colaresi and Thompson 2003). The most comprehensive tests report that with fixed effects, per capita income has no significant impact (Acemoglu et al. 2008). My own estimates using contestation as the dependent variable illustrate why this is so. Table 9.2 shows the usual strong positive effect of income when OLS is run on a pooled sample (Model 1) and a practically identical between-countries effect (Model 2). When we get separate estimates for the between-countries and within-countries effects, however, the between-countries effect is about the same as the overall effect. There is also a significant positive within-countries effect, but it is only about 30 percent as large (Model 3). To the extent that this finding would hold even when controlling for other

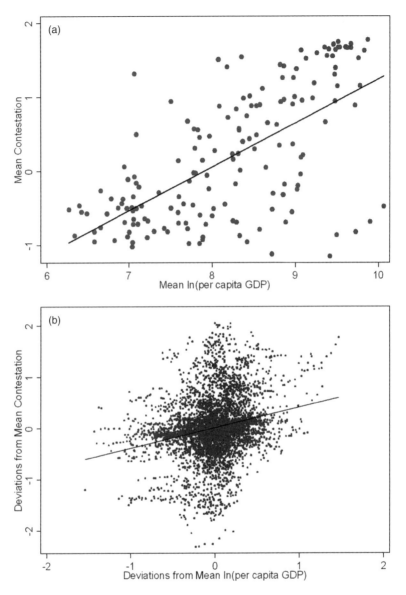

Figure 9.2   Income and Democracy: Between- versus Within-Country: (a) Between-Country Effects. (b) Within-Country Effects

factors – which I believe likely, as per capita GDP has long been the most robust correlate of democracy – it casts doubt on any interpretation (at least, any simple interpretation) of the empirical link between income and democracy as primarily a micro-modernization process. It also forces us to

Table 9.2. Estimates of the impact of per capita income on level of democracy

Model	1		2		3 Random effects with	
Estimator	OLS		Fixed effects		first-order autocorrelation	
Dependent variable	Mean contestation		Contestation		Contestation	
Independent variables	coeff.	s.e.	coeff.	s.e.	coeff.	s.e.
Intercept	−4.47	0.46	−4.52	0.48	−4.53	0.42
lnGDPpc	0.568	0.056	0.578	0.058		
lnGDPpc between					0.598	0.051
lnGDPpc within					0.182	0.045
R^2 within			0.057		0.059	
R^2 between			0.379		0.378	
R^2 overall	0.386		0.438		0.448	
N	164		5361		5233	
Countries	164		164		165	
rho					0.871	

Note: Coefficients in bold are significant. LnGDPpc is the natural log of per capita GDP.

reconsider why there is a long-term, cross-national relationship. This remains an empirical generalization in search of a theory. Until a more definite theory emerges and survives more rigorous testing, per capita GDP is an excellent control variable but an opaque explanatory one.

A related estimation technique, random effects, is a weighted average of the between-country and within-country estimates; it gives more weight to between-country estimates when their variance is larger and more to within-country estimates when their variance is larger (Castilla 2007). When democracy is the dependent variable, the variance of the between-country effect has been, and I predict always will be, greater, so random-effects estimates will always reflect mostly cross-national variation. Compare, for example, the two coefficients for ln(GDP per capita) in Model 3 of Table 9.2.[18] The fact that these two coefficients are significantly different from each other ($\chi^2 = 13.35$, $p = .0003$) suggests that random-effects estimation blurs the distinction between the relationships and should not be used when testing the relationship between income and the level of democracy. The findings of those who have used random effects – Gonick and Rosh (1988),

[18] Model 3 corrects for first-order autocorrelation because, as explained herein, serial autocorrelation – always present in TSCS democratization data – would otherwise give us false confidence in the significance of the within-effects coefficient.

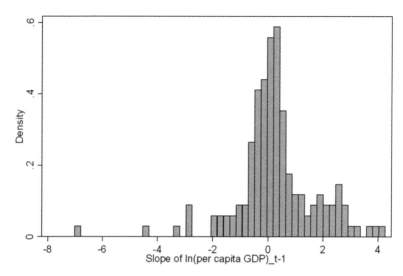

Figure 9.3   Distribution of Coefficients for Annual Cross-Sections: Regressing Contestation on Income. *Note:* Estimates are from 151 countries, 1950–2000, or whenever the country existed and data were available. Per capita GDP data are from the Penn World Tables 6.1; contestation is from Coppedge, Alvarez, and Maldonado (2008).

Burkhart and Lewis-Beck (1994), Burkhart (1997), Ross (2004), and Herb (2005) – should therefore be interpreted as findings about predictors of long-term cross-national variation.[19] Some of these studies use regional dummy variables that perform a function similar to fixed effects, but only to the extent that all the countries in each region have the same levels of income and democracy. For most regions, this is an inadequate substitute for fixed effects.

As noted earlier, fixed effects are only one of several patterns in the residuals that can threaten inferences. It is also possible to have different slopes for different cases, or causal heterogeneity. For example, it is possible that increasing income promotes democracy in some countries but undermines democracy in others. Although this may sound implausible, the empirical evidence strongly suggests that it is true. If contestation is regressed on the log of per capita GDP separately in each country over time (all independent years from 1950 to 2000), the coefficients of income are distributed as in Figure 9.3. The central tendency is a small positive effect, but the dispersion is quite wide, from very strong positive effects to equally strong negative effects,

---

[19] Jensen and Wantchekon (2004) report that their random-effect estimates were no different from their fixed-effect estimates, but their sample was limited to thirty-nine African countries.

many of which are statistically significant. The reasons for this are not yet clear. It may be a reflection of the disparate impact of economic growth in different regimes, which is discussed herein: growth seems to strengthen both democracies and nondemocracies, whereas economic decline may undermine both types of regime. The relationship between income and democracy may also depend on how countries earn their income. Some research suggests that high income promotes democracy less powerfully in states that profit from the export of oil or other minerals (Bueno de Mesquita and Smith 2009; Epstein et al. 2006; Finkel et al. 2007; Herb 2005; Ross 2001; Ross 2004; Smith 2004). It would also make sense that democracy would suffer where the economy is dominated by drug trafficking, thus leading to a negative relationship (Coppedge, Alvarez, and González 2008).

Scholars have tested such conditional relationships in several ways. The simplest technique is a dummy-variable interaction; that is, estimating different income coefficients for different groups of countries, which are identified by one or more dummy variables. Burkhart and Lewis-Beck (1994) used this technique to show that income (actually, per capita energy consumption) had a weaker impact on democracy in the semiperiphery and especially the periphery of the world system than it did in the core countries (Burkhart and Lewis-Beck 1994). It is also possible, and appropriate, to interact continuous variables when testing a hypothesis in which one variable conditions (magnifies, mediates, or modifies) the effect of another variable (Kam and Franzese 2007). For example, Rudra finds that trade openness harms democracy only when social spending is not increased to compensate the casualties of trade (Rudra 2005). The most flexible way to deal with conditional relationships, however, is hierarchical linear modeling (HLM), which allows researchers to nest models within models at different levels of analysis. Thus, a model need not be limited to an intercept, an error term, and a list of independent variables; it can also incorporate models of the determinants of the intercept and determinants of the coefficients each of the independent variables while allowing some of the additional models to have their own error terms. With HLM, Coppedge, Alvarez, and González (2008) found that the more a country's economy depends on drug trafficking, the more negative the impact of per capita GDP is on contestation. Hierarchical linear modeling is a powerful tool that has only begun to be exploited in comparative research on democratization.[20]

---

[20] Finkel et al. (2007) used HLM to model the cross-national determinants of countries' initial regimes and rate of democratization rather than to model determinants of their time-varying (within-country) explanatory variable coefficients.

Another common pattern in the residuals is heteroscedascity, which means that some cases are better predicted than others. This problem does not bias the coefficient estimates, but it does affect the standard errors of the explanatory variables, which makes it hard for analysts to know whether to trust their significance tests. There are two fundamentally different ways to fix this situation. The first, which is uncommon but, in principle, preferred, is to figure out why some cases are harder to explain and then to specify new variables that would make all of the units "well behaved" (equally well or poorly explained in the sense that their residuals have approximately the same variance). One could, for example, note that the variance in democracy scores over time is much smaller at the extremes of most democracy indexes than it is for the intermediate cases – perhaps because of the truncation of the indicator – and repair the problem by controlling for each country's distance from the nearest extreme of the index (Brinks and Coppedge 2006). In the same spirit, some researchers modeling the probability of a regime change have controlled for the number of past regime changes. The process modeled by these corrections is still somewhat vague, but they are good examples of specification fixes. The alternative is the statistical fix, which is even less informative but more common. The current standard is to calculate panel-corrected standard errors, which give better estimates of the precision of the coefficient estimates by using information about variation within countries over time (Beck and Katz 1995).

In democratization research, the most relentless pattern in the residuals is inertia (serial autocorrelation) because most countries do not change their level of democracy in most years. For example, the level of contestation in one year explains 93 percent of the variation in the level of contestation the next year.[21] Intuitively, it is quite easy to predict how democratic a country is this year if one knows how democratic it was last year. This inertia is a problem because it artificially shrinks standard errors, making us unduly confident of the significance of our findings. A more authoritative indicator of the presence of serial autocorrelation is the statistic rho, which is the correlation between current and lagged values of the dependent variable. If rho is small (closer to zero than to one), autocorrelation is not much of a problem and any of the available fixes will yield similar answers. But if rho is close to one (i.e., there is strong inertia), it is essential to correct for autocorrelation. How this is done is likely to have a big effect on inferences about one or more of the explanatory variables (Beck and Katz 2009). In democratization models, rho

---

[21] Coefficient of lagged dependent variable $= 0.971$, s.e. $= 0.003$, $t = 323$, $N = 7,361$.

is almost always huge (0.8 or greater), so this problem cannot be ignored. There is no one technique that is appropriate in all circumstances; rather, scholars must choose the technique that has the most plausible interpretation in the context of the theory and the data.

The most common *statistical* fix (first-order autogression, or AR1) is to multiply both sides of the equation by 1-rho before estimating the regression parameters.[22] This correction models a process in which all of the independent variables exert their impacts immediately, whereas any relevant omitted variables (captured by the error term) have a geometrically declining impact on the dependent variable starting in the next period. As Beck and Katz (2009) observe, it is hard to imagine a situation in which such a process would be plausible. The AR1 fix usually works, in the sense of helping researchers rule out any additional autocorrelation, but it is hard to defend on theoretical grounds.

The most common *specification* fix is to include a lagged dependent variable (LDV) as one of the explanatory variables. Achen (2002) argues that this fix can overcorrect, washing out the effect of other variables, especially when they trend in the same direction as the dependent variable. If this objection applies anywhere, it applies to democratization models, because a (one-year) lagged dependent variable typically has a highly significant coefficient very close to one and explains more than 90 percent of the variance. Beck and Katz (2009), however, argue that there is no purely statistical reason to avoid using a lagged dependent variable. It does not necessarily overpower other independent variables and, if it does, whether or not it should be included in the model is a theoretical question rather than a statistical one. These are conceptual and theoretical choices that must be made consciously and carefully.[23] In democratization research, an LDV model would imply that the independent variables have an immediate impact and that any later impact they (and any omitted variables) may have is completely channeled through the lagged dependent variable rather than exerted directly on current observations of the dependent variable. This strikes me as imperfect but more plausible for most democratization models than the assumptions behind the AR1 correction.[24]

---

[22] Serial autocorrelation can be assumed to occur at the same rate for all countries (i.e., contemporaneous serial autocorrelation) or at different rates for different countries (i.e., panel-specific serial autocorrelation).

[23] Directed acyclic graphs, developed by Judea Pearl to model Bayesian networks of causality, can be helpful for deciding how best to deal with unobserved confounders, or indeed whether there is any satisfactory way to model causal effects in a given problem. See Foster (2010).

[24] LDV and AR1 are special cases of the more general autoregressive distributed lag (ADL) models. Beck and Katz (2009) suggest that ADL can be a good place to start and that empirical testing can

Writing about political economy data, Beck and Katz also dismiss the concerns of economists that a lagged dependent variable may have a unit root (rho of one or greater), which would force the predicted values, and therefore the residuals, to spiral eventually toward infinity. The econometrics literature has worried that even rho estimates less than one could also be problematic because the closer they get to one, the harder it becomes to be sure that the "true" rho is not greater than one. Beck and Katz point out that many political-economy variables are proportions (e.g., shares of seats, percentages of a budget) that are necessarily bounded, unlike the production, inflation, trade, and growth variables modeled in econometrics (Beck and Katz 2009). One can therefore safely assume a theoretical model in which there can be no unit root, even though it is still imperative to model the strong inertial tendency in these processes in some way.[25] It is important to recall here that statistical analyses always presume that the theoretical model is correct; they do not tell us what the model should be. If the theoretical model tells us that infinite growth in bounded variables would be nonsensical, there is no need to worry that an estimated rho less than one is actually greater than one. The same argument should apply to indicators of democracy, which cannot become infinitely large.

The most radical fix for serial autocorrelation is to difference the dependent variable so that one is explaining change in democracy rather than its level (Allison 1990; Teorell 2010). This strategy effectively eliminates this type of autocorrelation but radically changes the question. Of course, the notion of short-term changes in democracy gets us closer to testing hypotheses about a short-term process, but it sacrifices information about longer-term changes in the level of democracy that show up as cross-national differences. Change is also much harder to explain than level: it is rare for a model to account for more than 20 percent of the variance (Brinks and Coppedge 2006). For example, Jan Teorell's *Determinants of Democratization*, the most thorough recent effort, seeks to explain upturns and downturns in democracy, as well as change in either direction (Teorell 2010). Despite testing more than thirty explanatory variables, he was able to explain only about 10 percent of annual change, although he had much greater success explaining long-term change (Teorell 2010).

guide decisions about which variables to lag and how many lags to use. A few researchers have used a five-year lag instead of the usual one year (Barro 1999; Gonick and Rosh 1988; Ross 2001).

[25] Beck and Katz argue for the lagged dependent variable followed by diagnostics to rule out additional serial autocorrelation.

Another pattern in the residuals is period effects: residuals that are systematically higher or lower for all countries in the same years. This phenomenon is well known in the democratization literature, which calls attention to waves of democracy: the second wave in the aftermath of World War II, the reverse wave of the 1960s and 1970s, the third wave that spread from Southern Europe to Latin America and beyond, and a possible fourth wave following the collapse of the Soviet Union. Once again, this kind of process can be treated as a substantive modeling issue or as a statistical problem in need of correction. The most common specification fix has been to model some sort of diffusion process (discussed subsequently). But it is more common to use the statistical fix of adding year or period dummy variables to the model (Brinks and Coppedge 2006; Gleditsch and Ward 2006; Jensen and Wantchekon 2004; Starr and Lindborg 2003; Wright 2008).[26] The drawback of this technique is that these dummies are ambiguous: they capture the impact of any events that occurred in those years, not merely the events the researcher had in mind. Does 1974 refer to the restoration of democracy in Greece, the Organization of the Petroleum-Exporting Countries oil embargo, the Portuguese revolution, or Watergate? Does 1989 refer to the fall of the Berlin Wall, the Chilean referendum lost by Augusto Pinochet, or the end of the Iran-Iraq War? Nevertheless, crude corrections are usually better than no corrections at all. Year or period dummies are appropriate when the historical patterns are obvious but hard to measure in any other way.

Spatial autocorrelation presents similar problems; the only difference is that errors are correlated not across years but rather across space. It includes the domino effect, coup contagion, diffusion, and globalization: any process in which countries are not self-contained, independent units rather are linked together. The links need not be literally spatial, as they are in the case of contiguous countries; they may be networks consisting of cultural affinities, common languages, trade and investment flows, or the movement of people and ideas across borders (Huntington 1991; Whitehead 1986). Most of us find such linkages plausible, but it is only recently that scholars have tested for them systematically. If they exist, failure to model them results in excessive confidence in the domestic determinants of democracy. Indicators of geographic clustering such as Moran's I consistently confirm that there are spatial patterns in the distribution of democracy and regime changes around the globe. Statistical fixes are available that are analogous to corrections for

---

[26] Panel-corrected standard errors also automatically correct for contemporaneous correlation (Beck and Katz 2009).

Table 9.3. The proliferation of dependent variables

Dependent variable	Mathematical definition	Research questions
Level of democracy	D_t	Why are some countries (or country-years) more democratic than others?
Probability of being democratic or not	$\mathrm{pr}(D_t > a^*)$	Why are some countries democratic and others undemocratic?
Magnitude of change in level	$D_t - D_{t-1}$ or ΔD	Why do some countries experience great changes toward democracy, others great changes away from democracy, and others something in between or little change at all?
Probability of transition (P_{AD})	$\mathrm{pr}(D_t > a \mid D_{t-1} < a)$ or $\mathrm{pr}(\Delta D > b^{**})$	Why do some nondemocracies become democracies in the current year?
Probability of breakdown (P_{DA})	$\mathrm{pr}(D_t < a \mid D_{t-1} > a)$ or $\mathrm{pr}(\Delta D < -b)$	Why do some democracies become nondemocracies in the current year?
Probability of regime change	$\mathrm{pr}(\mid \Delta D \mid > b)$	Why do some countries change their regime at all, in either direction?
Cumulative hazard of transition	$\mathrm{pr}(\Delta D > b \mid t)$	Why do some nondemocracies become more likely to become democracies in the long run, while others become less likely to do so?
Cumulative hazard of breakdown	$\mathrm{pr}(\Delta D < -b \mid t)$	Why do some democracies become more likely to become nondemocracies in the long run, while others become less likely to do so?

Note: * a is a threshold of democracy; ** b is the largest $\mid \Delta D \mid$ that can happen without a regime change taking place.

serial autocorrelation. However, it is better to try to model the process and learn from it than it is to correct for it without learning anything (Beck 2008; Franzese and Hays 2009).

Other dependent variables

One of the major trends in quantitative research on democratization has been the proliferation of dependent variables. This process may have been driven by the need to deal with statistical complications, but it has resulted in theoretical innovation. These variables are not merely different ways of measuring the same concept; they are measures of quite different concepts that correspond to new hypotheses. Much recent research is no longer focused on explaining levels of democracy. Table 9.3 defines these variables and the questions they pose.[27] There is little reason to expect that all of these questions have the same answers. Factors that cause small improvements may not move many countries across the cut point of a dichotomous indicator (Elkins 2000). A country could have reached its level of democracy (or crossed the threshold) via either a large, sudden change or an accumulation of incremental changes. The causes of breakdown are not necessarily the flip side of the causes of transition (Rustow 1970). Some factors may destabilize regimes without determining whether they will become more democratic or less so. Other factors may affect the long-term chances of a regime change without having a discernible impact in any given year. It may be possible to conceive of all of these variables as components of a single process: special cases of a more complex process. Eventually, we will probably reconverge on more holistic models that can estimate the magnitude and direction of a change, given the probability of change from one level to each other level (or type), as a function of elapsed time.

A change in the dependent variable gave rise to one of the major debates of the past decade: whether per capita GDP makes transitions more likely or merely helps existing democracies survive. Przeworski and Limongi (1997) and Przeworski and colleagues (2000) (commonly referred to as PACL, for Przeworski, Alvarez, Cheibub, and Limongi) upset decades of research when they calculated separate estimates for the probability of a transition from authoritarianism to democracy (P_{AD}) and the probability of a transition from democracy to authoritarianism (P_{DA}).[28] They are among a growing number of scholars who use event-history models to explain duration, or the probability of transition or breakdown as a function of elapsed time; or, as PACL put it, the life expectancy of regimes. It is the preferred method when we are trying to model pent-up, episodic change. Their conclusion was

---

[27] There is some other research that seeks to describe or explain transitions among regime types that do not lie on a single dimension of democracy (Geddes 2003; Hannan and Carroll 1981; Starr 1991). For example, military regimes and no-party regimes are distinct and yet may be equally undemocratic. Table 9.3 describes only dependent variables that can be derived from a unidimensional understanding of democracy.

[28] Earlier articles using categorical dependent variables had reported a positive impact of income that seemed consistent with modernization literature. Hannan and Carroll modeled transitions among five discrete regime types, one of which – multiparty systems – was equivalent to democracy (Hannan and Carroll 1981). Using event-history analysis, they found that high income inhibits regime changes of all kinds and helps prevent military coups. Londregan and Poole, even with a very rigorous model that specified a lagged dependent variable and fixed effects, concluded that income increases the probability of being a democracy (Londregan and Poole 1996). However, the effect they reported combined the impact of income on both transitions to democracy and the survival of democracy. In light of subsequent research, their estimate probably reflected mostly the latter.

that income had no effect on transitions; it only helped democracy survive in countries that became democracies for other reasons (Przeworski et al. 2000).

A pitched debate ensued. Boix and Stokes replied that PACL's own estimates actually supported a significant impact of income on transitions to democracy and that if a longer time-series were used, the effect of income on P_{AD} was actually larger than the effect on P_{DA} (Boix and Stokes 2003). Epstein and colleagues buttressed Boix and Stokes by pointing out that PACL had miscalculated a standard error, which led to an underestimate of the significance of the impact of income on transitions (Epstein et al. 2006). Epstein and colleagues also reported that the impact of income on transitions was about as large as the impact on breakdowns. In the meantime, Bernhard and colleagues (2004) replicated PACL's finding of a strong positive effect of income on survival but did not test for any impact on transitions. A stronger endorsement of PACL came from Gassebner and colleagues, who tested the robustness of the association between income and democracy by running more than 3 million regressions with all possible combinations of fifty-eight control variables, taken three at a time (Gassebner et al. 2009). They found that income had a significant association with the survival of democracy in 67 percent of the models, whereas it had a significant association with transitions to democracy in only 13 percent of the models. This would be a powerful confirmation if it were not for the principle that scholars should not engage in blind specification searches; if one of the models in the 13 percent is correct, then all of the millions of other estimates would be irrelevant.

Speaking directly to that point, Acemoglu and colleagues have shown that income rarely has a significant association with the level of democracy, the probability of transition to democracy, or the probability that democracy will survive, *if* models are estimated with fixed effects – a tweak that Gassebner and colleagues never tried (Acemoglu et al. 2008). Their finding confirms an ancillary finding by Colaresi and Thompson, who used the equivalent of fixed effects (XTGEE in Stata) and found no significant impact of log per capita GDP either in a panel model or in a cross-sectional model with change in Polity as the dependent variable (Colaresi and Thompson 2003). Acemoglu and colleagues argue that the well-known association between income and democracy is spurious: countries, especially former colonies, long ago set out on one of two self-reinforcing paths (Acemoglu et al. 2008). On one path, elites hoard both economic resources and political power and have no incentive to share either one more broadly. On the other path, both resources and power were initially dispersed, making it hard for elites to concentrate their control of either one, even though they might wish to do so. This theory strikes me as simplistic and unable to account for the many instances of democratization in highly unequal societies (e.g., India, South Africa, Brazil, and Bolivia). Nevertheless, evidence is mounting that there are powerful fixed effects in democratization. We must take them into account in our tests, even as we continue to debate what they are and how to model them.

Other explanatory variables

This section surveys the testing of many variables other than per capita GDP or modernization, which have monopolized our attention up to this point. These variables have been tested less frequently, so my conclusions are more tentative. Nevertheless, there is a great deal of interesting research to survey. I group these variables into three categories – relatively fixed predictors, stock variables, and dynamic variables – because each category tells us something about the kind of variation in democracy that these variables can explain.

Relatively fixed predictors

We have seen that there are strong fixed effects in TSCS democracy data: a tendency for countries to remain at a certain level of democracy for long periods of time. Fixed effects call for fixed causes. Intuitively, predictors that are constantly changing are not very promising candidates for explaining a relatively stable phenomenon. If we approach the problem inductively, it seems that the most promising explanatory factors would be those that change rarely, change little, change slowly, or do not change at all. Such factors have been tested often, and some of them have proved significant.[29] The drawback is that their relatively fixed nature makes it very hard to distinguish the effects of one fixed variable from another. This is a central theme in the literature on all of these variables.

Some of the first tests using relatively fixed variables were inspired by dependency theories holding that the countries on the "periphery" of the **world economic system** were exploited by countries in the "core" and, as a result, were less developed and less democratic (Wallerstein 1974). Several studies therefore included dummy variables for countries in the periphery and those

---

[29]   They are not guaranteed to be significant, however. For example, in large samples, land area is not significant (Finkel et al. 2007; Gassebner et al. 2009). These findings also cast doubt on the claim that islands tend to be democratic (Dahl and Tufte 1973).

in the semiperiphery and found that they had a negative association with levels of democracy (Bollen 1983; Bollen and Jackman 1985; Gonick and Rosh 1988; but see Muller 1995 for an exception). These results were statistically significant but only vaguely informative. They could have reflected a host of dimensions on which developing and developed countries tend to differ – social or economic modernization, culture, religion, geography, climate, trade, disease, diet, immigration patterns, political stability, and so on – only some of which were germane to the explanations elaborated by dependency theories. Dummy variables for world **regions**, such as South America, the Middle East, and sub-Saharan Africa, have yielded similar results and raised similar questions. Regional dummies are very often significantly associated with levels of democracy – some positively, others negatively, depending on which region serves as the reference category (Helliwell 1994; O'Loughlin et al. 1998; Ross 2001). They also tend to be associated with the magnitude of changes in democracy, which reflect which regions experienced a wave of democratization during the sample period (Brinks and Coppedge 2006; O'Loughlin et al. 1998). Finally, regional dummies have also been significant predictors of the probability of the rise, survival, and fall of democratic regimes (Bernhard et al. 2004; Starr and Lindborg 2003). These findings sometimes evaporate, however, when models add more rigorous controls (Bernhard et al. 2004; Hannan and Carroll 1981). This tendency suggests that region is not a very meaningful or useful explanation in itself; a satisfying explanation for democracy's inertial patterns should be more substantive.[30]

One substantive static factor is **presidentialism** – static because presidential democracies have hardly ever become parliamentary or vice versa. Juan Linz propounded an elaborate theory arguing that presidential democracies are more likely to break down than parliamentary ones (Linz and Valenzuela 1994). Presidents come into office believing that they have a more direct mandate than congress, he argued, yet they are less likely to have a working majority in the legislature, and so they are tempted to rule by decree or to circumvent the legislature in other ways. Given the fixed presidential term, the legislature has no way to remove the president from office. This stalemate can escalate into a constitutional crisis, leading to military intervention or some other unconstitutional resolution. Quantitative testing of this theory – usually limited to adding a dummy for presidential systems to a regression model – yielded contradictory results. Some found that presidential democracies

---

[30] See Mainwaring and Pérez Liñán (2005) for a defense of regional analysis that nevertheless agrees that it is important to specify why regions matter.

lasted longer, on average, than parliamentary democracies (Stepan and Skach 1993); some found no difference in duration (Gasiorowski and Power 1998). Przeworski and colleagues concluded, "Presidential democracies are simply more brittle under all economic and political conditions" (Przeworski et al. 2000, 136); this is consistent with Brinks and Coppedge (2006). Others found that presidential regimes were not more likely to change (Bernhard et al. 2004; Gasiorowski 1995; Pevehouse 2002b; Wright 2008). The contradictory findings were probably due to different samples (Should one include European parliamentary democracies? The parliamentary democracies of interwar Europe? Only developing countries?), different classifications of presidential systems (Should one code a regime as presidential if it is not democratic? How should one treat hybrid systems with both a president and a prime minister?), and different dependent variables (Is presidentialism supposed to explain the longevity of a regime, whether or not it is democratic, the level of democracy, the magnitude of a change in score, the probability of a regime change in any direction, or only the probability of a breakdown?).

In response to these inconclusive results, research bifurcated into two strands. One held that presidentialism by itself has no simple impact on regime survival; it is pernicious only in fragmented multiparty systems (Mainwaring 1993) or where more specific rules governing executive-legislative relations make interbranch conflict likely and hard to resolve (Mainwaring and Shugart 1997). The other strand holds that there is an empirical association between presidentialism and the breakdown of democracy, but that it is not a causal relationship. Linz was, in other words, right about the tendency but wrong about its cause (Cheibub and Limongi 2002). José Antônio Cheibub argues that what appears to be the fragility of presidential systems is actually the fragility of democracy in countries with a history of military intervention in politics (Cheibub 2006) – a different, fairly invariant explanatory factor. This research program is a good illustration of the difficulty of adjudicating among competing fixed effects in quantitative research.

States often have relatively stable characteristics – such as their ability to control territory, maintain public order, enforce laws, and prevent corruption – that might seem to be a promising explanation for stable levels of democracy. The less dramatic deviations from highly governable, ruly, strong states – such as bureaucratic rectitude and maintenance of the rule of law – have not yet been found to be significantly correlated with levels of democracy (Barro 1999; Kopstein and Reilly 2000; Ross 2004), although this may be because of the limitations of existing governance indicators. The more dramatic disruptions such as civil war are discussed herein as dynamic factors.

Levels of democracy are also associated positively with **capitalism** and negatively with **communism**, as one would expect, given that indicators of democracy were developed in the capitalist West (Gonick and Rosh 1988; Hadenius 1992; Muller 1995). There is a more interesting debate about a subtler distinction among economic systems: the extent to which a state depends on revenues from oil and other mineral exports as opposed to taxing its own citizens. Although this is not technically a fixed characteristic, it is approximately fixed because states tend to fluctuate within a narrow range of values for decades at a time. In a celebrated article, Michael Ross showed that these mineral-dependent **rentier states** indeed tend to be less democratic, other things being equal (Ross 2001; see also Hadenius 1992).[31] Michael Herb then challenged this result with the argument that although oil revenues have a negative, *direct* effect on democracy, they have an *indirect*, positive effect by raising per capita GDP, which raises the level of democracy; the indirect effect cancels out the direct effect (Herb 2005).[32] Teorell found no significant effect of rentierism on *change* toward or away from democracy (Teorell 2010). Ross also defined three variants of the rentier-state hypothesis and produced other tests that took him closer to identifying the causal mechanisms at work. I discuss these in the section on dynamic variables. However, Ross also reported that the more personnel the military had, the less democratic the country was; and that this was *not* part of the rentier effect (Ross 2001). There is, therefore, no scholarly consensus on this thesis, but it is a relatively recent line of investigation that will surely continue.

Religion, ethnicity, and the division of society along religious, ethnic, or linguistic lines are national characteristics that change little or change slowly. Comparativists have tested for associations between these features and each of the democracy variables. The results at first appear to be confused and contradictory, but by looking more closely at the methods used, we can draw the conclusion that religion is a more promising predictor of democracy than language or national identity. Where results are inconsistent, we should give the greatest weight to those that have been replicated with a different data and estimators; some weight to those that were produced by the most rigorous methods; and little weight to those produced with inferior methods.

Only a few relationships in this area have been uncontested (among the articles I have seen) or, better yet, repeatedly confirmed. First, countries with a

[31] Gervasoni finds a similar relationship at the subnational level in Argentina (Gervasoni 2010).
[32] Herb's finding rests on the assumption that if Iran did not have oil, it would be like Turkey and Pakistan; and if the Gulf States lacked oil, they would be like Jordan, Egypt, and Yemen. Some readers may not be persuaded.

high level of religious fractionalization are less politically stable: democracy is more likely to both rise and fall, and regimes are shorter lived, where society is split among multiple religious groups (Bernhard et al. 2004; Przeworski et al. 2000; Teorell 2010).[33] Second, the larger the nonreligious population, the lower is the average level of democracy (Barro 1999). Third, the larger the Catholic population, the more likely democracy is to survive (Przeworski et al. 2000). Although these last two findings are statistically credible, they are not necessarily causal. Countries with many atheists may be less democratic without the atheism being responsible for it. It is more likely that both were encouraged by a third factor, such as communist rule. Similarly, if Catholic democracies are more stable, is it because they are Catholic? The Catholic Church's active support for democracy in recent decades undoubtedly also played a role (Huntington 1991; Mainwaring 1999), but during much of the post–World War II period, the predominantly Catholic Latin American and Southern European democracies were also sustained by other forces – their level of development, their proximity to powerful stable democracies, and their cultural and economic ties to the democratic West.

More studies have reported that the Protestant percentage of the population has no significant association with the level of democracy (Barro 1999; Brunk et al. 1987; Burkhart 1997; Muller 1995) than have reported that it has a positive effect (Bollen and Jackman 1985; Ross 2004). However, Ross's analysis uses the largest sample and is the only one to lag the dependent variable, estimate panel-corrected standard errors, and correct for serial autocorrelation. Likewise, three studies find that Muslim countries are less democratic (Herb 2005; Ross 2001; Ross 2004), whereas two others report no significant difference (Barro 1999; Muller 1995). However, Ross (2001) obtained fixed-effects estimates, Herb had the largest sample and corrected for selection bias, and all three used panel-corrected standard errors. Similar comparisons of methods suggest that Muslim countries are also less likely to experience a transition to democracy (Gassebner et al. 2009). Nevertheless, overall, these relationships are not strong, and many of them have been disconfirmed by some tests. They could well be overturned by more rigorous research in the future.

The sole significant effect of ethnolinguistic, as opposed to specifically religious, fragmentation is on the growth curve of democracy in Finkel and colleagues' hierarchical linear model (Finkel et al. 2007). Its interpretation is

---

[33] Teorell, however, finds that religious fractionalization tends to trigger downturns but impede upturns (Teorell 2010).

that ethnically divided societies tend to be less democratic initially (in this case, around 1990, when the sample begins) but democratize more rapidly (until 2004, when the sample ends). It is hard to reconcile this result with the many null findings: that ethnolinguistic fragmentation has no association with the level of democracy (Ross 2001), the magnitude of democratic change (Colaresi and Thompson 2003; Hannan and Carroll 1981; Teorell 2010), or the probability or hazard of breakdown (Bernhard et al. 2003, 2004; Gasiorowski 1995; Hannan and Carroll 1981; Smith 2004; Wright 2008) or of transition to democracy (Gasiorowski 1995). It is possible that what Finkel and colleagues captured was the period effect of many divided societies in Africa and the former Soviet Union being caught up in the fourth wave of democracy, which coincided with the sample period. Once again, these relatively static explanatory factors are difficult to disentangle.

Language, religion, and other slowly changing features of society are often **legacies of past colonization**, which, upon independence, can be represented by a dummy variable. Most research has not shown any significant impact of colonization in general on the level of democracy (Barro 1999; Colaresi and Thompson 2003), the magnitude of change (Colaresi and Thompson 2003; Teorell 2010), or the probability of regime change (Gassebner et al. 2009; Przeworski et al. 2000). It has, however, repeatedly found a positive impact of a specifically British colonial legacy on the level of democracy (Bollen and Jackman 1985; Burkhart 1997; Jensen and Wantchekon 2004; Muller 1995), the magnitude of change (Brinks and Coppedge 2006; fixed-effects estimate), and the probability of survival (Bernhard et al. 2004; Przeworski et al. 2000). The two exceptions to this pattern (Barro 1999; Finkel et al. 2007) do not explore these relationships as carefully as the best article. Bernhard and colleagues (2004) differentiate among former British, French, Spanish, Portuguese, Dutch, and U.S. colonies and carry out subanalyses for certain groups of countries. They also replicate their results using years under colonial rule, a cross-nationally graded but within-country fixed effect in the sample period. Their analyses show powerfully positive effects of British colonial rule on the survival of democracy, which the authors believe came about through improvements in economic development and state-society relations. They also show negative effects of French, Dutch, and Portuguese rule in all models, and of Spanish rule in models controlling for development and social fragmentation. Their results explain why colonization in general is not significant: it is an average of positive and negative effects, and therefore is close to zero.

Nevertheless, colonial legacies are hard to distinguish from the other invariant predictors. Tests comparing them are essentially cross-sectional tests, with few degrees of freedom, and many of these variables are collinear (colonial legacy, world-system position, region, religion, language). Quantitative analysis is useful for ruling out some candidates for explaining the persistent cross-national differences in democracy such as land area and ethnicity, but it is not very useful for adjudicating among the hypotheses that are most likely to be correct. Those interested in this question would be better served by historical process tracing.

Stock variables

Economists and systems theorists make a distinction between stocks and flows. A stock is a quantity that can grow or shrink; a flow is a change in the stock. A bank balance is a stock; deposits and withdrawals are flows. Population is a stock; births and deaths are flows. Flows, as their name suggests, can fluctuate rapidly and greatly; stocks change more slowly and incrementally. Democratization variables that keep a running tally of a country's years of independence or experience with democracy can be considered stock variables in this sense. Unlike relatively fixed predictors, their values change over time, and this increases their potential for explaining variance. Like many relatively fixed predictors, however, they tend to be crude, opaque indicators that are hard to interpret. It can also be hard to distinguish their effects from those of other variables that follow similar trends.

One stock variable, national **population**, is clearly unimportant. Existing analyses indicate that it has no significant effect on the level of democracy (Barro 1999), the probability of any regime transition (Hannan and Carroll 1981), or the starting level of democracy or the subsequent rate of change (Finkel et al. 2007). Neither does the **age of the country** seem to matter for the level of democracy (Brunk et al. 1987; Pevehouse 2002a) or the probability of a transition (Hannan and Carroll 1981; Przeworski et al. 2000). It is neither surprising nor very interesting that the older a country is, the more years of democratic experience it has had, on average (Pevehouse 2002b). It is somewhat more interesting that countries founded after 1950 tended to become less democratic during the 1960–1992 period (Colaresi and Thompson 2003), but this probably reflects the quick failures of the newly independent democracies in Africa and the incomplete redemocratization of the continent as of 1992. This could, therefore, just as easily be a regional effect as an age effect. And Bernhard and colleagues' evidence shows that the extra frailty of democracy in Africa disappears when they control for religious and ethnic fractionalization and economic development (Bernhard et al. 2004).

Stock variables relating to the regime itself, however, often matter quite a bit. In particular, the number of **past transitions and breakdowns** is a powerful predictor of the probability of another regime change (Przeworski et al. 2000; Smith 2004). In fact, the Gassebner and colleagues study reports that the number of past regime transitions is the most robust of all available predictors of the probability of transitions to democracy (significantly positive in 87 percent of their more than 3 million models) and one of the most robust predictors of democratic survival (significantly negative 57 percent of the time) (Gassebner et al. 2009). What the number of past transitions actually measures, however, is open to interpretation. The most meaningful interpretation would be that powerful actors learn from past breakdowns and transitions that regime change is feasible and so attempt it more often, or that the lore of how to effect a regime change successfully is learned and passed down from one generation to the next. But it is equally possible that this variable is merely a proxy for other hard-to-measure conditions that repeatedly destabilize regimes.[34]

Dynamic variables

Factors that vary both within and across countries offer the best hope for explaining the variance in democracy that takes place within countries, which is smaller than the cross-national variance but closer to what we consider causal relationships. These factors fall into three categories: economic, institutional, and international.

There is little reason to expect **economic growth** to be a good predictor of the *level* of democracy because growth is dynamic while levels are relatively static: if growth rates mattered much for levels, then levels would change more often. It is not surprising, therefore, that tests of this proposition have yielded decidedly mixed results. One has found a positive association between change in per capita GDP and Freedom House but not Polity (Finkel et al.

---

[34] Perhaps for this reason, some analyses with different controls find no significant impact of past attempts at democracy on the probability of breakdown (Bernhard et al. 2003), of prior years of democracy on the survival of democracy, of prior years of nondemocracy on either transition or breakdown (Gasiorowski 1995; Gleditsch and Ward 2006), or of past regime failures on the probability of transition (Gleditsch and Ward 2006). Brinks and Coppedge find that the older a regime is (whether democratic or not), the less likely it is to change score (Brinks and Coppedge 2006); but Gasiorowski found no such relationship in a smaller sample (Gasiorowski 1995).

2007); some have found a positive association with Polity but not Freedom House (Jensen and Wantchekon 2004; Rudra 2005); and some have found a mix of nonsignificant or even negative relationships (Casper and Taylor 1996; Wright 2008).

Nevertheless, there is a good reason to expect economic growth to predict *changes* in level of democracy and the probabilities of transition and breakdown or survival. This is not because of a micro-modernization process. Rather, economic growth should operate through a completely different causal mechanism in which economic expansion enhances the legitimacy of governments and undercuts antiregime forces, whereas economic contraction feeds antigovernment and perhaps antiregime sentiment (Haggard and Kaufman 1995). This dynamic should affect democracies and nondemocracies alike. Most of the reported empirical relationships with survival or breakdowns are consistent with this hypothesis: democracies are less likely to break down when the economy is growing and more likely to break down when it is declining (Bernhard et al. 2004; Gasiorowski 1995; Gleditsch and Ward 2006; Pevehouse 2002b; Przeworski et al. 2000; Teorell 2010). This seems to be especially true in poor countries (Przeworski and Limongi 2007). One study argues that it is not so much that economic growth helps democracies survive as it is that economic crisis tends to make them fail, especially if the crisis occurs before two elections have been held (Bernhard et al. 2003). There are a few studies that have failed to confirm a significant impact of growth on survival or breakdowns (Epstein et al. 2006; Gassebner et al. 2009; Wright 2008), but it is supported more often than not. The research on growth and transitions to democracy also confirms this hypothesis fairly consistently (Epstein et al. 2006; Gassebner et al. 2009; Przeworski et al. 2000; Przeworski and Limongi 1997). There is some disconfirming evidence (Gleditsch and Ward 2006; Pevehouse 2002b). However, all of the studies cited in this paragraph support a significant positive relationship between economic decline and either breakdowns or transitions, if not both. We must regard this as one of the leading propositions.

Inflation would seem to be another good indicator of economic crisis. Unfortunately, it is difficult to imagine a causal story that makes sense of the empirical findings. There appears to be no significant relationship between inflation (or the log of inflation) and the probability of either *breakdown or transition* (Gasiorowski 1995; Gassebner et al. 2009). But some studies turn up a positive association between inflation and the *level* of democracy (Li and Thompson 1975; Rudra 2005). These have to be spurious relationships created by the clustering of both democracy and high inflation in certain regions and decades. This conclusion is consistent with Gasiorowski's finding that inflation inhibited transitions in the 1950s and 1960s but facilitated them in the 1980s, and with the fact that Rudra limited her sample to developing countries. Perhaps if inflation rates were normed by decade and region or country, so that they did a better job of indicating whether inflation rates were relatively high or low for that country at that time, then they would be better proxies for economic crisis and better predictors of regime change.

Income inequality is especially relevant for testing both modernization theories (Lipset 1959) and the more recent formal theories (Acemoglu and Robinson 2006; Boix 2003). It is common to assert that inequality changes very little, but the most complete data collection suggests that it can be surprisingly dynamic (Deininger and Squire 1996). Many have tried repeatedly, but without success, to use indicators of inequality to explain *levels* of democracy (Barro 1999; Bollen and Jackman 1985; Finkel et al. 2007; Hadenius 1992; Muller 1988). One exception is Burkhart's sophisticated model in which inequality is allowed to have a nonlinear effect on democracy while democracy also affects inequality (Burkhart 1997). He finds that where the richest fifth of the population receives less than 45 percent of national income, inequality is positively associated with the level of democracy, but that the relationship is negative where the richest fifth receives more than 45 percent: inequality hurts the level of democracy only beyond a certain threshold. If this is correct, it accounts for the others' null findings: fitting a linear model to this relationship would bias the inequality slope toward zero. It is surprising that no one has replicated this intriguing finding.

Scholars have been more successful using inequality to explain regime *change*. Both Muller and Przeworski and colleagues found that countries with great inequality tend to become less democratic and are more likely to break down if they are democracies (Muller 1988, 1995; Przeworski et al. 2000). Przeworski and colleagues also claimed that an increase in income inequality increases the chance of a breakdown, and that sectoral inequality may make transitions to democracy more likely. Teorell, however, found no impact of economic inequality on regime change, and Gassebner and colleagues found no significant impact of inequality (measured differently) on the probability of transitions or democratic stability (Gassebner et al. 2009; Teorell 2010).[35] All of the research on inequality, however, must be treated as very tentative because indicators of inequality are scarce and varied and not necessarily

---

[35] Gassebner and colleagues (2009) did not test for any impact on the probability of breakdowns per se, although this may be the inverse of the probability of survival.

comparable across countries. As a result, the samples on which these results were based consisted of about one hundred countries or fewer, and any time-series analyses simply copied the few inequality measurements or interpolated between them to fill in the missing years.

Thinking about both rentier states and the end of absolute monarchy inspires the notion that the dependence of the state on revenues raised from its own citizens renders it more accountable, and therefore more democratic (Chaudhry 1997; Downing 1992). Michael Ross's work provides some empirical support for a positive association between Polity and personal or corporate **tax collection** as a percentage of GDP (Ross 2001). However, Gassebner and colleagues found that neither income taxes nor tax revenues were robust predictors of transitions or the survival of democracy (Gassebner et al. 2009). On the **spending** side, it could be argued that government consumption would promote democracy, by either strengthening the state or providing services that empower citizens. But it could also be argued that a large, powerful state erodes checks on state power by private-sector actors. In his 2001 article, Ross found that government consumption and government spending as a percentage of GDP were negatively related to levels of democracy (Ross 2001). But in his 2004 article, he found that the size of government had no significant impact; rather, it is the ratio of taxes to spending that matters (Ross 2004). People do not rebel against paying taxes, per se; they rebel against getting too little for their tax dollar.[36] Another study suggests that it is not government spending that matters so much as how the government spends the money: Rudra demonstrated a strong, positive association between Polity and social spending in developing countries, especially where globalization (trade and portfolio flows) was intense (Rudra 2005). Her interpretation was that globalization can undermine democracy unless there is a government-provided safety net to cushion its victims.

Among the institutional variables, the **number of political parties**, or party-system fractionalization or fragmentation, necessarily has a positive relationship with the level of democracy if the range of variation includes some dominant- or hegemonic-party systems, simply because most definitions of democracy require competitive elections. Wright, therefore, finds that single-party governments are negatively associated with the initial level of democracy, and Casper and Tufis report that the positive relationship

---

[36] It is also possible that the relationship is nonlinear: Brunk and colleagues found that government spending as a share of GDP was associated with higher levels of democracy when it was less than 25 percent but with lower levels of democracy when it exceeded that threshold (Brunk et al. 1987). However, this was a small cross-sectional study that has not been replicated with TSCS data.

between the level of democracy and Rae's Index of Party-System Fraction-alization is the only one that survives all their robustness checks and holds regardless of how democracy is measured (Casper and Taylor 1996; Wright 2008). The higher degrees of fragmentation have been posited to threaten the *survival* of democratic regimes, but most research other than that of Teorell (Teorell 2010) – modeling change in democracy – has failed to confirm this expectation. Party-system fragmentation seems to help democracies last long enough for parties to alternate in power – one criterion for the consolida-tion of democracy (Gasiorowski and Power 1998). Overall, democracies with highly fragmented party systems seem to be no more likely to break down than those with something closer to a two-party system (Bernhard et al. 2003, 2004).[37] In *Democracy and Development*, Przeworski and colleagues reported that presidential democracies may be more likely to break down when the party system is moderately fragmented, especially when the largest party con-trols one-third to one-half of the legislative seats, perhaps because it is harder to form coalitions when there are a few parties of similar size (Przeworski et al. 2000). After a more careful analysis, however, one of the authors of that book later concluded that there was no causal connection between party-system characteristics and breakdown (Cheibub 2006).

Research on the consequences of **military involvement** has been incon-clusive. Is a democratic regime less likely to survive if its leader is a former military leader? The massive specification search says that it is, in 76 per-cent of the possible models (Gassebner et al. 2009). The only similar study reports nearly the opposite: when a military leader is in power in a democ-racy, democracy is more likely (Londregan and Poole 1996). This study is not completely comparable, however, because the dependent variable combines democratic survival and transitions to democracy. Are military regimes, as opposed to other types of nondemocratic regimes (e.g., single-party regimes or personal civilian dictatorships) more likely or less likely to experience a transition to democracy? Two studies conclude that they are more likely (Gasiorowski 1995; Geddes 2003), but one says they are less likely (Pevehouse 2002a). One of these studies also finds that nonconstitutional leadership has no significant impact on either survival or transition (Londregan and Poole 1996). These conflicting results are probably due to differences in the coding criteria used to identify military regimes and leaders. Sorting them out would require careful inspection and comparison of the data.

---

[37] One of Bernhard and colleagues' several regression models reported a parties coefficient that was more than twice its standard error, but it appears to be due to a misplaced decimal.

The only political variables that conclusively matter are the more dramatic problems of states, such as **political violence** and **state failure**, which have been shown to reduce the level of democracy. Countries in the throes of state failure are rated, on average, 0.77 points lower on the 13-point Freedom House index and 2 points lower on the 21-point Polity index. Widespread political violence and civil war also significantly lower the level of democracy (Finkel et al. 2007; Peceny 1999). The impact on the probability of regime change, however, is not clear. In nondemocracies, Pevehouse finds that internal violence increases the chances of a transition to democracy, but Gleditsch and Ward find that transitions are more likely when a state has been at peace for many years; and they find no significant impact of civil war (Gleditsch and Ward 2006; Pevehouse 2002a). Teorell concludes that peaceful demonstrations trigger improvements in the level of democracy (which is not the same as a higher probability of a transition) (Teorell 2010). Surprisingly, these studies report no relationship between internal violence or civil war and the probability that a democracy will survive or break down (Gleditsch and Ward 2006; Pevehouse 2002b). Remembering the experiences of Spain, Greece, revolutionary Mexico, and contemporary Iraq, it is difficult to believe that civil war and violence really have no impact on the probability of regime change. However, the relationships are probably complex and sensitive to the nature of the initial regime and the nature of the violence, which have not been adequately measured yet.

No man is an island; some countries are, but even so, no country can be regarded as completely self-determined and unaffected by the world beyond its borders. Some research has therefore examined international determinants of democratization, including trade, investment, war, diffusion, and international efforts to promote democracy. As we have seen here, each of these factors can be measured in a variety of ways, and their effects should be expected to vary depending on which aspect of democracy is being analyzed – its level, changes, the probability or hazard of transition, breakdown, or regime change in either direction.

One of the first studies to examine **trade** systematically was Axel Hadenius's cross-sectional analysis of developing countries (Hadenius 1992). Dependency theory had led him to expect that trade would make developing countries less democratic, but his results challenged that belief. He did find that the volume of trade with the European Community and the Soviet bloc countries was indeed negatively related to levels of democracy, but he also found that trade with the United States had a positive effect, as did the log of total trade. Overall, therefore, it was a positive effect. This was more consistent with Western promarket thinking of the 1990s, and it found some confirmation in a later study of the countries of the former Soviet Union (Kopstein and Reilly 2000) and in a more ambitious study of developing countries from 1979 to 1997 (Rudra 2005). Rudra, in fact, argued that the impact of trade dependence (usually operationalized as exports plus imports divided by GDP) was almost always positive and became more positive the more a government spent on social programs. An equally rigorous study of both developed and developing countries over a longer span of time (1960–1992), however, found no significant impact of trade dependence on the level of democracy (Colaresi and Thompson 2003), and one study found a negative impact of trade dependency on democratic change (Teorell 2010). It seems likely that the significant results reflected temporary regional associations between trade levels and democracy.

The evidence is not more persuasive about democracy and other international economic relationships, either. Epstein and colleagues' carefully executed, very large-sample ($N = 4,299$) analysis concluded that trade openness made democracies less likely to break down; but Gassebner and colleagues' simpler specification search found that this was not a robust effect (Epstein et al. 2006; Gassebner et al. 2009). None of the studies reviewed here has reported a conventionally significant impact of trade dependence on the probability of transition to democracy, and if there is an impact of trade on the hazard of a transition in either direction, it is either not significant or only barely so (Gasiorowski 1995; Hannan and Carroll 1981). Hadenius found that **investment** was associated with higher levels of democracy, but Rudra's superior analysis found that investment almost always has a net negative effect, although less so as governments spend more on social programs (Hadenius 1992; Rudra 2005). Gassebner and colleagues' study is the only study of the impact of investment on the probability of regime change, and it found no robust result for any of four indicators (Gassebner et al. 2009). The few findings there are in this area therefore typically rest on a single analysis.

There are only a few findings about the impact of **international conflict**. One study reports no significant relationship between conflict (the number of militarized interstate disputes, or MIDs) and the chances of breakdown or survival (Pevehouse 2002b). The same author found that regional conflicts (MIDs in the region) made transitions more likely when Polity data were used, but this result did not hold up using Gasiorowski's Political Regime Change data set (Pevehouse 2002a). Colaresi and Thompson, however, find that immediate international threats (the degree to which there is a relatively powerful rival nearby) tend to lower the level of democracy, especially in states that are more open to the international system; older threats do not matter (Colaresi and Thompson 2003).[38]

So far, almost all of the increasingly sophisticated hypotheses about the transnational **diffusion of democracy** that have been tested have been confirmed. Dummy variables for world-system position or some geographic regions are significant correlates of democracy and regime change, both in cross-sectional analyses (Bollen 1983; Bollen and Jackman 1985; Gonick and Rosh 1988) and with TSCS data (Burkhart and Lewis-Beck 1994; Gasiorowski 1995; Muller 1995). Democracies, transitions, coups, and other breakdowns are clustered in space and time (Gleditsch and Ward 2006; Li and Thompson 1975; O'Loughlin et al. 1998; Starr 1991; Starr and Lindborg 2003). The greater the proportion of democracies in the world, in a country's world region, or among its immediate neighbors, the more likely a country is to be a democracy and the less likely it is to break down (Bernhard et al. 2004; Gassebner et al. 2009; Przeworski et al. 2000; Wright 2008). Countries tend to adjust their regimes to match their neighbors' (in either direction) (Brinks and Coppedge 2006). Countries whose neighbors undergo transitions tend to become more democratic (Teorell 2010). And, among electoral authoritarian regimes, the stronger the country's linkages to the West, the more likely it is to transition toward democracy when incumbents experience a political crisis (Levitsky and Way 2006). The frequent confirmation of spatial hypotheses, despite their different form, different data, and different degrees of statistical rigor, has made the international dimension of democratization increasingly important. However, the measurement of these factors has been so rough that it is still impossible to identify causal mechanisms. The most specific findings are that (1) membership in regional organizations helps democracies survive, especially if the other members are themselves democracies (Pevehouse 2002a; Pevehouse 2002b; Teorell 2010); and (2) U.S. Agency for International Development spending on "democratic governance" programs is associated with small but significant improvements in the recipients' overall and disaggregated democracy scores (Finkel et al. 2007). Clearly, much work remains to be done in this relatively new line of investigation, and it will require ingenuity.

---

[38] Their estimates are more credible than the null finding of Peceny, who limited the sample to countries that had suffered international intervention and who specified no domestic control variables except for a fifty-year lag (Peceny 1999).

Conclusion

Given that the greatest strength of the quantitative approach is testing general propositions about average tendencies, what generalizations do they enable us to make about democratization? Before we can answer this question, we must recognize that democratization is a complex process. Quantitative researchers have broken it down into several different dependent variables, each of which requires different explanatory variables. Explaining cross-national differences calls for relatively fixed factors; explaining change within countries calls for more dynamic factors; probabilities of various regime changes call for still others, and it probably makes a difference whether the change is toward democracy or away from it. Also, some of the explanatory variables have a positive effect on one aspect of democratization and a negative effect on another aspect. This complexity makes it impossible to generalize about democratization; one can only discuss which factors are associated with each facet of democratization.

Table 9.4 summarizes the conclusions of the preceding section. Each row corresponds to a distinct facet of democratization.[39] Each column corresponds to the state of our confidence in the explanatory factors listed in the cells beneath. The first three columns contain factors that have been tested repeatedly and produced fairly consistent results. I have included them here even when there is some disconfirming evidence if the methods used in some studies make them much more credible than the others. The next column lists results that have been supported in one study and not yet either replicated or disconfirmed by other studies. The last column lists factors that have been tested repeatedly but yielded different results for reasons that are unclear. They may be due to differences in variables, samples, estimators, or controls, but only careful replications and comparisons – which have not been done – would pin down the reasons exactly, so the findings are inconclusive.

One lesson of this table is that quantitative research on democratization is still – after a half-century! – at an early stage. With a half-dozen dependent variables and about three dozen independent variables, many possible relationships remain untested. The level of democracy has been the most common dependent variable, especially its cross-national component, and

---

[39] In the interest of simplicity, the table does not distinguish between the probability of an outcome and the cumulative hazard of an outcome as a function of time. However, the text on which the table is based does keep this distinction straight.

Table 9.4. Summary of quantitative findings

Dependent variable	Most robust or credible results			Single studies	
	Positive effect	Negative effect	No effect	Negative effect (unless +)	Multiple inconclusive studies
Level (cross-national)	Income, core, democratic neighbors, capitalism, W. Europe, British legacy	State failure, Middle East, periphery, rentier state, communism	Land area, colonial rule, population, age of country, rule of law, linguistic fragmentation	Non-British legacy, violence/ civil war, international threat, inequality (nonlinear), Catholic population (+), nonreligious population, taxation (+), taxation: spending (+), no. military personnel, spending × trade (+)	Growth, trade, inequality (linear), Protestant population, Muslim population, state spending
Level (within-country)	British legacy		Linguistic fragmentation	Drug trafficking	Income, Muslim population
Magnitude of change	British legacy	Inequality	Population, linguistic fragmentation	Democratic neighbors (+), USAID "democratic governance spending" (+)	Presidentialism
Probability of change	Number of past transitions	Income	Population	Investment	Presidentialism
Probability or hazard of transition (P_{AD}) vs. survival of nondemocracy (P_{AA})	Number of past transitions, religious fragmentation, democratic neighbors	Income, growth	Age of country	Muslim population	Inflation, taxation, military rule, violence and/or civil war, trade openness, international conflict, or (only for breakdown) presidentialism
Probability or hazard of survival (P_{DD}) vs. breakdown of democratic regime (P_{DA})	Democratic neighbors, income, growth, British legacy	Number of past transitions, inequality, religious frag-mentation	Linguistic fragmentation	New country, membership in regional organization (+), non-British legacy	

Note: See text for explanations and sources.

there has been a substantial body of work on the probability of transitions and breakdowns, especially with the advent of event-history modeling in the past decade. But there has been relatively little research to explain levels of democracy within countries, the magnitude of changes in level, or the probability of change irrespective of its direction.

Only a few independent variables have been ruled out – land area, population, age of the country, rule of law (as currently measured), colonial rule (without differentiating among colonial powers), and linguistic fragmentation. This is certainly useful progress, bearing in mind that the job of scientists is disconfirmation, first and foremost. But only a few theoretically meaningful independent variables have been robustly confirmed as predictors of any aspect of democratization. Income (the log of per capita GDP) is associated with higher cross-national levels of democracy; income and economic growth are both associated with a higher probability of survival as a democracy and a lower probability of transition. Greater absolute changes in level and a higher probability of breakdown are found in the more unequal societies. Rentier states tend to be less democratic. And religiously fragmented societies are less stable: more likely to experience both transitions and breakdowns. All of the other independent variables that have robust effects are relatively static and opaque variables, many of them dummy variables that lend themselves to many interpretations. They include the core versus periphery distinction, the proportion of democratic neighbors, the distinction between capitalist and communist economies, the number of past regime transitions, a British colonial legacy, regional dummies, and the most opaque of all, the lagged dependent variable.

There has been tantalizing empirical support for a larger number of propositions that have not yet been contradicted only because they have been tested in only one study so far – at least among the five dozen studies reviewed in this chapter. Confirmation in a single study does not inspire much confidence, not least because of the file-drawer problem, or the tendency of scholars to leave null results in the file drawer because they are harder to publish (Gerber et al. 2001). But, for the same reason, these hypotheses should become a high priority for future research, especially (for between-country levels) non-British colonial legacies, taxation and spending levels, (for within-country levels) drug trafficking, (for the magnitude of change) democracy promotion efforts, (for the probability of change) investment, and (for the probability of survival) membership in international organizations. Comparative politics needs much more effort at replication (King 1995).

The evidence for many other propositions is more obviously inconclusive in part because they have been tested so often. These include tests addressing some of the central debates about democratization: the impact of inequality and Islam on the level of democracy, the fragility of presidential democracies, and the impact of internal or international conflict on regime transitions. As I noted in earlier chapters, large-sample quantitative testing is a poorly integrated approach. Each study is distinct in multiple ways, which makes it impossible to know why results differ without undertaking a meticulous replication and comparison of all of the relevant studies. A few articles do this, but it is too rare. It should be the normal practice.

It must be understood that all of these conclusions are provisional. Table 9.4 reflects my best judgment about what is likely to be true, based on the frequency of confirmation and the rigor of the methods employed. Any of these findings could be overturned by improved ways of measuring the key concepts, the inclusion of different control variables, tests using different samples of countries or years, or the choice of a different estimation method that rests on different assumptions about the error structure. The work of conscientious journal referees gives us some assurance that the most obvious misspecifications have been detected and corrected using some of the more popular techniques. But quantitative methods evolve rapidly and the standards for rigor rise constantly: none of the articles that were pathbreaking in the mid-1990s could be published in a top journal today. Yet, we still routinely overlook violations of the assumptions of regression analysis, simply because we have to, because data and expertise are limited.

Earlier, I stated that quantitative researchers tend to crunch first and ask questions later. This is an exaggeration; I think it is rare for a successful scholar to run randomly specified regressions and then invent a theory to fit whatever turns out to be significant. However, the theories that can be tested are so constrained by access to data and methodological expertise that this approach is heavily data-driven, in the sense of both what can be tested at all and what can be tested well. There is usually a gulf separating the theories we would like to test from the variables available to test them. As a result, this approach accumulates empirical generalizations that are consistent with several competing theories. The theoretical questioning may start before the crunching begins, but it usually continues, often with renewed vigor, after the crunching is done. The quality of the data is becoming the most limiting factor in democratization research. Significant progress in the future will require disaggregated indicators of diverse facets of democracy, more reliable indicators of civil war, more abundant and comparable indicators of inequality, and so on. The best example of the limitations imposed by data is the total absence of any quantitative testing whatsoever of propositions inspired by the strategic elite frameworks for understanding breakdowns and transitions (see Chapter 4). Why has quantitative research ignored one of the top frameworks in the democratization literature? It is only because testing its hypotheses would require radically disaggregated data collection. Data on country-years does not even begin to be relevant; what is required is data on subnational organizations and actors, observed at intervals of months or weeks rather than once a year.[40] Quantitative methods are not inappropriate for analyzing such processes; in fact, they would have distinct advantages. All that is lacking is the data.

That said, there are three fundamental holes in existing quantitative research on democratization that could be addressed by statistical methods that, so far, are underutilized. First, only a few studies have modeled endogenous relationships: chains of causation in which some variables are both causes and effects (Barro 1999; Bollen and Jackman 1985; Brinks and Coppedge 2006; Burkhart 1997; Burkhart and Lewis-Beck 1994; Helliwell 1994; Pevehouse 2002b; Przeworski et al. 2000; Smith 2004). Yet, much thinking about democratization speaks of sequences and stages, in which the outcome at one step influences what happens next. We have structural equations and other instrumental variables models that can handle such relationships, but most analyses have not taken advantage of them. Such models could also be used to improve the measurement of complex concepts when all of the available indicators are, taken separately, inadequate (Kaplan 2009). Second, because comparativists typically work with observational rather than experimental data, our samples are likely to contain missing data and sample-selection bias. In certain situations – when the researcher has access to more complete data that can be used to model the probability of being selected into the sample – it is possible to apply a correction for selection bias, thus reducing this kind of threat to inference (Brinks and Coppedge 2006; Finkel et al. 2007). Third, as this chapter has emphasized, democratization is a multilevel phenomenon. Much of the variation is cross-national and some is variation within countries over time (and some is international). Cross-sectional analyses confine their attention to variance among countries; panel models with fixed effects confine their attention to variation within countries; and most other research blurs the distinction between the levels. Yet, we now are able

---

[40] Conflict research has made some moves in this direction (Shellman 2008).

to model both levels simultaneously using hierarchical linear modeling or similar techniques. Multilevel modeling is ideal for the analysis of the TSCS data that is now de rigueur in democratization (and other comparative and international) research, but it is only starting to become familiar (Coppedge et al. 2008a; Finkel et al. 2007). I expect that it will become common in the near future, especially when testing hypotheses about levels of democracy.

The arguments and evidence in this chapter are aligned with the central thesis of this book: that each methodological approach achieves one goal well and two goals poorly. Large-sample quantitative analysis has been thin, as seen in the inadequacy of the data it uses and the simplicity of the hypotheses it tests. It is often not well integrated, as seen in the growing body of findings that are difficult to reconcile and in the tendency to test variables that are close at hand, whether or not they are relevant for the theory. (It is increasingly well integrated with respect to the central role of income, however: this debate has gone on for decades in an admirably cumulative fashion.) Nevertheless, large-sample quantitative analysis excels at the task of generalization: telling us which propositions hold true in extensive temporal and geographical domains, and how much confidence we can have in them. The concluding chapter takes stock of all three basic approaches, assessing what we know about democratization, what remains to be done, and the potential for multimethod research that combines the strengths of all three approaches.

10   An agenda for future research

Surveying democratization research in tandem with a critique of research methods has given us a more balanced and solid perspective on what we know and how confident we can be about it. Each type of research – conceptualization and measurement, checklists and frameworks, case studies, comparative history, formal models and theories, political culture, and quantitative analysis – is useful for developing certain kinds of knowledge but unhelpful for developing others. Chapters 2, 4, 5, 6, 8, and 9 concluded with a broad summary of findings and a critique of the methods used to produce them. This chapter pulls together what we have learned so far from all approaches and highlights the limitations of this understanding to focus attention on areas that should be high priorities for future research.

One priority is for each approach to do a better job of playing to its strengths: for comparative histories to generate more complex explanations, for formal modeling to produce more tightly integrated theories, and for quantitative methods to test general propositions more rigorously. Another priority, however, is for each approach to compensate for its weaknesses. Comparative historians could reach for greater generalization and a more systematic grounding in deductive propositions; formal models could become more realistic and make predictions that are more suitable for rigorous testing; and quantitative analysis could test more complex models and incorporate stronger theoretical guidance. The more these separate approaches compensate for their weaknesses, the closer we will get to a unified comparative method.

This overarching advice addresses a theme found throughout this book: our methodological choices have conceptual and theoretical consequences, and our concepts and theories influence our choice of methods. Methodological specialization has encouraged conceptual and theoretical divergence, and that divergence has eased our balkanization into different methodological camps. Although in some respects this is progress, it comes at the cost of a common language and a cumulative research agenda. It is in the best interests of the social sciences to resist these trends by encouraging multimethod research that leads to a more holistic understanding of democratization.

Concepts and indicators

The survey begins with four fundamental problems concerning concepts and indicators of democracy: disputed concepts, narrow indicators, unreliable indicators, and lack of theoretical guidance on aggregation. Disaggregation would help solve all four problems. Solving these problems should be the highest priority for the near future because all other democratization research depends on how we define and measure democracy.

All research on democratization presumes that we know what democracy is. It is dismaying that there is still so little consensus on the nature of the phenomenon we are studying, which is also a serious obstacle to progress of any kind. The best solution to this problem, however, is not to redouble efforts to forge a consensus on a single definition of democracy. It is an inherently contested concept: we all want to claim the right to the democratic label; we all care deeply about it, yet we use many incompatible criteria for deciding who deserves it (Gallie 1956). In this situation, the more we talk about it, the more we are likely to disagree. Nevertheless, it is easier to reach agreement on how to define and measure specific components of democracy, provided that we do not get sidetracked into debates about exactly which ones are essential for democracy and which are not (Coppedge et al. 2011).

Before proposing more definitions of democracy, we should, therefore, disaggregate the concept; that is, break it down into its constituent components and focus our attention on those specific institutions, practices, and conditions rather than on democracy as a whole. During this phase, we should be open minded about which attributes may be relevant. There are, as Chapter 2 made clear, many different models of democracy: ones that emphasize participation, deliberation, limited government, rule of law, national sovereignty, socioeconomic equality, and other principles (Held 2006). The more of them that we can include in our thinking, the more fully we will understand what democracy means to all who use the term. Of course, there is a trade-off in doing this: the more meanings democracy has, the more unwieldy the concept becomes. But this is a necessary step along the way toward an understanding of the components of democracy, which are concepts that would be easier to manage.

Let us keep in mind that concepts are merely tools that enable us to describe reality and analyze relationships. As long as we are dealing with disaggregated concepts and indicators, it does not matter much where the boundary lies between attributes of democracy and attributes of other concepts. For example, one could examine the relationship between the extent of the suffrage and levels of income inequality. If only suffrage is defined to be an attribute of democracy, then this can be understood as a relationship between income inequality and an aspect of democracy; if both suffrage and inequality are defined to be attributes of democracy, then this could be framed as a relationship between attributes of democracy. Only the theoretical frame changes; the empirical relationship remains the same. We should keep in mind that theoretical frames are merely intellectual constructs that we invent to make sense of the world. If they refer to cohesive aspects of reality that have regular, predictable relationships with other constructs, they are useful and we keep them; if not, they are a hindrance to understanding and should be discarded in favor of constructs that give us empirical traction.

Eventually, once we become accustomed to thinking about relationships among components of democracy, perhaps the dust will have settled enough for comparativists to return the question of where to draw the dividing line between democracy and related concepts such as human rights, equality, and the rule of law. It may be that certain attributes cohere, thus pointing to a natural division between democracy and other phenomena. Whether it is useful to group attributes together under the label "democracy" is in part an empirical question.

The second problem with concepts and indicators is that to the extent that political scientists in the United States agree on a definition of democracy, it is on a narrow concept of democracy – polyarchy or, even more narrowly, contestation. Almost all indicators of democracy measure aspects of democracy that are aligned with one or both of Robert Dahl's two dimensions of polyarchy: contestation and inclusiveness. Exploratory principal components analysis of the major indicators (Polity, Freedom House, Banks [1999], Cingranelli and Richards [2004], and others) reduces them to two components that account for about 75 percent of the variance (Coppedge, Alvarez, and Maldonado 2008). Most indicators primarily measure contestation. Only a few primarily reflect inclusiveness. Only a quarter of the variance in these indicators is unexplained, and it does not correspond to a single coherent dimension.

These are the dimensions of democracy that are most relevant to most U.S. political scientists. Narrowing the focus to polyarchy has made it possible to make progress on empirical research. It produced a partial working consensus that legitimated many indicators, which have been essential for research that has turned up many intriguing relationships. However, this research has begun to be constrained by the reduction of democracy to polyarchy, which is a Western, institutional and/or procedural, liberal version of democracy at the national level. Polyarchy omits many criteria that some theorists have included in their definitions of democracy, such as participatory democracy (the health of civil society organizations, authority and resources controlled by subnational governments, levels of democracy at the subnational level); deliberative democracy; egalitarian democracy (economic and social equality; protections for women and ethnic, religious, and linguistic minorities; descriptive representation); sovereignty, which is necessary for self-government; and even some additional aspects of liberal democracy (e.g., judicial independence, judicial effectiveness, term limits, turnover, majoritarian versus consensual styles of democracy, presidential versus parliamentary constitutions) (Coppedge et al. 2011; Held 2006). Some democracy indicators, especially those produced by Freedom House, purportedly capture some of these criteria, but if so, they do not significantly alter their primary focus on contestation. Polyarchy is also a fairly low standard for democracy that is not very useful for distinguishing degrees of democracy among the democracies. Such distinctions would have to be multidimensional.

We cannot really know whether it is useful to think about democracy in ways that are deeper and richer than polyarchy until we measure them. Useful concepts are in principle measurable; the most concrete definitions are operational. This may seem like an extremely inductive, realist approach to conceptualization, but actually it is a perfectly balanced one because it gives equal emphasis to theory and evidence. Just as valid indicators must link evidence to concepts that we find meaningful, useful concepts must be linked to evidence in concrete, reliable ways. When measurement is valid and concepts are useful, theoretical dimensions are aligned with empirical dimensions: the things that we expect to go together actually do. We may theorize all we like about questions such as the following: Is there a distinctive set of practices we can call participatory? Do they covary? Do the attributes of participatory democracy have more in common with one another than they do with liberal democracy or deliberative democracy? If not, these distinctions are not very useful. We cannot answer such questions without measuring these concepts. For this reason, a necessary step along the path to useful concepts and indicators of democracy, variants of democracy, or dimensions of democracy is the construction of indicators of their many attributes. The existing indicators that reflect only contestation and, to a lesser extent, inclusiveness, do not help us do this.

The third problem is imprecise measurement. Existing democracy indicators have been quite useful for making broad distinctions between democracies and nondemocracies, and sometimes a few gradations in between. Most are ordinal or nominal; very few are continuous, and most of those that appear to be continuous actually represent false precision. Rigorous analyses show that they are unable to make fine distinctions reliably (Pemstein et al. 2010). For example, nearly half of the countries rated by Polity in 2000 have a democracy score that is not significantly lower than that of the United States (Treier and Jackman 2008).

An important reason for this imprecision is the practice of adding up component variables that are probably not all unidimensional. This procedure would be expected to produce indicators that discriminate the most and least democratic extremes well, but not the countries with intermediate scores. This is exactly what we observe. Polity has been shown to have this problem (Gleditsch and Ward 1997), but other indicators do it in a less obvious way, by coding a single set of scores for complex component variables that are themselves multidimensional (Coppedge et al. 2011). This problem would be attenuated if we created distinct indicators or scales for distinct empirical dimensions. Measuring more specific dimensions of democracy would also reduce the truncation of indicators at their most democratic pole, which has led to a bunching up of relatively democratic scores.

Improving measurement accuracy is essential for advancing research on the causes and consequences of democracy. A simple distinction between democracies and nondemocracies is adequate for some models and ideal for duration analysis, which models the time elapsed between regime changes. If the phenomenon to be explained is the level of democracy, however, then the more levels an indicator can reliably distinguish, the more confidence we can have in the estimates of causal effects. Accurate measurement is even more critical for modeling changes in the level of democracy, which presuppose intervals of equal size and entail a higher level of measurement than the currently typical ordinal indicators. At this writing, only the Unified Democracy Scores can claim to attain interval-level measurement (Pemstein et al. 2010).

To be realistic, people care too much about something called democracy to completely abandon the concept in favor of its specific attributes. There will always be a demand for definitions and indicators of democracy, even if it is a complex, multidimensional phenomenon. The final problem, however, is that we have not thought enough about how to aggregate multidimensional components into indicators of thicker concepts of democracy. It is certainly possible to reduce several multidimensional variables into a single indicator.

For example, area, velocity, and per capita gross domestic product (GDP) are all constructed from variables that vary on independent dimensions (e.g., length and width, distance and time, income and population). But theoretical guidance is required do it properly. Only a few indicators are based on any aggregation formula other than a linear combination (Hadenius 1992; Munck 2005; Vanhanen 1990). Responsible multidimensional aggregation requires theoretical guidance on thresholds, weighting, and substitutability. It raises questions such as: How limited can electoral competition become before broad suffrage becomes irrelevant? How much more important for democracy are clean elections than an independent judiciary? How vibrant does civil society have to be to compensate for feckless political parties? We have barely begun to think about such issues. A disaggregated approach to conceptualization and measurement would encourage thinking along these lines.

Case studies and comparative histories

Authors of case studies and comparative histories can play to two strengths: theory generation and intensive testing. Their work has generated fundamental insights into the nature of democratization.[1] For example, first-wave democracy was not intentionally designed; it evolved as a series of incremental adjustments to preexisting institutions and practices that had their roots in the Holy Roman Empire and still earlier norms and traditions. Some of these adjustments were revolutionary, spurred by violence; some were peacefully negotiated accommodations; but all were bound up with struggles over land, monarchy, religion, class, gender, and national identity. These structural conditions provide an essential backdrop to any well-rounded account of democratization. In Chapter 5, I criticized this approach for being myopic. But if case studies and comparative histories are myopic, then any theory that takes this historical background for granted – such as a theory about institutions that does not wonder where they came from or a theory about strategic actors that does not explain how they became influential – is even

---

[1] Although I generally favor rigorous, systematic testing before claiming to have insights, I also argue (Chapters 3 and 7) that it is not necessary to test propositions for which there is no plausible counterargument. I am not aware of any school of thought that questions the notion that historical background matters in these general ways, so I do not think it necessary to test these basic ideas. What require testing are the more specific conclusions about whether this or that class or class alliance played a decisive role.

more myopic! One of the limitations of this approach is that it has focused its attention primarily on Europe and Latin America. There are notable exceptions, such as Moore (1966) and Skocpol (1979), but the political history of Africa, Asia, and the Middle East is comparatively undertheorized (pace Brownlee 2007; Hui 2005; Slater 2010). Expanding into non-Western regions is one way this approach could capitalize on its strengths.

Case studies and comparative histories also lend themselves to intensive testing: using evidence about processes unfolding over time to decide which of several competing explanations for specific events is most plausible. I do not attempt to summarize any findings of case studies because they are myriad and specific, along the lines of why General Golbery decided in 1974 to begin the *abertura*, or political opening, that led to Brazil's transition to democracy.[2] Comparative histories can claim similarly convincing specific explanations, albeit often supported by less detailed evidence. The utility of these studies for intensive testing would be enhanced if their authors would take greater care not to modify explanations in the course of testing them, which transforms their work into theory generation rather than testing.

It would be refreshing if the advocates of comparative history would abandon their claim that Millian comparisons of most-similar or most-different cases are a form of testing. As tests, they are so lax that a little historical knowledge and critical thinking could turn up many counterarguments to any conclusion that one cross-national difference or similarity explains another. It is extremely rare for such simple comparisons to achieve the basic goal of any science: disconfirming all plausible competing explanations. There are practically infinite differences, and almost as many similarities, between any two countries, and it is all too easy to build causal stories around them. Small-N cross-national comparisons are nearly useless for testing propositions.[3] For testing, the true forte of small-sample research is the comparison of each case with itself at different points in time and the examination of the fit of evidence with multiple competing explanations – intensive testing. If one wishes to test, it is almost always better to do a good study of a single case than to dilute one's efforts and evidence by studying two or three cases. However, if the goal is theory development, then comparisons of a few cases can often suggest novel hypotheses that are more likely to survive extensive testing.

---

[2] According to Alfred Stepan, General Golbery was persuaded by Juan Linz's argument in *Authoritarian Brazil* (Linz 1973) that the military would never be able to institutionalize an authoritarian regime (Stepan 2007)!

[3] I say this despite having published a paired comparison myself (Coppedge 1993). As paired comparisons go, the case selection in this one was relatively good, but the self-criticism is still valid.

Chapter 5 argues that the comparative historical literature is less integrated than it seems. Each major book proposes to explain a different mix of outcomes in different historical periods, in different sets of cases. These studies overlap without fully connecting, which makes it difficult to discern what findings they all support. They continue to disagree about questions as fundamental as whether or not the working class promoted democracy. Although these authors engage one another on questions large and small – Was the early modern English state bureaucratic or patrimonial? Is bourgeois impulse a useful concept? Was Weimar a successful transition to democracy or a failure? – there is too little agreement among them on basic concepts and arguments to sustain a dialogue that adds up to specific and meaningful conclusions.

All research on democratization would benefit from standardization of concepts, not just among comparative historians but also across different approaches – qualitative and quantitative and multimethod research, too. Although it is a distant goal, we should strive to develop a set of standard concepts and indicators that have been repeatedly shown to be useful because they (1) identify consequential attributes of the political world, and (2) have robust and plausible causal relationships with other useful concepts and their indicators. This does not require the creation of a central authority that certifies some concepts and indicators as useful and bans others, however. Rather, standardization could emerge naturally from the competitive efforts of many scholars and the judgment of their peers, who will slowly come to agree on the most useful ways to define and measure common concepts in comparative politics.

Case studies and comparative histories are inherently limited in geographic and temporal scope, but this is not incompatible with the kind of hierarchical general theory described in Chapter 3. Phenomena as complex as regime change certainly require different explanations in different contexts. This poses no obstacle to the development of general theory provided that we have metatheories that identify what is systematically different about each temporal-spatial context. For example, it seems reasonable to propose that first-wave democratization was more gradual or intermittent than later transitions, simply because democratizers were making things up as they went along; later democratizers had models to copy. Thus, perhaps the same processes of socioeconomic modernization were at work in first- and second-wave transitions, but the process was accelerated in the second wave. It is also possible that the diffusion of models from previous democracies has become such a powerful force that domestic conditions become less important:

cosmopolitan elites can adopt democratic institutions even in societies that are not developed enough to demand and preserve them. Such metatheories condition more basic theories; they could tell us when and where to apply which theory. Of course, they have to be tested just as any theory does. But before they can be tested, someone must propose them. Comparative historians are the scholars most qualified to play this role. To perform it, all they must do is speculate explicitly about the boundary conditions that limit the scope of their arguments. If these scholars do this, other scholars could test their conjectures, and we could all work together to assemble a more integrated nested theory of democratization.

Formal models and theories

The comparative advantage of formal models and theories is theoretical integration. In Chapter 6, I argued that this literature is less integrated than one would expect. One path to progress, therefore, would be to develop more models to fill in all the branches on the theoretical family tree. Modeling all of the combinations of assumptions among the models would tell us which assumptions decisively alter the implications. It would be useful to know which predictions are unaffected by the variety of assumptions and which are sensitive to apparently innocuous tweaks.

There seems to be little need to continue to vary the number of actors in positional models. We have models with two, three, four, and six actors, and Colomer's (2000) six-actor model subsumes the rest with respect to the number of actors, provided that they are involved only in pairs. With respect to other assumptions, however, positional models are in need of integration both upstream (integrating with models of earlier stages of democratization) and downstream (with later stages).

Downstream integration would entail adding each of the unique assumptions made by one model to models that lack these elements. More of the models could examine the expected consequences of specifying incomplete information about whether the rulers are hard-liners or soft-liners, the possibility of a foreign power propping up an authoritarian regime or leaving it high and dry, the option of offering amnesty to a dictator, and opposition and regime estimates of whether they can prevail in a confrontation.

Moving upstream, more could be done to combine models of transition with models of liberalization. Would the leaders of an authoritarian regime liberalize if they knew there was a chance that the outcome would be not just liberalized authoritarianism but also a democracy in which they could be held accountable for human rights abuses? How much more likely would the opposition be to mobilize if it knew that democracy was a possibility? How much less likely to mobilize would they be if they took into consideration the regime's calculations about the risk of democracy? Przeworski's (1991) and Crescenzi's (1999) models already answer these questions but only given their own particular assumptions. The answers could well be different when both rulers and opposition are subdivided or when any of a dozen other assumptions is changed. One could move still farther upstream by modeling who gets a seat at the bargaining table, where preferences come from, and what drives a sincere change in preferences. An imaginative scholar might even be able to integrate positional and economic models in the course of pursuing such depth of integration.

The economic models are already fairly well integrated. Acemoglu and Robinson (2006) incorporate almost all of the assumptions found in other models. However, they could still consider incorporating some of the findings of behavioral economics, which show that humans are willing to take great risks given the prospect of a gain but few risks given the prospect of a loss (Gould and Maggio 2007; Kahneman and Tversky 1979). They could also problematize transition negotiations, which, positional models show, are not straightforward. Two of the economic models work with three class actors and claim that varying the number of actors would not affect their main conclusions (Acemoglu and Robinson 2006; Boix 2003). This claim could be explored more thoroughly because it is likely that each additional actor adds a new dimension of strategy.

The foregoing suggestions are directed at improving what formal models already do well, compared to other approaches. More dramatic improvement could be achieved by trying to emulate the virtues of other approaches – thickness and generality. Formal models are exceptionally thin, especially in their concepts. It would be fantastic if positional models could overcome the circularity of defining the actors in terms of their preferred regimes by specifying instead the actual institutional roles they play – military officers, union leaders, party leaders, civilian dictator, and so on. This would complicate the model greatly because people in these positions have varied and dynamic regime preferences. But that is exactly why thickness is required: models that assume away these problematic correspondences do not match actual cases and cannot, therefore, be tested fairly. It is also critical for economic models to work with a concept of democracy that cannot be confused with utopian communism. Even if the median voter is influential in democracies, most actual democracies have not so far made dramatic strides toward an equal distribution of income. Owners of capital have little reason to fear confiscatory tax rates, and the poor have little reason to hope that democracy will raise them to the middle class. Models that did not ascribe these motives to the players would be more realistic.[4]

The assumptions of the models could also be made thicker. Positional models would be more realistic if they contemplated games involving more than two or three players, as O'Donnell and Schmitter's inductively inspired multilayered chess metaphor suggests is the case (O'Donnell and Schmitter 1986). And what would happen if actors had conflicting motives rather than a single-minded focus on maximizing one kind of payoff? They could be modeled as trying to maximize their gains in a two- or three-dimensional space, as is common in spatial models of voting and legislative behavior (Hinich and Munger 1997).

A more radical thickening would be to specify how to derive regime outcomes from alliances among actors. Przeworski, for example, asserts that democracy without guarantees to the old regime is the outcome of an alliance of the moderate opposition with both the radical opposition and the reformist rulers; but that authoritarianism continues if the reformist rulers ally with the hard-liners instead (Przeworski 1991). Similarly, Colomer claims that democracy happens when any two of his six actors settle on it as an equilibrium (Colomer 1991). Aside from the possibility that the other four actors might not be OK with this (if they exist; the model gives us no way to know), it is not clear that, say, the radical opposition and the radical hard-liners would be bargaining on a level playing field. At some point, power has to be brought into the equation. Finally, it is fundamentally important for these models to provide more reliable guidance for deciding which models apply where and when. This requires thickening the concepts and the assumptions so that the gap between the model and the actual cases is easier to bridge.

Advancement in this direction would also help with testing the assumptions and implications of these models. With more realistic assumptions, it would become possible to define a relevant universe, draw samples, and test predictions systematically. Tests could give us more confidence that we know

---

[4] Boix and Acemoglu and Robinson would surely respond that their theories explain why democracy is not very redistributive: governments have had to moderate distributive policies to appease owners of mobile assets. Perhaps this actually happened long ago and the Gramscian hegemony of capital leads us to take it for granted today (Gramsci 1971). If the privileged position of business, however, has become all-pervasive, then it is a constant that can no longer explain the dynamics of regime change (Lindblom 1977).

who the actors are, what their goals are, how much information is available to them, which choices confront them, and how they weigh the costs and benefits of different outcomes. Testing is being done already for applications of other formal models, although less than one would hope (Green and Shapiro 1994). Formal models of liberalization and transition, however, have not been tested frequently or rigorously. Part of what it means to be rigorous is testing against competing hypotheses; this has been done very little in the democratization literature. It is more typical for scholars to produce empirical illustrations that are consistent with their predictions without exposing hypotheses to a real test.

Political culture

For all of its advantages for achieving deep understanding, thick description, and cultural insights, the anthropological approach to political culture can say little about general processes of democratization. It can certainly be useful for informing case studies, which could suggest better theories. But the work of testing to see whether there is truth in any general cultural hypotheses about democratization requires survey research.

Research to date has turned up several fascinating paradoxes. First, trust in institutions has declined in the West, but support for democracy remains high (Norris 1999a). This paradox raises the question of what connection there is, if any, between institutional trust and democratic legitimacy. One would expect that if citizens judged the performance of democratic institutions to be poor, they would become disenchanted with democracy itself. Is it just a matter of time? Is there some lower threshold below which alarm bells suddenly start to ring? Are there only certain types of institutional failure that undermine legitimacy? Or is the whole answer Rose, Mishler, and Haerpfer's finding that democracy holds onto legitimacy as long as citizens can imagine no superior alternative regime (Rose et al. 1998)? Can we distinguish between legitimacy relative to other regimes and absolute legitimacy?

Second, democratic regimes can survive for years even when the public has little confidence in their parties, legislatures, and other institutions (Inglehart and Welzel 2005; Linz 1978). Are the disgruntled masses too powerless or passive to effect any change? Is this a failure to overcome the collective-action problem (Olson 1971)? Are there smaller, more powerful groups in the population whose opinions matter more? Who are they – military officers, legislators, judges, the media, intellectuals? Are they more sanguine in their judgments of institutional performance than the mass public is? Are they actively preventing antidemocratic mobilizations?

A third paradox is the low correlation between support for democracy and levels of democracy (Inglehart 2003). Because levels of support for democracy are generally high, this raises the opposite question: How is it that there are so many nondemocracies in which the population would prefer to live in a democratic regime? Clearly, citizens cannot simply will democracy into existence. This paradox also demands more detailed theories that connect public opinion to behavior and regime outcomes.

A fourth paradox is that trust in institutions is related to interpersonal trust cross-nationally but not at the individual level (Newton and Norris 2000; Seligson 2001). Perhaps this is just another instance of the ecological fallacy, and we should not be surprised. However, one of the most influential books in comparative politics gives us reasons to expect that there should be a relationship: interpersonal trust theoretically extends to others in one's extended network and the larger network of networks, thus producing more responsive institutions (Putnam et al. 1993). Nevertheless, it has been suggested that there is a possible causal mechanism that bypasses the individual level (Newton and Norris 2000): higher aggregate levels of interpersonal trust may produce greater trust in institutions generally, even if the people who have greater interpersonal trust are not the same people who have greater institutional trust. In fact, those who trust people less may trust institutions more precisely because they know that those who trust people more and institutions less are holding the institutions accountable! A clever research design would be required to test this hypothesis.

Finally, it is paradoxical that aggregate self-expression values predict levels of democracy well, even though this dimension barely exists at the individual level (Davis and Davenport 1999; Inglehart and Welzel 2005; Seligson 2002). This seems to be a real relationship, but it cannot be interpreted precisely the way Inglehart and Welzel have interpreted it. The different relationships at different levels of analysis imply that there is an influential variable that varies more across countries than among individuals and that this variable is associated with average levels of democracy and average levels of the variables composing the self-expression index. Chapter 9 identified several candidates for such fixed effects and explained why it is so difficult to distinguish them.

Research to resolve these paradoxes must begin with theory that specifies the causal mechanisms that bridge levels of analysis: which attitudes or beliefs held by which actors lead to what kind of actions that change regimes in which ways? Such a theory would distinguish between endogenous and exogenous forces and on the patterns of convergence and divergence they produce. It would recognize that a snapshot of attitudes from one survey says nothing about these patterns. This research program would therefore require frequently repeated panel surveys. It is crucial that they measure support for democracy better, without using the term *democracy*, and compare it to support for regime alternatives. If this kind of research is to address theories of transition rather than survival or breakdown, it must take place more frequently in nondemocratic settings, where survey research is more difficult. Cross-national survey analysis is beginning to employ multilevel modeling to properly estimate cross-national and individual-level relationships. If an improved theory refocused attention on elites, testing it would also require more elite surveys, preferably in panels – a potentially pathbreaking research design that has rarely been attempted with elite respondents.

Quantitative testing

Quantitative testing already has sophisticated methods for testing the general validity of hypotheses. In the spirit of playing to this strength, some would advise exploiting its technical sophistication more fully. In some respects, I agree. There are real benefits to be reaped by imputing missing data, correcting for selection bias, and using multilevel modeling to consistently distinguish within-country and cross-national effects. But more substantial progress is to be made by compensating for the thinness and lack of integration in quantitative methods.

The quantitative literature on democratization is full of empirical generalizations that are compatible with multiple theoretical explanations. There are numerous ways to thicken hypotheses to try to discover why these empirical relationships exist. Tests of thicker hypotheses would start to bridge the gap between the average tendencies identified by quantitative analysis and the specific causal mechanisms suggested by case studies, comparative histories, and formal models. All of this can be done with common quantitative techniques. A good place to start would be the dependent variable. A half-dozen different ways to operationalize democratization are in use, regardless of the specific indicator used. In addition to the familiar level of democracy, researchers are attempting to explain the magnitude of changes in level, the probability of being a democracy, the hazard of a transition, and the hazard of a breakdown. All of these could be considered facets of a single process with different moments and phases. If each facet and phase were independent of the others, we could safely model them separately. But we know that they are interconnected: the most democratic and least democratic countries are less likely to change than countries at intermediate levels; the number of past transitions is a powerful predictor of instability; and the most democratic countries tend to become less democratic, whereas the least democratic countries are more likely to become more democratic.

We would understand democratization better if we developed a way to test many of these different aspects of democratization at once: to explain the magnitude and direction of change within countries, given the cumulative hazards of transition or survival (depending on each country's initial level), controlling for static cross-national differences in level and a host of explanatory factors. Structural-equation models could be used more to model endogeneity appropriately. Doing this would also help tease apart cross-national and within-country effects. In addition, as we become increasingly able to measure dimensions of democracy other than contestation, the modeling options become richer and more interesting. For those who work with discrete regime typologies, it will be necessary to model transitions among qualitatively different regime types (Hannan and Carroll 1981); with continuous indicators, it will be important for comparativists to learn techniques for modeling movements of countries in a multidimensional space.

Comparativists are becoming increasingly aware of causal heterogeneity. Dealing with this requires paying more attention to conditional relationships and boundary conditions. The priority is not to make samples as large as possible but to make them large while preserving causal homogeneity. A much more ambitious project would be to develop fine-grained data at the level of actor-weeks rather than country-years. We will not be able to test hypotheses from the strategic elite frameworks until this is accomplished, perhaps starting with one case, then several, and then a large sample.

Among the findings of quantitative analysis to date, there are some robust but opaque relationships, some intriguing isolated findings, and many inconclusive sets of contradictory findings. Each set of findings calls for a different research agenda.

Robust but opaque fixed effects dominate most models of the level of democracy, whether they use cross-sectional or panel data. These static factors include region (especially the Middle East and North Africa), British legacy (which also seems to matter for the survival of democracy), and having a rentier state. Quantitative methods cannot disentangle these fixed effects; doing so will require intensive testing of multiple competing theories. Only when case studies and comparative histories give us a clearer understanding of the nature of the fixed effect will we be able to undertake statistical testing with thick indicators and highly disaggregated data.

Two dynamic variables have also been robust predictors of the level of democracy – income (per capita gross domestic product) and diffusion (usually levels of democracy in neighboring countries). These variables clearly matter, but it is not clear why. Why is per capita GDP an excellent control variable but an opaque explanatory variable? Why did the cross-sectional slope of per capita GDP drop dramatically after 1989? The reasons for or reasons why income predicts democracy could be explored by interacting it with other variables such as asset specificity, dependence on oil exports, having a rentier state, the availability of lootable wealth, economic dependence on drug trafficking, levels of violent conflict, and dependence on foreign aid (Ross 2001; Snyder and Bhavani 2005). This seems like a promising approach because the slope of democracy levels regressed on income are highly variable; some are even negative (Coppedge, Alvarez, and González 2008). This phenomenon demands an explanation. Diffusion of democracy (from democratic neighbors) is also a robust predictor of the probabilities of transition and survival, but the reasons are still hard to pin down. Future research will certainly make more use of geographic information systems to explore these spatial relationships, which seem to be among the most important, yet neglected, explanatory factors.

The literature contains many intriguing single studies that have identified relationships that may be important. Other things being equal, inequality, taxation levels, and drug trafficking affect the level of democracy; a large Muslim population makes transitions less likely; and a British legacy helps democracies survive. These findings need to be replicated, however, before they can be trusted to hold up with different samples, indicators, specifications, and estimators.

Finally, we have many inconclusive sets of contradictory findings. The guidance from published research says that economic growth, trade, inequality, religion, and state spending either raise or lower the level of democracy; and inflation, taxation, military rule, conflict, and trade openness may help spur transitions from authoritarianism, but they may also hinder them or have no effect. Similarly, inflation, taxation, military rule, conflict, trade openness, and presidentialism have been found to both help and hinder the prospects for the survival of democracy. To deal with these contradictory findings, it is crucial to backtrack to figure out why we get different estimates. It would be helpful if scholars would develop the habit of replicating the findings of other studies and then modifying one parameter of the specification at a time (e.g., the control variables, the indicators used, the sample, and the assumptions of the estimator) so that it would be clear to all why estimates differ.

Prospects for democratization research

Some of the suggestions here are practical and could be done tomorrow with existing data and methods. Others may not become possible for years, and still others may turn out to be inherently or practically impossible. We have learned a great deal about democratization already, although our knowledge is partial, probabilistic, conditional, and forever and always provisional. Nevertheless, if we work to improve how each approach does what it does best and also work on making these approaches less distinct from one another, I am optimistic that in the long run we can make astounding progress. Progress would mean knowledge that is (1) less partial and probabilistic because it identifies more of the relevant causal factors and leaves less to randomness or omitted variables; (2) more explicitly conditional, so that we develop both middle-range theories and metatheories that help us link them together in a more general theory; and (3) more certain, so that there is a much larger body of logically integrated theory that is considered a core, even though propositions on its periphery will continue to be uncertain and provisional.

In the long run, I expect democratization research to be transformed by two secular trends: homogenization and specialization. For millennia, the world has been undergoing a loss of diversity of many kinds – biological, linguistic, and cultural. I believe that the social sciences are losing methodological diversity as well and that this is a good thing. I do not mean that there are fewer methods at our disposal; on the contrary, there are more choices than ever. What I mean is that our discipline is becoming less polarized by methods. Younger political scientists increasingly have all of these methods at their disposal and view them all as complementary tools to be used in a consensually understood collective effort to understand politics. As they do so, they will produce thicker, more integrated, and more general knowledge. We will get closer to a methodological consensus and to a hierarchically integrated (but extremely complex) theory of politics.

At the same time, assuming that catastrophic climate change does not trigger the collapse of civilization and make political scientists an endangered species, I expect increasing specialization. All social sciences – indeed, all branches of knowledge – evolved by differentiation from ancient philosophy. Political science itself, as a profession, is barely a century old.

Democratization will probably subdivide itself into distinct research programs before we figure it out. It will likely be replaced with research on the causes of components or qualities of democracy, such as direct democracy practices, responsiveness, improvements in representation, and the protection of basic civil and political rights. In the process, we will come to understand democratization better even if we call it by different names.

References

Acemoglu, Daron, Simon Johnson, James A. Robinson, and Pierre Yared. 2008. "Income and Democracy." *American Economic Review* 98 (3):808–42.

Acemoglu, Daron, and James A. Robinson. 2001. "A Theory of Political Transitions." *American Economic Review* 91 (4):938–63.

———. 2006. *Economic Origins of Dictatorship and Democracy.* Cambridge: Cambridge University Press.

Achen, Christopher. 2002. "Toward a New Political Methodology: Microfoundations and ART." *Annual Review of Political Science* 5:423–50.

Adcock, Robert, and David Collier. 2001. "Measurement Validity: A Shared Standard for Qualitative and Quantitative Research." *American Political Science Review* 95 (3):529–46.

Adelman, Irma, and Cynthia Morris. 1965. "A Factor Analysis of the Interrelationship between Social and Political Variables and Per Capita Gross National Product." *Quarterly Journal of Economics* 79:555–78.

Adelman, Irma, and Cynthia Taft Morris. 1967. *Society, Politics, and Economic Development: A Quantitative Approach.* Baltimore: Johns Hopkins University Press.

Adorno, Theodor W., Else Frenkel-Brunswik, Daniel J. Levinson, and R. N. Sanford. 1950. *The Authoritarian Personality.* New York: Harper and Row.

Aldrich, John, and Charles F. Cnudde. 1975. "Probing the Bounds of Conventional Wisdom: A Comparison of Regression, Probit, and Discriminant Analysis." *American Journal of Political Science* 19 (3):571–608.

Alesina, Alberto, and Dani Rodrik. 1994. "Distributive Politics and Economic Growth." *Quarterly Journal of Economics* 112:465–90.

Allison, Graham T. 1971. *Essence of Decision: Explaining the Cuban Missile Crisis.* Boston: Little, Brown.

Allison, Paul D. 1990. "Change Scores as Dependent Variables in Regression Analysis." *Sociological Methodology* 20:93–114.

Almond, Gabriel, and G. Bingham Powell. 1966. *Comparative Politics: A Developmental Approach.* Boston: Little, Brown.

Almond, Gabriel, and Sidney Verba. 1965. *The Civic Culture: Political Attitudes and Democracy in Five Nations.* Boston: Little, Brown.

Altemeyer, B. 1981. *Right-Wing Authoritarianism.* Winnipeg: University of Manitoba Press.

Alvarez, Michael, José Antônio Cheibub, Fernando Limongi, and Adam Przeworski. 1996. "Classifying Political Regimes." *Studies in Comparative International Development* 31 (2):3–36.

Amodio, David M., John T. Jost, Sarah L. Master, and Cindy M. Yee. 2007. "Neurocognitive Correlates of Liberalism and Conservatism." *Nature Neuroscience* 10:1246–47.

Arat, Zehra F. 1988. "Democracy and Economic Development: Modernization Theory Revisited." *Comparative Politics* 21 (1):21–36.

Banfield, Edward C. 1958. *The Moral Basis of a Backward Society.* New York: Free Press.

Banks, Arthur S. 1979. *Cross-National Time-Series Data Archive Users' Manual.* Binghamton, New York: Center for Social Analysis, State University of New York.

———. 1999. "Cross-National Time-Series Data Archive." Binghamton, New York: Center for Social Analysis, State University of New York.

Banks, Arthur S., and Robert B. Textor. 1963. *A Cross-Polity Survey.* Cambridge, MA: MIT Press.

Barrie, James Matthew. 1991. *Peter Pan: The Complete and Unabridged Text.* New York: Viking Press.

Barro, Robert J. 1999. "Determinants of Democracy." *Journal of Political Economy* 107 (6):158–83.

Bates, Robert H., Rui J. P. de Figueiredo Jr., and Barry R. Weingast. 1998. "The Politics of Interpretation: Rationality, Culture, and Transition." *Politics and Society* 26 (4):603–42.

Beck, Nathaniel. 2008. "Time-Series Cross-Section Methods." In *The Oxford Handbook of Political Methodology,* 475–93, ed. J. M. Box-Steffensmeier, H. E. Brady, and D. Collier. Oxford: Oxford University Press.

Beck, Nathaniel, and Jonathan Katz. 1995. "What to Do (and Not to Do) with Time-Series Cross-Sectional Data." *American Political Science Review* 89 (3):634–47.

———. 2009. "Modeling Dynamics in Time-Series–Cross-Section Political Economy Data." Social Science Working Paper 1304, Pasadena: California Institute of Technology.

Beetham, David, Sarah Bracking, Iain Kearton, and Stuart Weir. 2002. *International IDEA Handbook on Democracy Assessment.* The Hague: Kluwer Law International.

Bendix, Reinhard. 1964. *Nation-Building and Citizenship: Studies of Our Changing Social Order.* New York: John Wiley and Sons.

Berg-Schlosser, Dirk, and Gisèle De Meur. 1994. "Conditions of Democracy in Interwar Europe: A Boolean Test of Major Hypotheses." *Comparative Politics* 26 (3):253–80.

Berlin, Isaiah. 1953. *The Hedgehog and the Fox: An Essay on Tolstoy's View of History.* London: Weidenfeld and Nicolson.

Bermeo, Nancy. 1997. "Myths of Moderation: Confrontation and Conflict During Democratic Transitions." *Comparative Politics* 29 (3):305–22.

———. 2003. *Ordinary People in Extraordinary Times: The Citizenry and the Breakdown of Democracy.* Princeton, NJ: Princeton University Press.

Bernhard, Michael, Christopher Reenock, and Timothy Nordstrom. 2003. "Economic Performance and Survival in New Democracies: Is There a Honeymoon Effect?" *Comparative Political Studies* 36 (4):404–31.

———. 2004. "The Legacy of Western Overseas Colonialism on Democratic Survival." *International Studies Quarterly* 48 (1):225–50.

Blasier, Cole. 1985. *The Hovering Giant: U.S. Responses to Revolutionary Change in Latin America, 1910–1985.* Pittsburgh, PA: University of Pittsburgh Press.

Blossfeld, Hans-Peter. 1996. "Macro-Sociology, Rational Choice Theory, and Time: A Theoretical Perspective on the Empirical Analysis of Social Processes." *European Sociological Review* 12 (2):181–206.

Boix, Carles. 2003. *Democracy and Redistribution.* New York: Cambridge University Press.

Boix, Carles, and Susan C. Stokes. 2003. "Endogenous Democratization." *World Politics* 55:517–49.

Bollen, Kenneth A. 1980. "Issues in the Comparative Measurement of Political Democracy." *American Sociological Review* 45 (3):370–90.

———. 1983. "World System Position, Dependency, and Democracy: The Cross-National Evidence." *American Sociological Review* 48 (4):468–79.

———. 1990. "Political Democracy: Conceptual and Measurement Traps." *Studies in Comparative International Development* 25 (1):7–24.

———. 1993. "Liberal Democracy: Validity and Method Factors in Cross-National Measures." *American Journal of Political Science* 37 (4):1207–30.

———. 1998. "Cross-National Indicators of Liberal Democracy, 1950–1990." Chapel Hill, NC and Ann Arbor, Michigan: University of North Carolina (producer) ICPSR (distributor).

Bollen, Kenneth A., and Burke D. Grandjean. 1981. "The Dimension(s) of Democracy: Further Issues in the Measurement and Effects of Political Democracy." *American Sociological Review* 46 (5):651–59.

Bollen, Kenneth A., and Robert W. Jackman. 1985. "Political Democracy and the Size Distribution of Income." *American Sociological Review* 50 (4):438–57.

Bollen, Kenneth A., Robert W. Jackman, and Hyojoung Kim. 1996. "Suffrage, Registration, and Turnout: A Comparative Analysis." Unpublished paper, Department of Sociology, University of North Carolina at Chapel Hill.

Bollen, Kenneth A., and Pamela Paxton. 1998. "Detection and Determinants of Bias in Subjective Measures." *American Sociological Review* 63 (3):465–78.

Brady, Henry E., and David Collier. 2004. *Rethinking Social Inquiry: Diverse Tools, Shared Standards.* Lanham, MD: Rowman and Littlefield.

Brinks, Daniel, and Michael Coppedge. 1999. "Patterns of Diffusion in the Third Wave of Democratization." Paper presented at the annual meeting of the American Political Science Association, Atlanta.

———. 2006. "Diffusion Is No Illusion: Neighbor Emulation in the Third Wave of Democracy." *Comparative Political Studies* 39 (4):463–89.

Brownlee, Jason. 2003. "Ruling Parties and Regime Persistence: Electoral Authoritarianism in Egypt and Malaysia." Paper presented at the annual meeting of the American Political Science Association, Philadelphia.

———. 2007. *Authoritarianism in an Age of Democratization.* New York: Cambridge University Press.

Brunk, Gregory C., Gregory A. Caldeira, and Michael S. Lewis-Beck. 1987. "Capitalism, Socialism, and Democracy: An Empirical Inquiry." *European Journal of Political Research* 15 (4):459–70.

Bueno de Mesquita, Bruce, and Alastair Smith. 2009. "Political Survival and Endogenous Institutional Change." *Comparative Political Studies* 42 (2):167–97.

Burkhart, Ross E. 1997. "Comparative Democracy and Income Distribution: Shape and Direction of the Causal Arrow." *Journal of Politics* 59 (1):148–64.

Burkhart, Ross E., and Michael Lewis-Beck. 1994. "Comparative Democracy: The Economic Development Thesis." *American Political Science Review* 88 (4):903–10.

Calabresi, Steven G. 2001. "The Virtues of Presidential Government: Why Professor Ackerman Is Wrong to Prefer the German to the U.S. Constitution." *Constitutional Commentary* 18 (1):51–104.

Camp, Roderic Ai. 2001. "Democracy Through Latin American Lenses." In *Citizen Views of Democracy in Latin America*, 3–23, ed. R. A. Camp. Pittsburgh, PA: University of Pittsburgh Press.

Cardoso, Fernando Henrique, and Enzo Faletto. 1971. *Dependencia y desarollo en América Latina*. Mexico City: Siglo Veintiuno.

Carothers, Thomas. 1999. *Aiding Democracy Abroad: The Learning Curve*. Washington, DC: Carnegie Endowment for International Peace.

Casper, Gretchen, and Michelle M. Taylor. 1996. *Negotiating Democracy: Transitions from Authoritarian Rule*. Pittsburgh, PA: University of Pittsburgh Press.

Castilla, Emilio J. 2007. *Dynamic Analysis in the Social Sciences*. London: Elsevier.

Central Intelligence Agency. 2003. "CIA World Factbook." Available at https://www.cia.gov/library/publications/the-world-factbook/.

Chaudhry, Kiren Aziz. 1997. *The Price of Wealth: Economies and Institutions in the Middle East*. Ithaca, NY: Cornell University Press.

Cheibub, José Antônio. 2006. *Presidentialism, Parliamentarism, and Democracy*. Cambridge: Cambridge University Press.

Cheibub, José Antônio, and Jennifer Gandhi. 2004. "A Six-Fold Measure of Democracies and Dictatorships." Paper presented at the annual meeting of the American Political Science Association, Chicago.

Cheibub, José Antônio, and Fernando Limongi. 2002. "Democratic Institutions and Regime Survival: Parliamentary and Presidential Democracies Reconsidered." *American Review of Political Science* 5:151–79.

Cingranelli, David, and David Richards. 2004. "The Cingranelli-Richards (CIRI) Human Rights Database Coding Manual." Online publication available at http://ciri.binghamton.edu/documentation/ciri_coding_guide.pdf.

Clark, Grenville. 1955. "Einstein Quoted on Politics." *New York Times*, April 22.

Clarke, Kevin A., and David M. Primo. 2007. "Modernizing Political Science: A Model-Based Approach." *Perspectives on Politics* 5 (4):741–53.

Cohen, Youssef. 1994. *Radicals, Reformers, and Reactionaries: The Prisoner's Dilemma and the Collapse of Democracy in Latin America*. Chicago: University of Chicago Press.

Colaresi, Michael, and William R. Thompson. 2003. "The Democracy-Economic Development Nexus: Does the Outside World Matter?" *Comparative Political Studies* 36 (4):381–403.

Coleman, James S., and Gabriel Almond. 1960. "Conclusion: The Political Systems of the Developing Areas." In *Politics of the Developing Areas*, 532–76. Princeton, NJ: Princeton University Press.

Collier, David, and Robert Adcock. 1999. "Democracy and Dichotomies: A Pragmatic Approach to Choices about Concepts." *Annual Review of Political Science* 2:537–65.

Collier, David, Henry E. Brady, and Jason Seawright. 2004a. "Sources of Leverage in Causal Inference: Toward an Alternative View of Methodology." In *Rethinking Social Inquiry*, 229–66, ed. H. E. Brady and D. Collier. Lanham, MD: Rowman and Littlefield.

Collier, David, and Steven Levitsky. 1997. "Democracy with Adjectives: Conceptual Innovation in Comparative Research." *World Politics* 49 (3):430–51.

Collier, David, Jason Seawright, and Gerardo L. Munck. 2004b. "The Quest for Standards: King, Keohane, and Verba's Designing Social Inquiry." In *Rethinking Social Inquiry*, 21–50, ed. H. E. Brady and D. Collier. Lanham, MD: Rowman and Littlefield.

Collier, Ruth Berins. 1999. *Paths toward Democracy: The Working Class and Elites in Western Europe and South America.* Cambridge: Cambridge University Press.

Collier, Ruth Berins, and David Collier. 1991. *Shaping the Political Arena.* Princeton, NJ: Princeton University Press.

Colomer, M. Josep. 1991. "Transitions by Agreement: Modeling the Spanish Way." *American Political Science Review* 85 (4):1283–1302.

———. 2000. *Strategic Transitions: Game Theory and Democratization.* Baltimore: Johns Hopkins University Press.

Coppedge, Michael. 1993. "Parties and Society in Mexico and Venezuela: Why Competition Matters." *Comparative Politics* 25 (3):253–74.

———. 1994. *Strong Parties and Lame Ducks: Presidential Partyarchy and Factionalism in Venezuela.* Stanford, CA: Stanford University Press.

———. 1997. "Modernization and Thresholds of Democracy: Evidence for a Common Path and Process." In *Inequality, Democracy, and Economic Development*, ed. M. Midlarsky, 177–201. Cambridge: Cambridge University Press.

———. 1999. "Thickening Thin Concepts and Theories: Combining Large N and Small in Comparative Politics." *Comparative Politics* 31 (4):465–76.

———. 2002. "Democracy and Dimensions: Comments on Munck and Verkuilen." *Comparative Political Studies* 35 (1):35–39.

———. 2005. "Explaining Democratic Deterioration in Venezuela through Nested Inference." In *Advances and Setbacks in the Third Wave of Democracy in Latin America*, 289–316, ed. F. Hagopian and S. Mainwaring. Cambridge: Cambridge University Press.

Coppedge, Michael, Angel Alvarez, and Lucas González. 2008. "Drugs, Civil War, and the Conditional Impact of the Economic on Democracy." Working Paper No. 341, Kellogg Institute, University of Notre Dame, Notre Dame, IN.

Coppedge, Michael, Angel Alvarez, and Claudia Maldonado. 2008. "Two Persistent Dimensions of Democracy: Contestation and Inclusiveness." *Journal of Politics* 70 (3):632–47.

Coppedge, Michael and John Gerring with David Altman, Michael Bernhard, M. Steven Fish, Allen Hicken, Matthew Kroenig, Staffan I. Lindberg, Kelly McMann, Pamela Paxton, Holli A. Semetko, Svend-Erik Skaaning, Jeffrey Staton, and Jan Teorell. 2011. "Conceptualizing and Measuring Democracy: A New Approach." *Perspectives on Politics* 9 (2): 247–67.

Coppedge, Michael, and Wolfgang Reinicke. 1990. "Measuring Polyarchy." *Studies in Comparative International Development* 25 (1):51–72.

Coronil, Fernando, and Julie Skurski. 1991. "Dismembering and Remembering the Nation: The Semantics of Political Violence in Venezuela." *Comparative Studies in Society and History* 33 (2):288–337.

Cox, Gary W. 1997. *Making Votes Count.* Cambridge: Cambridge University Press.

Crescenzi, Mark J. C. 1999. "Violence and Uncertainty in Transitions." *Journal of Conflict Resolution* 43 (2):192–212.

Crozier, Michel, Samuel Huntington, and Joji Watanuki. 1975. *The Crisis of Democracy.* New York: New York University Press.

Cutright, Phillips. 1963. "National Political Development: Measurement and Analysis." *American Sociological Review* 28:253–64.

Cutright, Phillips, and James A. Wiley. 1969. "Modernization and Political Representation: 1927–1966." *Studies in Comparative International Development* 5:23–44.

Dahl, Robert A. 1971. *Polyarchy: Participation and Opposition.* New Haven, CT: Yale University Press.

———. 1989. *Democracy and Its Critics.* New Haven, CT: Yale University Press.

Dahl, Robert A., and Edward R. Tufte. 1973. *Size and Democracy.* Stanford, CA: Stanford University Press.

Dalton, Russell J. 2002. *Citizen Politics: Public Opinion and Political Parties in Advanced Industrial Democracies.* New York: Seven Bridges and Chatham House.

Davis, Darren W., and Christian Davenport. 1999. "Assessing the Validity of the Postmaterialism Index." *American Political Science Review* 93 (3):649–64.

Deininger, Klaus, and Lyn Squire. 1996. "A New Data Set Measuring Income Inequality." *World Bank Economic Review* 10 (3):565–91.

Department of State. 2003. *Background Notes.* Washington, DC: Department of State.

Diamond, Jared M. 1997. *Guns, Germs, and Steel: The Fates of Human Societies.* New York: W. W. Norton.

Diamond, Larry. 1992. "Economic Development and Democracy Reconsidered." In *Reexamining Democracy,* 93–139, ed. G. Marks and L. Diamond. Newbury Park, CA: Sage Publications.

———. 1993a. "Causes and Effects." In *Political Culture and Democracy in Developing Cultures,* 411–35. Boulder, CO: Lynne Rienner.

———. 1993b. "Introduction: Political Culture and Democracy." In *Political Culture and Democracy in Developing Cultures,* 1–33. Boulder, CO: Lynne Rienner.

———. 1999. *Developing Democracy: Toward Consolidation.* Baltimore: Johns Hopkins University Press.

Diamond, Larry, Juan J. Linz, and Seymour Martin Lipset. 1988. *Democracy in Developing Countries.* Boulder, CO: Lynne Rienner.

———. 1995. "Introduction: What Makes for Democracy?" In *Politics in Developing Countries: Comparing Experiences with Democracy,* 1–66, ed. L. Diamond, J. J. Linz, and S. M. Lipset. Boulder, CO: Lynne Rienner.

Diamond, Martin. 1959. "Democracy and the Federalist: A Reconsideration of the Framers' Intent." *American Political Science Review* 53 (1):52–68.

Diermeier, Daniel. 1996. "Rational Choice and the Role of Theory in Political Science." In *The Rational Choice Controversy,* 59–84, ed. J. Frieden. New Haven, CT: Yale University Press.

Dion, Douglas. 1998. "Evidence and Inference in the Comparative Case Study." *Comparative Politics* 30 (2):127–45.

DiPalma, Giuseppe. 1990. *To Craft Democracies: An Essay on Democratic Transitions.* Berkeley: University of California Press.

Domínguez, Jorge, and Abraham Lowenthal, eds. 1996. *Constructing Democratic Governance: Latin-America and the Caribbean in the 1990s.* Baltimore: Johns Hopkins University Press.

Downing, Brian. 1992. *The Military Revolution and Political Change: Origins of Democracy and Autocracy in Early Modern Europe.* Princeton, NJ: Princeton University Press.

Duverger, Maurice. 1972. *Party Politics and Pressure Groups*. New York: Thomas Y. Crowell.

Eckstein, Harry. 1975. "Case Study and Theory in Political Science." In *Handbook of Political Science: Strategies of Inquiry*, 79–138, ed. F. I. Greenstein and N. W. Polsby. Reading, MA: Addison-Wesley.

————. 1988. "A Culturalist Theory of Political Change." *American Political Science Review* 82 (3):789–804.

Elkins, David J., and Richard E. B. Simeon. 1979. "A Cause in Search of Its Effect, or What Does Political Culture Explain?" *Comparative Politics* 11 (2):127–45.

Elkins, Zachary. 2000. "Gradations of Democracy? Empirical Tests of Alternative Conceptualizations." *American Journal of Political Science* 44 (2):293–300.

Elkins, Zachary, and Beth Simmons. 2005. "On Waves, Clusters, and Diffusion: A Conceptual Framework." *Annals of the American Academy of Political and Social Science* 598 (1):33–51.

Epstein, David, Robert Bates, Jack Goldstone, Ida Kristensen, and Sharyn O'Halloran. 2006. "Democratic Transitions." *American Journal of Political Science* 50 (3):551–69.

Ertman, Thomas. 1997. *Birth of the Leviathan: Building States and Regimes in Medieval and Early Modern Europe*. Cambridge: Cambridge University Press.

Evans, Peter B., Dietrich Rueschemeyer, and Theda Skocpol, eds. 1985. *Bringing the State Back In*. Cambridge: Cambridge University Press.

Fearon, James D. 1991. "Counterfactuals and Hypothesis Testing in Political Science." *World Politics* 43 (2):169–95.

Feng, Yi, and Paul J. Zak. 1999. "The Determinants of Democratic Transitions." *Journal of Conflict Resolution* 43 (2):162–77.

Finkel, Steven E., Aníbal Pérez Liñán, and Mitchell A. Seligson. 2007. "The Effects of U.S. Foreign Assistance on Democracy Building, 1990–2003." *World Politics* 59 (3): 404–39.

Fish, M. Steven. 2005. *Democracy Derailed in Russia: The Failure of Open Politics*. New York: Cambridge University Press.

Fitzgibbon, Russell H. 1951. "Measurement of Latin-American Political Phenomena: A Statistical Experiment." *American Political Science Review* 45 (2):517–23.

Foster, E. Michael. 2010. "Causal Inference and Developmental Psychology." *Developmental Psychology* 46 (6):1454–80.

Franseze, Robert J., Jr. 2005. "Empirical Strategies for Various Manifestations of Multilevel Data." *Political Analysis* 13 (4):430–46.

Franzese, Robert, and Jude C. Hays. 2009. "Empirical Models of Spatial Interdependence." In *Oxford Handbook of Political Methodology*, 570–604, ed. J. M. Box-Steffensmeier, H. E. Brady, and D. Collier. Oxford: Oxford University Press.

Freedom House. 2002. *Political Rights and Civil Liberties*. New York: Freedom House.

————. 2003. *Freedom in the World*. New York: Freedom House.

Friedman, Milton. 1953. "The Methodology of Positive Economics." In *Essays in Positive Economics*, 3–43. Chicago: University of Chicago Press.

Fudenberg, Drew, and Eric Maskin. 1986. "The Folk Theorem in Repeated Games with Discounting or with Incomplete Information." *Econometrica* 54 (3):533–54.

Fukuyama, Francis. 1992. *The End of History and the Last Man*. New York: Free Press.

Gallie, W. B. 1956. "Essentially Contested Concepts." *Proceedings of the Aristotelian Society* 56:167–220.

Gasiorowski, Mark J. 1995. "Economic Crisis and Political Regime Change: An Event-History Analysis." *American Political Science Review* 89 (4):882–97.

Gasiorowski, Mark J., and Timothy J. Power. 1998. "The Structural Determinants of Democratic Consolidation." *Comparative Political Studies* 31 (6):740–71.

Gassebner, Martin, Michael J. Lamla, and James R. Vreeland. 2009. "Extreme Bounds of Democracy." Working Paper 224, KOF Swiss Economic Institute, Zurich.

Geddes, Barbara. 1997. "Paradigms and Sandcastles: Research Design in Comparative Politics." *APSA-CP: Newsletter* 8 (1):18–20.

———. 2003. *Paradigms and Sand Castles: Theory Building and Research Design in Comparative Politics*. Ann Arbor: University of Michigan Press.

———. 2007. "What Causes Democratization?" In *The Oxford Handbook of Comparative Politics*, 316–39, ed. C. Boix and S. Stokes. Oxford: Oxford University Press.

Geertz, Clifford. 1973. *The Interpretation of Cultures: Selected Essays*. New York: Basic Books.

George, Alexander L., and Andrew Bennett. 2005. *Case Studies and Theory Development in the Social Sciences*. Cambridge, MA: MIT Press.

Gerber, Alan S., Donald P. Green, and David Nickerson. 2001. "Testing for Publication Bias in Political Science." *Political Analysis* 9 (4):385–92.

Gerring, John. 2001. *Social Science Methodology: A Critical Framework*. Cambridge: Cambridge University Press.

———. 2011. "Large-N Observational Data Analysis (aka Messy Data): A Modest Defense." *Qualitative and Multi-Method Research* 9 (1):8–17.

Gervasoni, Carlos. 2010. "A Rentier Theory of Subnational Regimes: Fiscal Federalism, Democracy, and Authoritarianism in the Argentine Provinces." *World Politics* 62 (2):302–40.

Giugni, Marco. 1999. "How Social Movements Matter: Past Research, Present Problems, Future Developments." In *How Social Movements Matter*, xiii–xxxiii, ed. M. Giugni, D. McAdam, and C. Tilly. Minneapolis: University of Minnesota Press.

Gleditsch, Kristian, and Michael D. Ward. 1997. "Double Take: A Reexamination of Democracy and Autocracy in Modern Polities." *Journal of Conflict Resolution* 41:361–83.

———. 2006. "Diffusion and the International Context of Democratization." *International Organization* 60 (4):911–33.

Goertz, Gary. 2006. *Social Science Concepts: A User's Guide*. Princeton, NJ: Princeton University Press.

Goertz, Gary, and James Mahoney. 2005. "Two-Level Theories and Fuzzy-Set Analysis." *Sociological Methods and Research* 33 (4):497–538.

Goldthorpe, John H. 1991. "The Uses of History in Sociology: Reflections on Some Recent Tendencies." *British Journal of Sociology* 42 (2):211–30.

Gonick, Lev S., and Robert M. Rosh. 1988. "The Structural Constraints of the World-Economy on National Political Development." *Comparative Political Studies* 21 (2):171–99.

González, Luis Eduardo, and Charles Guy Gillespie. 1994. "Presidentialism and Democratic Stability in Uruguay." In *The Failure of Presidential Democracy*, 151–78, ed. J. J. Linz and A. Valenzuela. Baltimore: Johns Hopkins University Press.

Gould, Andrew C. 1999. "Conflicting Imperatives and Concept Formation." *Review of Politics* 61 (3):439–63.

Gould, Andrew C., and Andrew K. Maggio. 2007. "Democracy, Dictatorship, and Economic Development: A Model of Reference-Dependent Choices with Experimental Data." In

Regimes and Democracy in Latin America: Methods and Applications, 231–45, ed. G. L. Munck. Oxford: Oxford University Press.

Gramsci, Antonio. 1971. "The Modern Prince." In *The Modern Prince and Other Writings* 164–88. New York: International Publishers.

Granger, C. W. J. 1969. "Investigating Causal Relations by Econometric Models and Cross-Spectral Methods." *Econometrica* 37 (3):424–38.

Granovetter, Mark. 1978. "Threshold Models of Collective Behavior." *American Journal of Sociology* 83 (6):1420–43.

Green, Donald P., and Ian Shapiro. 1994. *Pathologies of Rational Choice Theory: A Critique of Applications in Political Science*. New Haven, CT: Yale University Press.

Hadenius, Axel. 1992. *Democracy and Development*. Cambridge: Cambridge University Press.

Hadenius, Axel, and Jan Teorell. 2005. "Assessing Alternative Indices of Democracy." Working paper, Committee on Concepts and Methods, Mexico City.

Haerpfer, Christian W., Patrick Bernhagen, Ronald F. Inglehart, and Christian Welzel, eds. 2009. *Democratization*. Oxford: Oxford University Press.

Haggard, Stephan, and Robert R. Kaufman. 1995. *The Political Economy of Democratic Transitions*. Princeton, NJ: Princeton University Press.

Hall, Peter A. 2003. "Aligning Ontology and Methodology in Comparative Research." In *Comparative Historical Research in the Social Sciences*, 373–404, ed. J. Mahoney and D. Rueschemeyer. Cambridge: Cambridge University Press.

Hannan, Michael T., and Glenn R. Carroll. 1981. "Dynamics of Formal Political Structure: An Event-History Analysis." *American Sociological Review* 46 (1):19–35.

Hanushek, Eric, and John Jackson. 1977. *Statistical Methods for Social Scientists*. Orlando, FL: Academic Press.

Hartlyn, Jonathan. 2002. "Contemporary Latin America, Democracy, and Consolidation: Unexpected Patterns, Re-elaborated Concepts, Multiple Components." In *Democratic Governance and Social Inequality*, 103–30, ed. J. Tulchin and A. Brown. Boulder, CO: Lynne Rienner.

Hartlyn, Jonathan, and Arturo Valenzuela. 1994. "Democracy in Latin America Since 1930." In *The Cambridge History of Latin America*, 99–162, ed. L. Bethel. Cambridge: Cambridge University Press.

Heckman, James J. 1979. "Sample Selection Bias as a Specification Error." *Econometrica* 47 (1):153–62.

Held, David. 1996. *Models of Democracy*. Stanford, CA: Stanford University Press.

———. 2006. *Models of Democracy*. 3rd ed. Stanford, CA: Stanford University Press.

Helliwell, John. 1994. "Empirical Linkages between Democracy and Economic Growth." *British Journal of Political Science* 24 (2):225–48.

Hempel, Carl G. 1965. *Aspects of Scientific Explanation and Other Essays in the Philosophy of Science*. New York: Free Press.

Herb, Michael. 2005. "No Representation without Taxation? Rents, Development, and Democracy." *Comparative Politics* 37 (3):297–316.

Hermens, Ferdinand. 1972. *Democracy or Anarchy? A Study of Proportional Representation*. New York: Johnson Reprint Corporation.

Higley, John, and Michael G. Burton. 1989. "The Elite Variable in Democratic Transitions and Breakdowns." *American Sociological Review* 54 (1):17–32.

Hinich, Melvin J., and Michael C. Munger. 1997. *Analytical Politics*. New York: Cambridge University Press.

Holowchak, M. Andrew. 2007. *Critical Reasoning and Science: Looking at Science with an Investigative Eye*. Lanham, MD: University Press of America.

Horowitz, Donald L. 1985. *Ethnic Groups in Conflict*. Berkeley: University of California Press.

Hui, Victoria Tin-bor. 2005. *War and State Formation in Ancient China and Early Modern Europe*. New York: Cambridge University Press.

Human Rights Watch. 2003. *World Report: Events of 2002*. New York: Human Rights Watch.

Huntington, Samuel. 1991. *The Third Wave: Democratization in the Late Twentieth Century*. Norman: University of Oklahoma Press.

———. 1993. "The Clash of Civilizations." *Foreign Affairs* 72 (3):22–49.

Hyde, Susan D. 2007. "The Observer Effect in International Politics: Evidence from a Natural Experiment." *World Politics* 60 (1):37–63.

Inglehart, Ronald. 1977. *The Silent Revolution*. Princeton, NJ: Princeton University Press.

———. 2003. "How Solid Is Mass Support for Democracy – And How Can We Measure It?" *PS: Political Science and Politics* 36 (1):51–57.

Inglehart, Ronald, and Christian Welzel. 2005. *Modernization, Cultural Change, and Democracy: The Human Development Sequence*. New York: Cambridge University Press.

International Labor Organization. 2003. *Indicators on Income and Economic Activity*. New York: Department of Statistics, United Nations.

Jackman, Robert W. 1973. "On the Relation of Economic Development and Democratic Performance." *American Journal of Political Science* 17 (3):611–21.

Jensen, Nathan, and Leonard Wantchekon. 2004. "Resource Wealth and Political Regimes in Africa." *Comparative Political Studies* 37 (7):816–41.

Johnson, John J. 1958. *Political Change in Latin America: The Emergence of the Middle Sectors*. Stanford, CA: Stanford University Press.

Kahneman, Daniel, and Amos Tversky. 1979. "Prospect Theory: An Analysis of Decision under Risk." *Econometrica* 47 (2):263–91.

Kam, Cindy J., and Robert Franzese. 2007. *Modeling and Interpreting Interactive Hypotheses in Regression Analysis*. Ann Arbor: University of Michigan Press.

Kanai, Ryota, Tom Feilden, Colin Firth, and Geraint Rees. 2011. "Political Orientations Are Correlated with Brain Structure in Young Adults." *Current Biology* 21 (8):677–80.

Kaplan, David. 2009. *Structural Equation Modeling: Foundations and Extensions*. Thousand Oaks, CA: Sage Publications.

Karl, Terry Lynn. 1997. *The Paradox of Plenty: Oil Booms and Petro States*. Berkeley: University of California Press.

Katz, Richard S. 1997. *Democracy and Elections*. New York: Oxford University Press.

Kaufmann, Daniel, Aart Kraay, and Massimo Mastruzzi. 2007. "Governance Matters VI: Aggregate and Individual Governance Indicators, 1996–2006." Working paper, World Bank Policy Research, World Bank, Washington, DC.

Keck, Margaret, and Kathryn Sikkink. 1998. *Activists beyond Borders: Advocacy Networks in International Politics*. Ithaca, NY: Cornell University Press.

King, Gary. 1995. "Replication, Replication." *PS: Political Science and Politics* 28 (3):443–99.

King, Gary, Robert Keohane, and Sidney Verba. 1994. *Designing Social Inquiry: Scientific Inference in Qualitative Research*. Princeton, NJ: Princeton University Press.

Klingemann, Hans-Dieter, and Pippa Norris. 1999. "Mapping Political Support in the 1990s: A Global Analysis." In *Critical Citizens: Global Support for Democratic Governance*, 31–56. New York: Oxford University Press.

Knight, Alan, and Roderic Ai Camp. 2001. "Polls, Political Culture, and Democracy: A Heretical Historical Look." In *Citizen Views of Democracy in Latin America*, 223–42. Pittsburgh, PA: University of Pittsburgh Press.

Kopstein, Jeffrey, and David A. Reilly. 2000. "Geographic Diffusion and the Transformation of the Postcommunist World." *World Politics* 53 (1):1–37.

Kreps, David M. 1990. *Game Theory and Economic Modelling*. Oxford: Oxford University Press.

Kuhn, Thomas S. 1996. *The Structure of Scientific Revolutions*. Chicago: University of Chicago Press.

Kuran, Timur. 1989. "Sparks and Prairie Fires: A Theory of Unanticipated Political Revolution." *Public Choice* 61 (1):41–74.

———. 1991. "Now Out of Never: The Element of Surprise in the East European Revolution of 1989." *World Politics* 44 (1):7–48.

Labovitz, Sanford. 1970. "The Assignment of Numbers to Rank Order Categories." *American Sociological Review* 35 (3):515–24.

Laitin, David D. 1986. *Hegemony and Culture: Politics and Religious Change among the Yoruba*. Chicago: University of Chicago Press.

———. 2007. "Culture, Rationality, and the Search for Discipline." In *Passion, Craft, and Method in Comparative Politics*, 601–48, ed. G. L. Munck and R. Snyder. Baltimore: Johns Hopkins University Press.

Lakatos, Irme. 1970. "Falsification and the Methodology of Scientific Research Programmes." In *Criticism and the Growth of Knowledge*, 8–101, ed. I. Lakatos and A. Musgrave. Cambridge: Cambridge University Press.

———. 1978. *The Methodology of Scientific Research Programmes: Philosophical Papers*. Edited by J. Worrall and C. Gregory. Cambridge: Cambridge University Press.

Lalman, David, Joe Oppenheimer, and Piotr Swistak. 1993. "Formal Rational Choice Theory: A Cumulative Science of Politics." In *Political Science: The State of the Discipline II*, 77–104, ed. A. Finifter. Washington, DC: American Political Science Association.

Landman, Todd. 2008. *Issues and Methods in Comparative Politics: An Introduction*. New York: Cambridge University Press.

Lane, Jan-Erik, and Svante Ersson. 2005. *Culture and Politics: A Comparative Approach*. Aldershot, UK: Ashgate.

Lange, Matthew K. 2009. *Lineages of Despotism and Development: British Colonialism and State Power*. Chicago: University of Chicago Press.

LatinoBarómetro. 2004. *Informe – Resumen LatinoBarómetro 2004: Una década de mediciones*. Santiago, Chile: LatinoBarómetro.

———. 2005. *Informe – Resumen LatinoBarómetro 2005: Una década de mediciones*. Santiago, Chile: LatinoBarómetro.

Lave, Charles A., and James G. March. 1993. *An Introduction to Models in the Social Sciences*. Lanham, MD: University Press of America.

Lerner, Daniel. 1958. *The Passing of Traditional Society*. New York: Free Press.

Levi, Margaret, and Laura Stoker. 2000. "Political Trust and Trustworthiness." *Annual Review of Political Science* 3:475–507.

Levine, Daniel H. 1973. *Conflict and Political Change in Venezuela*. Princeton, NJ: Princeton University Press.

Levitsky, Steven, and Lucan Way. 2006. "Linkage versus Leverage: Rethinking the International Dimension of Regime Change." *Comparative Politics* 38 (4):379–400.

Li, Richard P. Y., and William R. Thompson. 1975. "The 'Coup Contagion' Hypothesis." *Journal of Conflict Resolution* 19 (1):63–88.

Lichbach, Mark Irving, and Alan S. Zuckerman, eds. 2009. *Comparative Politics: Rationality, Culture, and Structure*. 2nd ed. New York: Cambridge University Press.

Lieberman, Evan. 2005. "Nested Analysis as a Mixed-Method Strategy for Cross-National Research." *American Political Science Review* 99 (3):435–52.

Lieberson, Stanley. 1992. "Small Ns and Big Conclusions: An Examination of the Reasoning in Comparative Studies Based on a Small Number of Cases." In *What Is a Case? Exploring the Foundations of Social Inquiry*, 105–18, ed. C. C. Ragin and H. S. Becker. Cambridge: Cambridge University Press.

Lijphart, Arend. 1977. *Democracy in Plural Societies: A Comparative Exploration*. New Haven, CT: Yale University Press.

————. 1999. *Patterns of Democracy: Government Forms and Performance in Thirty-Six Countries*. New Haven, CT: Yale University Press.

Lindblom, Charles E. 1977. *Politics and Markets*. New York: Basic Books.

Linz, Juan J. 1973. "The Future of an Authoritarian Situation or the Institutionalization of an Authoritarian Regime: The Case of Brazil." In *Authoritarian Brazil: Origins, Policies, Future*, 233–54, ed. A. Stepan. New Haven, CT: Yale University Press.

————. 1975. "Totalitarian and Authoritarian Regimes." In *Handbook of Political Science*, 175–357, ed. F. I. Greenstein and N. W. Polsby. Reading, MA: Addison-Wesley.

————. 1978. *The Breakdown of Democratic Regimes: Crisis, Breakdown, and Reequilibration*. Baltimore: Johns Hopkins University Press.

Linz, Juan J., and Alfred Stepan. 1978. *The Breakdown of Democratic Regimes*. Baltimore: Johns Hopkins University Press.

————. 1996. *Problems of Democratic Transition and Consolidation: Southern Europe, South America, and Post-Communist Europe*. Baltimore: Johns Hopkins University Press.

Linz, Juan J., and Arturo Valenzuela, eds. 1994. *The Failure of Presidential Democracy*. Baltimore: Johns Hopkins University Press.

Lipset, Seymour Martin. 1959. "Some Social Requisites of Democracy: Economic Development and Political Legitimacy." *American Political Science Review* 53 (1):69–105.

————. 1960. *Political Man: The Social Bases of Politics*. Garden City, NY: Anchor Books.

————. 1994. "The Social Requisites of Democracy Revisited: 1993 Presidential Address." *American Sociological Review* 59 (1):1–22.

Lipset, Seymour Martin, Kyoung-Ryung Seong, and John Charles Torres. 1993. "A Comparative Analysis of the Social Requisites of Democracy." *International Social Science Journal* 45 (2):154–75.

Lohmann, Susanne. 1994. "The Dynamics of Informational Cascades: The Monday Demonstrations in Leipzig, East Germany, 1989–91." *World Politics* 47 (1):42–101.

Londregan, John B., and Keith T. Poole. 1996. "Does High Income Promote Democracy?" *World Politics* 49 (1):1–30.

Loveman, Brian. 1994. "Protected Democracies and Military Guardianship: Political Transitions in Latin America, 1978–1993." *Journal of Interamerican Studies and World Affairs* 36 (2):105–89.

Lowenthal, Abraham. 1991. "The U.S. and Latin American Democracy: Learning from History." In *Exporting Democracy: The United States and Latin America.* Baltimore: Johns Hopkins University Press.

Luebbert, Gregory M. 1987. "Social Foundations of Political Order in Interwar Europe." *World Politics* 39:449–78.

———. 1991. *Liberalism, Fascism, or Social Democracy: Social Classes and the Political Origins of Regimes in Interwar Europe.* New York: Oxford University Press.

Machiavelli, Niccoló. 1988 [1513]. The *Prince.* Translated by R. Price. Edited by Q. Skinner and R. Price. Cambridge: Cambridge University Press.

Mahoney, James. 2003. "Knowledge Accumulation in Comparative Historical Research: The Case of Democracy and Authoritarianism." In *Comparative Historical Analysis in the Social Sciences*, 208–40, ed. J. Mahoney and D. Rueschemeyer. Cambridge: Cambridge University Press.

———. 2008. "Toward a Unified Theory of Causality." *Comparative Political Studies* 41 (4–5): 412–36.

Mahoney, James, and Dietrich Rueschemeyer. 2003. "Comparative Historical Analysis: Achievements and Agendas." In *Comparative Historical Analysis in the Social Sciences*, 1–38, ed. J. Mahoney and D. Rueschemeyer. Cambridge: Cambridge University Press.

Mainwaring, Scott. 1993. "Presidentialism, Multipartism, and Democracy: The Difficult Combination." *Comparative Political Studies* 26 (2):198–228.

———. 1999. "The Surprising Resilience of Elected Governments." *Journal of Democracy* 10 (3):101–14.

Mainwaring, Scott, Daniel Brinks, and Aníbal Pérez-Liñán. 2001. "Classifying Political Regimes in Latin America, 1945–1999." *Studies in Comparative International Development* 36 (1):37–65.

Mainwaring, Scott, and Aníbal Pérez-Liñán. 2003. "Level of Development and Democracy: Latin American Exceptionalism, 1945–1996." *Comparative Political Studies* 36 (9):1031–68.

———. 2005. "Regional Effects and Region-Wide Diffusion of Democracy: Why Regions of the World are Important in Comparative Politics." Kellogg Institute Working Paper 322, Notre Dame, IN.

Mainwaring, Scott, and Matthew Soberg Shugart. 1997. "Conclusion: Presidentialism and the Party System." In *Presidentialism and Democracy in Latin America*, 394–439, ed. S. Mainwaring and M. S. Shugart. Cambridge: Cambridge University Press.

Malloy, James M., and Eduardo Gamarra. 1988. *Revolution and Reaction: Bolivia, 1964–1985.* New Brunswick, NJ: Transactions Books.

Marks, Gary. 1992. "Rational Sources of Chaos in Democratic Transition." *American Behavioral Scientist* 35 (4–5):397–421.

Marks, Gary. 1992. "Rational Sources of Chaos in Democratic Transitions." In *Reexamining Democracy: Essays in Honor of Seymour Martin Lipset*, 47–69, ed. G. Marks and L. Diamond. Newbury Park, CA: Sage Publications.

Marshall, Monty G., and Keith Jaggers. 2002. *Dataset Users' Manual*. College Park: University of Maryland.

Marx, Karl, and Friedrich Engels. 1932. *Manifesto of the Communist Party*. New York: International Publishers.

Mattes, Robert, and Michael Bratton. 2003. "Learning about Democracy in Africa: Awareness, Performance, and Experience," Afrobarometer Working Paper 31, Cape Town.

McClosky, Herbert. 1964. "Consensus and Ideology in American Politics." *American Political Science Review* 58:361–82.

———. 1983. *Dimensions of Tolerance: What Americans Believe about Civil Liberties*. New York: Russell Sage Foundation.

McCoy, Jennifer L. 1989. "Labor and the State in a Party-Mediated Democracy: Institutional Change in Venezuela." *Latin America Research Review* 24 (2):35–67.

Michels, Robert. 1962. *Political Parties: A Sociological Study of the Oligarchical Tendencies of Modern Democracy*. New York: Free Press.

Mill, John Stuart. 1843. *A System of Logic, Ratiocinative and Inductive, Being a Connected View of the Principles of Evidence, and the Methods of Scientific Investigation*. London: John W. Parker.

Miller, John H. 2007. *Complex Adaptive Systems: An Introduction to Computational Models of Social Life*. Princeton, NJ: Princeton University Press.

Moon, Donald J. 1975. "The Logic of Political Inquiry: A Synthesis of Opposed Perspectives." In *Handbook of Political Science*, 131–95, ed. F. I. Greenstein and N. W. Polsby. Reading, MA: Addison-Wesley.

Moore, Barrington, Jr. 1966. *Social Origins and Dictatorship and Democracy: Lord and Peasant in the Making of the Modern World*. Boston: Beacon Press.

Moreno, Alejandro. 2001. "Democracy and Mass Belief Systems in Latin America." In *Citizen Views of Democracy in Latin America*, 27–50, ed. R. A. Camp. Pittsburgh, PA: University of Pittsburgh Press.

Morton, Rebecca B. 1999. *Methods and Models: A Guide to the Empirical Analysis of Formal Models in Political Science*. Cambridge: Cambridge University Press.

Muller, Edward N. 1988. "Democracy, Economic Development, and Income Inequality." *American Sociological Review* 53 (1):50–68.

———. 1995. "Economic Determinants of Democracy." *American Sociological Review* 60 (4):966–82.

Muller, Edward N., and Mitchell A. Seligson. 1994. "Civic Culture and Democracy: The Question of Causal Relationships." *American Political Science Review* 88:635–52.

Munck, Gerardo L. 2005. "Democratic Development Indicators." In *Democracy in Latin America: Towards a Citizens' Democracy*, 77–129. New York: United Nations Development Program.

Munck, Gerardo L., and Jay Verkuilen. 2002. "Conceptualizing and Measuring Democracy: Evaluating Alternative Indices." *Comparative Political Studies* 35 (1):5–34.

Naím, Moisés. 1993. *Paper Tigers and Minotaurs: The Politics of Venezuela's Economic Reforms*. Washington, DC: Carnegie Endowment for International Peace.

Neubauer, Deane E. 1967. "Some Conditions of Democracy." *American Political Science Review* 61 (4):1002–1009.

Newton, Kenneth, and Pippa Norris. 2000. "Confidence in Public Institutions: Faith, Culture, or Performance?" In *Disaffected Democracies: What's Troubling the Trilateral Countries?*, 52–73, ed. S. J. Pharr and R. D. Putnam. Princeton, NJ: Princeton University Press.

Norris, Pippa. 1999a. "Conclusions: The Growth of Critical Citizens and its Consequences." In *Critical Citizens: Global Support for Democratic Governance*, 257–72, ed. P. Norris. New York: Oxford University Press.

———. 1999b. "Introduction: The Growth of Critical Citizens?" In *Critical Citizens: Global Support for Democratic Governance*, 1–27, ed. P. Norris. New York: Oxford University Press.

———. 2002. *Democratic Phoenix: Reinventing Political Activism.* Cambridge: Cambridge University Press.

———. 2004. "From the Civic Culture to the Afrobarometer." *APSA-CP* 15 (2):6–11.

O'Donnell, Guillermo. 1973. *Modernization and Bureaucratic-Authoritarianism: Studies in South American Politics.* Berkeley: Institute of International Studies, University of California.

———. 1993. "On the State, Democratization, and Some Conceptual Problems: A Latin American View with Glances at Some Post-Communist Countries." *World Development* 21 (8):1355–69.

———. 1994. "Delegative Democracy." *Journal of Democracy* 5 (1):57–64.

———. 1998. "Horizontal Accountability and New Polyarchies." Working Paper No. 253, Kellogg Institute, Notre Dame, IN.

———. 2002. "Human Development, Human Rights and Democracy." Paper presented at the workshop on "Calidad de la Democracia y Desarrollo Humano en América Latina," San José, Costa Rica.

O'Donnell, Guillermo, and Philippe C. Schmitter. 1986. *Transitions from Authoritarian Rule: Tentative Conclusions about Uncertain Democracies.* Baltimore: Johns Hopkins University Press.

O'Donnell, Guillermo, Philippe C. Schmitter, and Laurence Whitehead, eds. 1986. *Transitions from Authoritarian Rule: Comparative Perspectives.* Baltimore: Johns Hopkins University Press.

O'Loughlin, John, Michael D. Ward, Corey L. Lofdahl, Jordin S. Cohen, David S. Brown, David Reilly, Kristian S. Gleditsch, and Michael Shin. 1998. "The Diffusion of Democracy, 1946–1994." *Annals of the Association of American Geographers* 88 (4):545–74.

Olson, Mancur. 1971. *The Logic of Collective Action.* Cambridge, MA: Harvard University Press.

Ordeshook, Peter, and Olga Shvetsova. 1994. "Ethnic Heterogeneity, District Magnitude, and the Number of Parties." *American Journal of Political Science* 38:100–23.

Owolabi, Olukunle. 2005. "Blessing or Curse? The Impact of British Colonial Rule on the Success of Liberal Democracy in Africa and the Caribbean." Paper presented at the annual meeting of the Midwest Political Science Association, Chicago.

Palmer, David Scott. 1980. *Peru: The Authoritarian Tradition.* New York: Praeger.

Parry, Geraint. 1969. *Political Elites.* New York: Praeger.

Pateman, Carole. 1970. *Participation and Democratic Theory.* Cambridge: Cambridge University Press.

Paxton, Pamela. 2000. "Women's Suffrage in the Measurement of Democracy: Problems of Operationalization." *Studies in Comparative International Development* 35 (3):92–110.

Peceny, Mark. 1999. "Forcing Them to Be Free." *Political Research Quarterly* 52 (3):549–82.

Pemstein, Daniel, Stephen Meserve, and James Melton. 2010. "Democratic Compromise: A Latent Variable Analysis of Ten Measures of Regime Type." *Political Analysis* 18 (4): 426–49.

Pérez Liñán, Aníbal. 1998. "Assessing the Quality of Democracy: A Citizens' Perspective." In *A Citizens' Audit on the Quality of Democracy: A Proposal*, ed. M. Gutiérrez-Saxe and J. Vargas Cullell. Notre Dame, IN: Helen Kellogg Institute of International Studies, University of Notre Dame.

Persson, Torsten, and Guido Tabellini. 1994. "Is Inequality Harmful for Growth? Theory and Evidence." *American Economic Review* 84 (3):600–21.

Peters, B. Guy. 1998. *Comparative Politics: Theory and Method.* New York: New York University Press.

Pevehouse, Jon C. 2002a. "Democracy from the Outside-In? International Organizations and Democratization." *International Organization* 56 (3):515–49.

———. 2002b. "With a Little Help from My Friends? Regional Organizations and the Consolidation of Democracy." *American Journal of Political Science* 46 (3):611–26.

Pierson, Paul. 2004. *Politics in Time: History, Institutions, and Social Analysis.* Princeton, NJ: Princeton University Press.

Popper, Karl. 1968. *The Logic of Scientific Discovery.* New York: Harper and Row.

Poulantzas, Nicos. 1973. *Political Power and Social Classes.* London: NLB Press.

Prebisch, Raul. 1949. "El desarollo económico de la América Latina y algunos de sus principales problemas." *Trimestre Económico* 16 (93):175–245.

Proyecto Estado de la Nación. 2001. *Informe de la auditoría ciudadana sobre la calidad de la democracia.* San José, Costa Rica: Proyecto Estado de la Nación.

Przeworski, Adam. 1986. "Problems in the Study of Transition to Democracy." In *Transitions from Authoritarian Rule: Comparative Perspectives*, 47–63, ed. G. O'Donnell, P. C. Schmitter, and L. Whitehead. Baltimore: Johns Hopkins University Press.

———. 1987. "Democracy as a Contingent Outcome of Conflicts." In *Constitutionalism and Democracy*, 59–80, ed. J. Elster and R. Slagstad. Cambridge: Cambridge University Press.

———. 1991. *Democracy and the Market: Political and Economic Reforms in Eastern Europe and Latin America.* Cambridge: Cambridge University Press.

Przeworski, Adam, Michael E. Alvarez, José Antonio Cheibub, and Fernando Limongi. 1996. "What Makes Democracies Endure?" *Journal of Democracy* 7 (1):39–55.

———. 2000. *Democracy and Development: Political Institutions and Well-Being in the World, 1950–1990.* Cambridge: Cambridge University Press.

Przeworski, Adam, and Fernando Limongi. 1997. "Modernization: Theories and Facts." *World Politics* 49 (2):155–83.

Przeworski, Adam, and Henry Teune. 1970. *The Logic of Comparative Social Inquiry.* New York: John Wiley and Sons.

Purcell, Edward A., Jr. 1973. *The Crisis of Democratic Theory: Scientific Naturalism and the Problem of Value.* Lexington: University Press of Kentucky.

Putnam, Robert D. 1995. "Bowling Alone." *Journal of Democracy* 6:65–78.

Putnam, Robert D., Robert Leonardi, and Raffaela Y. Nanetti. 1993. *Making Democracy Work: Civic Transitions in Modern Italy.* Princeton, NJ: Princeton University Press.

Putnam, Robert D., Susan J. Pharr, and Russell J. Dalton. 2000. "Introduction: What's Troubling the Trilateral Democracies?" In *Disaffected Democracies: What's Troubling the Trilateral Countries?*, 3–27, ed. S. J. Pharr and R. D. Putnam. Princeton, NJ: Princeton University Press.

Pye, Lucian W. 1985. *Asian Power and Politics: The Cultural Dimensions of Authority.* Cambridge, MA: Belknap Press, Harvard University Press.

Ragin, Charles C. 1987. *The Comparative Method: Beyond Qualitative and Quantitative Strategies.* Berkeley: University of California Press.

———. 2000. *Fuzzy-Set Social Science.* Chicago: University of Chicago Press.

———. 2008. *Redesigning Social Inquiry: Fuzzy Sets and Beyond.* Chicago: University of Chicago Press.

Ragin, Charles C., and Howard S. Becker. 1992. *What Is a Case? Exploring the Foundations of Social Inquiry.* Cambridge: Cambridge University Press.

Riggs, Fred W. 1988. "The Survival of Presidentialism in America: Para-Constitutional Practices." *International Political Science Review* 9 (4):247–78.

Robinson, William S. 1950. "Ecological Correlations and the Behavior of Individuals." *American Sociological Review* 15:351–57.

Rodrik, Dani. 2005. "Why We Learn Nothing from Regressing Economic Growth on Policies." Unpublished paper. Cambridge, MA: Harvard University.

Rose, Richard, William Mishler, and Christian Haerpfer. 1998. *Democracy and Its Alternatives: Understanding Post-Communist Societies.* Baltimore: Johns Hopkins University Press.

Rosendorff, B. Peter. 2001. "Choosing Democracy." *Economics and Politics* 13 (1):1–29.

Ross, Marc Howard. 1997. "Culture and Identity in Comparative Political Analysis." In *Comparative Politics: Rationality, Culture, and Structure*, 42–80, ed. M. I. Lichbach and A. S. Zuckerman. Cambridge: Cambridge University Press.

Ross, Michael 2001. "Does Oil Hinder Democracy?" *World Politics* 53 (3):325–61.

Ross, Michael. 2004. "Does Taxation Lead to Representation?" *British Journal of Political Science* 34:229–49.

Rudra, Nita. 2005. "Globalization and the Strengthening of Democracy in the Developing World." *American Journal of Political Science* 49 (4):704–30.

Rueschemeyer, Dietrich. 1991. "Different Methods, Contradictory Results? Research on Development and Democracy." *International Journal of Comparative Sociology* 32 (1–2):9–38.

Rueschemeyer, Dietrich, John D. Stephens, and Evelyne Huber Stephens. 1992. *Capitalist Development and Democracy.* Chicago: University of Chicago Press.

Rustow, Dankwart. 1970. "Transitions to Democracy: Towards a Dynamic Model." *Comparative Politics* 2 (3):337–63.

Sagan, Carl. 1980. "Encyclopaedia Galactica." Episode 12, *Cosmos.* PBS: December 14, 1980.

Sartori, Giovanni. 1970. "Concept Misformation in Comparative Politics." *American Political Science Review* 64 (4):1033–53.

———. 1976. *Parties and Party Systems.* Cambridge: Cambridge University Press.

———. 1987. *The Theory of Democracy Revisited.* Chatham, NJ: Chatham House.

Schaffer, Frederic C. 2000. *Democracy in Translation: Understanding Politics in an Unfamiliar Culture.* Ithaca, NY: Cornell University Press.

Schedler, Andreas. 2002. "The Nested Game of Democratization by Elections." *International Political Science Review* 23 (1):103–22.

———. 2003. "Comparative Politics As a Resource." *APSA-CP* 14 (2):7–10.

———. 2004. *Verstehen*. Edited by A. Schedler. Mexico City: Committee on Concepts and Methods.

Schmitter, Phillippe C., and Terry Lynn Karl. 1991. "What Democracy Is . . . and Is Not." *Journal of Democracy* 2 (3):76–80.

Schneider, Carsten Q., and Claudius Wagemann. 2006. "Reducing Complexity in Qualitative Comparative Analysis (QCA): Remote and Proximate Factors and the Consolidation of Democracy." *European Journal of Political Research* 45 (5):751–86.

Scott, James C. 1976. *The Moral Economy of the Peasant: Rebellion and Subsistence in Southeast Asia*. New Haven, CT: Yale University Press.

Seawright, Jason. 2007. "Democracy and Growth: A Case Study in Failed Causal Inference." In *Regimes and Democracy in Latin America: Theories and Methods*, 179–98, ed. G. L. Munck. Oxford: Oxford University Press.

Sekhon, Jasjeet. 2004. "Quality Meets Quantity: Case Studies, Conditional Probability, and Counterfactuals." *Perspectives on Politics* 2 (2):281–93.

———. 2009. "Opiates for the Matches: Matching Methods for Causal Inference." *Annual Review of Political Science* 12:487–508.

Seligson, Mitchell A. 2001. "Costa Rican Exceptionalism: Why the Ticos Are Different." In *Citizen Views of Democracy in Latin America*, 90–106, ed. R. A. Camp. Pittsburgh, PA: University of Pittsburgh Press.

Seligson, Mitchell A. 2002. "The Renaissance of Political Culture or the Renaissance of the Ecological Fallacy." *Comparative Politics* 34:273–92.

Shadish, William R., Thomas D. Cook, and Donald T. Campbell. 2001. *Experimental and Quasi-Experimental Designs for Generalized Causal Inference*. Boston: Houghton Mifflin.

Shellman, Stephen M. 2008. "Coding Disaggregated Intrastate Conflict: Machine Processing the Behavior of Substate Actors over Time and Space." *Political Analysis* 16 (4): 464–77.

Shin, Doh Chull. 1994. "On the Third Wave of Democratization: A Synthesis and Evaluation of Recent Theory and Research." *World Politics* 47 (1):135–70.

Shively, Phillips W. 1998. *The Craft of Political Research*. Upper Saddle River, NJ: Prentice-Hall.

Sikkink, Kathryn. 1988. "The Influence of Raúl Prebisch on Economic Policy Making in Argentina." *Latin American Research Review* 23 (2):91–114.

Skocpol, Theda. 1973. "A Critical Review of Barrington Moore's Social Origins of Dictatorship and Democracy." *Politics and Society* 4 (1):1–34.

———. 1979. *States and Social Revolutions: A Comparative Analysis of France, Russia, and China*. Cambridge: Cambridge University Press.

———. 1984. "Sociology's Historical Imagination." In *Vision and Method in Historical Sociology*, 1–24, ed. T. Skocpol. New York: Cambridge University Press.

Slater, Daniel. 2010. *Ordering Power: Contentious Politics and Authoritarian Leviathans in Southeast Asia*. New York: Cambridge University Press.

Smith, Benjamin. 2004. "Oil Wealth and Regime Survival in the Developing World, 1960–1999." *American Journal of Political Science* 48 (2):232–46.

Snyder, Richard, and Ravi Bhavani. 2005. "Diamonds, Blood, and Taxes: A Revenue-Centered Framework for Explaining Political Order." *Journal of Conflict Resolution* 49 (4):563–97.

Starr, Harvey. 1991. "Democratic Dominoes: Diffusion Approaches to the Spread of Democracy in the International System." *Journal of Conflict Resolution* 35 (2):356–81.

Starr, Harvey, and Christina Lindborg. 2003. "Democratic Dominoes Revisited: The Hazards of Governmental Transitions, 1974–1996." *Journal of Conflict Resolution* 47 (4):490–519.

Stepan, Alfred. 1971. *The Military in Politics: Changing Patterns in Brazil.* Princeton, NJ: Princeton University Press.

———. 2007. "Democratic Governance and the Craft of Case-Based Research." In *Passion, Craft, and Method in Comparative Politics*, 392–455, ed. G. L. Munck and R. Snyder. Baltimore: Johns Hopkins University Press.

Stepan, Alfred, and Cindy Skach. 1993. "Constitutional Frameworks and Democratic Consolidation: Parliamentarism and Presidentialism." *World Politics* 46 (1):1–22.

Stevens, S. S. 1946. "On the Theory of Scales of Measurement." *Science* 103 (2684): 677–80.

Stolle, Dietlind, and Marc Hooghe. 2004. "Review Article: Inaccurate, Exceptional, One-Sided or Irrelevant? The Debate about the Alleged Decline of Social Capital and Civic Engagement in Western Societies." *British Journal of Political Science* 35:149–67.

Stone, W., G. Lederer, and R. Christie. 1992. *Strength and Weakness: The Authoritarian Personality Today.* New York: Springer Verlag.

Sullivan, John L., and John E. Transue. 1999. "The Psychological Underpinnings of Democracy: A Selective Review of Research on Political Tolerance, Interpersonal Trust, and Social Capital." *Annual Review of Psychology* 50:625–50.

Summers, Lawrence H. 1991. "The Scientific Illusion in Empirical Macroeconomics." *Scandinavian Journal of Economics* 93 (2):129–48.

Sussman, Leonard. 1988. "An Index of Press Freedom." In *Freedom in the World: Political Rights and Civil Liberties*, 53–98, ed. R. Gastil. New York: Freedom House.

Sutter, Daniel. 1995. "Settling Old Scores: Potholes along the Transition from Authoritarian Rule." *Journal of Conflict Resolution* 39 (1):110–28.

Swaminathan, Siddharth. 1999. "Time, Power, and Democratic Transitions." *Journal of Conflict Resolution* 43 (2):178–91.

Teorell, Jan. 2009. "Determinants of Democratization: Explaining Regime Change in the World, 1972–2002." Lund, Sweden: University of Lund.

———. 2010. *Determinants of Democratization: Explaining Regime Change in the World, 1972–2006.* New York: Cambridge University Press.

Teorell, Jan, Sören Holmberg, and Bo Rothstein. 2006. "The Quality of Government Dataset." Electronic dataset. Quality of Government Institute, Göteborg University. Available at http://www.qog.pol.gu.se/data/.

Tessler, Mark. 2002. "Islam and Democracy in the Middle East: The Impact of Religious Orientations on Attitudes toward Democracy in Four Arab Countries." *Comparative Politics* 34 (3):337–54.

Thompson, E. P., and Dorothy Thompson. 2001. "Historical Logic [excerpt from *The Poverty of Theory and Other Essays*]." In *The Essential E. P. Thompson*, 245–302. New York: New Press.

Tilly, Charles. 1975. *The Formation of National States in Western Europe.* Princeton, New Jersey: Princeton University Press.

Tocqueville, Alexis de. 1969. *Democracy in America.* Edited by J. P. Mayer. Garden City, New York: Anchor Books.

Transparency International. 2008. *Transparency International Corruption Perceptions Index.* London: Transparency International Centre for Innovation and Research.

Treier, Shawn, and Simon Jackman. 2008. "Democracy as a Latent Variable." *American Journal of Political Science* 52 (1):201–17.

Valenzuela, Samuel J. 1992. "Democratic Consolidation in Post-Transitional Settings: Notion, Process, and Facilitating Conditions." In *Issues in Democratic Consolidation: The New South American Democracies in Comparative Perspective*, 57–104, ed. S. Mainwaring, G. O'Donnell, and J. S. Valenzuela. Notre Dame, IN: University of Notre Dame Press.

van Deth, Jan W., and Elinor Scarborough. 1995. *The Impact of Values.* New York: Oxford University Press.

Vanhanen, Tatu. 1990. *The Process of Democratization.* New York: Crane Russak.

———. 2000. "A New Dataset for Measuring Democracy, 1810–1998." *Journal of Peace Research* 37 (2):252–65.

Varshney, Ashotosh. 2003. *Ethnic Conflict and Civic Life: Hindus and Muslims in India.* New Haven, CT: Yale University Press.

Verba, Sidney, and Gabriel Almond. 1980. "On Revisiting the Civic Culture: A Personal Postscript." In *The Civic Culture Revisited*, 394–410. Boston: Little, Brown.

Wallerstein, Immanuel. 1974. *The Modern World-System: Capitalist Agriculture and the Origins of the European World-Economy in the Sixteenth Century.* New York: Academic Press.

Waterbury, John. 1999. "Fortuitous Byproducts." In *Transitions to Democracy*, 261–83, ed. L. Anderson. New York: Columbia University Press.

Webb, Robert L. 1980. *Modern England: From the Eighteenth Century to the Present.* New York: Harper and Row.

Weber, Max. 1958. *The Protestant Ethic and the Spirit of Capitalism.* New York: Charles Scribner's Sons.

Wedeen, Lisa. 2002. "Conceptualizing Culture: Possibilities for Political Science." *American Political Science Review* 96 (4):713–28.

Weiner, Myron. 1987. "Empirical Democratic Theory." In *Competitive Elections in Developing Countries*, eds. M. Weiner and E. Özbudun, 3–34. Durham, NC: Duke University Press.

Weingast, Barry R. 1997. "The Political Foundations of Democracy and the Rule of Law." *American Political Science Review* 91 (2):245–63.

Welch, Stephen. 1993. *The Concept of Political Culture.* New York: St. Martin's Press.

Whitehead, Laurence. 1986. "International Aspects of Democratization." In *Transitions from Authoritarian Rules: Comparative Perspectives*, 3–46, ed. G. O'Donnell, P. C. Schmitter, and L. Whitehead. Baltimore: Johns Hopkins University Press.

———. 2002. *Democratization: Theory and Experience.* Oxford: Oxford University Press.

Wiarda, Howard J. 2004. *Corporatism and Authoritarianism in Latin America – Revisited.* Gainesville: University of Florida Press.

Winkler, Robert L., and William L. Hays. 1975. *Statistics: Probability, Inference, and Decision.* New York: Holt, Rinehart, and Winston.

Wood, Elisabeth. 2001. "An Insurgent Path to Democracy: Popular Mobilization, Economic Interests and Regime Transition in South Africa and El Salvador." *Comparative Political Studies* 34 (8):862–88.

World Bank. 1999. *World Development Report: Knowledge for Development.* New York: Oxford University Press.

Wright, Joseph. 2008. "Political Competition and Democratic Stability in New Democracies." *British Journal of Political Science* 38:221–45.

Zak, Paul J., and Yi Feng. 2003. "A Dynamic Theory of the Transition to Democracy." *Journal of Economic Behavior and Organization* 52:1–25.

Zielinski, Jakub. 1995. "The Polish Transition to Democracy: A Game-Theoretic Approach." *Archives Européennes de Sociologie* 36 (1):135–58.

———. 1999. "Transitions from Authoritarian Rule and the Problem of Violence." *Journal of Conflict Resolution* 43 (2):213–28.

Index